the story of contemporary art

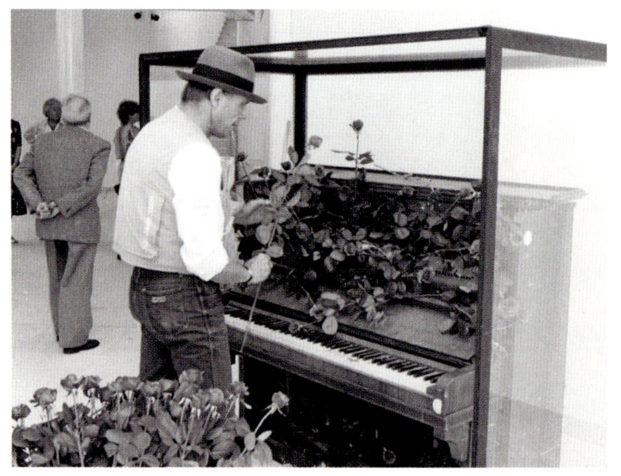

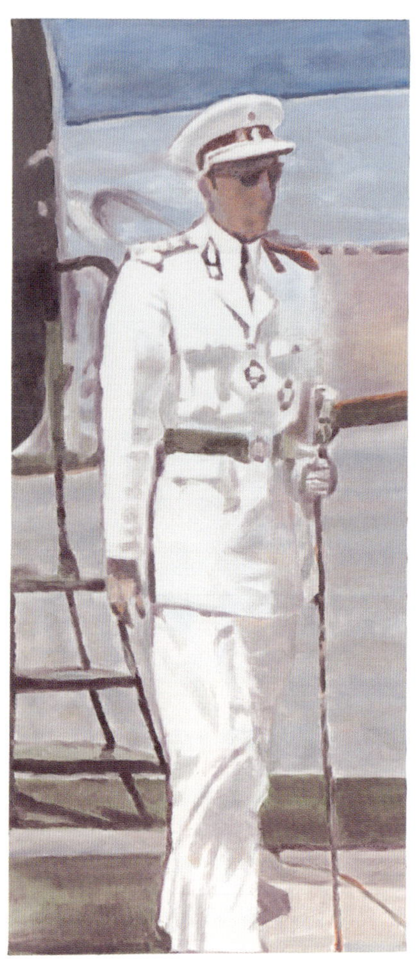

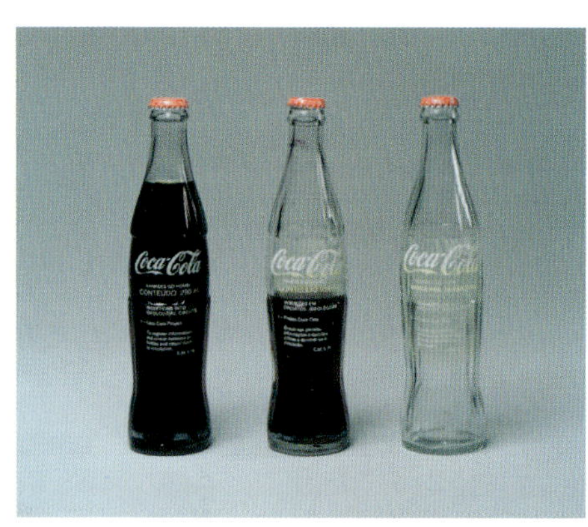
Coca-Cola
Coca-Cola
Coca-Cola

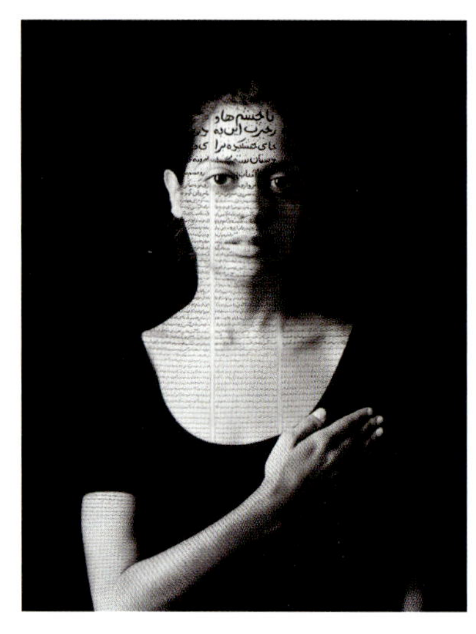

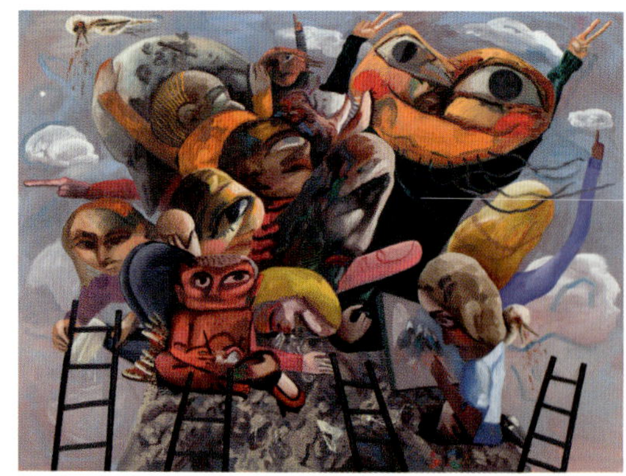

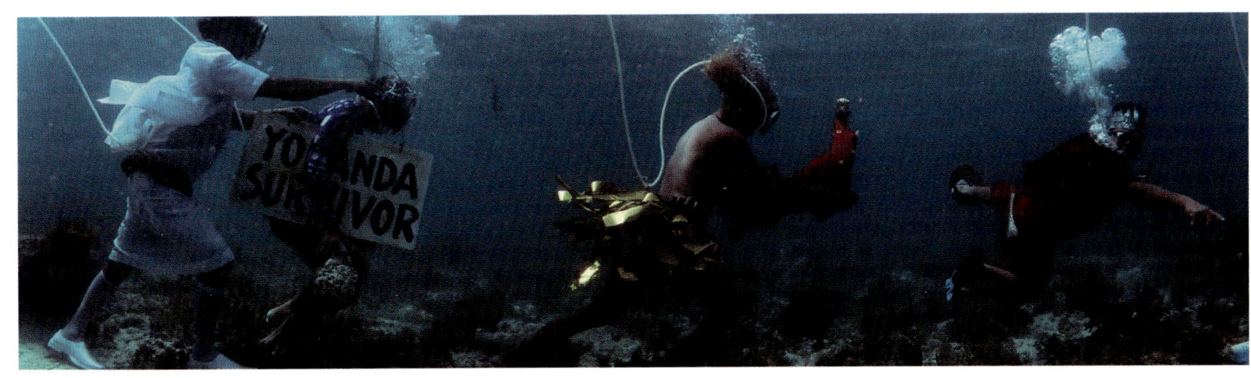

the story of contemporary art

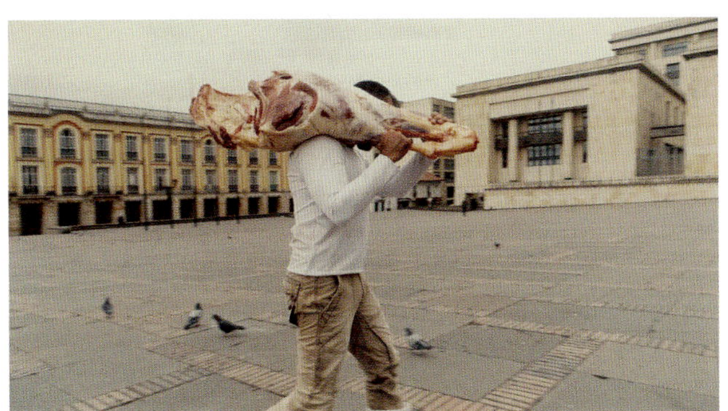

Tony Godfrey

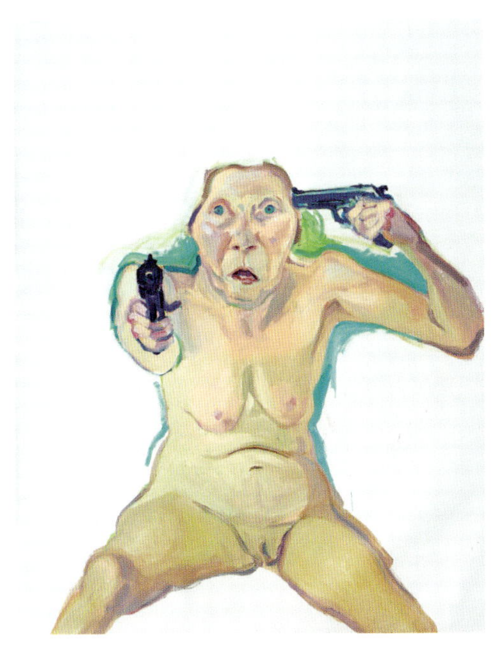

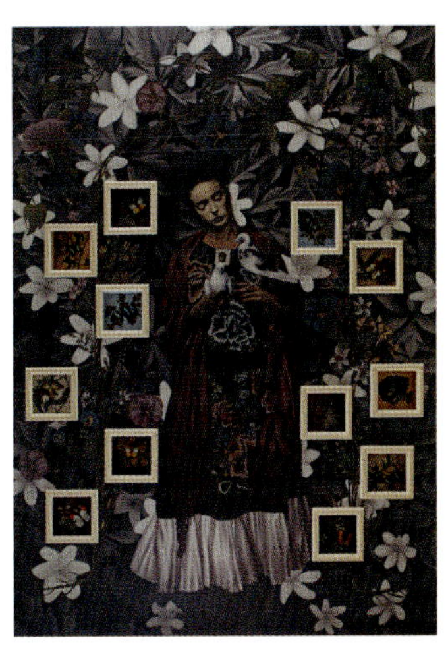

The MIT Press | Cambridge, Massachusetts

Published by arrangement with Thames & Hudson Ltd, London,
by the MIT Press

Library of Congress Catalog Control Number 2019951474

ISBN 978-0-262-04410-3

Printed and bound in Slovenia by DZS-Grafik d.o.o.

The MIT Press
Massachusetts Institute of Technology
Cambridge, Massachusetts 02142
http://mitpress.mit.edu

Contents

Preface

People are intrigued but often puzzled by contemporary art. I have spent the last forty years of my life trying to explain it and, even more importantly, trying to get people to enjoy and think about it. Often, someone will ask me to recommend a book to act as an introduction to this curious subject. But although there are many books on contemporary art, it is hard to think of one that I would recommend without reservation: they are either too partial or partisan, written in the dense language more suited to a PhD thesis than the general reader, or else too much like a mail-order catalogue, gushy and uncritical.

Some months ago, I picked up for the first time in many years a copy of Ernst Gombrich's *The Story of Art*, and was struck by how clear and readable it is. No wonder it is said to be the best-selling art book of all time! Could one, I wondered, tell the story of contemporary art with similar clarity and readability? Gombrich wrote in the preface to his book that it was 'intended for all who feel in need of some first orientation in a strange and fascinating field ... In writing it I thought first and foremost of readers in their teens who have just discovered the world of art for themselves ... I have striven to avoid these pitfalls [pretentious jargon and bogus sentiment] and to use plain language even at the risk of sounding casual or unprofessional ... I would not write about works I could not show in the illustrations; I did not want the text to degenerate into a list of names.'[1] Could one write such a book on contemporary art, I asked myself? Why not?

Contemporary art, despite its name, is not just art made *now*. Rather, it is a certain type (or types) of art, as well as the attitudes towards it. So, it must have a story. But when does that story begin? In 1945, 1960, 1968, 1973, 1980, 1989, 2001? You can make an argument for any of these dates. For me, however, as we shall see, 1980 was the decisive moment when how art was made, shown and collected seemed to change.

If contemporary art *is* a story, then what is the storyline? What are the plots and subplots? Who are the main characters – the heroes, heroines and villains? Which artists best typify the millions of other artists working today?

Significantly, I don't think there can be such a clear narrative of progress as there would seem to be in Gombrich's book. Instead, the story of contemporary art must be told as a series of often turbulent crises, conflicts and arguments about what art (and society) is or should be, with many of these arguments remaining unresolved and potent to this day: the exhaustion of modernist art, painting versus conceptual art, appropriation versus neo-expressionism, the national versus the global, etc. One of the things that makes contemporary art so exciting is that it is often about the pressing issues of our day: identity, environmental disaster and virtual life. As we look at individual artists, we might forget about that overall story, but we will keep coming back to it.

And who, you may ask, am I, your narrator? Well, I was born and raised in England, and began to teach and write about art in the late 1970s. I lived in London but travelled often around Europe, the United States and Mexico. In 2009, I went to live and work in South East Asia. That made me see the world of contemporary art very differently.

But before we move to the 1980s and the beginnings of contemporary art, we must first of all think broadly about what contemporary art is, and, secondly, about what was happening in the art world prior to that decade. It is also important to remember that a book about the art of our time can only ever be personal. Sometimes you might disagree with my opinion, but that's great! It means we are having a discussion. And contemporary art is all about discussion.

T. G., November 2019

Introduction

ON CONTEMPORARY ART AND ARTISTS

'What does that mean?' 'Is that really art?' 'Why does that cost so much money?' These are some of the questions I am often asked about contemporary art. They are not the questions that E. H. Gombrich felt compelled to answer in 1950, in his famous book *The Story of Art*. The questions he sought to tackle were very different: 'What is beauty in art?' 'Should art be true to nature?' 'What is harmony?' To illustrate his answers to such questions, Gombrich called on Raphael, Dürer, Rembrandt and other great masters of European painting.

Contemporary art seems often to be utterly different from what went before. Indeed, Gombrich felt unable to integrate it into his larger story: even in 1994, when he made what would be his final revisions to the book, the only contemporary artworks he condescended to illustrate were a painting by Lucian Freud and a photographic work by David Hockney – figurative pieces that such nineteenth-century artists as Manet or Degas would have had no difficulty comprehending. Gombrich included nothing that showed the impact of Pop, minimalist or conceptual art, those 'movements' of the 1960s that initiated what we still call 'contemporary' art.

Without doubt, Gombrich would have had no sympathy for either *White Flower* (page 10) or *The Pencil Story* (page 11), by Agnes Martin and John Baldessari respectively. Where, he may have asked, is the skill in such work? All the former has done is draw rows of straight lines, while the latter has simply scribbled some words under a pair of photos. But the very point of Baldessari's piece is that it shows no manual dexterity: we can all write, take snapshots like these and sharpen our pencils. What defines the work as art is not the medium, which for Gombrich would have meant exclusively drawing, painting or sculpture, but the way it questions what art actually is. At a certain point in the 1960s, several artists like Baldessari stopped making art, that is to say, any traditional form of art, and started to ask, 'What *is* art?' It was difficult to pose this question, however, by knocking off another drawing, painting or sculpture. Indeed, to show that a chasm had opened up between what he had made before this loss of faith, Baldessari cremated all his old Abstract Expressionist paintings – and, as we shall see later, made a new artwork out of this destructive act.

Agnes Martin, *White Flower*, 1960
Oil on canvas, 182.6 × 182.9 cm (71⅞ × 72 in.)

Why should it matter to Baldessari and others what art is? Why should it be so important a question to you? Why should we keep asking this question? I believe it's because art can be defined as that which is different, that which is special, as something that is meaningful. We see it this way because of its associations with such terms as 'genius', 'individuality', 'originality', 'profundity' and 'beauty'. We dedicate entire museums to it; people pay vast sums for it; we care for it and strive to preserve it.

Despite the disdain that Gombrich would probably have had for Agnes Martin's work, I doubt he would have disagreed with Martin when she said: 'When I think of art I think of beauty. Beauty is the mystery of life. It is not just in the eye. It is in the mind. It is our positive response to life.'[1] Even if the forms produced by artists had changed, many of their intentions had not. The presence here of Martin and her written words points to two things that are remarkably rare in Gombrich's book: women artists, and the words that artists spoke or wrote. In fact, it was only in 1989, with the publication of the fifteenth edition, that an illustration of a work by a female artist, Käthe Kollwitz, appeared in the *The Story of Art*. You will find many more women artists in the book you hold in your hands. Indeed, key to the story of this book is how the perception that art is made almost exclusively by white

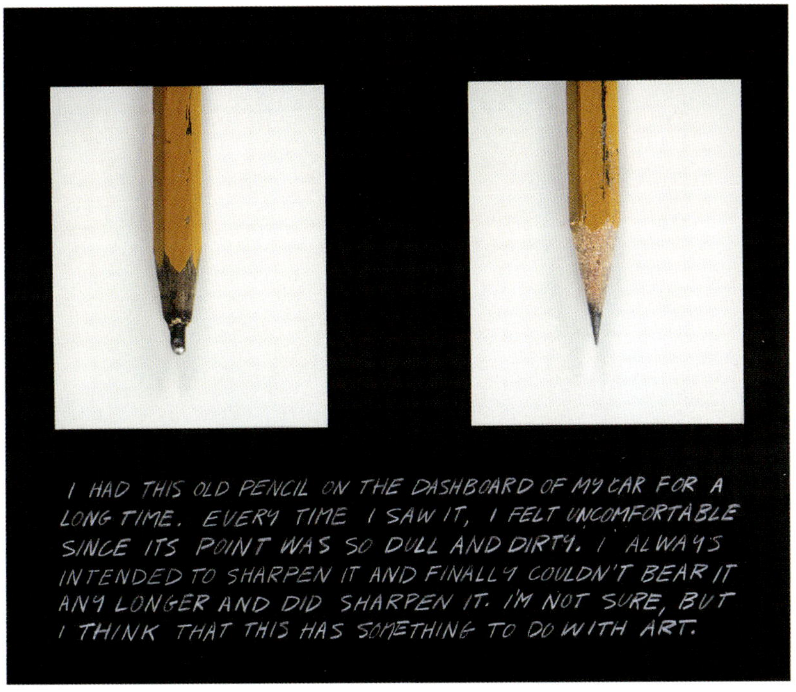

John Baldessari, *The Pencil Story*, 1972–73
Two colour photographs and coloured pencil on board, 55.8 × 69.2 cm (22 × 27¼ in.)

men from North America and Western Europe has expanded into one that art is made by men and women of all colours from all parts of the world.

Gombrich rarely quoted artists. Of course, we have no letters or diaries by Hieronymus Bosch, and no one recorded the conversations of Rembrandt. But even such artists as Constable or Cézanne, whose letters and conversations have survived, are quoted scantily by Gombrich. Like a magisterial headmaster, he felt he could speak on behalf of his boys. That would be impossible now: artists are frequently interviewed, while many write and publish. As art has become more varied and, often, more difficult, artists have felt a greater need both to explain and to discuss it. Some even see writing as part of their work.

We live in an increasingly global world. Artists from many different countries, with different cultures and different traditions – ones barely touched on by Gombrich, or ignored completely – now show their work internationally. Gombrich did mention, albeit briefly, Moghul miniatures in his token chapter on Asian art, but the art of Australian indigenous people he passed by in silence. When Shahzia Sikander studied traditional miniature painting in Lahore, few other students were interested in the form. However, she was neither motivated by nostalgia nor seeking to preserve the tradition as some sort of heritage activity; rather,

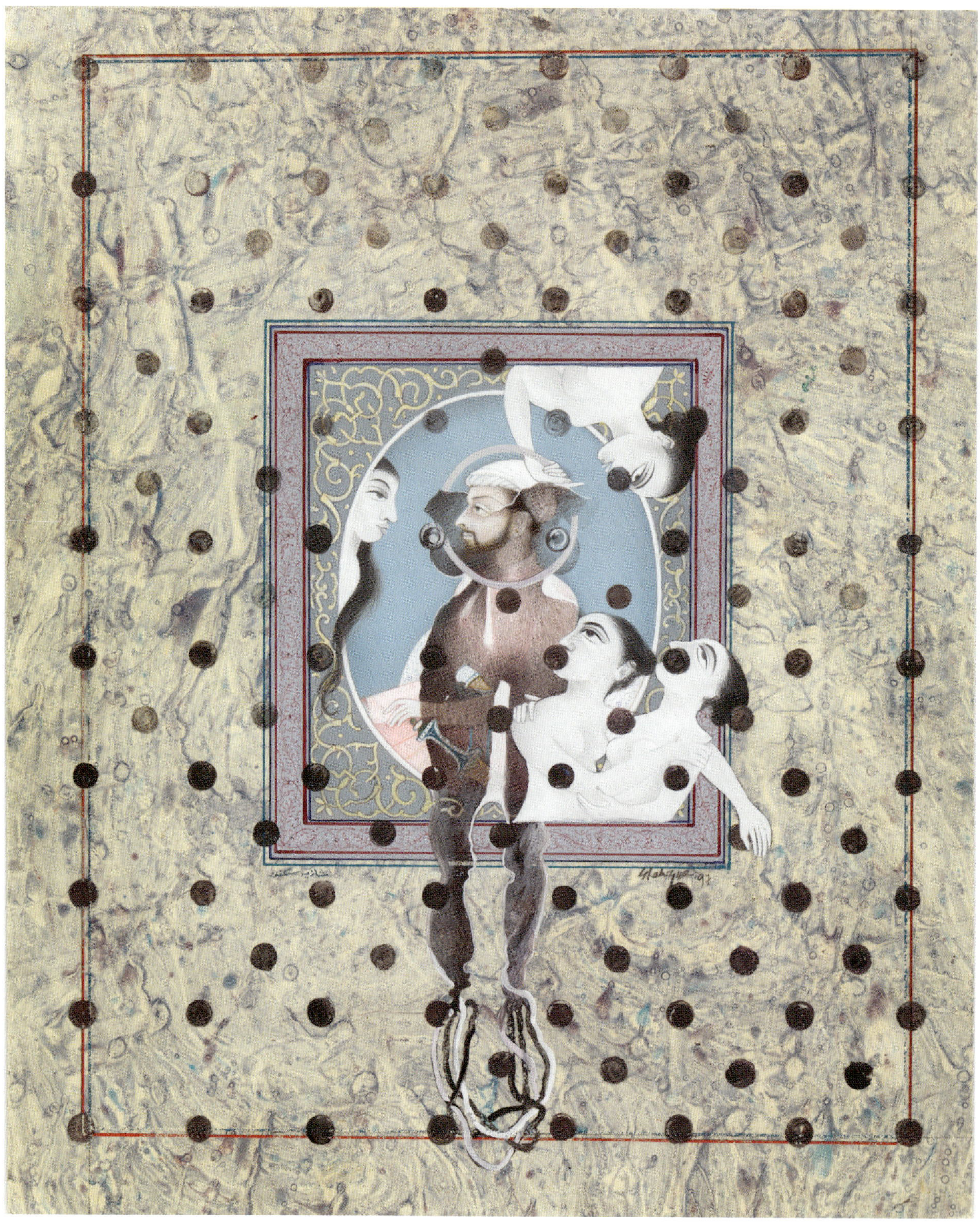

Shahzia Sikander, *Perilous Order*, 1989–97
Vegetable colour, dry pigment, watercolour and gold-leaf on wasli paper, sheet: 26.4 × 20.8 cm (10⅜ × 8¼ in.)

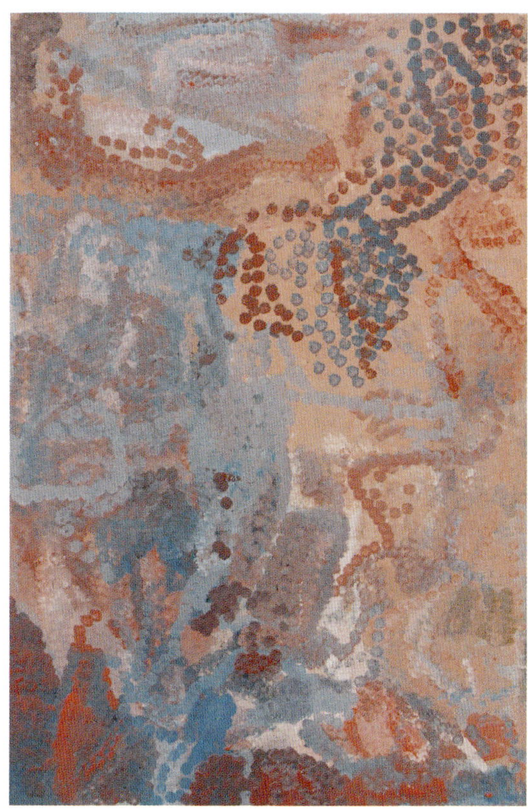

Emily Kame Kngwarreye, *Untitled (Alhalkere)*, 1993
Acrylic on polyester, 185 × 119 cm (72⅞ × 46⅞ in.)

she was intent on expanding it, using it to say something about her experience *now*. As Sikander herself has noted, 'My interest was and still is to create a dialogue with a traditional form – how to use tradition while engaging in a transformative task.'[2]

At the age of twenty-three, Sikander decided to leave her native Pakistan and move to New York. She arrived at a time when the words 'identity' and 'identity politics' were much in use. But, like many artists today, she is not fixed in one place or in one identity: 'I began to see my identity as being fluid, something in flux.'[3] This is a period in which many artists have become nomadic, moving from one country to another, responding to new contexts and ways of thinking.

In contrast to Sikander, the indigenous Australian artist Emily Kame Kngwarreye never travelled overseas and always painted her own country: Alhalkere in Central Australia, the land of her family and ancestors. 'I was born on this country – right here. This is my country. When I'm been a little girl we walked around in this bush. I been grown up here, Alhalkere Country – my country. I've been never moved from this country.'[4] Emily's work evolved out of the nine ancestral 'dreamings' she had inherited, about a sense of place and belonging. Where Sikander sought to combine, transform or morph traditions, Emily wished to save one, although it too has been touched by the materials of Western abstract art and shares its forms.

I once asked a British sculptor how often she visited the Victoria and Albert Museum in London, where the National Collection of Sculpture is held. She said she had been there once – with her father to look at carpets.[5] This rang true: most sculptors today have little or no attachment to the tradition that stretches back from Henry Moore to the ancient Greeks via Rodin and Michelangelo. The work of the American artist Sarah Sze, for instance, shows little influence of either classical or modernist sculpture. Viewing one of her assemblages or installations is more like viewing a film or a scientific model: our eyes move across a multitude of details – simple, everyday objects combined.

By contrast, many painters still have a strong sense of belonging to a tradition – and still respond to it. In the UK, both abstract and figurative painters can often be found in London's National Gallery looking at works by the old masters; similarly, in New York, painters are as likely to be studying a Rembrandt in the Met or a Matisse in MoMA as trawling the contemporary galleries. With affordable air travel, international publishing and the Internet, the old masters are available globally, allowing painters to feed off them or reject them. But unlike Gombrich's generation, we are far more open now as to who we consider an old master. When, during a period of personal anguish, the Filipina painter Geraldine Javier sought

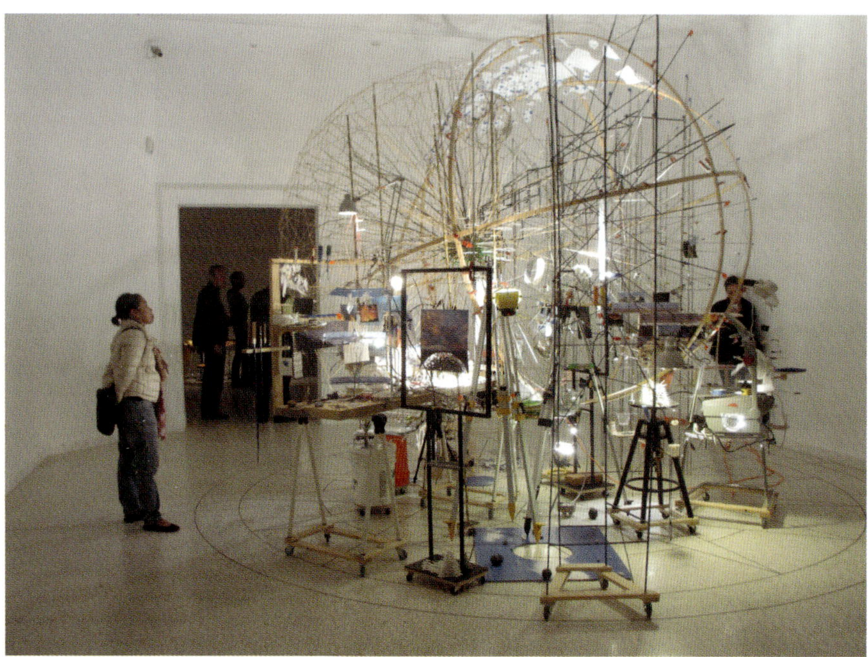

Sarah Sze, *Triple Point (Planetarium)*, 2013
Wood, steel, plastic, stone, string, fans, overhead projectors, photograph of rock printed on Tyvek, mixed media, 632.5 × 548.6 × 502.9 cm (249⅛ × 216 × 198 in.)

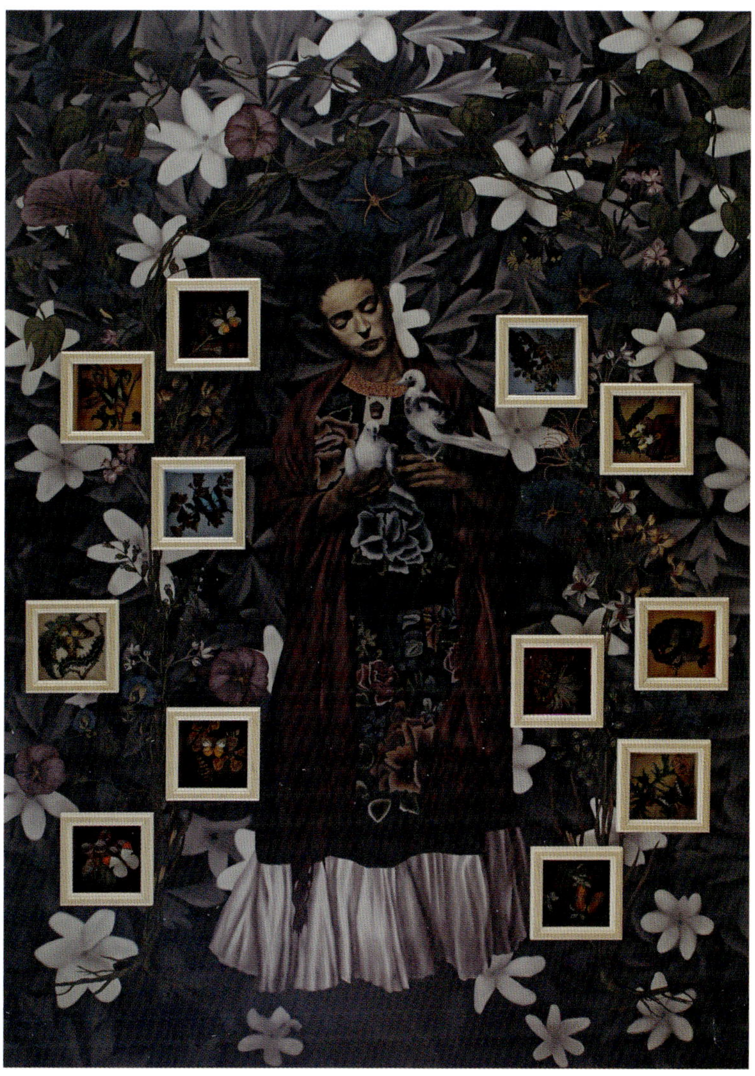

Geraldine Javier, *Ella amo' apasionadamente y fue correspondida*
(For she loved fiercely, and she is well-loved), 2010
Oil on canvas and framed embroidery with preserved butterflies, 228.5 × 160 cm (90 × 63 in.)

someone from the past as a soulmate and source of inspiration, it was the Mexican painter Frida Kahlo to whom she turned. We can see that Javier, like many artists today, is happy to adapt photographic images to her own needs, as well as using such non-traditional materials as embroidery and preserved insects.

Two other questions Gombrich sought to answer were, first, 'Why is art often new?' (here the writer chose Caravaggio to illustrate his answer), and, secondly, 'How does art seek expressiveness?' (Picasso). These questions seem just as relevant today. As we have seen, many things *have* changed, but not everything. Initially, conceptual art was seen as new and difficult, something that the popular press could mock and lampoon, but from the 1980s onwards many conceptual-style

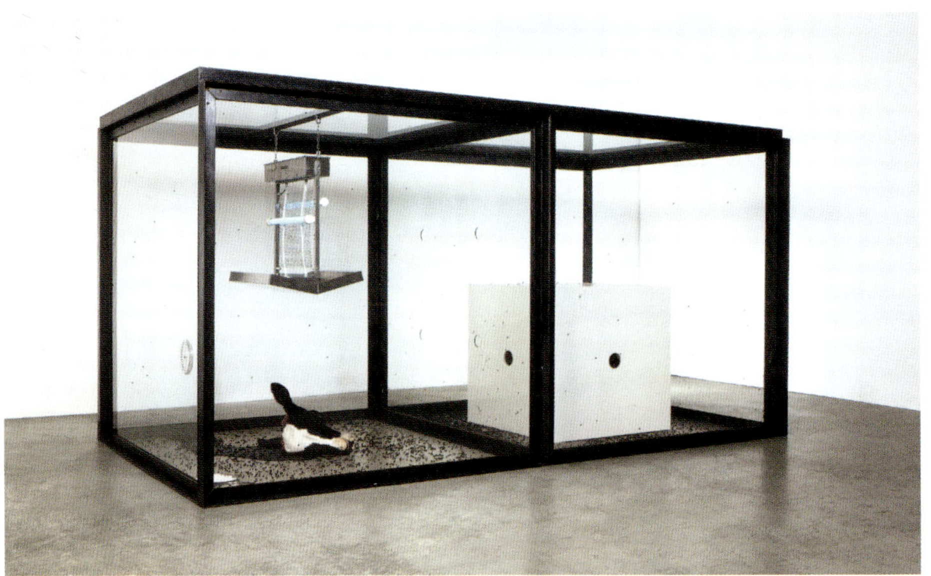

Damien Hirst, *A Thousand Years*, 1990
Glass, steel, silicone rubber, painted MDF, insect-o-cutor, cow's head, blood, flies, maggots, metal dishes, cotton wool, sugar and water, 207.5 × 400 × 215 cm (81.7 × 157.5 × 84.7 in.)

artists began to reach a wide audience. Their work was new, just as Caravaggio's had been, but it dealt with real concerns, the kind that anyone could relate to: Damien Hirst, for example, was obsessed with death, Kiki Smith with the vulnerability of the human body. Their work seemed very new – shocking, even – and although it wasn't expressive painting like Picasso's, people understood what was meant and responded emotionally: Hirst and Smith were staging our fear of death and our disgust at bodily functions.

In Hirst's *A Thousand Years* (above), flies hatched, ate sugar, had sex, laid eggs in a cow's head and, sooner or later, were zapped by an Insect-O-Cutor. One could see an entire life cycle – fascinating, but repellent, especially when the cow's head began to rot and stink. In *Untitled* (opposite), Smith's man and woman, in contrast to the noble figures carved by the likes of Michelangelo, are abject, purposeless, streaked with bodily fluids. We may not find them beautiful, but we are drawn to them nonetheless – much as we are drawn to medical dramas. Smith is making tangible the trauma we feel at seeing our bodies, or perhaps those of our parents, age and begin to fall apart. Compared to the days of high modernism, when abstraction ruled, the human body and all our fears about it – as well as our delight in it – are once again at the centre of much art being made now.

Today, we can no longer define art by its forms or materials. What, for example, do a pair of helter-skelters by Carsten Höller (page 18) and a painting by Beatriz

Milhazes (page 19) have in common, apart from both being called 'art'? Very little, it would seem: each has a different scale, different materials, different aesthetics. But they both offer particular experiences. The most important thing in soccer, said the charismatic football manager Jürgen Klopp, is not trophies or medals but 'the moment itself, the memory of being there at the game, that you were part of it. That's what it's all about! The experience!'[6] So it is with art. However precious the object, picture or installation, it is the experience we might have when viewing and thinking about it that truly matters.

Höller is one of a number of artists who, in the 1990s, began placing the emphasis on the experience rather than the object. The average person, whether a child or a grown-up, enjoys sliding down a helter-skelter. By calling this 'art', Höller is asking the participants to think a little bit differently about the experience. By considering whether it can be an 'art experience', they might end up with a sharper sense of their everyday interactions with the world.

At first glance, Milhazes's painting might not seem to offer such a visceral experience as Höller's slides. It is, after all, only a picture! But if we start to look at the painting carefully, moving back and forth in front of it, if we respond to the colours and rhythms, if we sense the complex and varied textures, then we begin to have a not-so-different experience after all. We need to let go, just as you let go when you go down a slide. As Rothko said, 'A painting is not about experience,

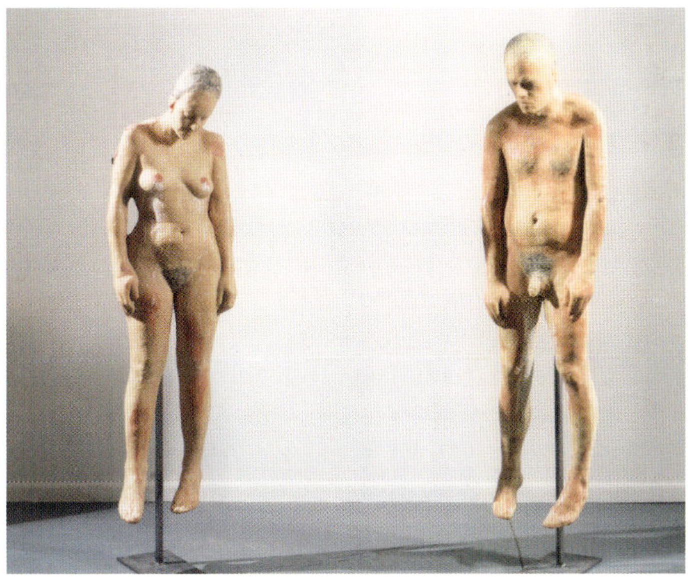

Kiki Smith, *Untitled*, 1990
Beeswax and microcrystalline wax figures on metal stands, overall: 198.1 × 181.6 × 54 cm (78 × 71½ × 21¼ in.)

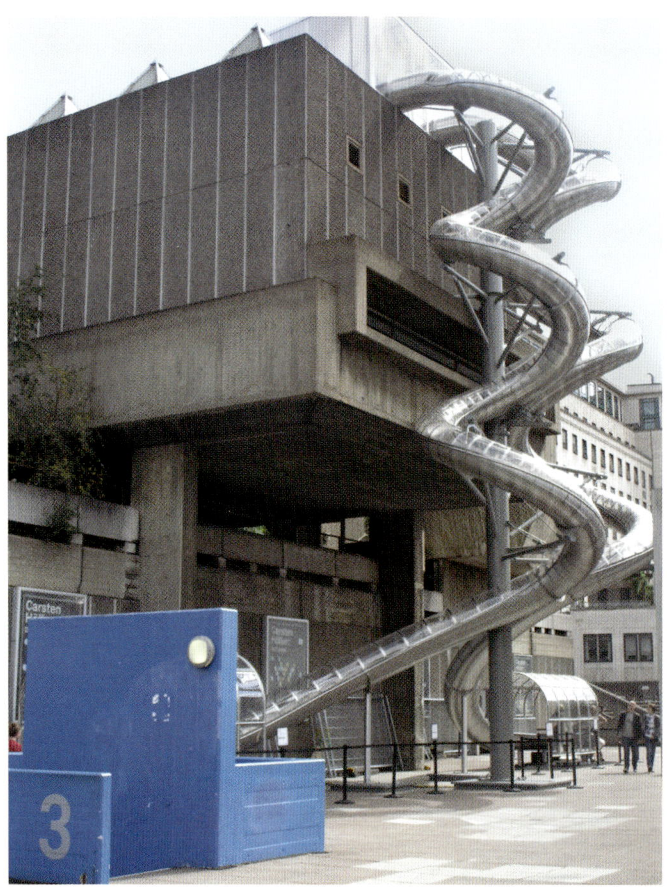

Carsten Höller, *Isometric Slides*, 2015
Installation view, Hayward Gallery, London

it is an experience.'[7] Although Milhazes is not a *carnivalesca* herself, perhaps – as a Brazilian – she intuitively understands the meaning of carnival: the exuberance, the delight and, underneath it all, a certain uncertainty, even melancholy. This is a gaiety very different from the happy babble of Disneyland.

Clearly, it matters where and how art is installed. Would people recognize one of Höller's slides as art if it were not attached to a gallery or museum? No wonder, then, that many artists have become obsessed with how their work is shown. Back in 1982, the American artist Donald Judd wrote, with typical crustiness, that 'the installation and context for the art being done now is poor and unsuitable ... Most owners of art install it badly; little can be expected. The museum should be serious and competent and much is expected but it's a disappointment.'[8] Judd's solution was to convert an old military base in Marfa, Texas, into a set of buildings in which art by him and his contemporaries could be shown permanently (page 20).

Other artists might not seek such a 'perfect' environment, preferring one that, for historical, social or poetic reasons, becomes part of the work. At the 2008 Sydney Biennale, a recording of the Berlin-based Scottish artist Susan Philipsz singing

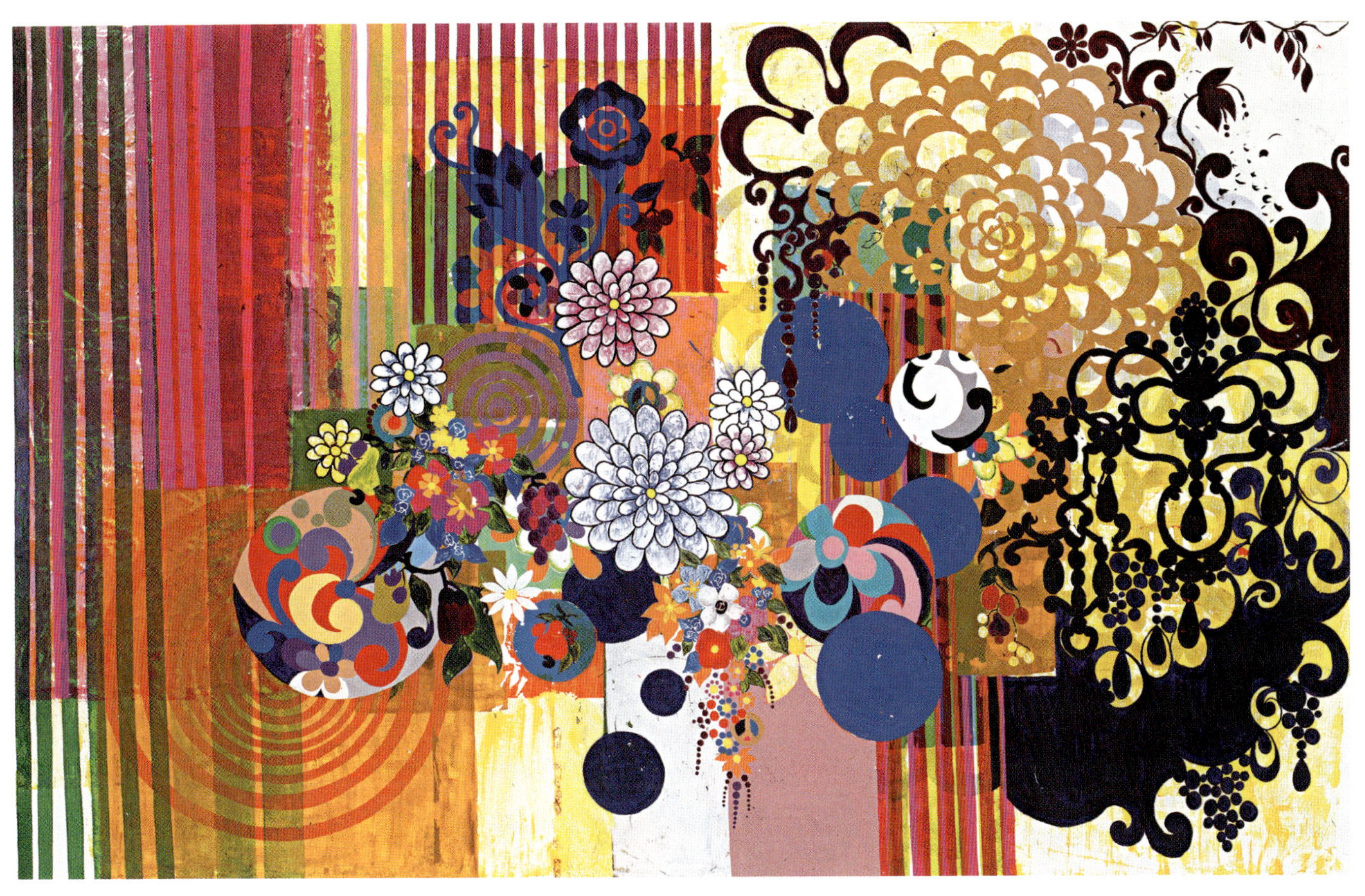

Beatriz Milhazes, *O Elefante Azul* (The Blue Elephant), 2002
Acrylic on canvas, 189 × 299 cm (74½ × 117¾ in.)

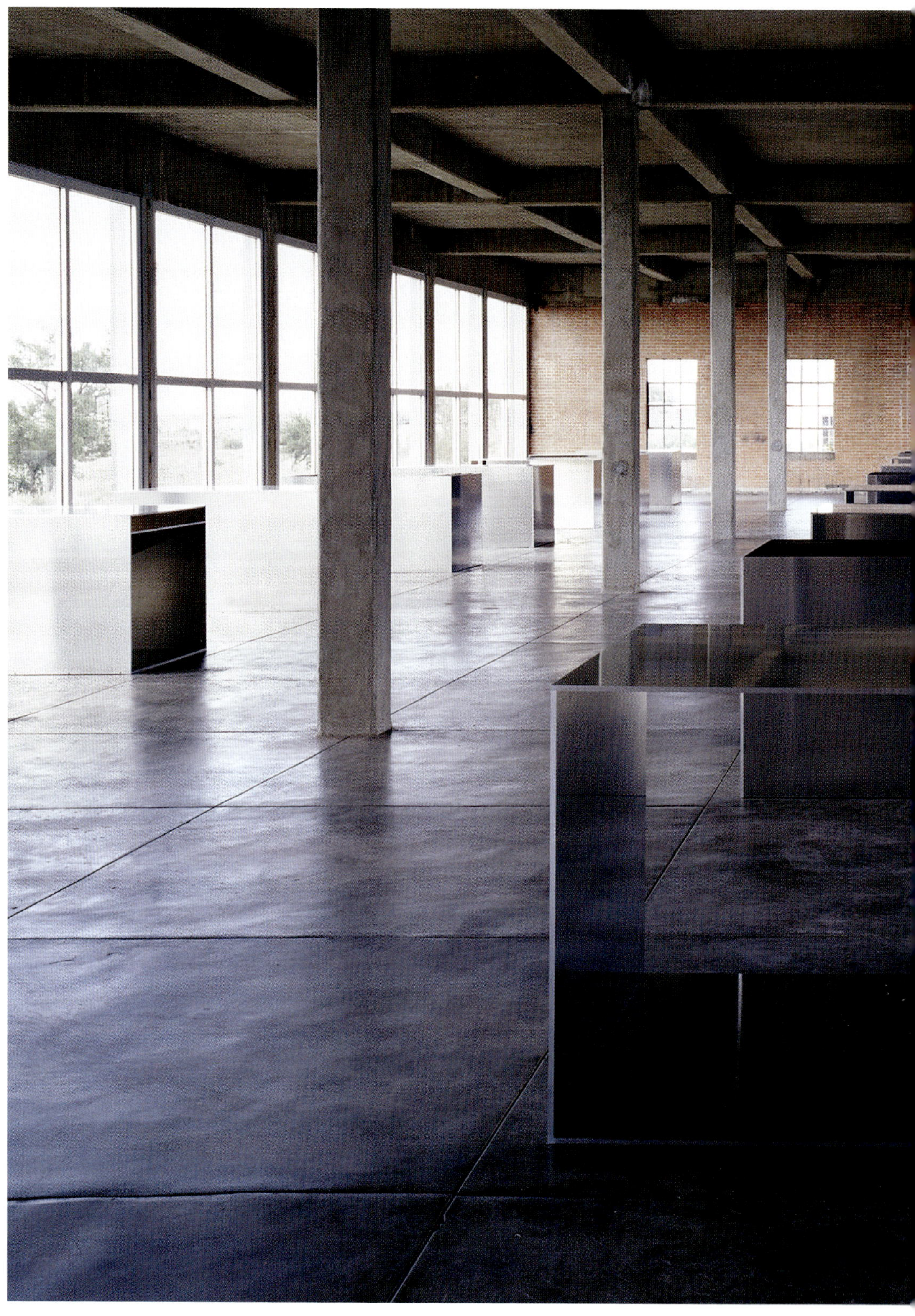

Donald Judd, *100 untitled works in milled aluminum*, 1982–86
Each 104.1 × 129.5 × 182.9 cm (41 × 51 × 72 in.), as installed in Chinati Foundation, Marfa, Texas

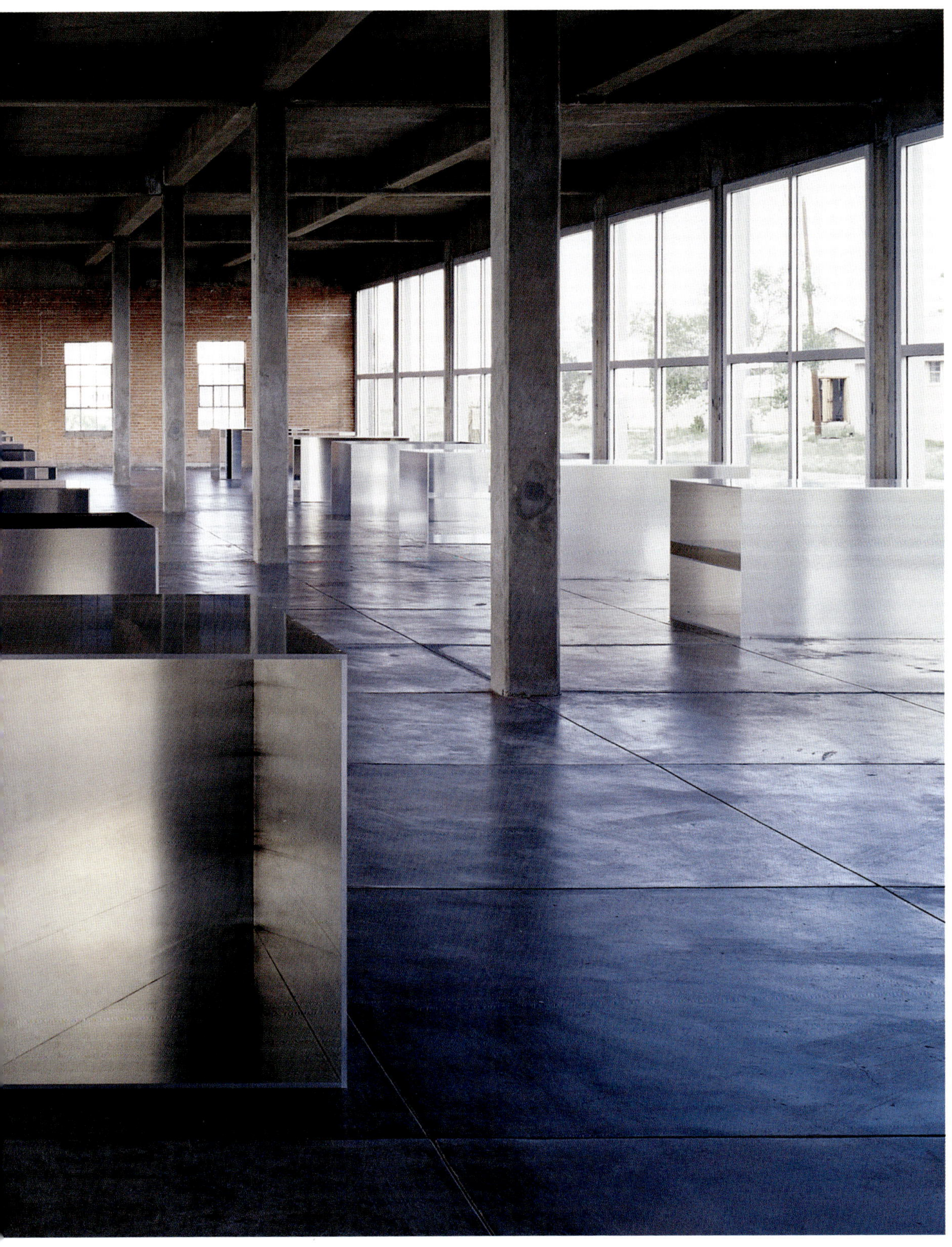

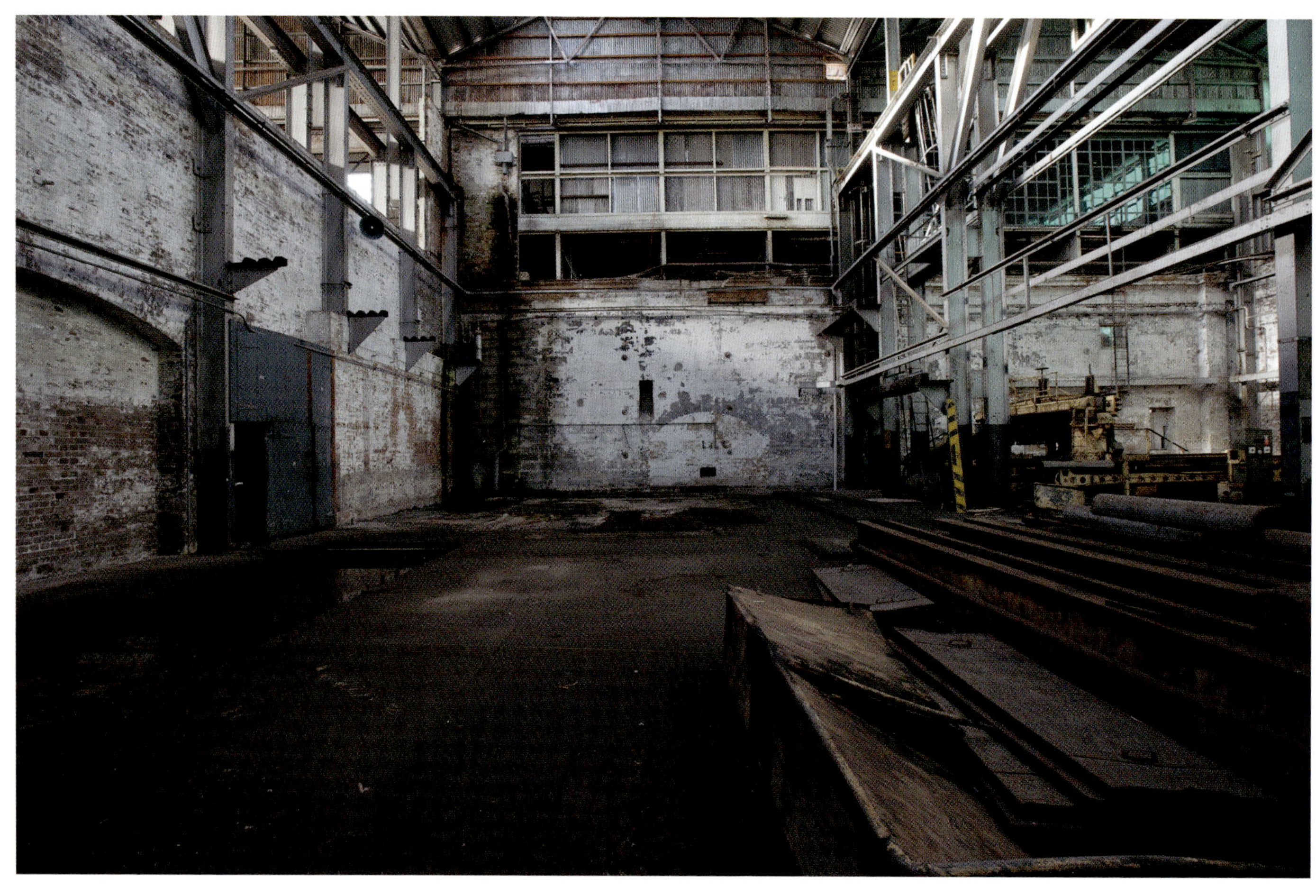

Susan Philipsz, *The Internationale*, 1999
Sound installation, Turbine Hall, Cockatoo Island, Sydney, 2:10 minutes

'The Internationale' could be heard playing non-stop in a vast, derelict naval factory that was empty save for some rusting machinery (opposite). 'My work', says Philipsz, 'deals with the spatial properties of sound and with the relationship between sound and architecture. I'm interested in the emotive and psychological properties of sound and how it can be used as a device to alter individual consciousness. I have used sound, and more recently song, as a medium in public spaces to interject through the ambient noises of the everyday. Using my own voice, I attempt to trigger an awareness in the listener, to temporarily alter their perception of themselves in a particular place and time.'[9] 'Workers of the world unite!' she sang in Sydney; and in the desolation of the abandoned building, one wondered where the workers had gone. What had happened to their struggle? Her singing filled the space, allowing one to appreciate its scale and stillness. A single woman's voice where once only men had toiled: not so much a call to revolution as a lament.[10]

Nowadays, in contrast to the art world Gombrich knew, art is no longer confined to galleries, museums, palaces and sacred buildings. Indeed, since his death in 2001, art fairs (where commercial galleries show artists), biennales (which, in theory at least, are non-commercial) and auctions of contemporary art have proliferated around the world. These new 'venues' not only change the way we *perceive* art, they also have an effect on how artists *make* art.

Although art fairs may seem glamorous and exciting to many, to others they are not only a poor environment in which to appreciate art – too crowded, too chaotic, too pressurized – but constitute, at their most repulsive, the spectacle of art reduced to prestige baubles that only the new super-rich can afford to buy. When commissioned to make a work specifically for an art fair in London, the American Richard Prince, whose work has often celebrated – or sneered at – US popular culture, displayed something one would normally expect to see only at a low-grade car show: a 'hot car' with a scantily dressed woman draped across it. It is, of course, a cynical piece, because, at the same time as mocking such fairs and the new glitzy art market, Prince makes a good living from them. And there's the rub: the extraordinary quantities of money that have flowed into the art world in recent years may have enabled many things, in particular allowing more artists to live by selling work, but has it not also been corrupting?

On 5 October 2013, the Chinese artist Zeng Fanzhi's *The Last Supper* (page 25) sold at Sotheby's Hong Kong for a record-breaking $23,269,070. That was and is a lot of money, far more than most of us will earn in a lifetime. Art, as always, mirrors society at large: in an age of extreme income disparity, where 0.01 per cent of the population supposedly owns 50 per cent of the wealth,[11] the prices for the most desirable art can seem obscenely high.

Is *The Last Supper* a good painting? Is it a good investment? Was it worth that much? It is certainly an interesting painting by a very serious, hardworking artist. Personally, I would say it is a good painting, but others may disagree. As to whether it is a good investment, I haven't the faintest idea: the market for so-called key or iconic work is overheated, and no one knows if these prices can be sustained or for how long.

What some call the 'Western tradition' in painting, the Chinese sensibly refer to as 'oil painting'. The medium, its history and traditions – even such images as Leonardo's *Last Supper*, on which Zeng based his work – do not belong solely to a single culture. In Zeng's painting, 'Jesus' and his 'true disciples' wear the red scarf of the Young Pioneers, a communist youth movement, but 'Judas' wears a gold tie. According to Zeng, 'The golden tie represents money and Western capitalism, and China only started wearing these ties after the mid-1980s.'[12] The religious texts on the walls, remnants of a past era, point to something else that has been lost in the new China, now a dynamic capitalist nation – albeit one without democracy.

Does an artist belong in his studio or in the world outside? If we look at Alexander Liberman's mid-1960s portrait of Mark Rothko (page 26), we see an image of a man removed from the world, his clothes paint-stained, smoking a cigarette in his own private space, lost in contemplation of his work. Fast-forward some fifty years, and, in a photograph from 2012 (page 27), we see the Singaporean artist Zhao Renhui not in his studio but in Yogyakarta, Indonesia, where he was exhibiting his own photographic work. His studio, aka his laptop, is travelling with him.

Whereas Rothko's move to the United States as a child was that of an exile, Zhao's travels have been those of a student (to London) or as an artist to residencies in such countries as Japan, Thailand and Wales. Rothko left America for the first time in 1950, aged forty-seven, and only three more times before his death in 1970. In contrast, by the age of thirty, Zhao had lost count of the number of times he had travelled outside Singapore. Of course, it is not only that Zhao, like many artists today, travels frequently, but also that he is rarely disconnected from the world. Although he too has a studio to retreat to occasionally, his laptop and smartphone give him a connectivity Rothko could never have imagined.

We can make a few other observations based on these images: like many of his generation, Rothko became famous late in life, whereas Zhao was exhibiting globally at an early age; painting dominated the art world Rothko knew, but now artists are just as likely to use a camera; and today, we cannot look only to New York, Paris or London for the best or most lively art, but must also consider many other cities – Yogyakarta and Singapore included.

In 1987 the American critic Donald Kuspit claimed that contemporary art was 'caught in a tug-of-war between what can be called the media and the therapeutic conditions of art'.[13] Or, to put it another way: is art now about making the world better, or is it merely a 'sophisticated entertainment'?[14] For Kuspit, '[Andy] Warhol was on one side, [Joseph] Beuys on the other.'[15] Warhol, as Kuspit saw it, represented narcissism and necrophilia. His identification with and uncritical appropriation of media images denied imagination and reduced the world to mere surface.

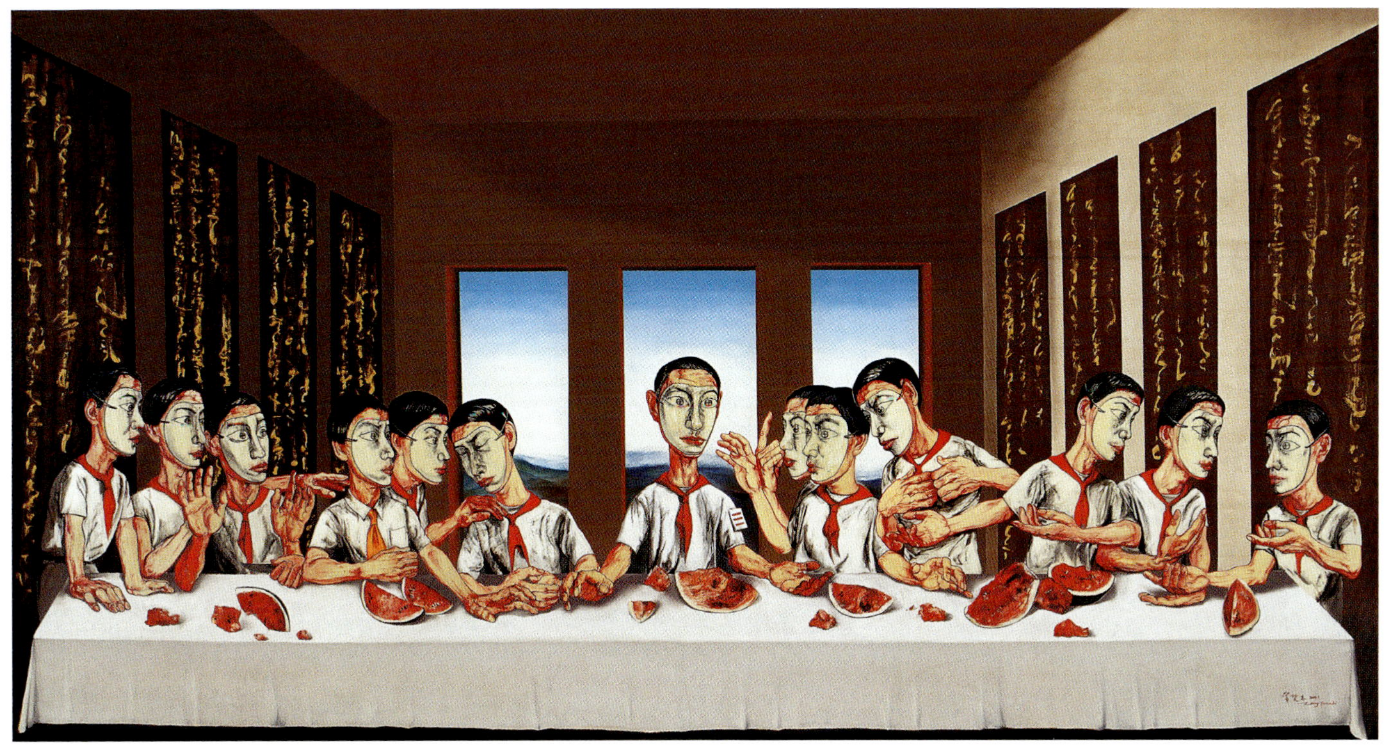

Zeng Fanzhi, *The Last Supper*, 2001
Oil on canvas, 220 × 400 cm (78¾ × 157½ in.)

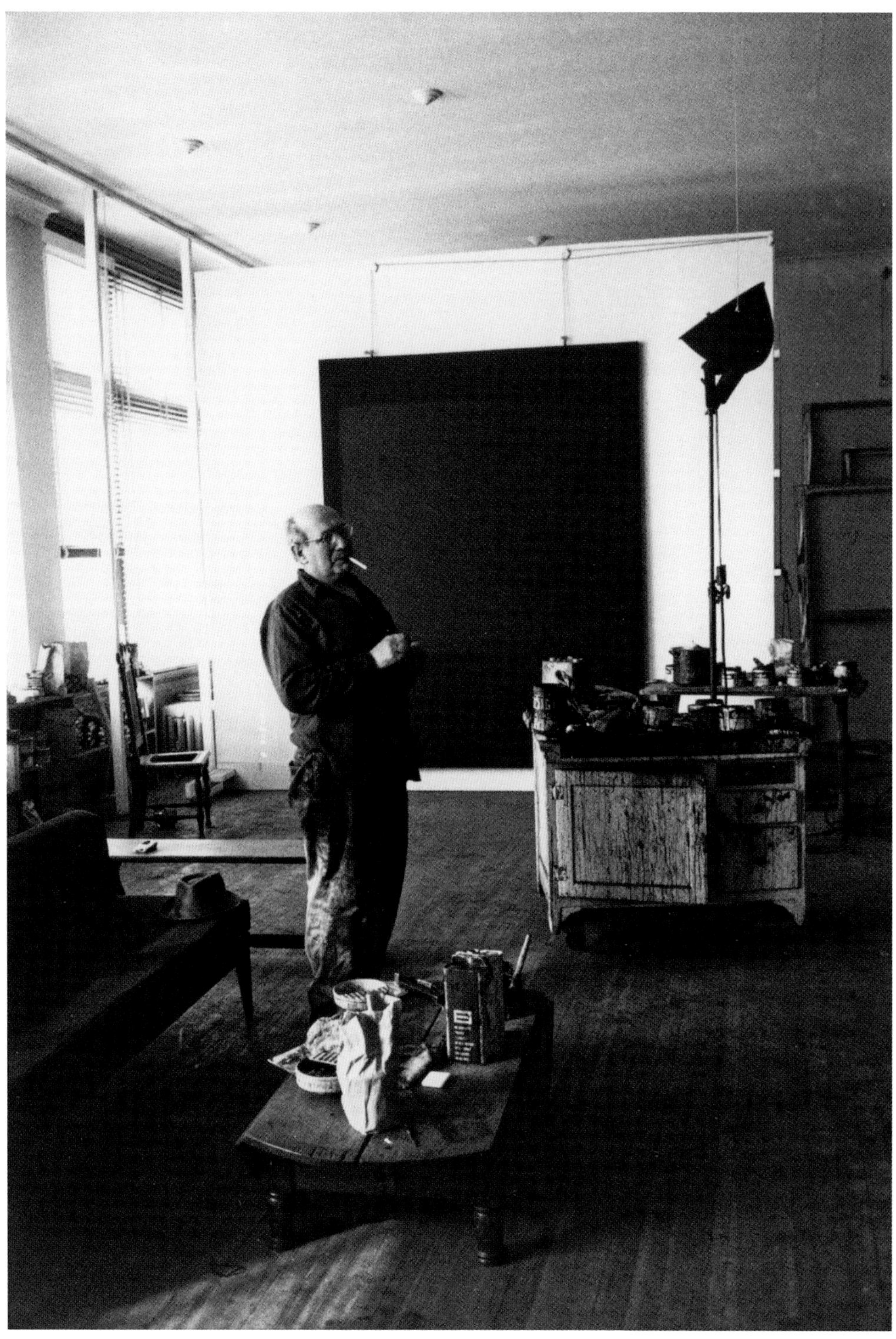

Mark Rothko in his studio, photographed by Alexander Liberman, 1964–68

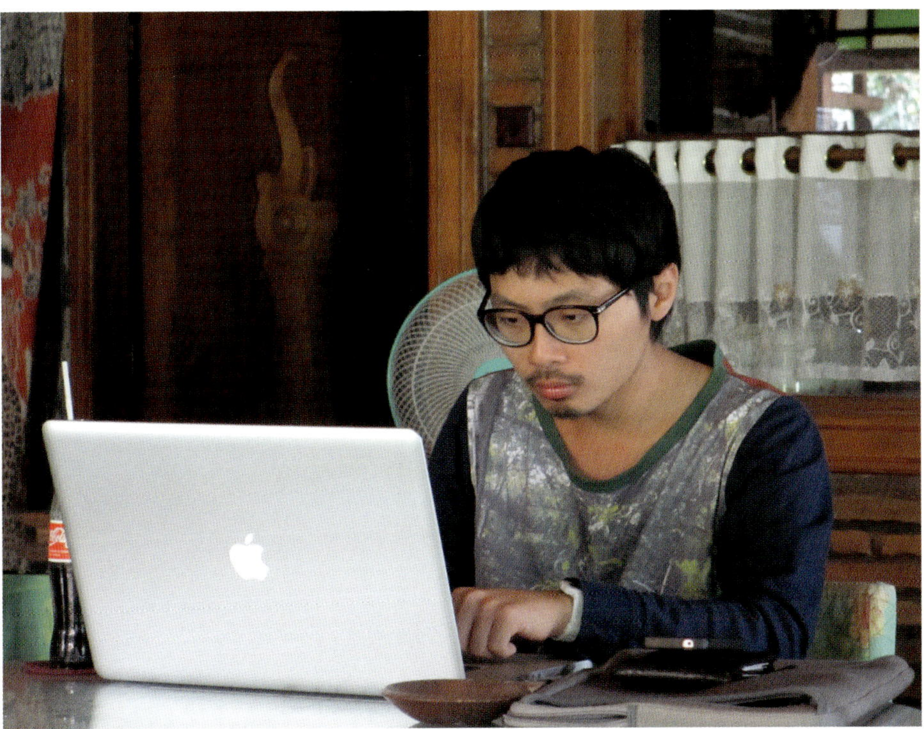

Robert Zhao Renhui in Yogyakarta, 2012

By contrast, Beuys was concerned with an art that dealt with psychoanalytical processes, and which could heal. Beuys was a utopian interested in changing the world; Warhol was interested in fame and the world of art.

Kuspit's question, albeit in a different form, is worth repeating: who do you believe in, Beuys or Warhol? Your answer will reveal much about how you view life and the world at large. Ask the same question of any two artists you find in the later chapters of this book. Who do you believe in?

As then, in the late 1980s, so it is now. Contemporary art, in all its many manifestations, echoes the problems we face in our daily lives: how to act, how to think, what to believe. Contemporary art can be entertaining, provocative, even irritating. Occasionally it is stunning, often it is difficult, but it is always alive. That is why it makes us think, why it puzzles and intrigues us – it is our world.

In the end, of course, we can never fully explain the most interesting and intriguing works of art. If we could, there would have been little point in making them. What is essential is that we experience them and think about them for ourselves. In writing this book, my aim has been to provide a context in which to better understand and experience the artworks of today by sharing my own experiences and thoughts.

Obviously, the world of art today is very different from the one that Gombrich wrote about, but much of what he said still rings true: 'One never finishes learning

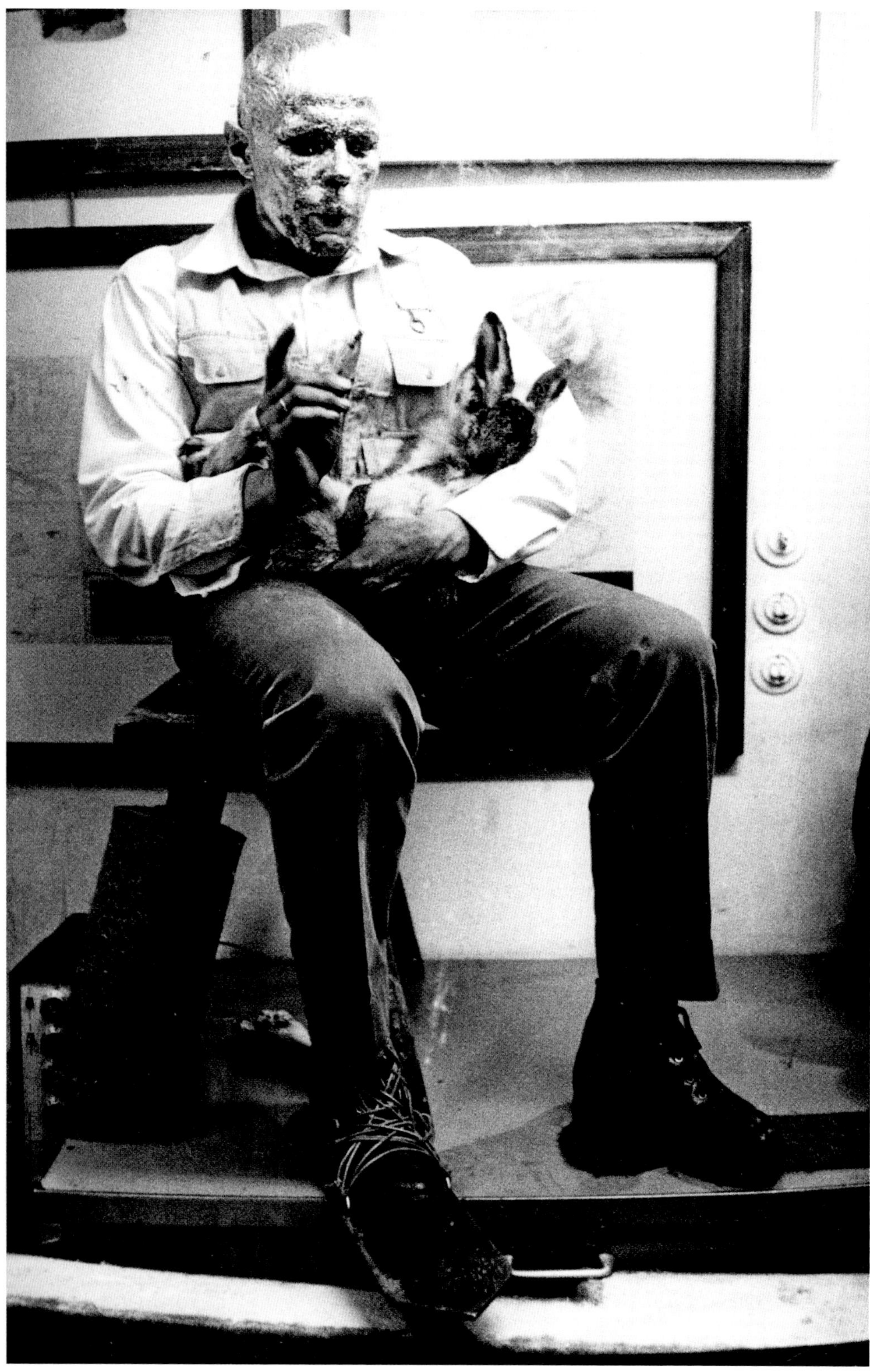

Joseph Beuys, *How to explain pictures to a dead hare*, 1965
Performance in the Schmela Gallery, Düsseldorf, 26 November 1965

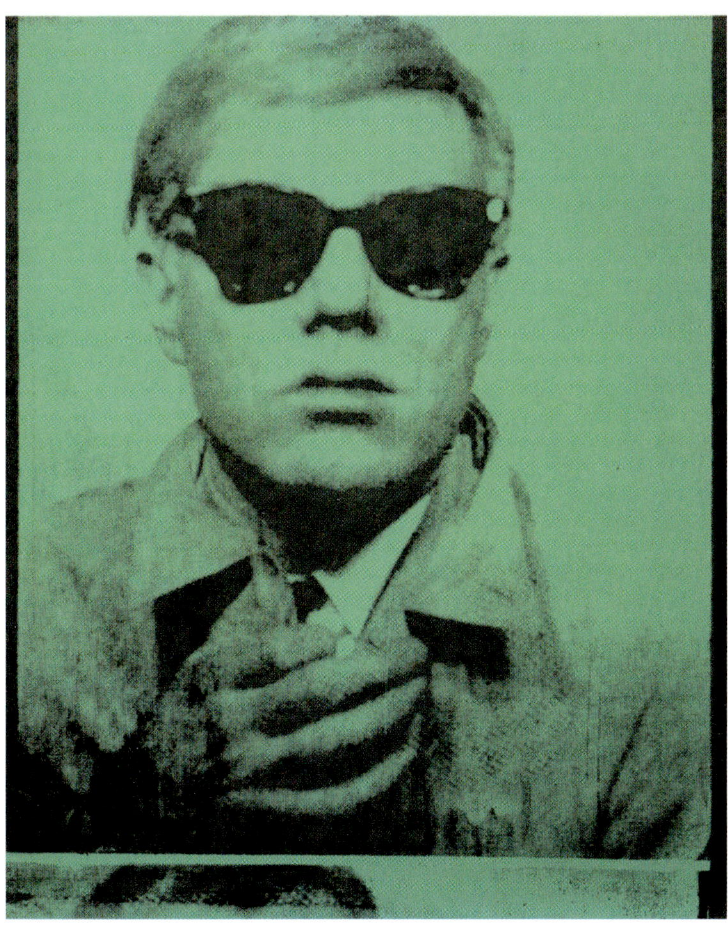

Andy Warhol, *Self-Portrait*, 1964
Silkscreen ink and acrylic paint on canvas, 50.8 × 40.6 cm (20 × 16 in.)

about art. There are always new things to discover. Great works of art seem to look different every time one stands before them. They seem to be as inexhaustible and unpredictable as real human beings. It is an exciting world of its own with its own strange laws and its adventures. Nobody should think he knows about it all for nobody does. Nothing, perhaps, is more important than just this: that to enjoy these works we must have a fresh mind, one which is ready to catch every hint and to respond to every hidden harmony: a mind, most of all, not cluttered up with long high-sounding words and ready-made phrases.'[16]

Chapter 1

THE WRECKAGE OF MODERNISM AND AFTER

1945–1979

After the War

Where do we look first?

Prior to the Second World War, Paris had been the traditional centre of the art world for more than two hundred years; but after the war, people began to realize that New York was more active – and richer. With Europe and Japan in ruins, the United States was now the most powerful nation in the world. Elsewhere, enormous changes were underway: the great empires of the nineteenth century were starting to collapse, and a new, post-colonial world was beginning to emerge. So let us look first of all at both New York and Yogyakarta, the revolutionary capital of the Republic of Indonesia, whose independence from the Netherlands was declared on 17 August 1945 by the nationalist leader Sukarno.[1]

Seko: Guerrilla advanced guard (page 32), by the Indonesian artist S. Sudjojono, and *Untitled (Violet, Black, Orange, Yellow on White and Red)* (page 31), by the American painter Mark Rothko, were both made in 1949. Clearly, they look very different from each other, but they were also made for different reasons. Rothko's painting, an example of the modernist abstraction pioneered by the likes of Mondrian and Kandinsky, is concerned with essentially private emotions: 'confronting and transcending loss' is one interpretation. It has no given title, no obvious subject, and was meant to be experienced by the individual privately. We look at the painting for its beauty; perhaps we also feel a sense of loss or something spiritual. Sudjojono's work, by contrast, was intended as a public expression of anger and pride: anger at the Dutch for destroying part of Yogyakarta; pride that his fellow Indonesians had fought back against the colonizers. The painting is meant to be a communal experience: art for Sudjojono had a role in nation building (specifically, the unification of a diverse body of nations connected only by their previous subjugation by the Dutch).

Paradoxically, Sudjojono wanted to make art that was outside Western modernism, to make a specifically 'Indonesian' art, but *Seko* is clearly modernist

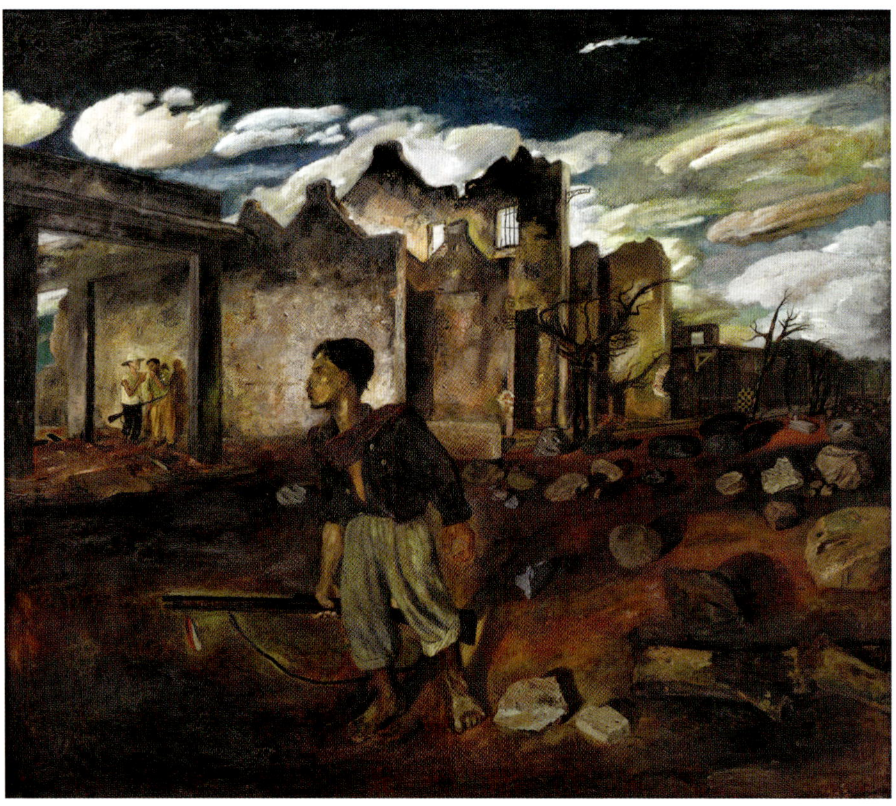

S. Sudjojono, *Seko: Guerilla advanced guard*, 1949
Oil on canvas, 173 × 194 cm (68⅛ × 76½ in.)

in its lineage, stretching back to Manet, Degas and so on. Or, to put it another way, the painting shows how Sudjojono ingested or cannibalized Western modernism to the point where it became his own language. Indeed, automatically labelling modernism as 'Western' is now seen as problematic: although its roots might lie in the West (albeit much influenced by Japanese prints and African and Oceanic sculpture), over the course of the twentieth century other peoples contributed to its development, making it more of a global tradition and way of thinking and making.

For Sudjojono, as for other artists in similar, newly independent countries, or where communism had become dominant, art was about action – communal action. This was the opposite of what Rothko and his peers were seeking. Soon after making *Seko*, Sudjojono joined the Communist Party (he would give up membership in 1958; see Chapter 2) and began depicting reality more exactly and dispassionately.

In effect, Sudjojono and Rothko were asking two questions that are crucial to contemporary art: *who* is art for, and *what* is art for?

In 1952 the Japanese artist On Kawara painted *Thinking Man*. The man is naked, emaciated and blotched, isolated in an empty room. The outline of his body is covered

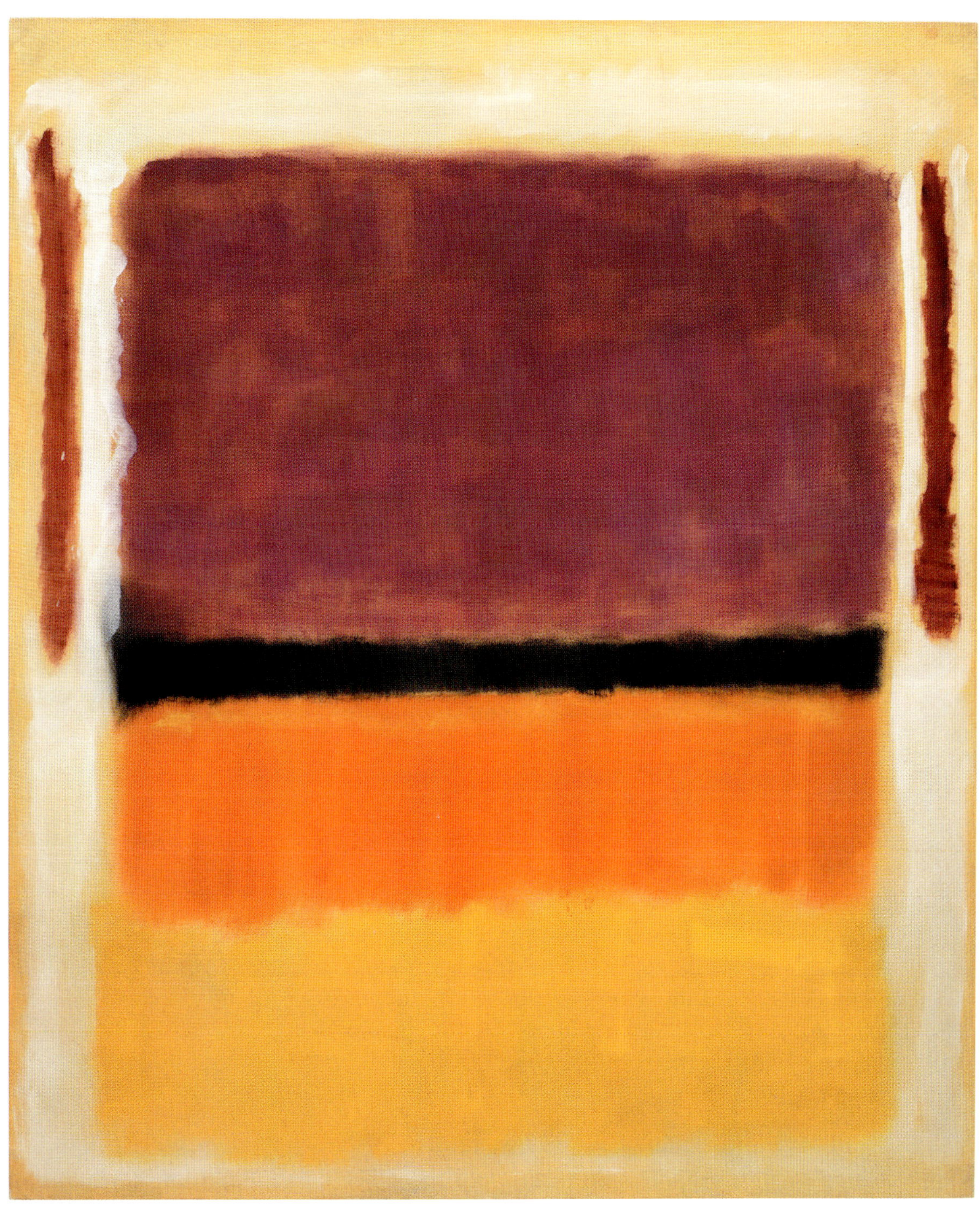

Mark Rothko, *Untitled (Violet, Black, Orange, Yellow on White and Red)*, 1949
Oil on canvas, 207 × 167.6 cm (81½ × 66 in.)

with prickles or stitches. The figure seems pained and anxious, and so does the act of making this pared-down work. It seems to express the horror of the war in Japan and its subsequent effects: radiation sickness, starvation, a loss of faith. But this is not social realism: Kawara was seeking a new way to express such sensations of angst and dislocation. When he was thirteen the atomic bomb dropped and Japan surrendered. Kawara's world and the belief system he had been brought up with collapsed. 'Recently,' he wrote in 1955, 'the notion of humanity has been threatened by matter. In daily life I feel this every moment. Political and economic anxieties overwhelm individuals.'[2]

The post-war trauma included a crisis of faith – indeed, a crisis of meaning. To many people, all the old belief systems seemed discredited: what could you now believe in? This loss of faith, and the need for it, was most acute in Japan: 'Japan's defeat and the subsequent collapse of a traditional order had shaken many to the core so that the chaos of post-war was also experienced as a personal crisis of existence.'[3] In 1945 the number of officially registered religions in Japan was 43; but once the emperor had been shown to be merely human, the country experienced what has been called 'the rush hour of the gods': by 1951, another 677 religions had been registered.[4]

People wanted more than ever to believe in God (or gods) and a better world. For many, however, retaining their faith proved very difficult. Nowhere is this more apparent than in the paintings of the New Zealand artist Colin McCahon. From the start of his career, McCahon had a sense that 'true communism means true Christianity, and I believe that by my painting I help to bring it about'.[5] But what he fixated on was a scene of doubt: that moment when Christ, nailed to the cross, cries out, asking why God has forsaken him.

Like many others, McCahon wobbled from sect to sect: from Presbyterian to Quaker to Catholic. He had visions of a landscape before God – and a benevolent god at that – but his faith was always insecure: 'I could never call myself a Christian,' he once said.[6] An avant-garde artist in a conservative country, he was much maligned, suffered, and drank too much. By the 1950s, images of people had disappeared from his paintings and been replaced with words. He prefigured much of what would happen a decade later, but he was ten thousand miles away from New York, on the periphery, unknown. At the end of his life, he remarked: 'I think I am a Christian – perhaps I am.'[7] With their giant scale and biblical or poetic phrases, his late paintings seem like statements of faith, such as a prophet might make. But they are really attempts to find faith and some certainty. Above all, McCahon wanted to reach out to an audience and be understood.

Uncertainty gives birth to questions and experiments. In 1956, at an exhibition of the avant-garde Gutai group, recently founded in Japan, Atsuko Tanaka appeared wearing her *Electric Dress* (page 36), an outfit composed of 190 light bulbs or tubes, half of them painted in various colours, which blinked on and off sporadically. Another of her pieces, *Work (Bell)* (1955), consisted of a series of electric bells spread out on the floor; the viewer (or listener) was invited to activate the bells by pressing

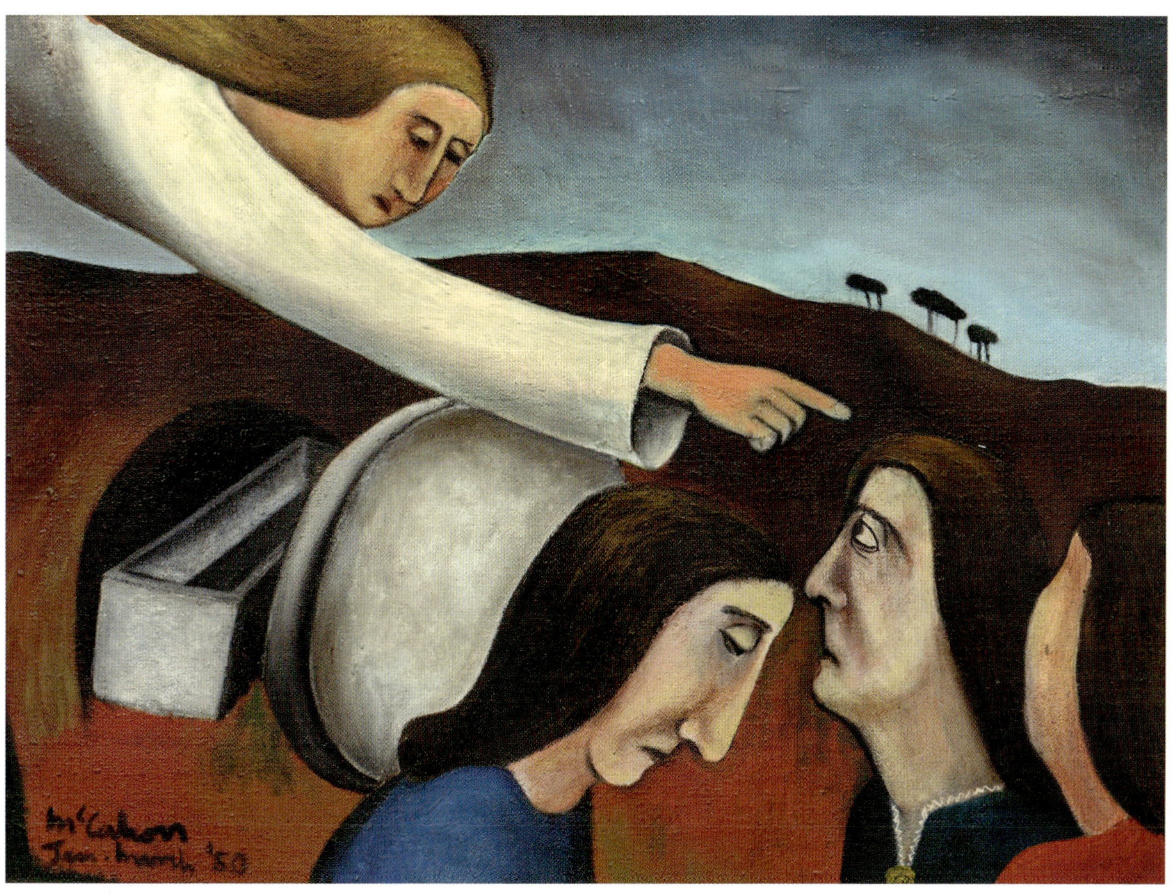

Colin McCahon, *The Marys at the Tomb*, 1950
Oil on canvas on hardboard, 80.6 × 105.4 cm (31¾ × 41½ in.)

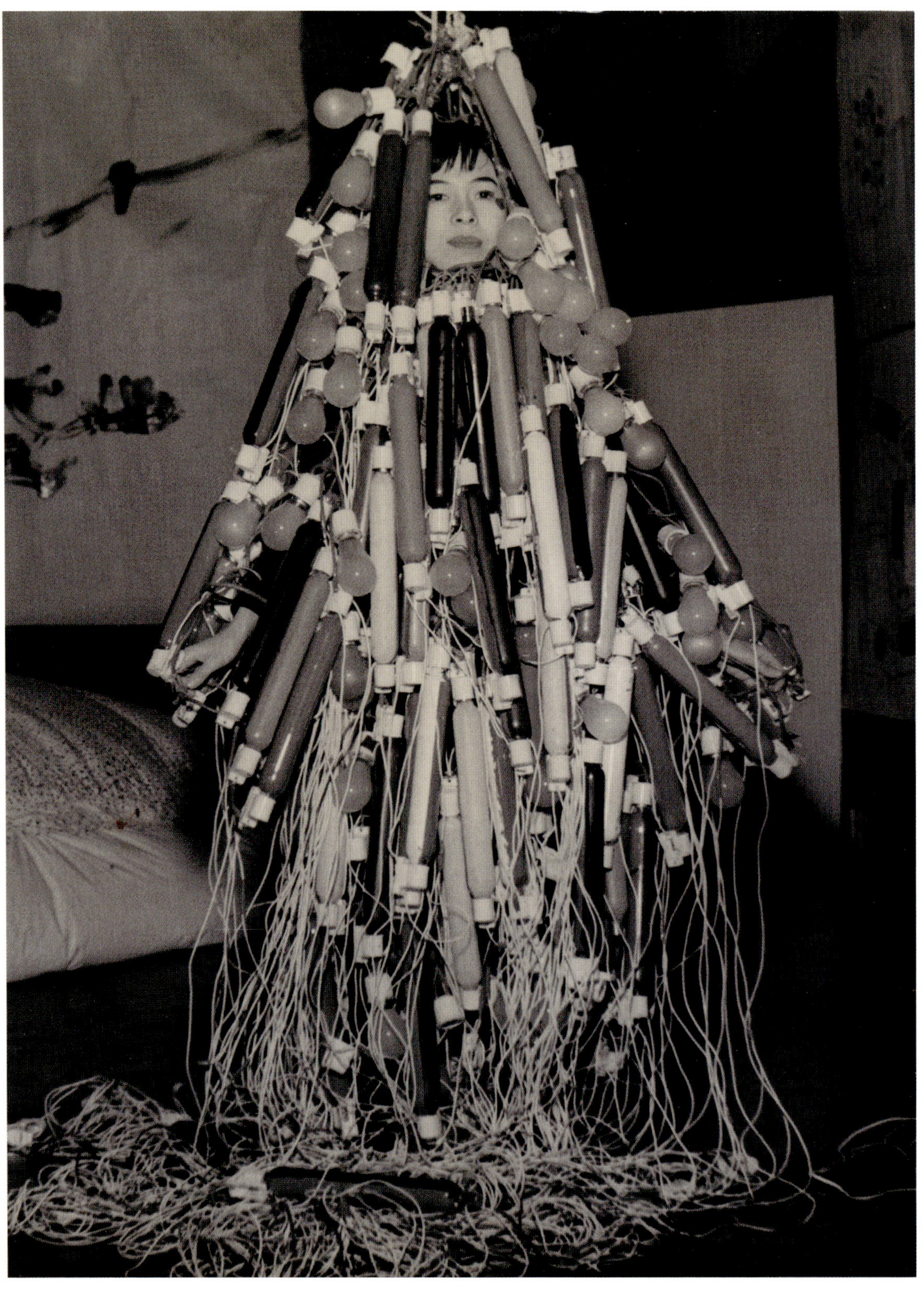

Atsuko Tanaka wearing her *Electric Dress*, 1956
Installation view, 2nd Gutai Art Exhibition, Ohara Hall, Tokyo

a switch. In its use of nondescript, functional objects and its invitation to participate, *Work (Bell)* anticipated much later work. But like her Gutai contemporaries, Tanaka stopped making such experimental pieces, instead producing paintings that, although derived from the idea of electric circuits, were effectively abstract, looking not so different from all the other abstract paintings being made around the world – Art Informel in France, Abstract Expressionism in the United States. There was a market and context for such painting, but there was as yet no context, let alone a market, for more experimental work.

Tanaka and her peers had, however, been among the first artists to ask the third question that underlies contemporary art: *what* is art anyway?

The 1960s

In 1960 the Indonesian artist Srihadi Soedarsono travelled to the United States to begin a two-year MFA at Ohio State University in Columbus. He was greeted by Roy Lichtenstein, who, as an artist-in-residence at the university, was making heavily textured abstract paintings. Although Srihadi had started his career in the 1940s, designing posters for the forces fighting to free Indonesia from Dutch colonial rule, he had chosen a modernist education and turned to abstraction. However, on returning to Indonesia, where the economy had collapsed in 1962, he was appalled by the poverty he saw. Suddenly, abstraction seemed strangely irrelevant. He wanted to make paintings that felt contemporary, but which also bore witness to what he saw around him: hungry people (page 38).

Everywhere there was a feeling that abstract painting had become too predictable and empty. By 1962, Lichtenstein had also forsaken abstraction and was helping to initiate Pop art. Like the London-born Pauline Boty, one of the few female artists in the Pop movement, Lichtenstein wanted an art that seemed NOW.[8] They both looked to advertising and consumer goods for imagery and style. Boty's painting *5-4-3-2-1* (page 39) is exuberant, funny and a statement of active female sexuality – 'Oh for a fu ...', reads the text in the speech bubble.

In 1964 the American artist Donald Judd claimed that 'Abstract Expressionism is dead. It sure looks dead.'[9] The collector Robert Scull certainly thought so. On 13 October 1965, Scull sold off most of the Abstract Expressionist paintings in his collection. He made good money because, although the Abstract Expressionists were still alive and painting, they had been given the status of old masters – with equivalent prices. Scull wanted to spend the money from the sale on the new art of his time: Pop art. This was a shock to many. It showed, some claimed, Scull was vulgar, the nouveau-riche owner of a taxi-cab business.

Although, arguably, Pop art had begun in England, its chief practitioner and philosopher, Warhol, was American. When Scull commissioned Warhol to produce

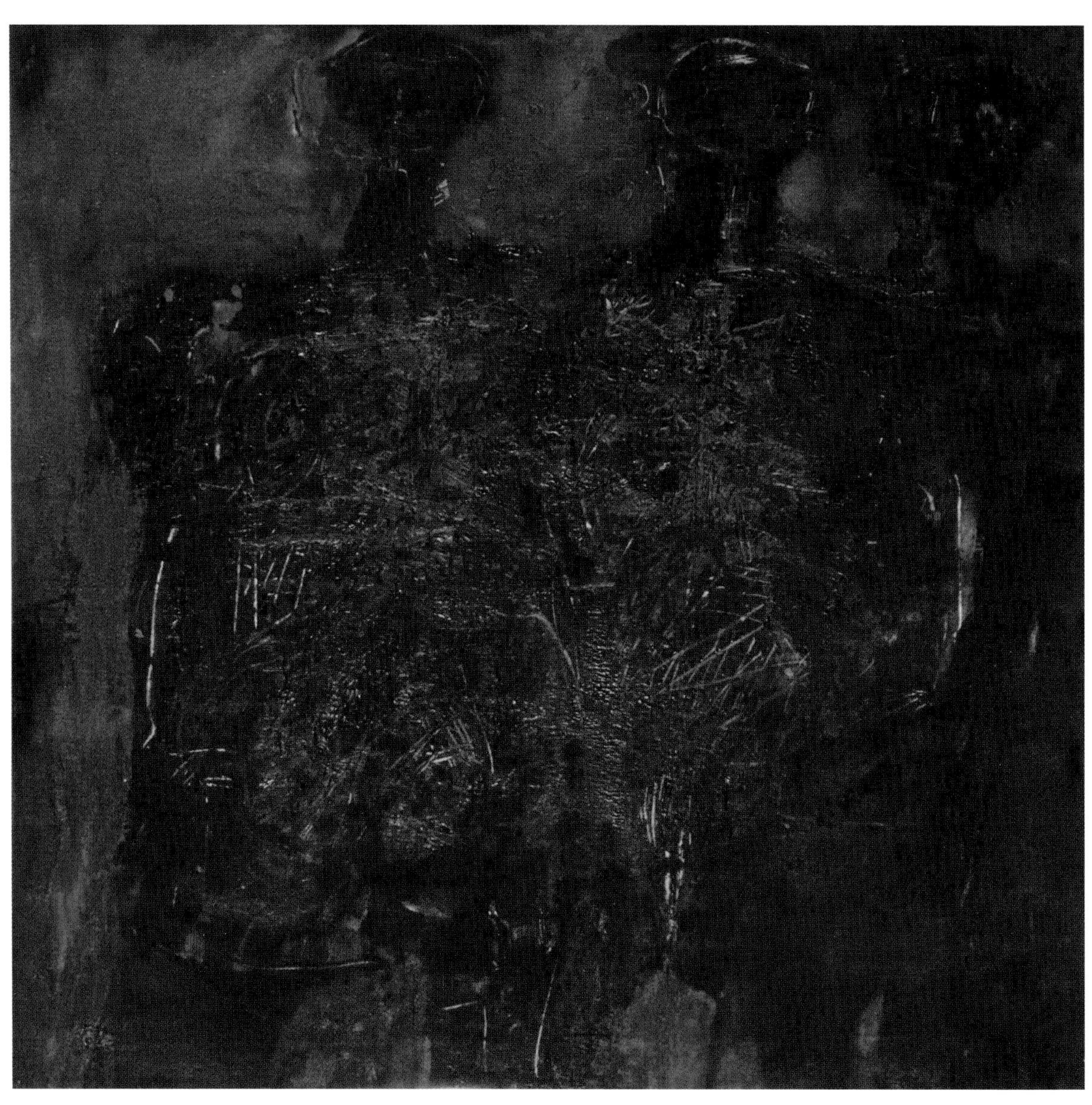

Srihadi Soedarsono, *Orang-Orang Lapar* (The Hungry People), 1962
Oil on canvas, 130 × 130 cm (51¼ × 51¼ in.)

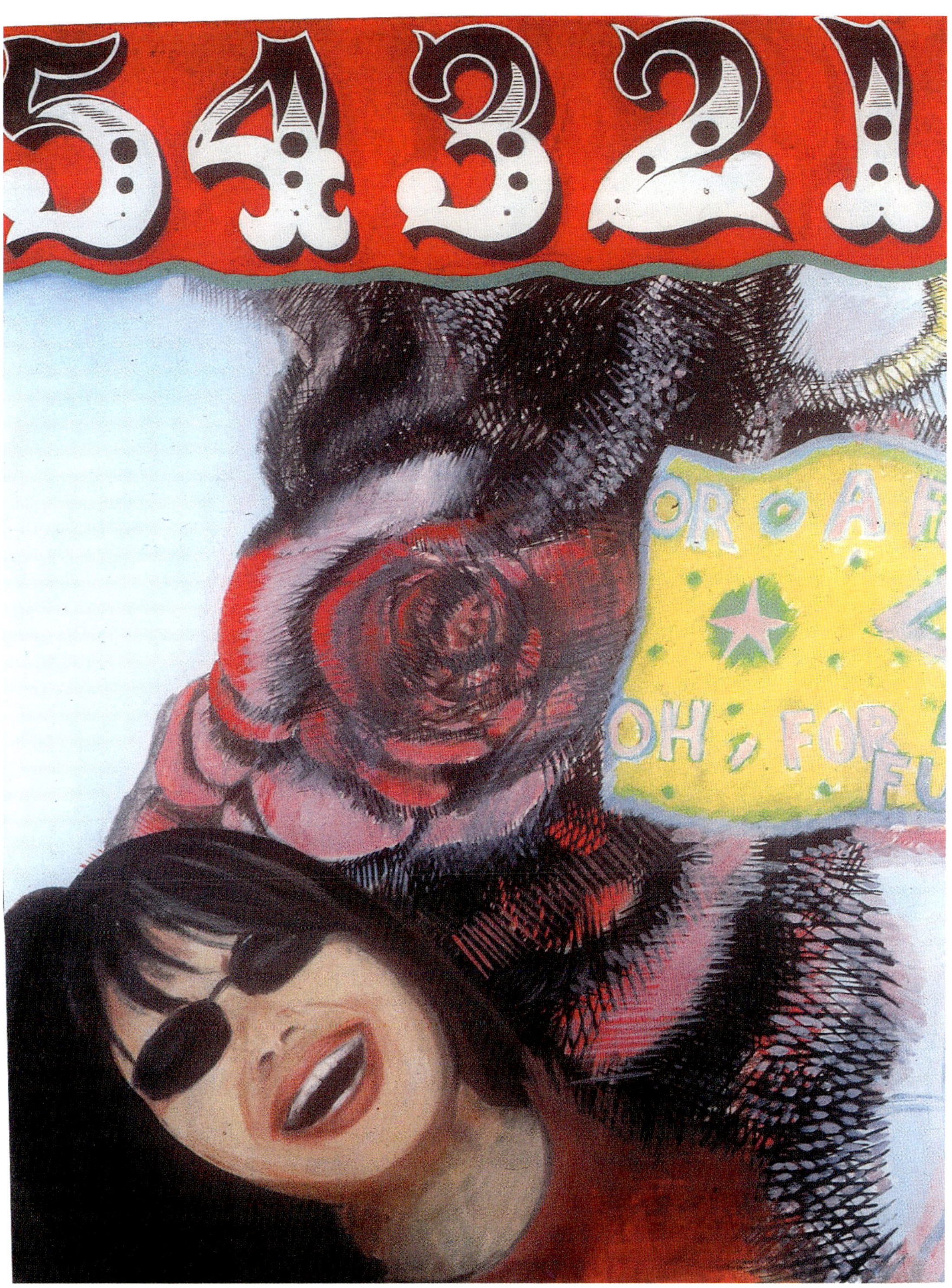

Pauline Boty, *5-4-3-2-1*, 1963
Oil on canvas, 125 × 100 cm (49¼ × 39¼ in.)

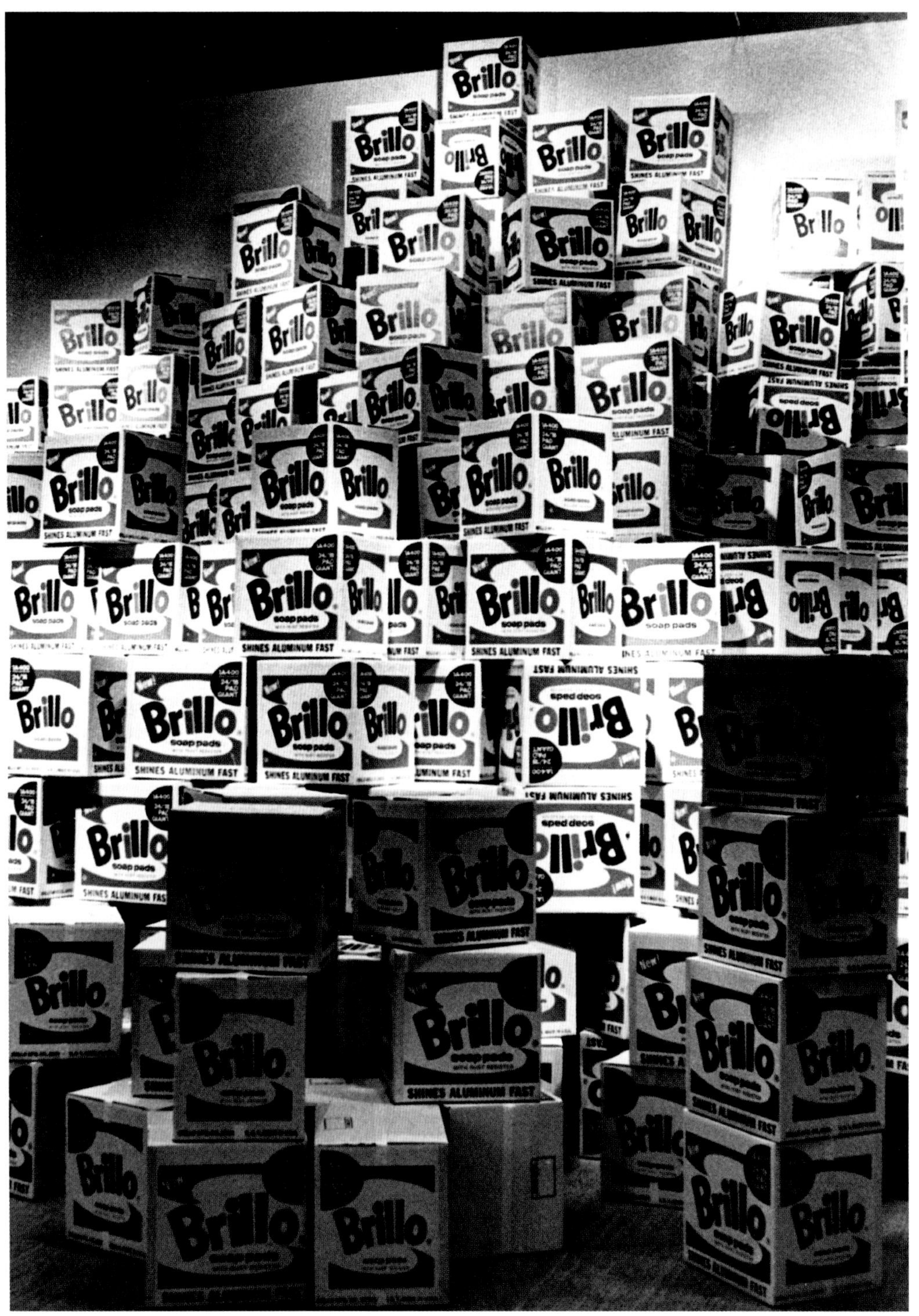

Brillo soap pads boxes at Warhol's retrospective
at Moderna Museet, Stockholm, 1968

a portrait of his wife, Ethel, in 1963, Warhol took her to a photo booth, asked her to pose in various ways, then silkscreened thirty-four of the resulting photos – two of them twice, in reverse – to produce a composite portrait, *Ethel Scull 36 Times*. The following year, at the Stable Gallery in New York, Warhol exhibited hundreds of packing boxes for Brillo pads, Del Monte peach halves, Campbell's tomato juice and Heinz tomato ketchup. The boxes were laid out in rows or stacked somewhat randomly on the floor or on window sills, as if they had just been delivered and the workers had been too rushed to pile them neatly. The boxes were not, however, the 'real' thing. Instead, they had been made by Warhol's assistants from wood and then silkscreened. They were simulacra.

The philosopher Arthur C. Danto was intrigued. If this was art, who decided that it was and that the original Brillo box was not? Danto answered his own question in an essay entitled 'The Artworld', published in the October 1964 edition of the *Journal of Philosophy*. Warhol's *Brillo Box* was art, Danto argued, because it was shown in a gallery and people in the art world accepted it as such. It did not need some magic ingredient, some 'artiness', to make it art. 'With the *Brillo Box*,' wrote Danto, 'the true character of the philosophical question of the nature of art had been attained.'

Four years later, in 1968, the Moderna Museet in Stockholm staged the first museum-based retrospective of Warhol's work. The budget was too small to ship over Warhol's original Brillo boxes, so instead the museum contacted the Brillo company in New York, ordered 500 of the actual delivery boxes at 20 cents each, and had them flat-packed and sent to Stockholm. The museum staff then assembled the boxes and stacked them up for the exhibition (opposite). Nobody seemed to notice. Indeed, one could argue that, by playing the game of real/simulacra, the museum staff were acting like artists too.[10] Today, of course, Warhol's Brillo boxes fetch huge amounts of money at auction; in 2010, for example, one sold for $3,050,500.[11] Sealed within protective Perspex containers, the boxes are displayed reverentially as icons of contemporary art.

As was the culture of advertising and commodities it reflected, Pop art became an international phenomenon. It was smart, up to date and easy to understand. Soon there were Pop artists in Germany, Japan, Venezuela, Australia ... It was also at this time that the first genuinely global avant-garde artists' group emerged, Fluxus. Founded by George Maciunas in the early 1960s, it involved poets and musicians as well as artists. Fluxus events constituted experimental art at its most chaotic or anti-sense, closer to vaudeville than any form of 'high art', sometimes funny, often silly. Collaborations were a key part of these events – inluding one between the Korean émigré Nam June Paik and Joseph Beuys, who billed themselves as the world's worst two piano players.

In 1962 Paik had himself performed for the first time his *One for Violin Solo*, in which he took a violin and smashed it on a table. He insisted that the piece should always be performed with a high-quality violin, ideally a Stradivarius,

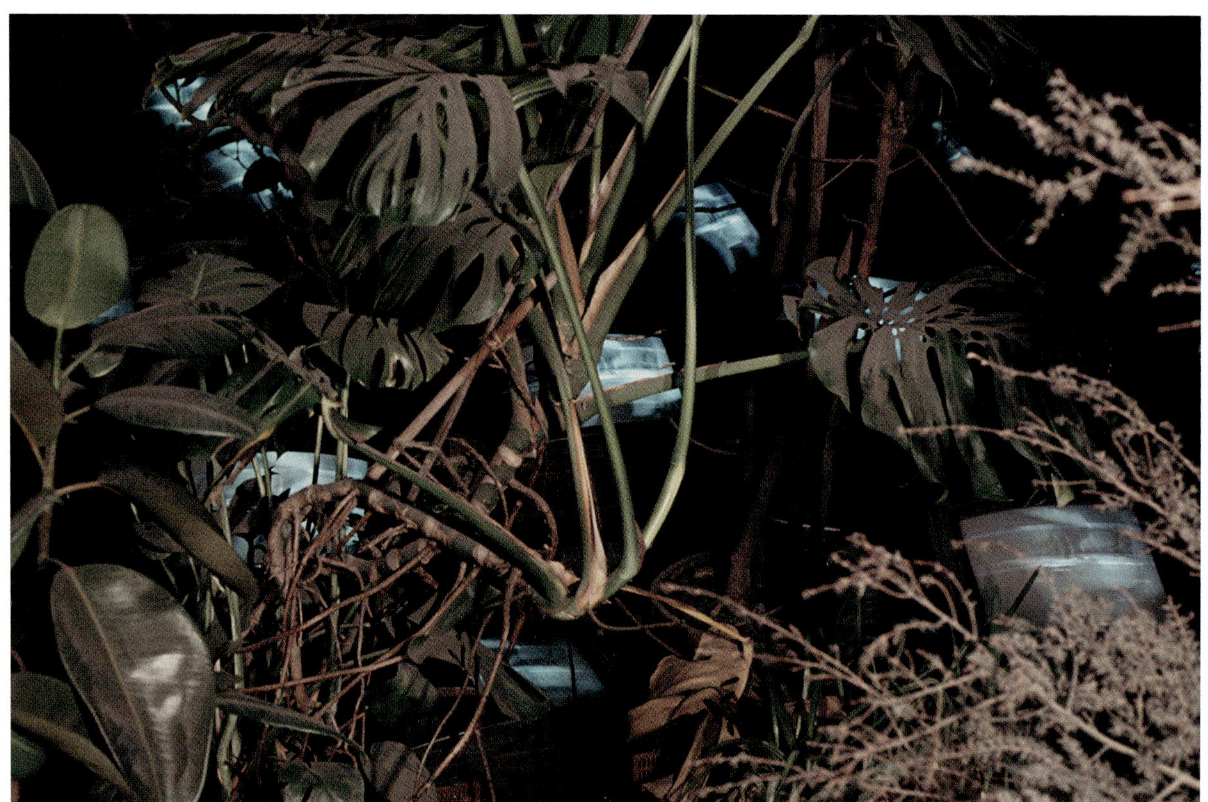

Nam June Paik, *TV Garden*, 1974
Installation view, documenta 6, Kassel, Germany, 1977

so that a good sound could be obtained. Paik's great innovation, however, was in working with video – distorting the signals, mixing the images and, above all, treating the television as a sculptural object. In his *TV Garden* (above), for example, numerous televisions, surrounded by pot plants, show a helter-skelter melange of moving imagery.

For his part, Beuys liked the 'anything goes' attitude of Fluxus, but his performances – or 'actions', as he called them – were more like ceremonies or rites of passage. Spending a week in a cage with a coyote, sweeping the street and putting all the rubbish in a vitrine, spending eight hours hidden in a roll of felt, a dead hare at each end of the roll – these and other such actions were meant to demonstrate his philosophy, the need for psychic healing, a deeper awareness of nature. We can be healed, our lives transformed, he believed, through his concept of 'social sculpture'. Everything in life, said Beuys, can be art: boxes of fat or peeling a potato or sealing up an old piano.

Beuys's *Revolutionary Piano* consisted of an upright piano filled with red roses. Contained within a glass vitrine marked with a brown cross, the piano was for ever silent. The roses, faded but preserved, were symbolic of the revolutionary writer and activist Rosa Luxemburg ('Red Rosa'), who was murdered by right-wing thugs in 1919. When the work was installed in the Museum Abteiburg, Mönchengladbach, in 1982, Beuys had himself photographed remaking it (below)– for that too was an action. The piano remains sealed and silent in perpetuity.

The notion that art could be both an event and therapeutic was also held by the Japanese artist Yayoi Kusama – although it was therapy for herself, rather than society at large, that interested her. Kusama moved to New York in 1958, aged twenty-nine, and became known for her 'infinity net' paintings.[12] Working non-stop for up to fifty hours at a time, she would cover each canvas with tiny loops. As a child she had suffered from hallucinations, patterns often spreading over everything she could see – an experience that may have induced such obsessional behaviour. 'I did not have any purpose,' Kusama has lamented. 'I felt that art and life were useless. I painted boredom, which is more important in life than the effect of sunlight which the Impressionists painted.'[13] In the 1960s she began applying her practice to sculptures and environments, covering everything in polka dots

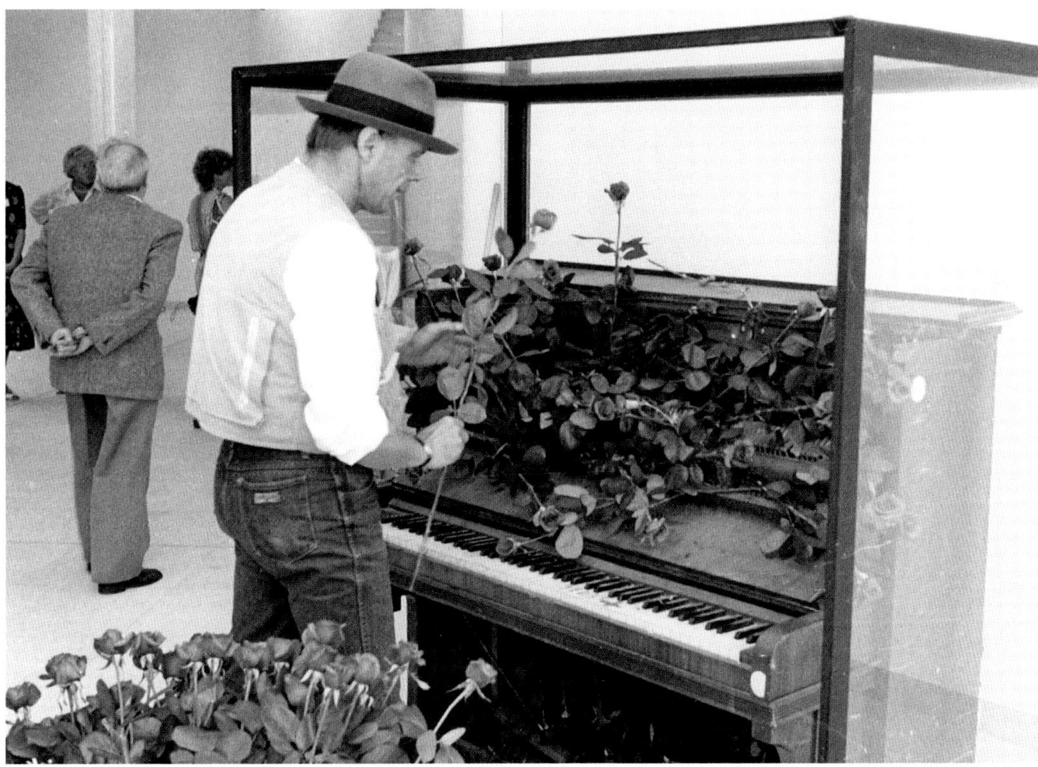

Joseph Beuys, *Revolutionary Piano* (*Revolutions Klavier*), 1969
Installation view, opening of Museum Abteiburg, Mönchengladbach, Germany, 1982

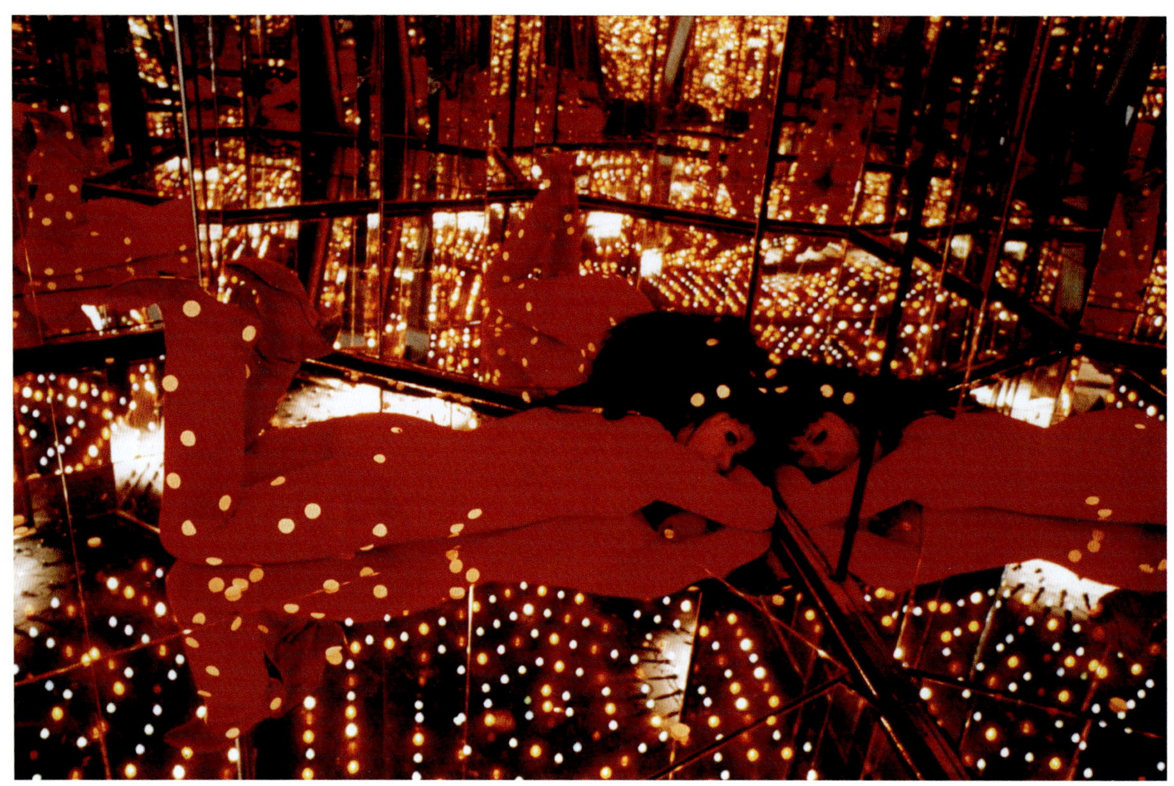

Yayoi Kusama pictured in her *Infinity Mirror Room – Love Forever*, 1966
Installation view, 'Kusama's Peep Show: Endless Love Show', Castellane Gallery, New York

or penis-shaped cloth appendages. The work seemed to be ego-less; but Kusama, wishing to embody the concepts that lay behind her creations, loved being photographed either in front of or lying on top of them.

The most ambitious of Kusama's environments was her 'peep show' (opposite), a 2.4-metre-wide (8 ft) mirror-covered hexagonal chamber that people could look into through one of two apertures. On the ceiling, arranged in hexagonal patterns, were Christmas lights that flashed on and off, creating infinite reflections in the mirrors. At the same time, observed the art critic Peter Schjeldahl after experiencing the work for himself, 'a loud tape of Beatles songs blends in your ears with the lively rattle (like metal popcorn) of the light switches, reinforcing your sense of having been removed to another, rather awesome, world.'[14] Subsequently, Kusama focused on performance pieces, often getting other people to take their clothes off in public and be painted with polka dots. Very 1960s! Very cool!

Minimalism

In such exhibitions as 'Primary Structures', held at the Jewish Museum, New York, in 1966, Donald Judd, Carl Andre and other artists showed their rejection of Abstract Expressionism – and of the notion of the artwork as the unique expression of a unique genius – by using industrial materials and simple, repeated forms. Judd had box-like structures fabricated, to be seen singly or in groups; Andre, meanwhile, laid out ordinary bricks or identical metal plates in lines or grids. Such repetition was associated with industrial production, not artistic freedom. What was crucial was the thinking that surrounded these artists' works, and how they were intended to be experienced – in time, by being walked around or, in Andre's case, walked on. (Andre wanted art to be experienced directly by the body, by the feet as well as the eyes. Sadly, however, few museums today will allow visitors to walk on his works.) Placement was also crucial: for Judd and Andre, the meaning of their work depended on its relation to the space it was installed in.

Around 1968 a group of artists in Japan known as *Mono-ha* (School of Things) began to exhibit together. Their work was as simple as that of Judd or Andre, but more likely to be made from materials found in nature, such as earth, stone and wood. Often, two materials would be combined – rock and metal, for example. The Korean-born Lee Ufan, the best known of the *Mona-ha* artists, called his works 'encounters'. Talking about his art in 2010, Lee said: 'In America, Minimalism [reduced] art to the very object itself. But the irony is that when you reduce art to that level, then all of a sudden the viewer's attention shifts from the object itself to everything else. What kind of space is it in? What kind of time is it? ... The aim of my work, from the outset, is to show everything else.'[15]

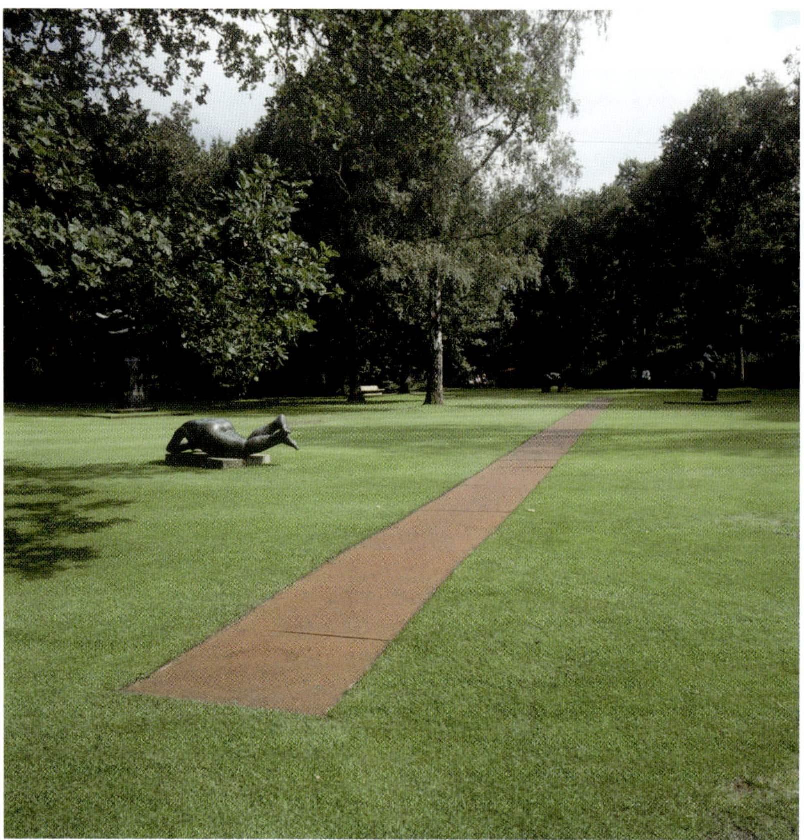

Carl Andre, *43 Roaring Forty*, 1988
Cold rolled steel, 43 squares, each 100 × 100 cm (39⅜ × 39⅜ in.)

Unlike Judd, Lee was inclined to think of his work as poetic and transcendent. In a 1997 essay titled 'Stand Still a Moment', he asked:

> Agitated, busy people, stop and stand still for just a moment. Look at the blue sky. Close your eyes and take a deep breath.
>
> If you will do this, you will change and the world will come to life.
>
> Bashō expressed this in a poem:
>
> The ancient pond –
> A frog jumps in,
> The sound of water.
>
> The poet was able to sense the reverberations of a larger universe in this tiny, momentary event.
>
> My own work is aimed at creating stimulating moments of this kind in the impassive world of everyday life.[16]

Lee goes on to point out that Bashō, a Japanese poet writing in the seventeenth century, used words to create indirect images, whereas art produces direct encounters. Tellingly, Lee's work is always most effective when sited in a beautiful garden or an old building (page 48, top).

Another approach to sculpture was to put the emphasis on exploring process. Such an approach was epitomized by the American Richard Serra's 'Verb List', written in 1967–68 as a sort of manifesto for art-making, a list of ninety verbs and sixteen conditions: 'to roll, to crease, to fold, to store, to bend ... of location, of context, of time.'[17] Location, context and time are crucial to a work such as Serra's *Spin Out (for Robert Smithson)*, installed in the sculpture park of the Kröller-Müller Museum in the Netherlands (page 48, bottom). Three large plates of steel are partly embedded in a bowl-shaped hollow; one can walk between them, or walk along a ridge above and look down on them through the trees. The work seems very different in spring and autumn. It is a simple, precise intervention in the world, creating multiple, intriguing experiences.

Conceptual Art

What was conceptual art? And why did it happen? It could emerge in many forms, for example, the presentation of a ready-made, the documention of some act or proposition, often as a photograph, language with no image, or an intervention in space. A simplistic definition is that it's a form of artistic practice where the idea or concept is more important than the actual object. A more appropriate definition, however, would focus on its uncertainty. Whenever you see a painting or sculpture, you instantly know it is art; it's as if the painting acts like a statement: 'I am a painting, therefore I am a work of art!' But when you see a photo of a field or a pile of stones, you have no such certainty. We could say, therefore, that a conceptual artwork functions more like a question: 'Could I be a work of art?'

This uncertainty, this doubt, runs deep. Conceptual art has been described as 'Modernism's nervous breakdown'.[18] Now, what does that mean? That art until then had been healthy and sane, albeit increasingly stressed, but had then collapsed suddenly, unable to continue? The notion promoted by modernists – that modernism was a coherent logical progression, and that there was only one way to make modern art – had been teased by Marcel Duchamp and subsequently mocked by Warhol and others. Now it was taking a kicking. Crudely speaking, modernism had been seen as a relay race: Gustave Courbet, the first off the blocks, had handed the baton to Manet, who had handed it to Cézanne, who had handed it to Picasso, who had handed it to Jackson Pollock, who had handed it to another abstract painter ... but then confusion! The baton had been dropped. There was no longer a race going in one direction, no evident line of progression. It was as if the runners had stopped mid-race to ask what the race was actually all about.

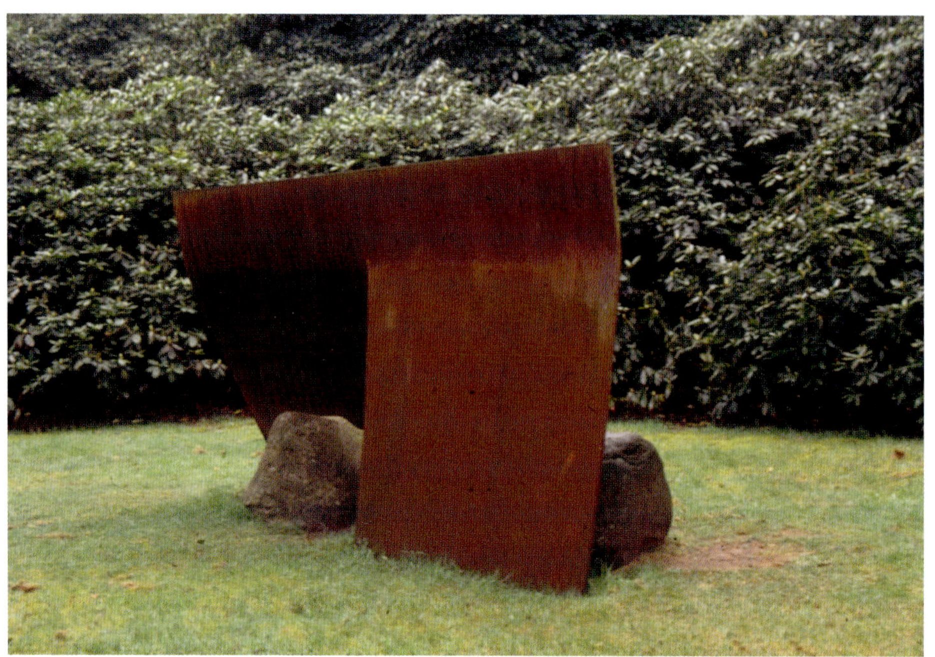

Lee Ufan, *Relatum*, 1979–80
Steel, stone, 197 × 105 × 402 cm (77⅝ × 41⅜ × 158⅜ in.)

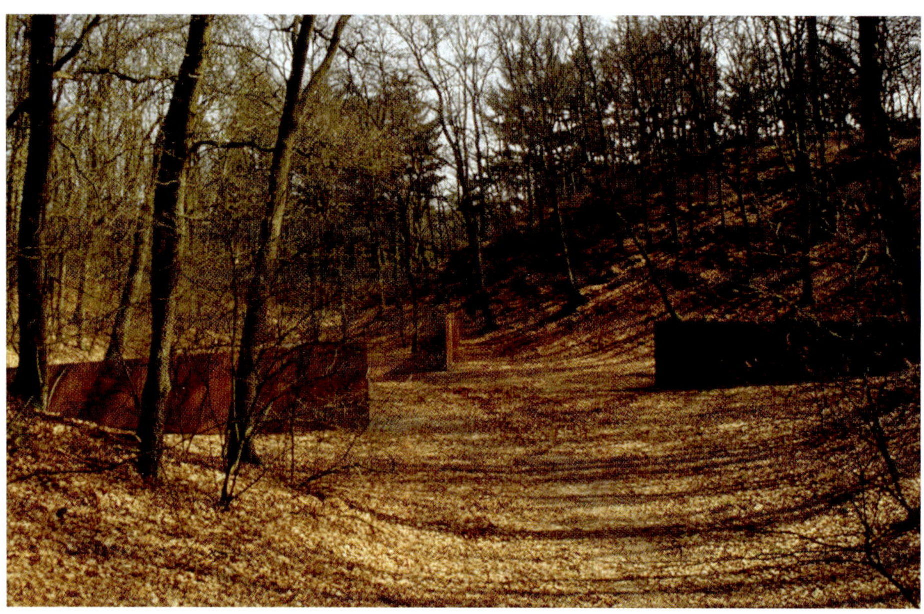

Richard Serra, *Spin Out (for Robert Smithson)*, 1972–73
Cor-ten steel, 3 parts, each 250 × 120 × 4 cm (98½ × 47¼ × 1⅝ in.)

But how could you make art out of doubt?

Certainly, Warhol – like Duchamp before him – had made art that poked fun at the art world's pretensions, but the conceptual art that emerged in the late 1960s was different in both its seriousness and its analytical approach. Crucially, it appeared more or less simultaneously in several cities before spreading like a virus across the world; or, as others maintained, like a breath of clean, fresh air. In some places it mutated. In others, it transpired that something like conceptual art was happening already.

This was not just a rejection of modernist progress; it also came from a conviction that something fundamental was wrong with the modern world. There were too many corrupt or tyrannical governments, too many old men in charge, an unfair distribution of wealth, and increasing ecological degradation. Above all else, however, there was the Vietnam War. By the start of 1968 there were more than half a million US soldiers in Vietnam, although few of them could have told you why they were there. It was turning out to be a bloody, pointless, humiliating quagmire.

Conceptual art was made in the shadow of the Vietnam War. But in what sense was Richard Long's straight line walked through grass (page 51), or John Baldessari's *Pencil Story* (page 11), a protest against America's involvement in the war? It would require very special pleading to turn either of these works into an anti-war poster, yet they both challenged accepted norms: of what an artist does, of what an artwork is, of what the art world is.

There were, of course, many protests against the Vietnam War, both in America and beyond. There were even explicit protests within the art world. The New York-based Art Workers' Coalition (AWC), for example, not only made posters based on photographs of the Mai Lai massacre, in which up to five hundred unarmed Vietnamese civilians were murdered by US troops, but also posed with the posters in front of *Guernica*, Picasso's famous denunciation of fascist atrocities, then on display at the Museum of Modern Art, New York. The protest was featured on the cover of *Studio International*, one of the magazines that were disseminating information about conceptual art internationally. The AWC believed that many of the museum's trustees were among a group of industrialists getting rich by supplying weapons to the army. One critic claimed that 'it is these art-loving, culturally committed trustees who are waging the war in Vietnam.'[19]

But to return to our earlier question: how can Richard Long's or John Baldessari's work be seen as a protest against the war? It must be admitted that the few statements made by Long early in his career gave no hint of any political views; indeed, he explicitly said, 'I am not interested in politics.'[20] But did the importance he gave to walking and being in nature have political connotations? Indirectly, yes. Later, in the 1980s, he wrote that, 'In the mid-sixties the language and ambition of art was due for renewal. I felt art had barely recognised the natural landscapes which cover this planet, or had used the experiences those places could offer ... I like the idea of using the land without possessing it.'[21] At this time he also said: 'My work really is just about being a human being, about living on the planet and using nature as a source.'[22]

In short, Long's work was – and is – about walking, and about sharing that experience as best he can. In 1967, when he was twenty-three, Long travelled from his college in London to the countryside. Finding an empty field, he began walking back and forth along a straight line until the grass had been trampled flat. Before the grass had time to spring upright again, he took a photograph of the mark he'd created, calling it *A Line Made by Walking*. It's an unpretentious photo, and Long would talk later of wanting his photographs, like all his work, to be 'simple and straightforward'.[23] But why should *A Line Made by Walking* be claimed as one of the key, revolutionary works of twentieth-century art?[24] Because it was so radically simple: a simple line, the simple act of walking.

By 1968 Long was also making simple structures in the landscape, or even in galleries, using stones or twigs. Indeed, he regarded all his works – whether presented as a photo, markings on a map or stones in a gallery – as sculpture. 'When I made my first straight ten-mile walk in England in 1968,' he explained, 'there was a physical pleasure actually just doing the walk ... but it was also enjoyable because of the fact that I knew I was making a very original, a unique and dynamic work of art which had a new scale to it, which was a sculpture which was invisible and in many other ways was interesting as art.'[25] As with the works of Lee Ufan, our response to Long's simple shapes and marks can re-awaken that playful and imaginative feeling for space that we tend to lose in our everyday lives.

When one abstract painter jeered at conceptual art, stating that 'conceptual art is just pointing at things',[26] John Baldessari decided to turn the gibe into a project. Accompanied by a friend, the artist walked through his hometown of San Diego and photographed his friend as he pointed at things he found interesting. Baldessari then showed the photos to assorted 'Sunday' artists whose work he had seen at country fairs, asking each of them to choose a photo and paint it. Next, under each of the fourteen resulting paintings, he employed a professional signwriter to add the name of the person who had painted it. Finally, Baldessari exhibited the canvases as his own work. We normally think of the artist as the one wielding the paintbrush, but Baldessari claimed that right as initiator. It was his idea, his concept; he curated it. The fun lay in befuddling our normal expectations of authorship. We might also ask: was each painting a work of art in its own right, or did all fourteen constitute the artwork?

Was conceptual art a paradigm shift? Could art ever be the same again? While Duchamp had worked in relative isolation, conceptual art was diffuse: by the early 1970s, there were thousands of artists around the world, from Seattle and Singapore to Manaus and Manila, either thinking about such art or making conceptual-like works. A further major question was posed again and again: if the notion of art has changed, then what is an artist? You didn't have to train as an artist to be a conceptual artist: some had trained as philosophers or worked as writers or dealers.

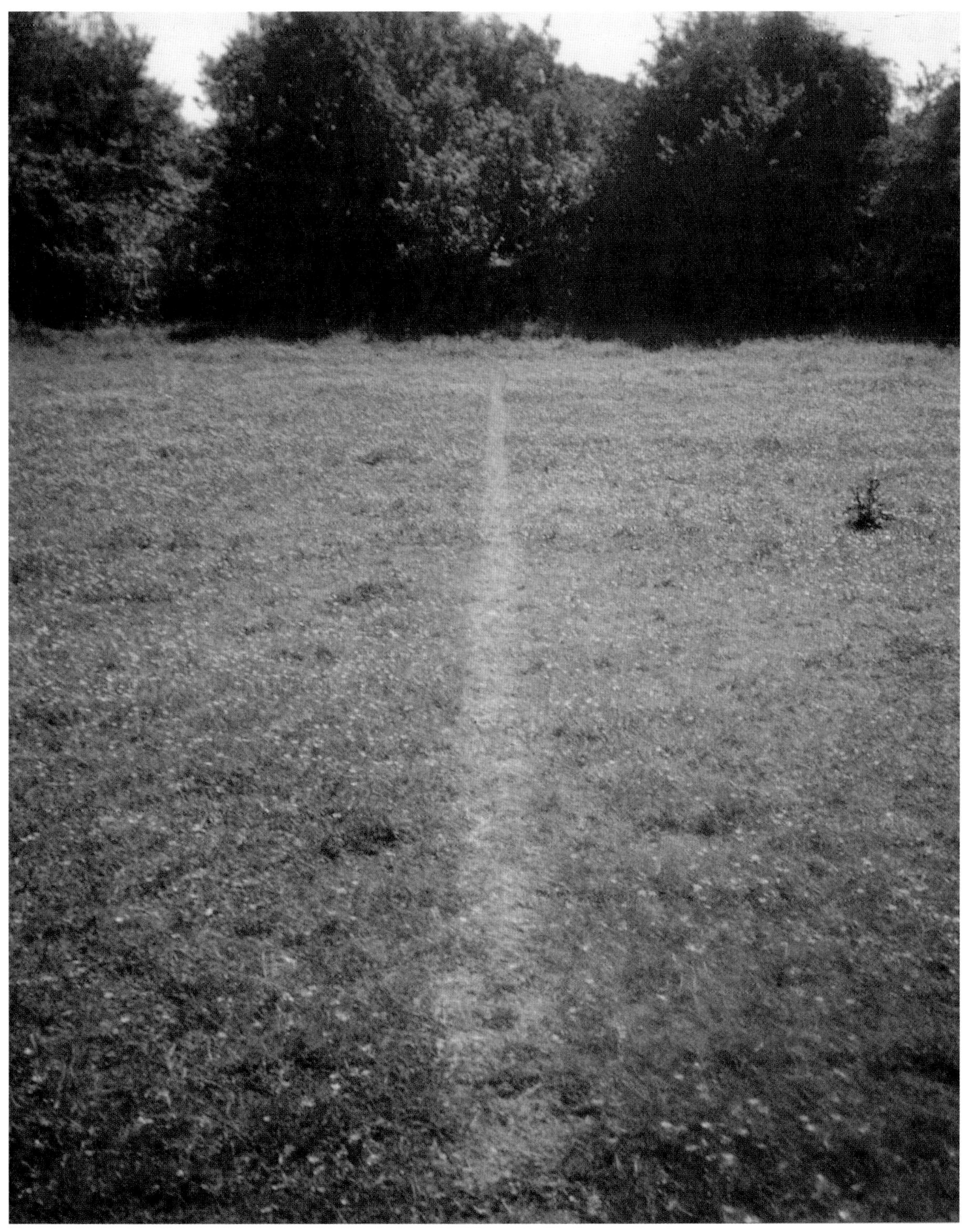

Richard Long, *A Line Made by Walking*, England, 1967
Gelatin silver print on paper, 37.5 × 32.4 cm (14⅞ × 12⅞ in.)

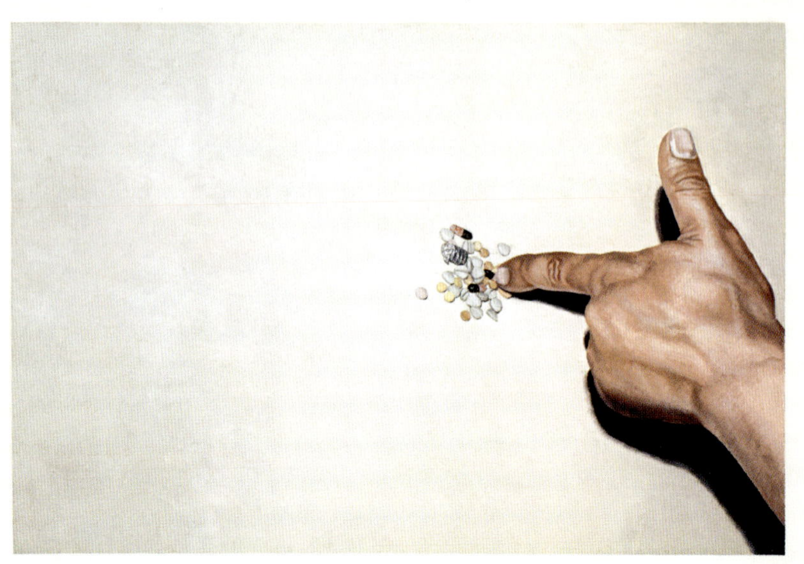

John Baldessari, *Commissioned Painting: A Painting by Edgar Transue*, 1969
Acrylic and oil on canvas, 150.5 × 115.6 cm (59⅞ × 45⅝ in.)

Moreover, if their definition or self-definition had changed, then how had their relationship to collectors, curators and critics changed?

None of these artists liked the label 'conceptual artist': it made their work seem rather academic. Many of them had no interest in actually getting rid of the object and replacing it with just a 'concept'. More than one artist would have preferred the term 'context art', believing that what they did was always made in response to a context, physical or social. In a term that would soon become widespread, they were making 'interventions'.

Despite the success he had had with his earlier paintings, On Kawara was dissatisfied with them. In 1959 he gave almost all his existing work to the National Museum of Modern Art in Tokyo, left for Mexico, and tried to live differently. On 4 January 1966 – some seven years after leaving Japan, and having destroyed most of the work he'd produced in the intervening period – Kawara created his first 'date painting'. By the time of his death in 2014, he had made almost three thousand of them. Meticulously crafted, each painting features the date of its creation in the language and linguistic conventions of whichever country the artist was in at the time (or Esperanto, if he was in Japan or China). There were eight alternative sizes, four alternative colours. If the painting had not been completed by midnight on the day it named, it was destroyed.

What did these paintings 'say'?

Nothing, save the date on which they were made. Kawara no longer believed that art could communicate personal experiences; expressionism was a fraud. Instead, he saw the date paintings as a form of meditation, as a way of escaping the ego, of putting aside distractions. Of course, as with his *One Million Years* (1999; a two-volume artist's book listing all the years from 998,031 BC to AD 1,001,992) and a series of telegrams composed of nothing but the words 'i am still alive' and the date, Kawara's date paintings could also make one think about time and mortality. Initially, he would place each date painting in a box with a cutting from that day's newspaper; eventually, however, he did away with this final connection with history and let the paintings 'speak' for themselves.

What does an artist do if they don't believe in painting anymore? In 1964 the American Bruce Nauman, at that time a postgraduate student, elected to stop making paintings. He was told to go to his studio and make art. 'Basically,' he explained, 'I would have to start over every day and figure out what art was meant to be about.'[27] What does an artist do when they go to their studio? He or she might sweep the floor, have a cup of coffee, smoke a cigarette, do some exercises. So Nauman began to make drawings, photographs or short films of those very things, including *Coffee Spilled Because the Cup was Too Hot*, a photograph, and *Dance or Exercise on the Perimeter of a Square* (page 54), a film. (Once the Sony Portapak became available in the late 1960s, he like other artists started making videos.)

This may sound random and rather banal, but Nauman approached each problem analytically. Like many artists of that period, he was much affected by philosophy – in his case the work of Ludwig Wittgenstein, which persistently questioned how language worked. If Nauman made objects, they were not about the formal issues of sculpture, but echoed how Wittgenstein explored the disconnection between words and things in the world; Nauman's *From hand to mouth* (page 55), a cast of his then wife's arm made with wax and cloth, plays on the everyday English phrase that means 'getting by on not very much'. Importantly, Nauman's was also no longer an art of looking at other people, but one of using his own body as a subject, much as

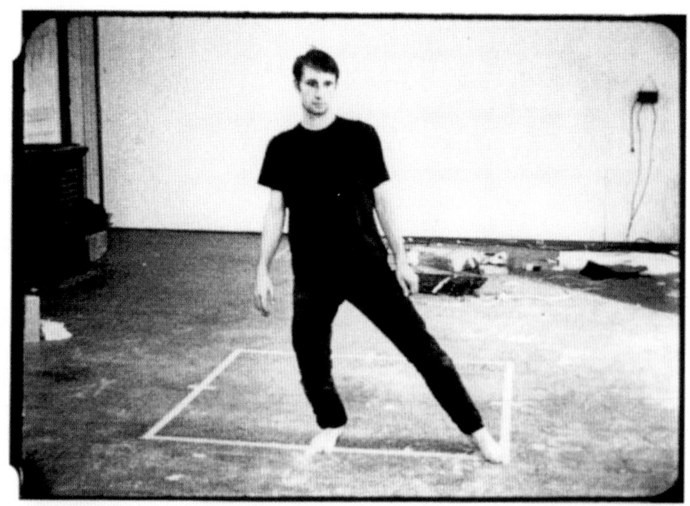

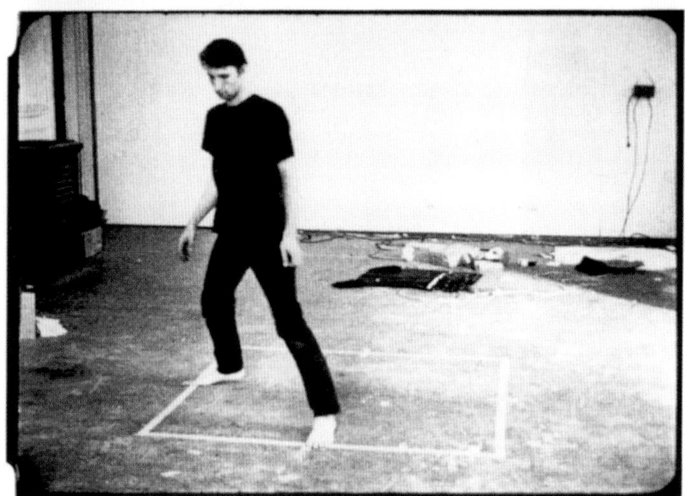

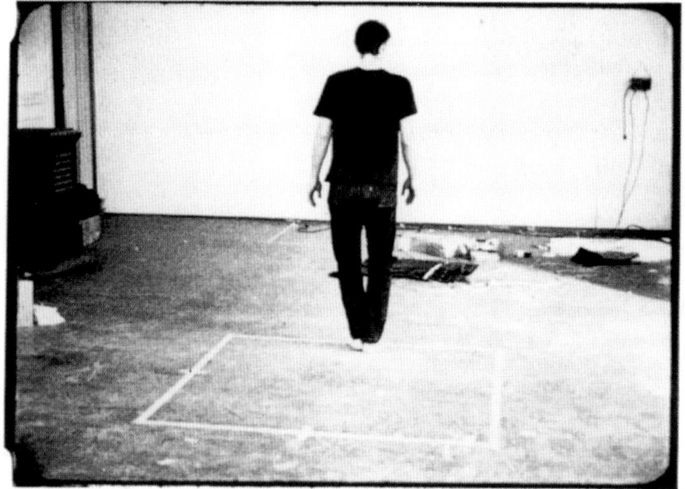

Bruce Nauman, *Dance or Exercise on the Perimeter of a Square (Square Dance)*, 1967–68
16mm film, 8:24 minutes

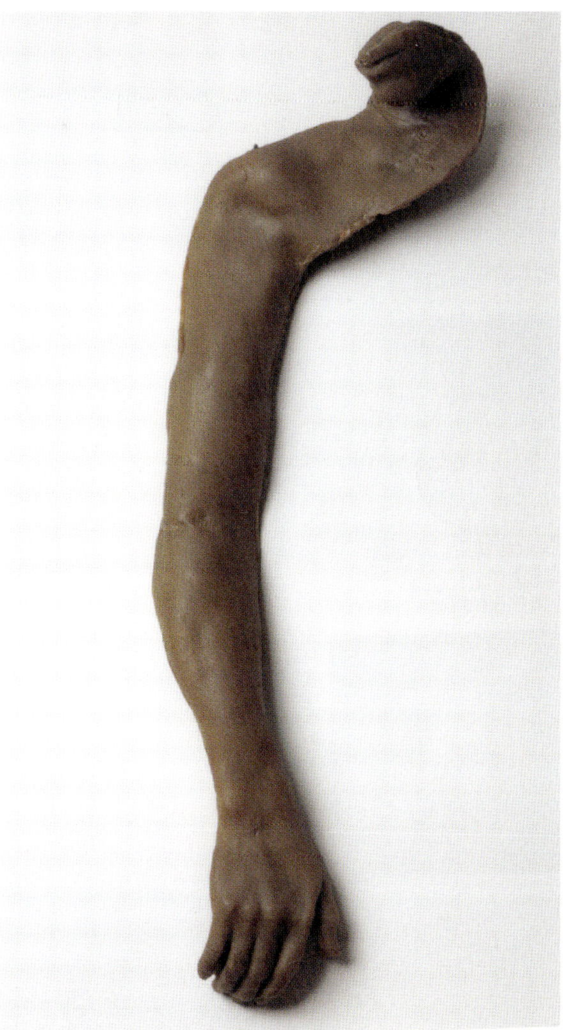

Bruce Nauman, *From hand to mouth*, 1967
Wax over cloth, 71.1 × 25.7 × 10.2 cm (28 × 10⅛ × 4⅛ in.)

a behavioural scientist might. In a world where surveillance was increasingly the way in which power was maintained, Nauman presented himself both as subject and as master of surveillance. Such a fascination with surveillance would prove prescient.

In Eastern Europe and Latin America, conceptual art tended to be more political or ideological – a way of fighting against prevailing ideas. The Brazilian artist Cildo Meireles's *Coca-Cola Project* (page 56) is a case in point. Every time Meireles found a Coca-Cola bottle, he would add a new label. Featuring such slogans as 'Yankees Go Home', the labels also included a more reflective message: '*Gravar nas garrafas, opiniões criticas, e devolve-las à circulação*' (Record in bottles, critical reviews, and return them to circulation). It was, he hoped, an intervention into the flow of everyday life: perhaps someone would pick the bottle up, read the label and start to think about how a Coca-Cola bottle can be part of an ideological 'circuit'.

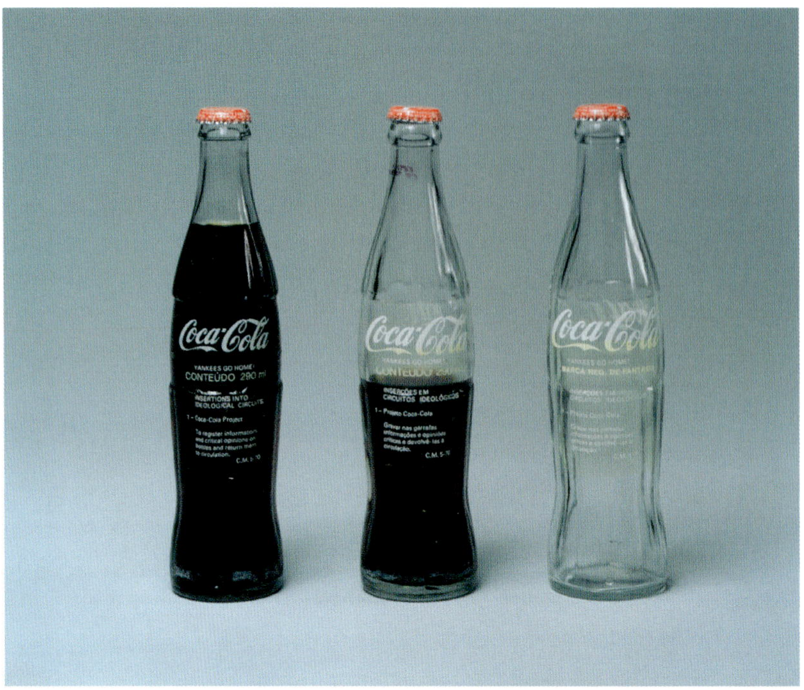

Cildo Meireles, *Insertions into Ideological Circuits: Coca-Cola Project*, 1970
Three glass bottles and adhesive labels with text, each 15.5 × 5.5 cm (6⅛ × 2⅛ in.)

The 1970s

It is clear that there is no single point when we can say contemporary art started. There are, however, several important moments, or stages, when what we understand to be contemporary art, or the contemporary art world, begins to crystallize. We have already noted 17 August 1945, a date on which post-colonialism can be said to have started. Other key dates might include 6 November 1962, when the first Pop art show opened in the United States; 27 April 1966, when the exhibition 'Primary Structures' established minimalism as, if not a movement *per se*, a sort of paradigm shift; and 22 March 1969, when the exhibition 'Live in Your Head' at the Kunsthalle Bern brought a large number of conceptual artists together. Pop, minimalism and, above all, conceptual art form the basis of much, if not most, of the art made since. We are still rethinking and reworking their issues and ideas today.

We could also say that the late 1960s/early 1970s was when the contemporary art world and art market developed and started to become a global phenomenon. In 1967 the Art Cologne art fair was launched (as Kölner Kunstmarkt); three years later, Art Basel was launched as a direct competitor.[28] Another key date is 18 October 1973, when Sotheby's in New York sold a further fifty works from Robert Scull's collection. This time, Scull needed the money not to buy a different kind of art but to pay for his divorce. The art he was selling was new to the auction market; it was also a new type of auction. 'I put the sale together as if I was making an exhibition,' Scull said, 'tried to give it balance, see that things worked with each other.'[29] The catalogue was an elegant hardback book, while the sale itself was a society event that the press filmed and reported on avidly. Outside the auction, members of Women in the Arts protested that only one of the fifty works being sold was by a woman; other demonstrators, from Taxi Rank and File Coalition, carried placards directed at Scull: 'Robbing Cabbies is His Living, Buying Artists is His Game'. Inside the auction, works by Pop artists were sold for record amounts: a flower painting by Warhol fetched $135,000; *Painted Bronze (Ale Cans)*, a small sculpture by Jasper Johns, went for $90,000 (Scull had bought it for $960). Although it was marketed as a modern-art event (Sotheby's didn't yet do contemporary sales), it set a yardstick for the future hype, excitement and high prices at auctions of contemporary art.

The presence outside Sotheby's of Women in the Arts reflected the emergence at this time of many women artists who, whether feminists or not, were determined to face down male prejudice and be seen as equals. One such artist was the Cuban-American Ana Mendieta. Following the rape and murder of a fellow student, Mendieta invited her friends and colleagues to visit her apartment, where they found her bound to a table, naked from the waist down and covered with blood. How else could she protest, not only against the rape and murder, but also against the deluge of photographic pornography that was by then pouring into bookshops? Hers was always an art about the body, about what could be done to it, and what it could do.

'It was during my childhood in Cuba', Mendieta once recalled, 'that I first became fascinated by primitive art and cultures. It seems as if these cultures are provided with an inner knowledge, a closeness to natural resources. And it is this knowledge which gives reality to the images they have created. This sense of magic, knowledge and power found in primitive art has influenced my personal attitude towards art making.'[30] When she was twelve years old, Mendieta was sent to live in the United States by her parents, who were opposed to Castro's anti-Catholic government. This experience left her with a profound sense of disconnection: a search for identity would be another driver of her art. As a student, Mendieta was influenced by the notion of 'intermedia' – the idea that art should be inter-disciplinary – and many of her performances were made specifically to be photographed or filmed. Often, as if making a ritual, she would pose in the landscape to be photographed or filmed, covered with flowers or blood and feathers (page 58), or, having made an impression of her body in the earth, would fill it with leaves, ash or flaming gunpowder.

'The main idea of my whole work is the body,' Marina Abramović has said.[31] Like Mendieta, performance was central to what she did. 'It is all about pushing

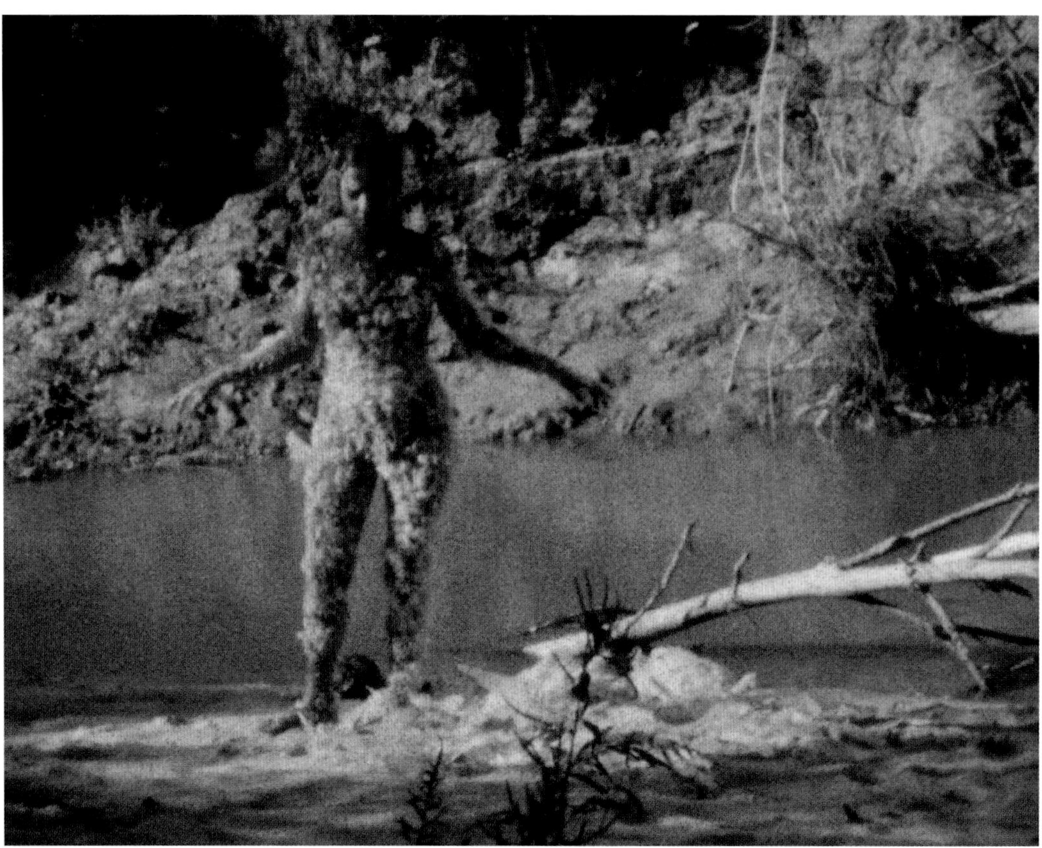

Ana Mendieta, *Blood + Feathers*, 1974
Super 8mm film transferred to high-definition digital media, colour, silent, 3:12 minutes

the body to the mental and physical limits ... how we could transform our inner body physically and mentally.'[32] Indeed, her performances, which she talks of as 'purifications', have often involved danger or endurance. A key word to her is 'energy' – 'a direct energy between me and the public.'[33] Like Joseph Beuys, she has always wanted her audience to be energized too. She has also been a charismatic, influential but exceptionally demanding teacher, expecting her students to undergo the same sorts of privation that she has – for example, going on a ten-hour walk after not talking or eating for four days.

Beuys watched one of Abramović's early performances, *Rhythm 5* (opposite). Staged in her native Yugoslavia, she had a star – the symbol of communism as well as a shape used in magic – constructed out of wooden rails. In between the rails were piles of wood shavings soaked in petrol. She set these alight, walked around the star and then began cutting her hair and nails. 'Every time I threw a piece of my hair or my nails in the fire it released a kind of light,' she later said, 'and that light was a rhythm for me.'[34] She then lay down inside the star, surrounded by

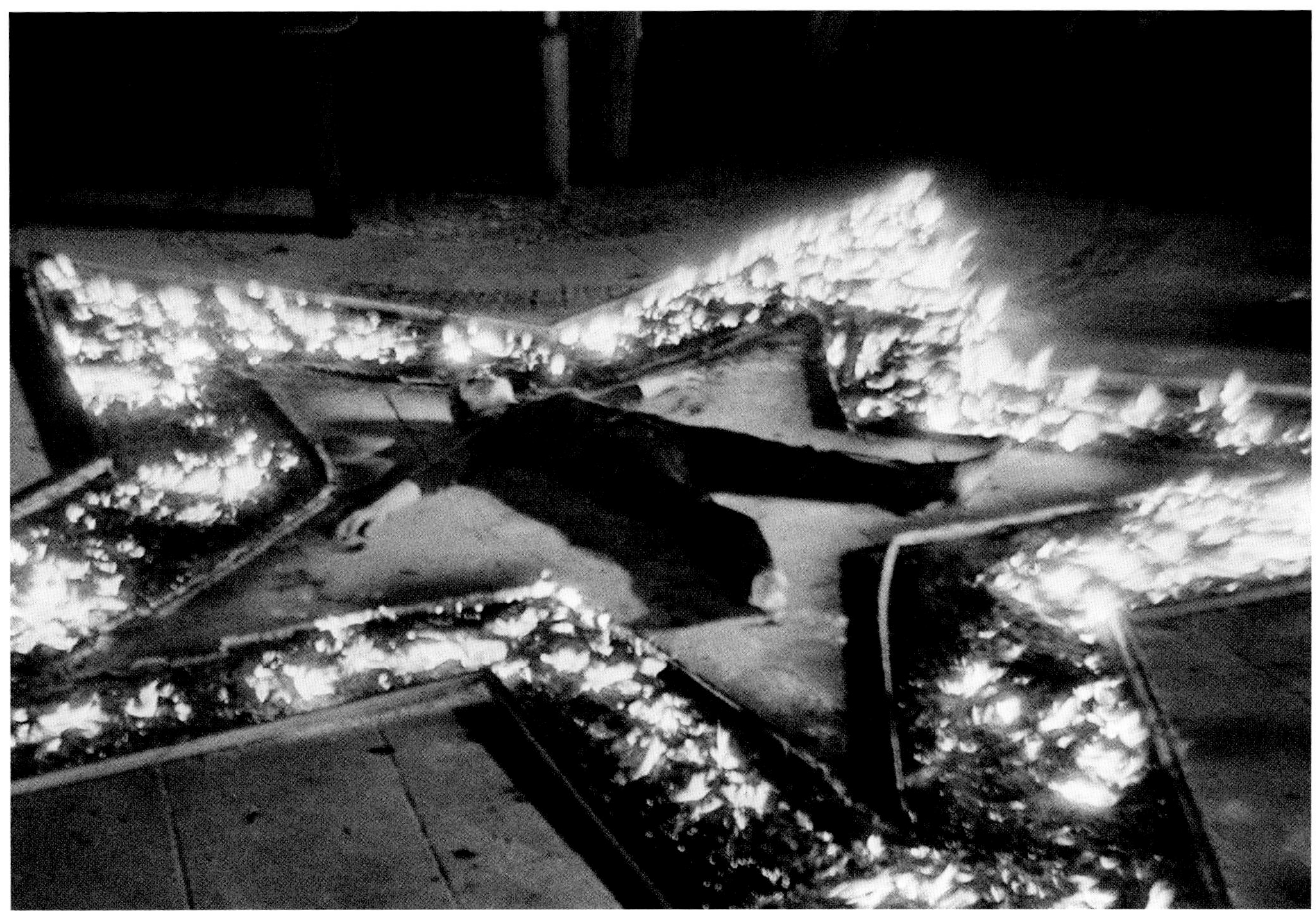

Marina Abramović, *Rhythm 5*, 1974
Performance, 90 minutes, Student Cultural Centre, Belgrade

flames. Fortunately, someone realized that she had passed out because the flames were consuming all the oxygen, and that she was in great danger: they jumped into the star and carried her out.

The American-born Susan Hiller – a very different character from Abramović – trained as an anthropologist but wanted to be an artist. In changing disciplines, she had to fight against the entrenched assumption that scientists deal with reason and artists with imagination. Everyone, she believed, has to deal with both. Hiller opposed other binaries, too: mind–body, matter–intellect. She studied and made work using dreams, pottery shards, Punch and Judy shows, the urge to collect, but always from the position of an engaged participant, not an academic observing from outside.

For *Dedicated to the Unknown Artists* (page 60), Hiller collected postcards of stormy seas, waves breaking on piers, and beaches – as sent by people on seaside holidays. In her accompanying notes, she wrote: 'I have been able to extend the work of the unknown artists, I have collaborated with them.' At first glance, the piece looks

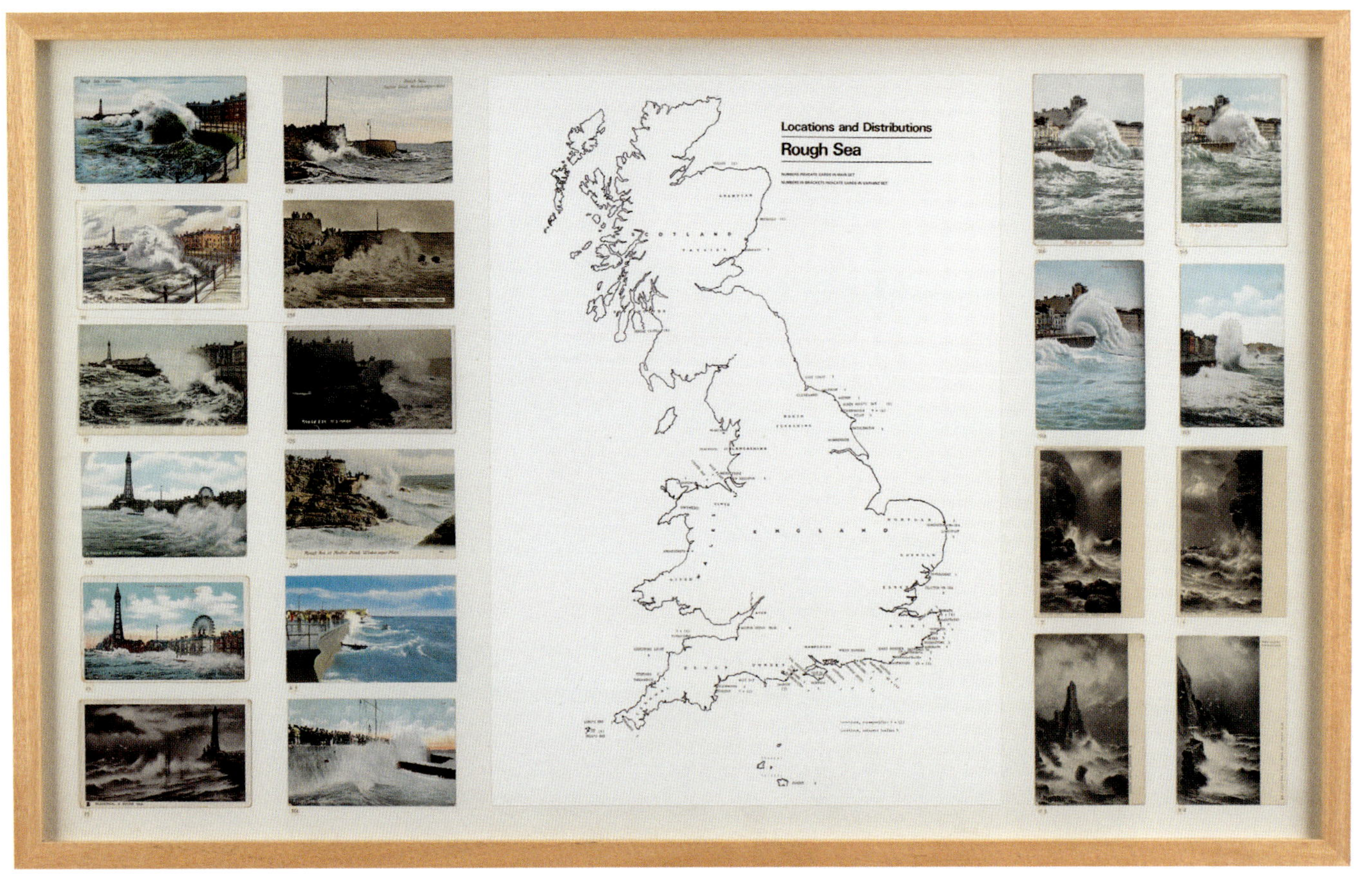

Susan Hiller, *Dedicated to the Unknown Artists*, 1972–76
305 postcards, charts, maps, one book, one dossier, mounted on 14 panels, each 66 × 104.8 cm (26½ × 41½ in.)

like the research of a social anthropologist, but the more one looks at the postcards and reads the texts, the more complex it seems; many of the images, for example, are hand-tinted, each in a very different way. Why? What led so many people to both make and send these cards? ‘My conviction’, said Hiller, ‘is that popular formats may well be art … Aspects of imagination, fantasy or whatever enters the process inevitably. Human beings are not machines; they express their creativity in their gestures, in their ordinary, mundane working gestures. And it’s those sorts of things I am trying to bring out in [this] piece.’[35] She later added: ‘What I am looking at is a set of cultural ideas that basically come down to certain obsessions about nature in relation to culture. I mean the sea threatening the buildings. Notions of sexuality come into that, notions of male and female, active and passive.’[36] For Hiller, a work of art was not an object, but ‘a place where one thinks, feels and acts. Here we can collectively begin to visualize and construct new knowledges.’[37]

If Nam June Paik used video in an almost Dadaistic manner, and Bruce Nauman used it analytically, Bill Viola has used it to tackle big, humanistic subjects. Speaking in 1990, Viola said: 'I think it's a great failure that critical discourse today in art, which exists supposedly on the edge of some of the higher aspirations we have as human beings, does not encompass the very, very human qualities of our emotional lives. You never hear love coming up in critical discourse today. I get somewhat frustrated that more people aren't thinking of the great themes in life as being in the domain of art.'[38]

For Viola, video can be an equivalent to individual consciousness, a means of illuminating the inner life. In *The Reflecting Pool* (below), Viola himself walks on screen, stands at the pool's edge, then leaps. But his image is frozen mid-air, his body in a foetal position, while the water below continues to shimmer. Eventually, Viola's image begins to fade before disappearing altogether. Outside the pool, nothing changes; inside it, we see disembodied reflections of other people. The pool darkens then lightens again, and Viola, now naked, climbs out and walks off into the trees. Not so much a dream as a metaphor for some kind of spiritual transformation. Today, we might view the special effects as crude and clunky, but the work retains its naive charm.

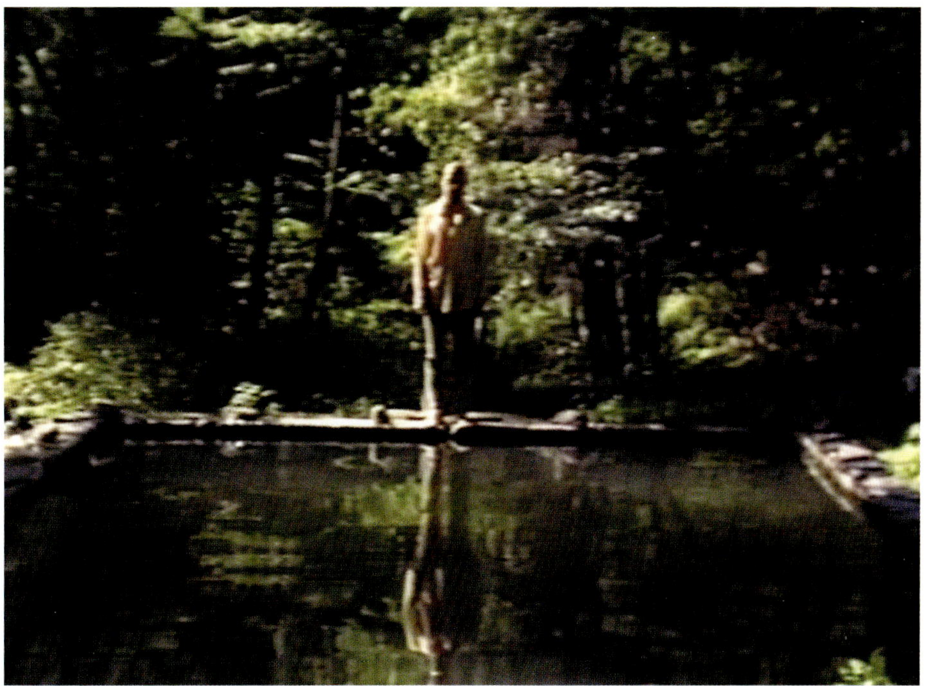

Bill Viola, *The Reflecting Pool*, 1977–79
Videotape, colour, mono sound, 7 minutes

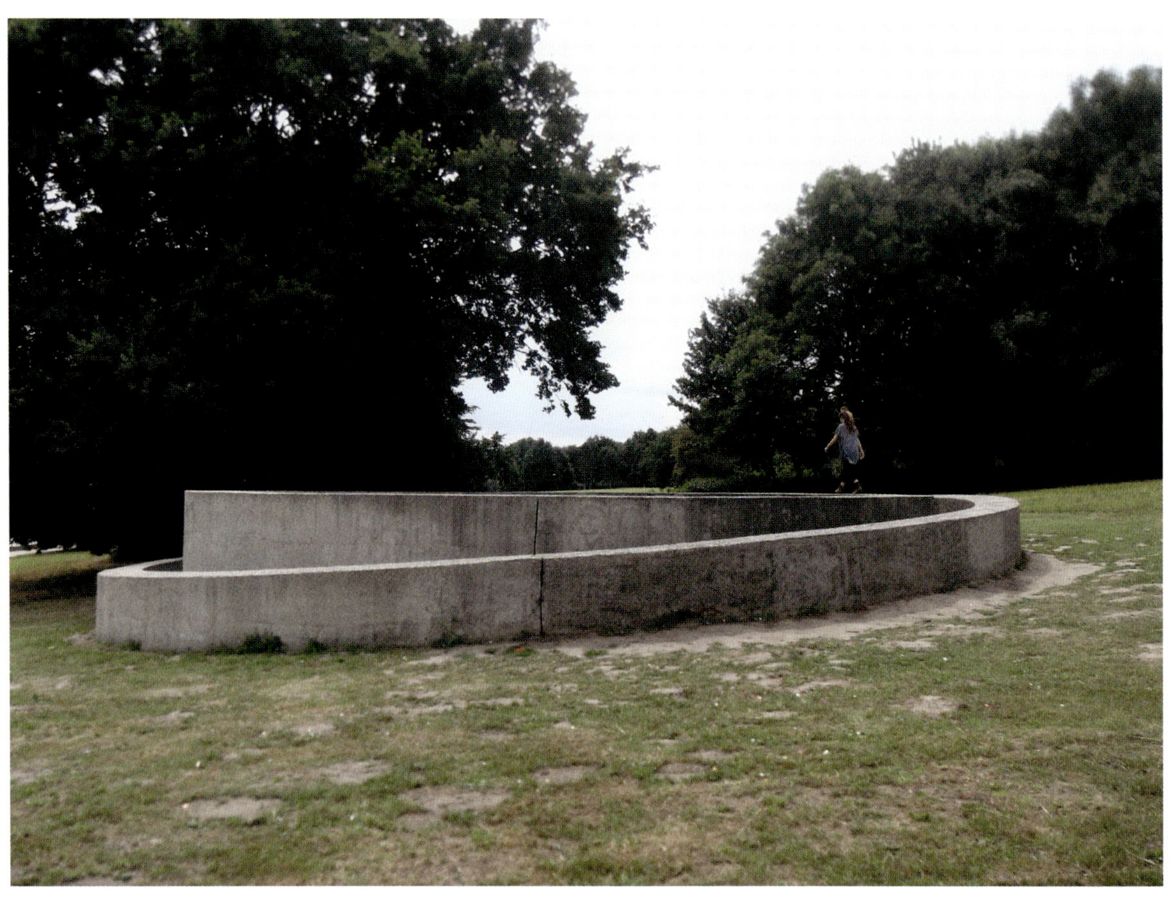

Donald Judd, *Untitled*, 1977
Two rings nested concrete, outer ring: 90 × 60 cm (35½ × 23⅝ in.), diameter 15 m (590⅝ in.); inner ring: height varies between 90 and 210 cm (35½ and 82¾ in.), diameter 13.5 m (531½ in.)

In 1977 the curators at the art museum in Münster, West Germany, were so distressed and aggravated by the inability of their public to like or understand contemporary sculpture, or accept it in public spaces, that they decided they had to do something. They asked a young curator, Kasper König, to curate an exhibition in the city that they hoped would demonstrate what contemporary sculpture was all about and, hopefully, win the public over. This was the first Skulptur Projekte Münster.

Of the participating artists, Carl Andre took ninety-seven steel plates and laid them out near a lake; Donald Judd made two concrete rings, the inner one horizontal, the outer tilted to the same degree as the hillside on which the rings sat (opposite); and Joseph Beuys took casts of the space under an ugly access ramp (Münster had been badly bombed during the Second World War, and most post-war redevelopments were dire), using them to make enormous sculptures of beef and mutton fat. Beuys referred to it as 'extracting a tooth to show its state of decay'.[39]

The exhibition did not win the townspeople over, but the city council were persuaded to buy and make two pieces permanent,[40] and to allow the museum to invite König back ten years later. What had surprised them was how many people had visited the town to see the exhibition: there really was an audience for this strange stuff!

Chapter 2

THE RETURN TO PAINTING

The Early 1980s

This was not what was supposed to happen.

As we saw in Chapter 1, painting had been consigned to the dustbin of history as an outmoded, exhausted, obsolete and reactionary project. Yet at the start of the 1980s, it returned with apparent vigour. Two exhibitions – 'A New Spirit in Painting' at the Royal Academy in London (1981), and 'Zeitgeist' in West Berlin (1982) – seemed to demonstrate not only that painting was still a plausible way to make art, but also that it was in fact a form possessed of a new vitality. Perhaps even more unexpectedly, the paintings in these two exhibitions were predominantly figurative. Why had painting come back? It had been presumed to be 'dead', the monochrome paintings of the 1970s – grey, white, black – representing a formal dead end.

Instead, one of the curators of 'A New Spirit', Christos Joachimides, gushed in his introduction to the catalogue that 'the artist's studios are full of paint pots again and an abandoned easel in an art school has become a rare sight. Wherever you look in Europe or America you find artists who have rediscovered the sheer joy of painting.'[1] Joachimides talked of these new paintings as having 'an intensive poetic force and piercing imagination'.[2] It was unfortunate that the painting that would come to dominate the 1980s was very often spoken of in such hyperbolic terms: to its critics, this seemed more the language of the market than of serious criticism. And this would be a time when the art market, which had been in the doldrums since 1973, started to boom again.

The key claim being made at the Royal Academy was that the works on show demonstrated an unbroken continuity in painting. Close to works by the German artist Georg Baselitz, then little known, hung the late paintings of Picasso, which, until then, had received a poor press. But Joachimides felt otherwise, asserting that Picasso, right to the end of his long life, had made 'powerful, expressive work'.[3] He had not just been an old modernist churning out slight and sloppy pastiches of his earlier work, but a *contemporary* artist. The late works of Philip Guston, recent poetic paintings by Cy Twombly and pieces by several senior English painters were also on show, but it was the work of Baselitz and other German painters,

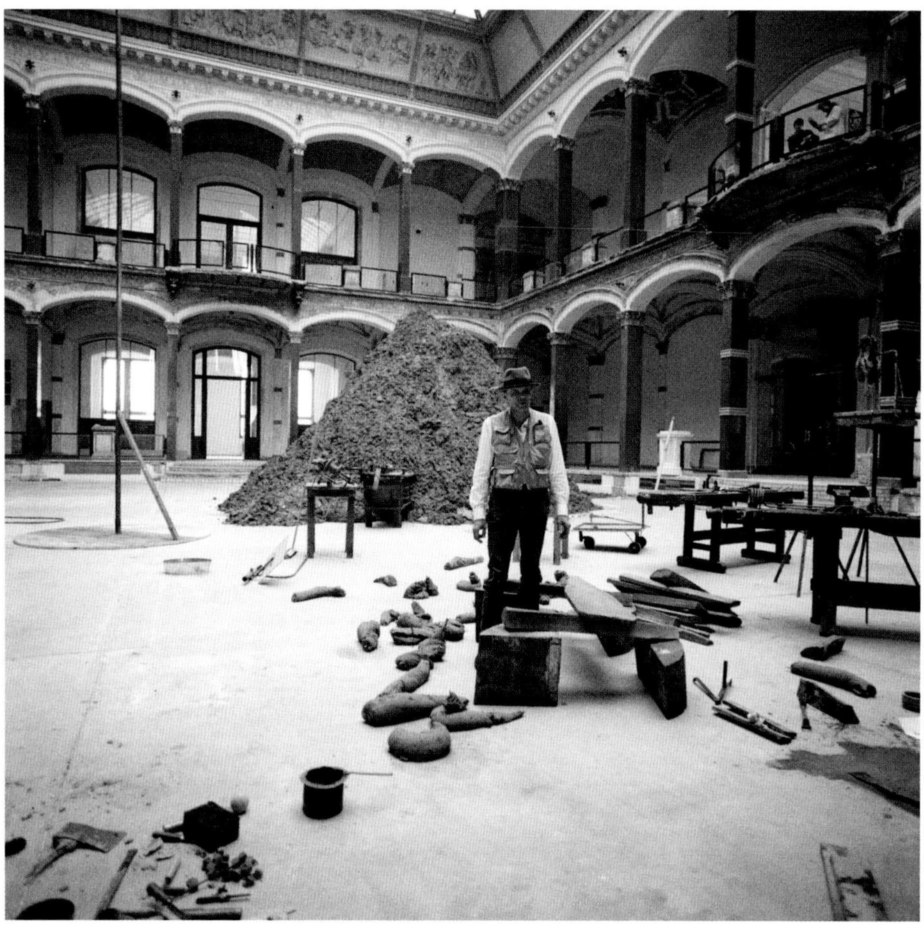

Joseph Beuys, *Stag Monument*, 1982
Installation view, 'Zeitgeist', West Berlin, 1982

such as Anselm Kiefer and Sigmar Polke, that gave the exhibition a raw, assertive and often uncomfortable edge. There had recently been a revival of interest in such German expressionists as Max Beckmann, Ernst Ludwig Kirchner and Emil Nolde, so, inevitably, the term 'neo-expressionism' was quickly applied to the work of Baselitz *et al.* As with all such labels, it was an over-simplification. Likewise, the term 'return to painting' was a misnomer, for although some younger artists who had been working in performance, film or rock music started painting again, at the core of this movement stood those older artists who had been painting throughout the 1970s and, in many cases, the 1960s.

Importantly, what these artists offered, and what the time called for, was not just expressive painting but a way to reconnect with myth and history. This desire for a myth-like approach to history and narrative had been prefigured by a number of events outside visual art, including the making of such films as Francis

Ford Coppola's *Apocalypse Now* and Ridley Scott's *Alien*, both released in 1979. At a more popular level, the incredible success of George Lucas's *Star Wars* (1977) also showed a need for myth, fable and allegory – if not to explain the contemporary world and its origins, at least to fictionalize in accessible and entertaining ways a new generation's fears and aspirations. Above all, perhaps, it was the extraordinary production of Wagner's *Der Ring des Nibelungen* at the 1976 Bayreuth Festival (below; first shown on television in 1980) that best encapsulated the mixed metaphors that characterized such new work.

After the Second World War, because of its associations with Hitler and the Nazi Party, the annual Wagner festival in the city of Bayreuth had eschewed Victorian realism in favour of vaguely archetypal settings. In 1976, in a further break with Germanic traditions, the French composer and conductor Pierre Boulez and the French designer Patrice Chéreau were employed. Their staging mixed up not only myths but also time periods; at the beginning, for example, the Rhinemaidens appear as high-class Victorian prostitutes cavorting against the backdrop of a hydro-electric dam. In Chéreau's hands, Wagner appeared as a contemporary, his narratives played out as psychodramas rather than pompous fustian.

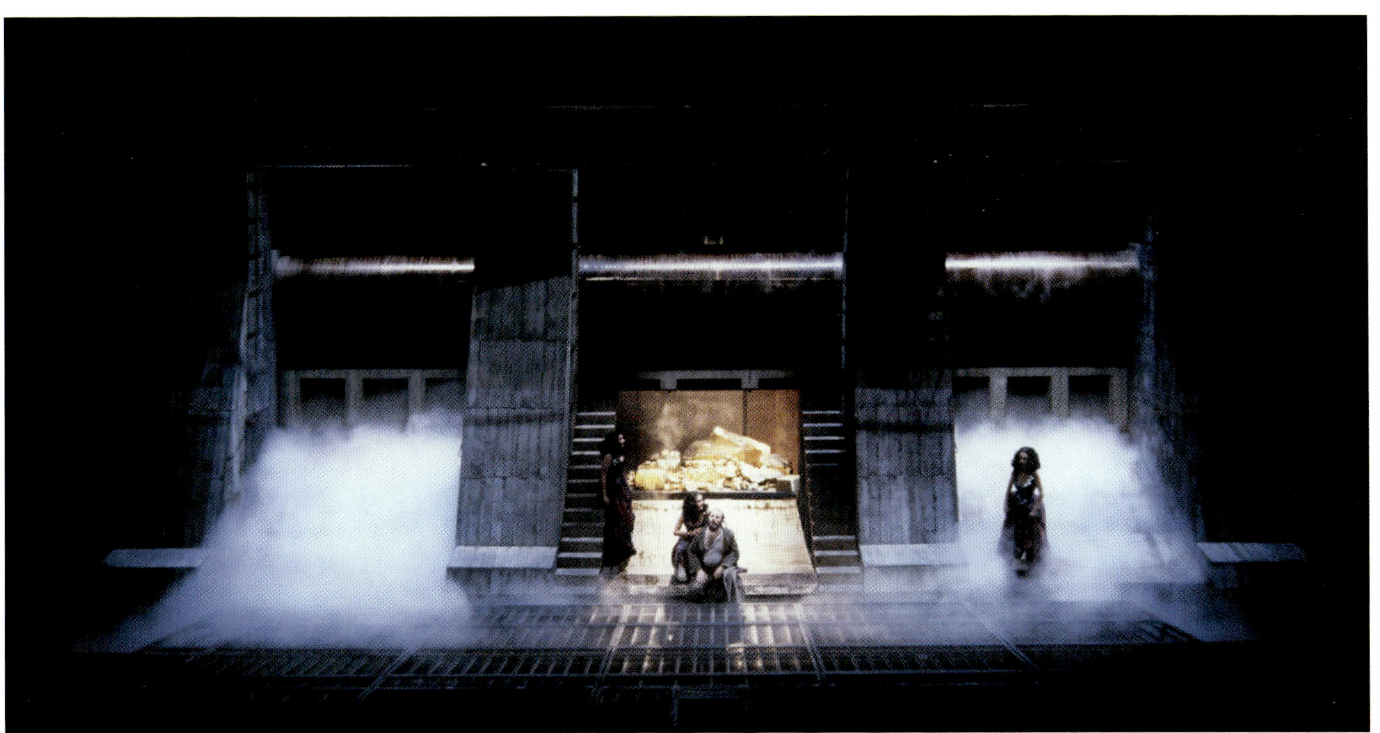

Chereau/Boulez, staging of Richard Wagner's *Rheingold*, 1976
Opening scene with Rhinemaidens against hydro-electric dam

Boulez and Chéreau's production of *Der Ring* was also a foretaste of how the 1980s would become a very German decade. Few outside Germany had noticed either the proliferation there of contemporary art galleries and modern art museums since 1945, or the work ethic and ambition of German artists. The location of the exhibition 'Zeitgeist' was symbolic: in a building right next to the Berlin Wall. The wall now came to be seen as symbolic not just of a divided Germany (and Europe), but also of a divided psyche in which past memories had been suppressed. The building, once an Arts and Crafts museum, then taken over by the Gestapo (its cellars used for torture), gutted by British night bombers and blighted by its proximity to the wall, was still semi-derelict. All in all, an extraordinary site for an exhibition about the art of the time, the *Zeit*.

For me, visiting 'Zeitgeist' was a revelation: the context and energy of the work made it seem very alive and absolutely of its time. By comparison, much of the conceptual art and abstract painting (fifth-generation Abstract Expressionism) that had been exhibited in the late 1970s looked tired and derivative. In retrospect, many of the paintings by the younger artists at 'Zeitgeist' were formally weak and lacked complexity, but they were nevertheless energetic. They seemed alive! They seemed to matter.

On the walls of the building's atrium were large, specially commissioned paintings by some of these younger artists, while at the atrium's centre was a vast, sprawling installation, *Stag Monument*, by Joseph Beuys (page 66). It looked like a workshop. Scattered around a huge mound of clay were workbenches and, on the floor, large sausage-like objects. The implication was that these were primordial life forms made by some now-absent creator. A simple wooden structure represented the stag. If it was a monument, it was one made with everyday stuff – Beuys's point being that the mythical or spiritual could be found in such everyday objects, and that making, even blood sausages, was creative and therapeutic.

That someone who, as a teacher, had derided painting should now be at the centre of an exhibition dedicated to the form was the greatest irony in an exhibition that generally sought to be expressive rather than ironic. But Beuys's focal presence was appropriate. His call to exhibit 'one's wound', both physical and spiritual, as well as his use of such 'magic' materials as hare's blood, could be seen elsewhere in the exhibition – in the straw- and lead-covered paintings of Kiefer, for example, or in the works of the American painter Julian Schnabel, with their broken plates and deer antlers (see below). Beuys had always been confrontational, and so were these painters – none more so than Baselitz, who, on this occasion, irritatingly, had hung his paintings far above eye level.

Provocation and controversy had marked the start of Baselitz's career in 1963. 'I'd read about the poet Brendan Behan, who had opened his fly at a reading', he explained many years later. 'To me that seemed a powerfully provocative move ... It was Behan that gave me the idea of painting a figure with a huge head and

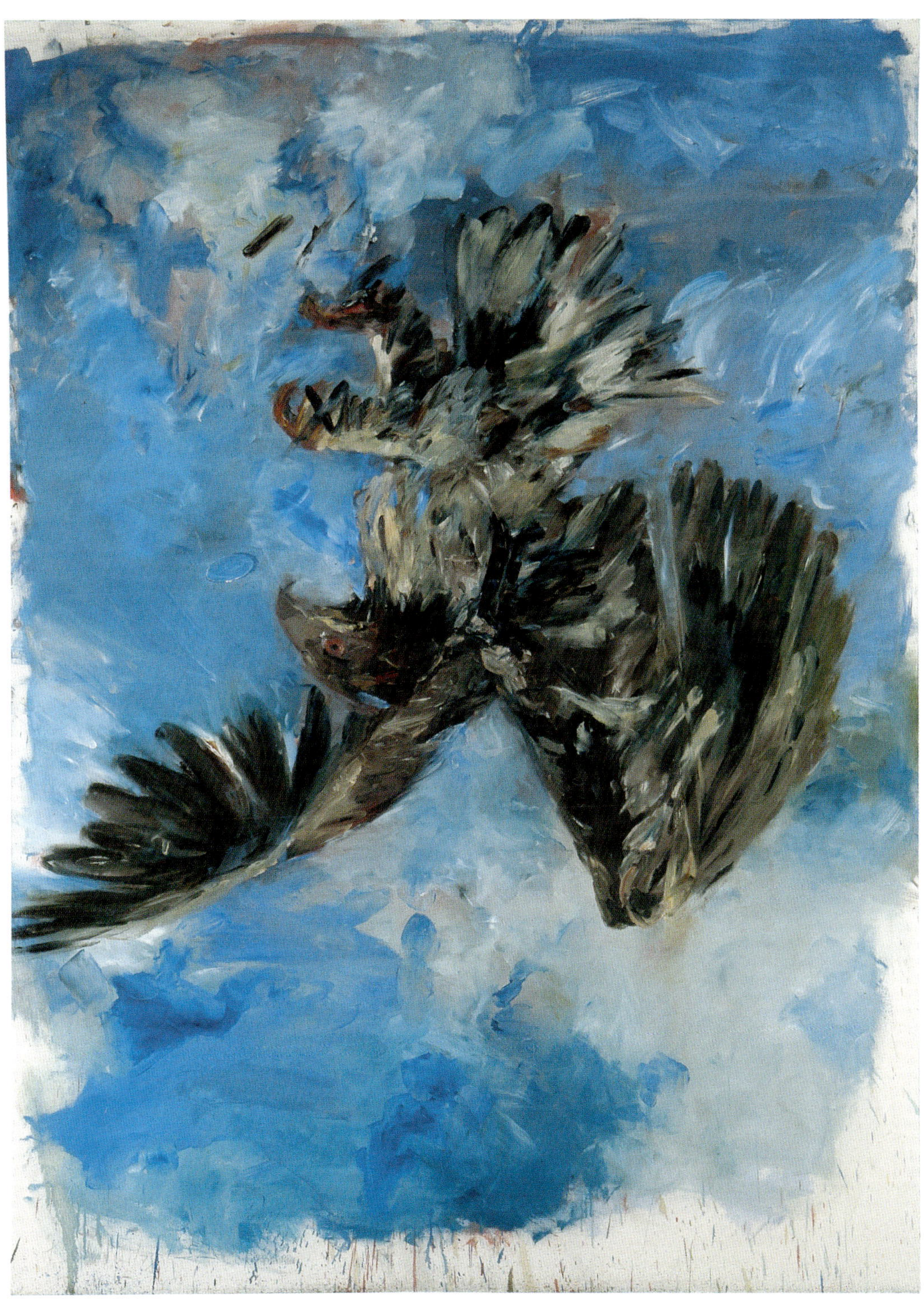

George Baselitz, *Finger Painting – Eagle*, 1972
Oil on canvas, 249.5 × 180.3 cm (98¼ × 71 in.)

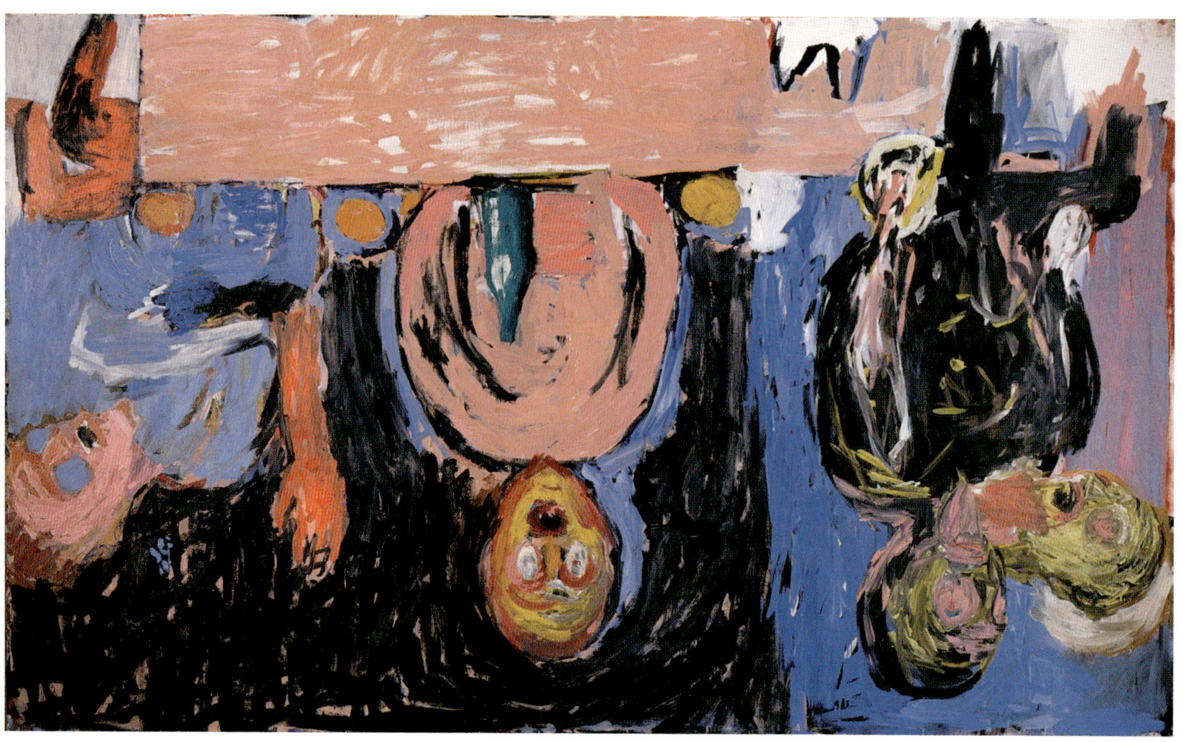

George Baselitz, *Last Supper in Dresden*, 1983
Oil on canvas, 280 × 450 cm (110¼ × 177¼ in.)

an almighty penis.'[4] The resulting work, *The Big Night Down the Drain*, was exhibited at Baselitz's first solo show, reported to the authorities as immoral,[5] and seized by the police. A refugee from East Germany, Baselitz loathed the polite, international-style abstraction that dominated West German art as much as he loathed the doctrinaire socialist realism he had been trained to paint in the East. His disgust and sense of being an outsider fuelled his early paintings, in which mutated beings and pin-headed heroes wander across a desolated landscape. He always emphasized both how German his work was and that he had grown up in a cultural disaster area: 'I was born into a destroyed order, a destroyed landscape, a destroyed people, a destroyed society ... I was forced to question everything, to be "naive", to start again ... I'm brutal, naive and Gothic.'[6]

In 1969 Baselitz started painting his subjects upside down. 'This is the best way to empty the contents out of what one paints', he later explained. 'The object expresses nothing. Painting is not a means to an end. On the contrary. Painting is autonomous.'[7] Baselitz painted ordinary things and traditional motifs: portraits, nudes, landscapes, birds. In theory, the paintings had become abstract; but the imagery, as well as the often brutal but sometimes surprisingly delicate handling, inevitably evoked very emotional responses.

Baselitz has always been contrary. On the one hand, he would deny being influenced by the expressionists, but then, on the other, would refer to them directly in such paintings as *Last Supper in Dresden* (opposite), which depicts Kirchner and other members of the German expressionist group Die Brucke, as well as associating them with the Last Supper of Christ. *Last Supper in Dresden* signalled a shift in Baselitz's work towards bright, acid colours and looser, broader handling. Some saw a visionary, ecstatic quality to such paintings, others saw them as a burlesque. Traditionalists were offended by what they saw as Baselitz's heavy-handed brushwork. He was not an easy artist to like, but his work always evoked a strong reaction.

The awkwardness and intensity of the generation of German artists to which Baselitz belongs has much to do with the peculiarity of the post-war division of Germany and the repression of much twentieth-century German history. Anselm Kiefer, for example, felt obligated to uncover what had been repressed. 'We see train tracks somewhere and think of Auschwitz', he lamented. 'That will remain for a long time ... I am one of the butchers, at least on a theoretical level, because I cannot know what I would have done at that time. Mankind is capable of anything. That is the explanation of my affliction.'[8] As a young man, he had had himself photographed in cities once conquered by the Nazis, wearing his father's old Wehrmacht jacket and giving the Nazi salute. 'I wanted', he explained, 'to ask myself the question, 'Am I a fascist?' It's very important, and one cannot give a swift answer. The authority, the spirit of competition, the feeling of superiority ... these are aspects of me just as they are of each one of us ... I wanted to depict the experience before the response.'[9]

Kiefer's actions were documented in the books he made in the 1970s, as well as in a series of watercolours that reveal a more gentle, lyrical and private personality, very different from the one inferred by the large and imposing paintings that would soon make him famous. Typically, in the watercolour illustrated here (page 72), he adds a mystical element: a personal 'dome of heaven'. The large paintings were so heavy with lead, straw and other materials that they were more like sculptures, prompting a very visceral, physical response from viewers.

No German city has had such a stigmatized name as Nuremberg. It is where the Nazi Party held its rallies, and where Nazi war criminals were tried after the war. It also has a rich cultural history – the birthplace of Albrecht Dürer and the setting for Wagner's opera *Die Meistersinger von Nürnberg* – while architecturally, before being largely destroyed by British bombing, it was the archetypal old German town. In his painting *Nürnberg* (page 73), Kiefer shows us a ploughed field with a solitary church in the background. The surface is heavy with shellac (a type of resin) and straw. Four charred posts have been tied to the painting, while in the bottom right-hand corner the words *Festspiel Wiese* (festival ground) identify the field as the site of the Nuremberg rallies. Above all, one's response to such a painting as this is visceral: it is as much a wall of stuff and things as an image. In their hurry

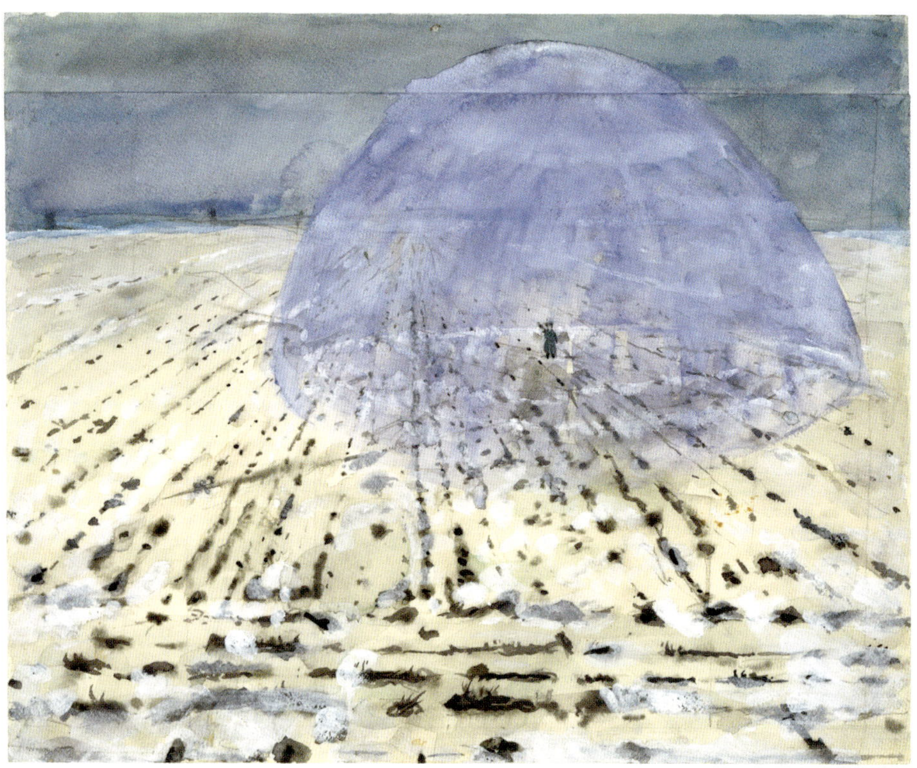

Anselm Kiefer, *Everyone stand under his own dome of Heaven*, 1970
Watercolour, gouache and graphite on joined paper, 40 × 48 cm (15¾ × 18⅞ in.)

to unlock symbols – either about the Nazis and the war or about burning stubble to regenerate the earth – critics often overlook this heavy materiality. What is true about Kiefer's work is that it tends to be ambivalent, often juxtaposing emblems of creativity with those of destructive forces – for example, an artist's palette made from the alchemical material of lead, set against square pillars similar to those used by Albert Speer in the buildings he designed for Hitler. Kiefer's avowed aim was to heal German culture, not to accuse it. Or, more precisely, to embody that culture in its forgotten wholeness: 'My paintings grow in sediments. These layers are laid in me. I am also a sediment. I am about two thousand years old.'[10]

Part of this culture was of course Jewish. From the poetry of Heinrich Heine to the music of Gustav Mahler and the theories of Karl Marx and Sigmund Freud, German culture had been enriched by Jewish intellectuals. An extended series of Kiefer's paintings and watercolours took as its starting point a poem by the Jewish writer Paul Celan, 'Todesfugue', in which he laments the death of both ashen-haired Jew Shulamith and blonde-haired Aryan Margarethe. In Kiefer's works, the words 'dein goldenes Haar Margarete, dein aschenes Haar Shulamith' recur throughout, along with images of ash, straw and burning cities.

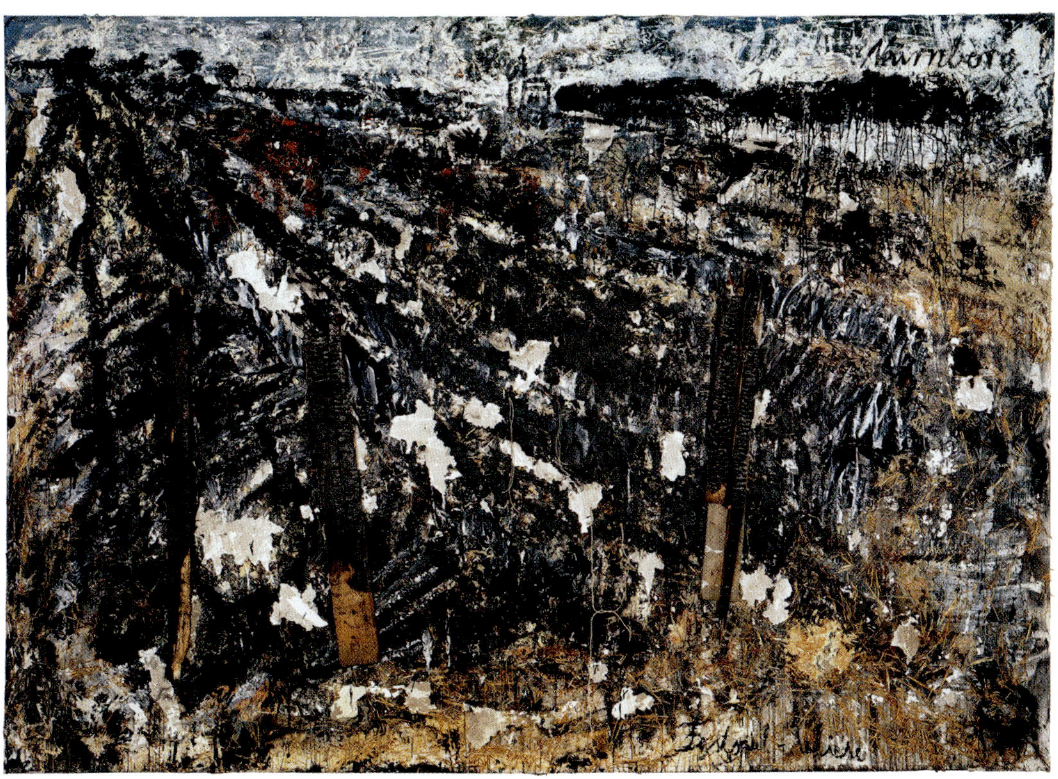

Anselm Kiefer, *Nürnberg*, 1982
Burnt wood, oil, acrylic, emulsion and straw on photograph on canvas, 290 × 390 cm (114⅛ × 153½ in.)

If an act of mourning is about reintegrating what has been lost with one's psyche, then Kiefer's paintings are just that: acts of mourning. The smaller pieces have a delicacy that is often overlooked; the scale, weight and use of everyday materials in the larger works could be seen as necessary to making an intrinsically private act a communal one.

Where Kiefer and Baselitz were exceedingly earnest, Sigmar Polke was witty and playful. In the 1960s he had made Pop art paintings full of witticisms ridiculing modernism. In the 1970s he had spent his time travelling and taking photographs. It was his 1960s spoofs of the all-too-serious art being made around him that he returned to in the 1980s. Rather than looking like a footnote to American Pop, he began to be seen as having a major position: part joker, part seer.

Whether chance or inspiration led to Polke's particular juxtapositions of styles and images – such as minimalism with kitschy Delft tiles in *Carl Andre in Delft* (page 74) – was never certain. Jokes on petty-bourgeois life, the art world and spirituality abounded. When asked later why he had started to add bits of gold leaf to his work, he answered that because his paintings were now so expensive, he felt obliged to include expensive materials. Characteristically,

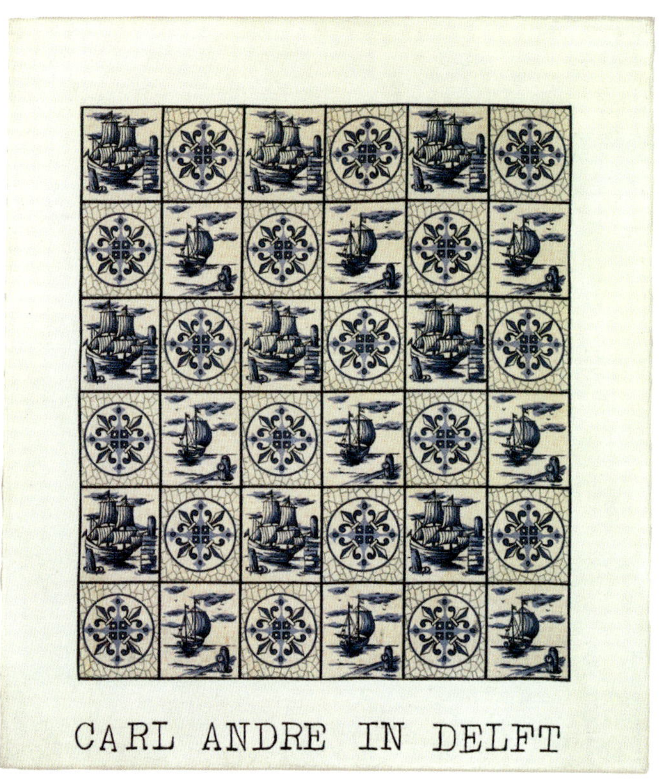

Sigmar Polke, *Carl Andre in Delft*, 1968
Acrylic on patterned fabric, 87.5 × 75 cm (34½ × 29⅝ in.)

he threw the gold leaf on in a casual, cack-handed manner. Nevertheless, and despite the very uneven nature of his production, the best works can easily persuade one of Polke's sincerity. His ambivalent posture as prankster and magus would make him, of all his contemporaries, perhaps the greatest influence on a younger generation.

At the same time as, or soon after, what many saw as the re-emergence of a specifically German painting tradition, groups of painters all working in a more or less expressionistic, figurative way emerged from other countries of Europe: Italy, France, Austria, Spain, Scotland, etc. All were claimed to be specifically Italian, French, Austrian, Spanish or Scottish. Neither those committed to the internationalism of modernism or the anti-nationalism of conceptual art were prepared for this new nationalist focus. The market, however, was. It boomed.

Most importantly, the hegemony of New York – the assumption that what happened there determined what would happen elsewhere – was destroyed: suddenly, what happened in Cologne or Rome or Glasgow could have equal consequences. There were also young painters emerging in the US, many of them connected to the graffito art of the period.

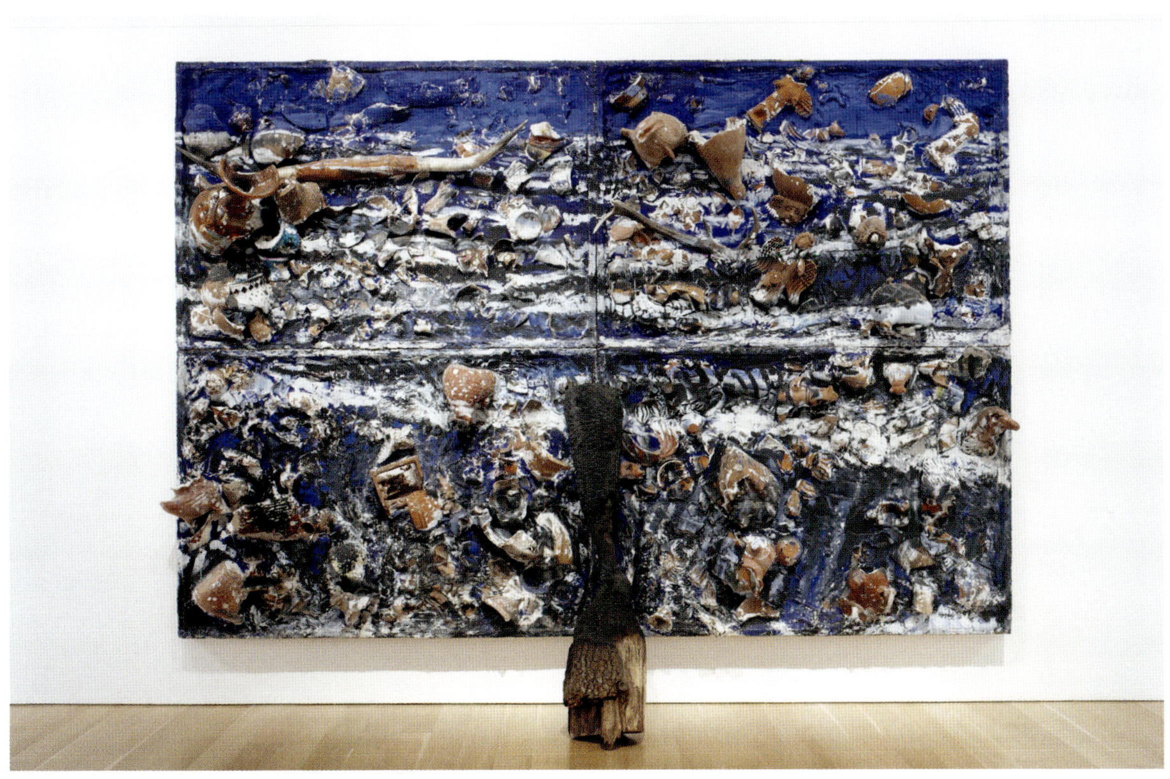

Julian Schnabel, *The Sea*, 1981
Oil, Mexican pots, plates, burnt wood, plaster, styrofoam, antlers, bondo on wood, 274.3 × 396.2 cm (108 × 156 in.)

The young Julian Schnabel could be as eclectic and ironically wilful as Polke: his large paintings might bring together references to the likes of Caravaggio, cartoon imagery, as well as unusual objects and materials. Long, structural brush-marks were employed to hold it all together. Unlike Polke, however, Schnabel's work could be emotional, operatic even. But the paintings seemed to come from a hollow world; or, as Schnabel himself put it in 1987, talking of his plate paintings: 'These paintings really are not about aggressive surfaces, but about an imagistically focussed inarticulateness, which shows itself as agitation. I don't really want my works to overwhelm people, but to bring out into the open inarticulateness which is the core of the most intimate sense of self. This anxious inarticulateness is perhaps most evident in the light that shines in my work and that nobody has noticed.'[11]

Along with what some saw as his vaulting ambition, Schnabel was an especially inventive artist. His paintings on velvet or broken plates, for example, were and remain eye-catching and memorable. Moreover, with New York collectors and critics witnessing an unexpected wave of European 'neo-expressionist' painters arriving in the city's galleries, they looked, inevitably, for an American equivalent. In the now hyperactive art market of New York, he was a star. And in Europe, too, people were

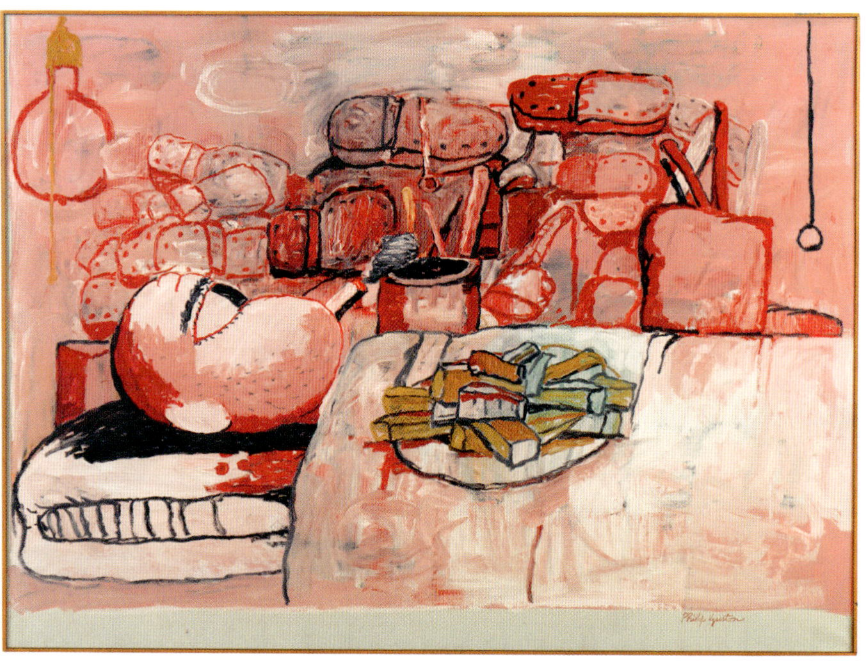

Philip Guston, *Painting, smoking, eating*, 1973
Oil on canvas, 196.8 × 262.9 cm (77½ × 103⅝ in.)

fascinated by Schnabel: he was included in both the 'New Spirit of Painting' and 'Zeitgeist' exhibitions. *The Sea* (above), heavy with broken Mexican pots and against which a charred stump leans, was one of five paintings of his shown at 'Zeitgeist'. In both Europe and the US he was a controversial artist: the traditionalists disliked his work; the Museum of Modern Art, bastion of modernist good taste, had promised never to buy a work by him; while the anti-painting brigade thought his work bombastic and vulgar. But for others, more than any other artist, he had something of the baroque – both its stylishness and its longing for excess and high passion.

However, if people expected Schnabel to be a flash in the pan, as many young painters of this period turned out to be, he would prove them wrong, not only by continuing to make paintings – often of immense size, extending at times into portraiture – but also by being the most successful of his generation of artists, Cindy Sherman among them, who had a go at directing movies, his films including *The Diving Bell and the Butterfly* (2007) and *At Eternity's Gate* (2018). In 2015 MoMA finally swallowed its pride and bought one of Schnabel's early paintings.

Also important at this time as models for a more figurative or poetic way of painting were two older American artists – one of whom, Philip Guston, was indeed already dead. Guston had been a revered Abstract Expressionist, but in the late 1960s he became radically disillusioned with abstract art: '[W]hen the 1960s came along I was feeling split, schizophrenic. The [Vietnam] war, what was happening in

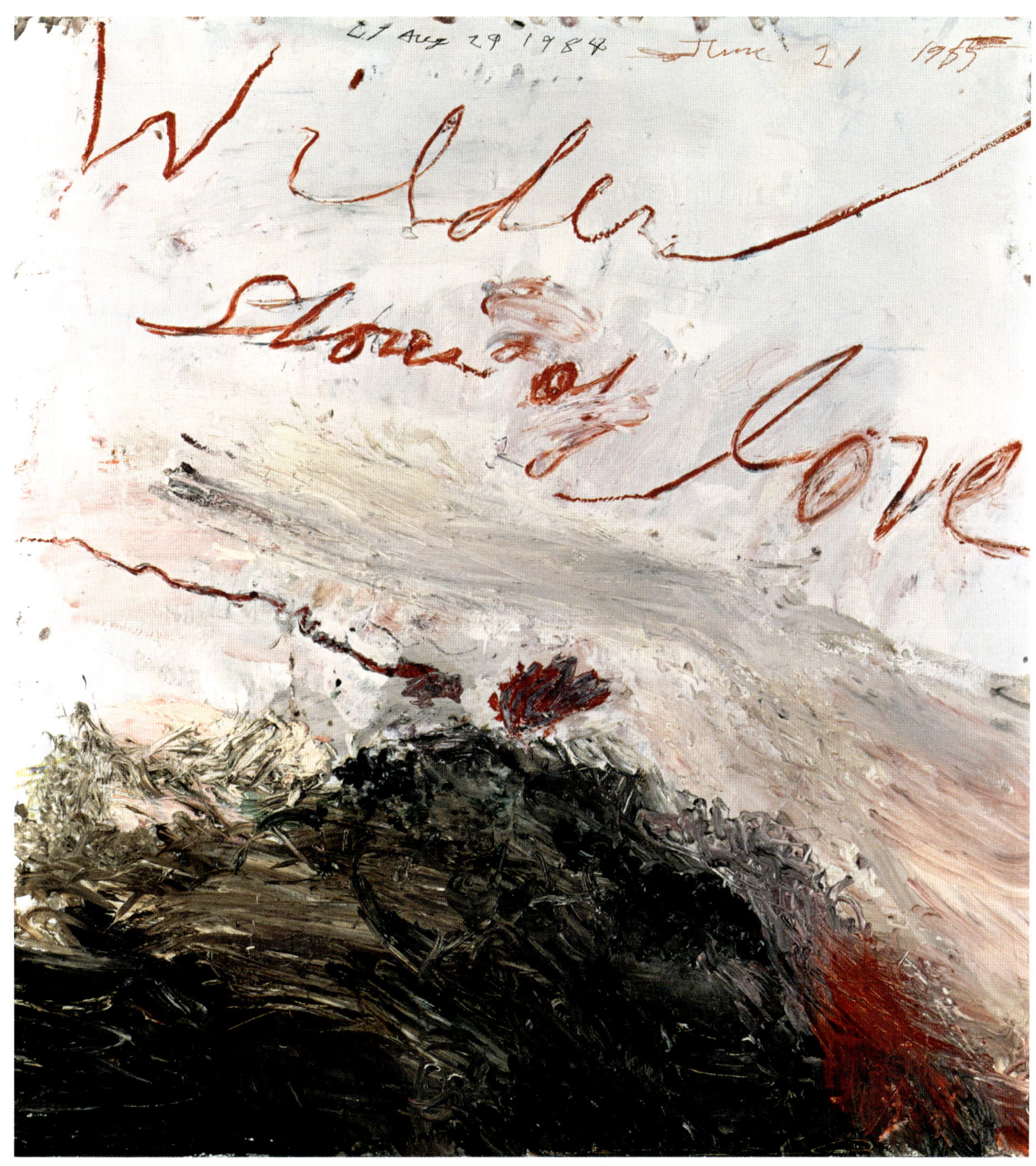

Cy Twombly, *Wilder Shores of Love*, 1985
Oil-based house paint, oil paint (paint stick), coloured pencil and lead pencil on wooden panel, 140 × 120 cm (55⅛ × 47¼ in.), second version

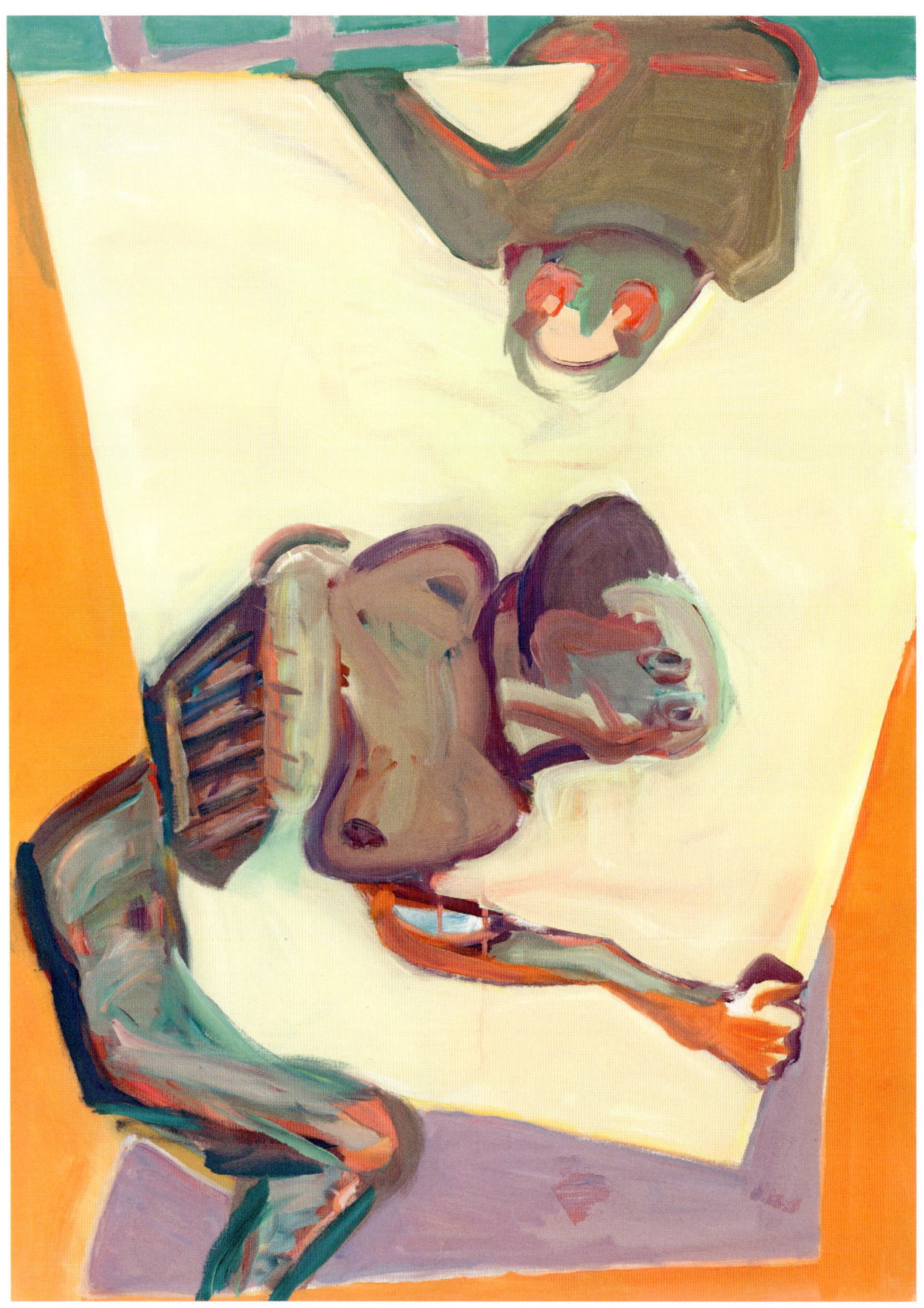

Maria Lassnig, *Die innige Verbindung von Maler und Leinwand* (The Intimate Connection Between Painter and Canvas), 1986
Oil on canvas, 200 × 140 cm (78¾ × 55⅛ in.)

America, the brutality of the world. What kind of man am I, sitting at home, reading magazines, going into a frustrated fury about everything – and then going into my studio *to adjust a red to a blue*. I thought there must be some way I could do something about it. I knew ahead of me a road was laying. A very crude, inchoate road. I wanted to be complete again, as I was when I was a kid ... Wanted to be whole between what I thought and what I felt.'[12] His utter repulsion at the art he had been associated with was seen in notes found after his death in 1980: 'American abstract art is a lie, a sham, a cover-up for a poverty of the spirit. A mask to hide the fear of revealing oneself ... Where are the wooden floors – the light bulbs – the cigarette smoke? Where are the brick walls? Where is what we feel – without notions – ideas – food intentions? No, just conform to the banks – the plaza – monuments to the people who own this country – give everyone the soothing lullaby of "art". We all know what this is – don't we?'[13]

Following his rejection of abstraction, Guston began making drawings and small paintings of everyday items – shoes, light bulbs, books, etc. Soon he moved to more heroically scaled paintings, but continued to populate them with commonplace objects, as well as cartoon-like figures. It is hard not to see *Painting, smoking, eating* (page 76) as a self-portrait: a man reduced to one gigantic eye and an aperture for cigarettes and, presumably, the plate of chunky fries on his chest; behind him, a pile of shoes, such as one might have found at Auschwitz, and a bare light bulb. Of course, these works were influenced by cartoons, but they were also imbued with a deep understanding of art history; a charismatic teacher, Guston would lecture, above all else, on the fifteenth-century Italian painter Piero della Francesca. What made Guston's work so different from Pop was the way he joined high art with low, not to be cool and ironic, but to speak and paint directly – as if it mattered.

Cy Twombly, unlike most of his American contemporaries, had left the United States, settling in Italy in 1957. He was as interested in the ancient arts of the Mediterranean as in the contemporary, and as fascinated by literature as by visual art. When, in 1991, a curator tried to interview Twombly about his work, he would talk only of poetry and his fear that it was a waning art form[14] – just as people had believed painting was a dying art form in the 1970s. Twombly's work frequently evokes poetry: 'I never separated painting and literature because I've always used reference,' he once explained.[15] In his paintings and drawings, he often wrote (he would say 'drew') the names or words of poets: Virgil, Ovid, Keats, Rilke. In so doing, he was trying to name and evoke a deep sense of culture. *Wilder Shores of Love* (page 77) takes its title from a 1954 book by Lesley Blanch about four nineteenth-century women from the West who travelled through the Middle East. Mediterranean culture, and those who had lived in it, were clearly important to him.

Twombly's subject matter is often sophisticated, arcane even, but his method of working – graffiti-like in its scrawling, dirtying way – seems pretty basic or child-like. Certainly, it was very physical. Such a combination of ostensible erudition and an apparently messy way of working – scratching, smudging, smearing paint – fascinated other artists. They were also intrigued by the complex way Twombly's work had evolved. Like Guston, Twombly was widely seen as a role model; yet also like Guston, he was difficult to copy or imitate without producing mere clumsy pastiches.

Every painter now had to find their own language.

What Twombly, Baselitz, Guston and others proved was that painting could still present arguments and provoke debate. It could also be both visually striking and embody complex, many-layered emotions. There were types of painting possible other than formalist abstraction or traditional figure painting.

But what about female artists? Had they not been making such work? It was noted by numerous observers that of the thirty-eight artists featured in 'A New Spirit in Painting', not one was female; likewise, of the forty-six artists in 'Zeitgeist', only one was a woman, Susan Rothenberg. For many, this stigmatized both exhibitions as male braggadocio, an archaic glorification of the male hero. Indeed, these were probably the last two major shows to ignore female artists in this way.

In retrospect, it is difficult to understand why the Austrian painter Maria Lassnig had not been included in either exhibition. If such artists as Baselitz, Schnabel and Guston emphasized visceral bodily experiences, Lassnig's work was a more focused and analytic examination of what it is to have a body. Lassnig made a crucial distinction between what she called 'inner-body awareness' and 'the retinal view of my body, the external view'.

Lassnig had begun making such 'inner-body awareness' paintings in 1951. In the 1970s she moved from her native Austria to New York but was ignored, her paintings seen as pathological. In response, she started painting more realistically, although self-portraits continued to dominate. In 1980 she returned to Austria and focused again on an inner sense of the body. 'Paint a picture in a particular body position,' she wrote in 1980, 'for example sitting down. Resting on one arm, one feels the shoulder blade, of the arm itself only the upper part, the palms of the hands like the grips on a crutch ... I feel the points where my backside presses into the divan, my stomach because it is filled like a sack, my head is sunken into the cardboard box of the shoulder blades, the skull is open at the back, in my face I feel the nasal opening, as big as a pig's, and around it I feel the skin burning. I'll paint it red.'[16]

While protesting the exclusion of female artists from major exhibitions was one aspect of the feminist movement in the arts, another was to rediscover forgotten or neglected female artists from the past: Artemisia Gentileschi, Berthe Morisot, Gwen John, Helene Schjerfbeck. Perhaps the most influential of these rediscoveries was Frida Kahlo, who had died in 1953. The exhibition of her work at London's Whitechapel Gallery in 1982 was the first to be staged outside her native Mexico. Apart from the sheer romance of her life – love affairs with Diego Rivera and Trotsky, involvement in radical politics, a terrible injury – her emphasis on bodily experiences and masquerade, her endless self-representation in both painting and photography, chimed with a later generation of female artists.

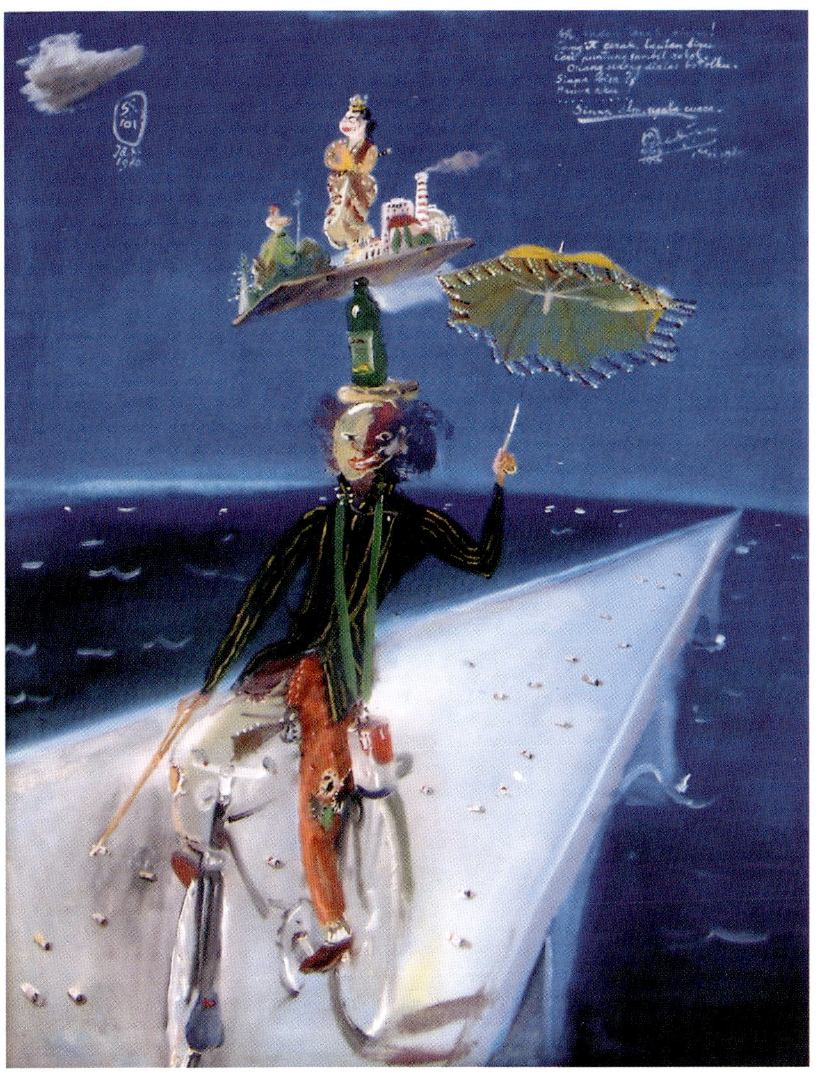

S. Sudjojono, *Fit Under Any Kind of Weather*, 1980
Oil on canvas, 90 × 70 cm (35½ × 27⅝ in.)

As we have noted, the 1980s were also a time when Europe began thinking once again in terms of national schools of painting. In an increasingly homogenous, global world, this seemed like a necessary search for 'roots' or a sense of place. Why, then, did an exhibition such as 'Zeitgeist' not include any artists from outside Western Europe or the United States? It seems that no one in the West realized that, just as there had been a very different and unsuspected history of art in Germany, so there were diverse histories of painting in other parts of the world. No one thought, for example, to look at the work of the many painters in Latin America, Asia and Eastern Europe who were just as committed to an expressive and imaginative use of the figure.[17]

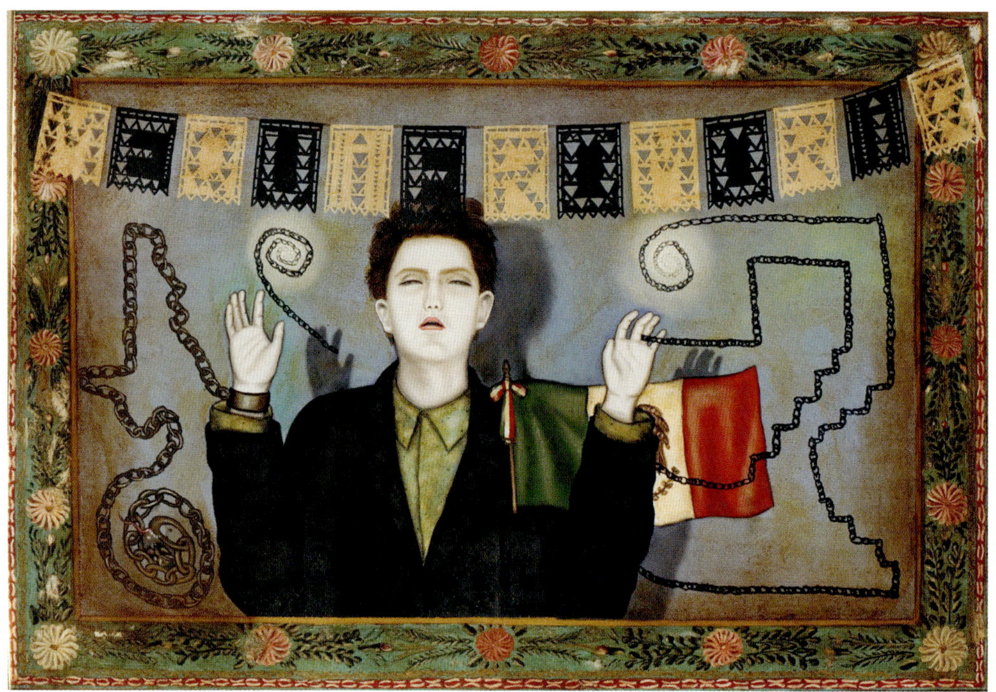

Julio Galán, *Me quiero morir* (I want to die), 1985
Oil on canvas, 132 × 187 cm (52 × 73⅝ in.)

One such artist was S. Sudjojono, whom we first encountered in Chapter 1. He had resigned from the Communist Party because their actions and ideology no longer represented his principles or beliefs. His life had also been changed by marrying the beautiful singer Rose Pandanwangi. In turn, his art became more expressive, with fantastical imagery. *Fit Under Any Kind of Weather* (page 81) is a self-portrait, a beer bottle balanced on the artist's head and the beloved Rose on top of that. Life under the repressive Suharto regime was hard, but Sudjojono's painting was about carrying on, simultaneously in the real world and that of the imagination. The text in the top right-hand corner of the painting translates as follows: 'Ah so beautiful is my country! / Clear skies, blue seas, / Collecting cigarette butts while smoking, / On top of my bottle people are happy. / Who is to handle this? / Only me! / No problem in any kind of weather.'

Would not the Mexican painter Julio Galán have also fitted into 'Zeitgeist' and enriched it? Galán raided the heritage of Mexican dress and decoration, popular culture and kitsch, that Frida Kahlo had celebrated. But while Kahlo wanted to embed herself in the traditional, Galán was more detached and ironic. Like her, he often included his own features in his paintings; yet, however heartfelt they were, there was always an element of masquerade. In *Me quiero morir* (above), Galán appears manacled in front of the Mexican flag, but do we really believe he wants to die?

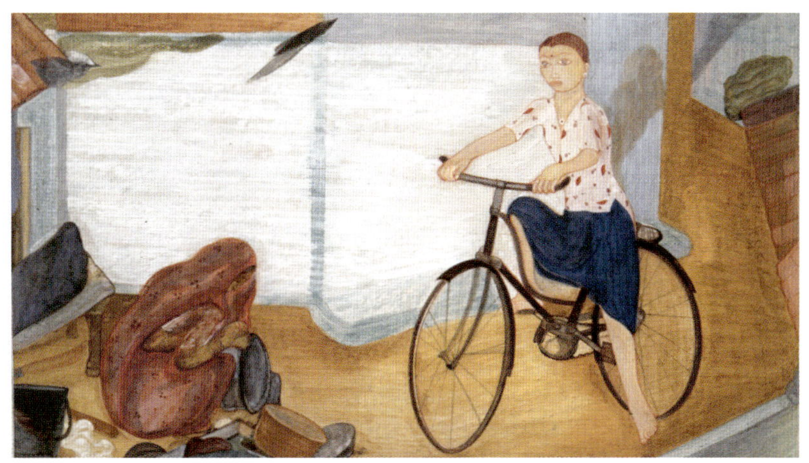

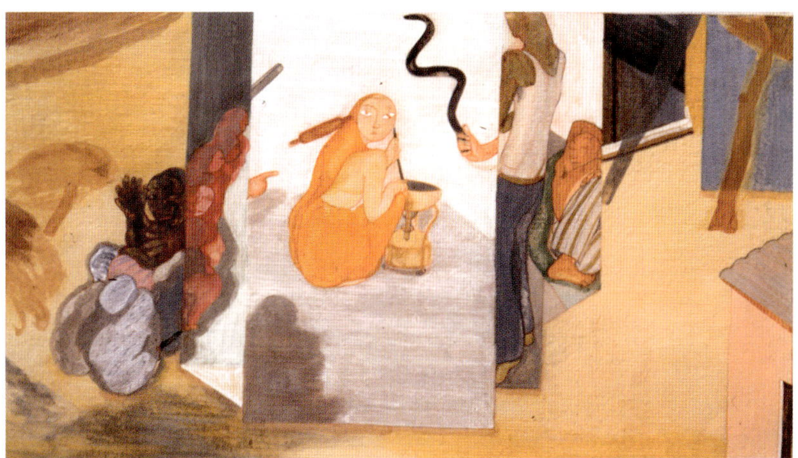

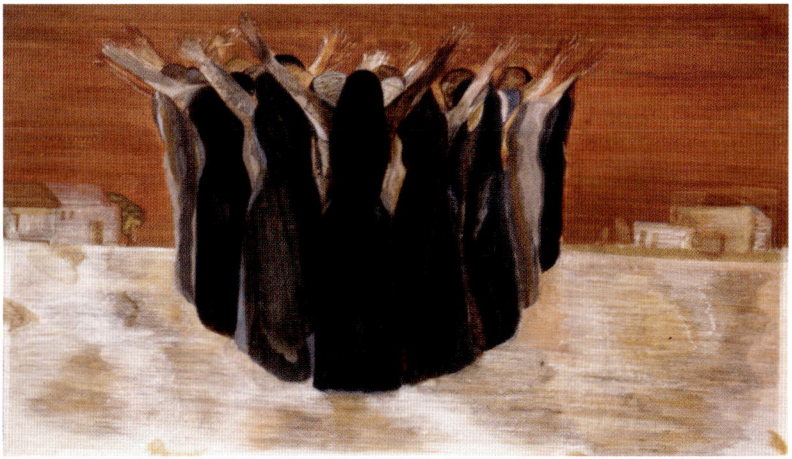

Nilima Sheikh, *When Champa grew up*, 1984
Gum tempera on wasli paper, set of 12, each 30.5 × 40.5 cm (12⅛ × 16 in.)

Galán's early work was driven by his experiences as a gay man living in an avowedly macho culture, although his imagery referred to his situation only indirectly. After moving to New York in 1984, he was able to be more open about his sexuality, depicting himself in drag or masked in cosmetics. Galán was one of many artists who began actively celebrating their homosexuality in the 1980s. Indeed, this would be the decade when identity politics, based around being gay or Hispanic etc., came to the fore.

Moreover – and surely this is no surprise – there were of course female artists from outside the West who could also have been included in 'Zeitgeist'. One such was the India-based Nilima Sheikh. In 1984 Sheikh completed a set of twelve paintings on paper, 'When Champa Grew Up'. The series, she tells us, 'was based on a real-life incident of a girl I knew; she played in the park where my children also played. She was the daughter of a class IV employee of Baroda University, where my husband and I lived. She was pretty, a darling of her indulgent parents I was told, and possessed a quietly independent spirit. But she was married off before she became an adult and after a while I found out that she had been killed. I came upon a group of women keening in ritualised mourning. It was a dowry killing.'[18] This was a time when India was becoming aware of 'the brutalisation and torture of very young brides to exhort more money from their families, often leading to murder'.[19]

When Sheikh exhibited 'When Champa Grew Up', she added texts in the form of Gujarati songs, partly to help tell the story clearly, and partly to enhance the poetry. For although this was passionate social campaigning, the twelve individual works were poetic and symbolic, rather than realist. Sheikh was also consciously using elements of the traditional mediums of Rajasthani and Pahari miniature painting. Just as European painters were looking at their own national traditions of painting, so Sheikh was looking at her own indigenous painting traditions.

'We don't need more paintings', declared the American artist Eric Fischl in 1985; 'What we need is meaning, more meaning.'[20] Fischl was one of many artists of his generation who, having been taught by conceptual artists, had no grounding in traditional life-drawing skills. He therefore had to teach himself how to paint figures. Fischl's subject matter is suburban life, its traumas and rites of passage. 'I would like to say', he wrote in 1982, 'that central to my work is the feeling of awkwardness and self-consciousness that one experiences in the face of profound emotional events in one's life. These experiences, such as death, loss, or sexuality, cannot be supported by a life style that has sought so arduously to deny their meaningfulness, and a culture whose fabric is so worn out that its public rituals and attendant symbols do not make for adequate clothing. One, truly, does not know how to act! Each new event is a crisis, and each crisis is a confrontation that fills us with much the same anxiety that we feel when, in a dream, we discover ourselves naked in public.'[21]

Fischl has always maintained that his famous, or rather *in*famous, painting *Bad Boy* (opposite) started out as a still life, and that only gradually, as he worked

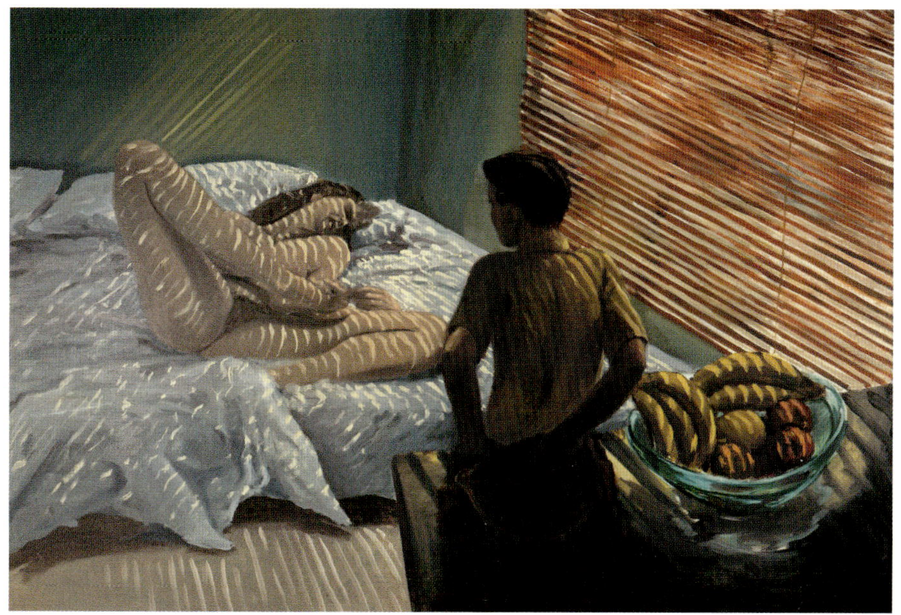

Eric Fischl, *Bad Boy*, 1981
Oil on canvas, 168 × 244 cm (66 × 96 in.)

intuitively, did it become a Freudian scene of a boy stealing from his mother's purse while he stares at her naked on a bed. For Fischl, the painting is as much about the bowl of fruit and the light that filters through the blind. It is a realist work of art, but totally unlike the work of any earlier American realist: larger and seemingly sloppier. 'I think my style is a kind of bourgeois realism that was developed in the first place by Manet and Degas', Fischl has said. 'It's a nineteenth-century tradition that has all these nice qualities to it: it's simple, it's fresh, it's intimate. Like a direct way of talking to somebody. You feel the paint strokes have a casualness that's like language – you're chatting, describing. Describing just enough detail to build content.'[22]

One of the most articulate of artists, Fischl was certainly no neo-expressionist. In many ways, his interests were to be found in the work of photographers, rather than fellow painters. But his commitment to painting would grow over time.

In contrast to the conceptual artists of the previous chapter, whose work was often presented coldly and anonymously, the artists discussed here made much of their unique personal vision. The popular press talked of them as equivalents to the painting heroes of a previous age – Van Gogh, Picasso, Pollock – even occasionally referring to them as 'geniuses'. But how good were they? As their work grew and developed, how did they compare to such 'masters'? Can we say that Baselitz *et al.* are *that* good? We shall return to such questions in our final chapter, when we consider these artists' later work, made in the twenty-first century.

Chapter 3

TAKING THE PHOTOGRAPH SERIOUSLY

The 1980s Continued

In the early 1970s, having participated in exhibitions of conceptual art, the Canadian artist Jeff Wall began to focus instead on art history, gaining a PhD in the subject and then teaching it. Although he had stopped making art, he had continued to think about it, especially photography. Like other conceptual artists, he had originally used photography as a way of documenting his concepts and actions; now, however, he began to produce photographs that, as he saw it, brought together his two loves: painting and film. For years, staged photography had been decried as fake or inauthentic, but it was exactly this type of photography that Wall now turned to, carefully setting up a scene and actors just as one would in a movie.

Wall's *Picture for Women* (page 88) is consciously based on Édouard Manet's *A Bar at the Folies-Bergère* (1882). Behind the bar at the Parisian music hall there was a curved mirror; in Manet's painting, the mirror shows not only the spectacle of the music hall but also the reflection of the back of a barmaid facing a moustachioed customer. If we work out the perspective of the mirror, we realize that, as viewers, we stand exactly where the customer had stood. We see what he saw. By 1979 it was known that a barmaid at the Folies-Bergère would probably have been expected to supplement her wages with part-time prostitution. Seen from the front, the barmaid in Manet's painting looks us in the face. Was the moustachioed man asking for champagne, or whether the young woman was 'working' that night? Manet is putting us on the spot: what would we have asked?

In Wall's remake, it is a camera that stares directly at us, while a woman looks at us from the side. Wall himself stands to the right, occupying the position of the male customer's reflection. And we are no longer looking at a glittering place of entertainment but at an empty classroom, the whole scene viewed entirely in the mirror. As Wall himself has noted, *Picture for Women* is a theoretical work relating to the male gaze – the persistent, possessive and objectifying way in which men have tended to look at women. Size was important too, Wall's photograph being larger than Manet's painting. Wall felt that this allowed for a more intimate relationship with the viewer,[1] but one that is also confrontational: the question is no longer,

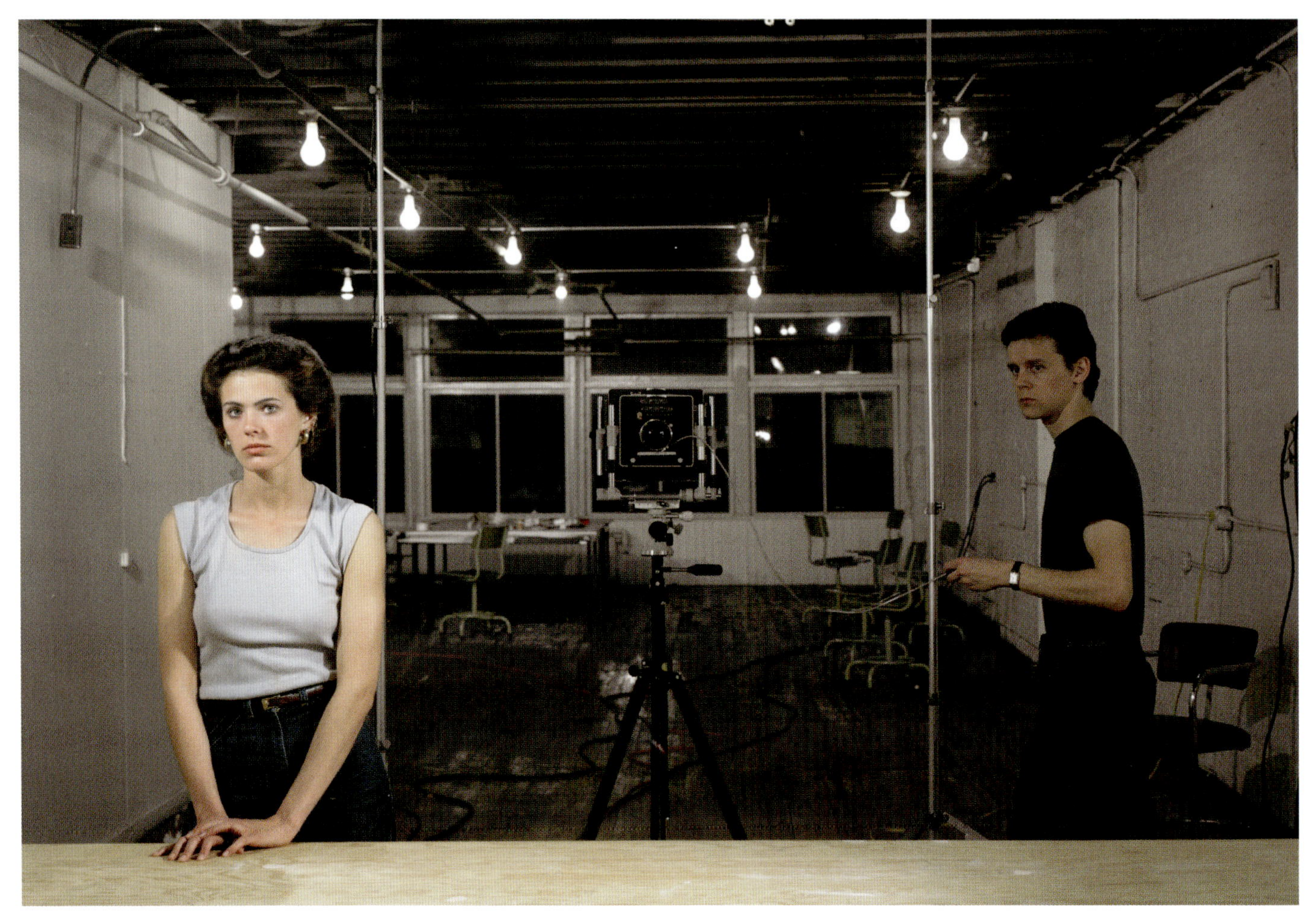

Jeff Wall, *Picture for Women*, 1979
Transparency in lightbox, 142.5 × 204.5 cm (56⅛ × 80⅝ in.)

'Are you working tonight?' but, 'How does the act of looking determine gender relationships?' – making this a deliberately problematic work. Wall had become what the poet and essayist Charles Baudelaire believed artists *should* be: a painter of modern life, someone who was engaged with the issues of the day.

Conceptual art had changed the way artists used photography, although this became obvious only in the 1980s. When Richard Long, John Baldessari or Ana Mendieta took photographs, they tried to make them not 'arty' but straightforward and informational: first and foremost, they were documentation. These were artists using photography, not photographers making art. But many of them did become very interested in the photograph – in how it was used in advertising and the media to influence people, and in how it could be used for other purposes in art.

At the start of the 1980s, it was clear that there was an underlying need to make pictures of people. The only question was whether to make these pictures out of paint or using photography. If neo-expressionism harked back to earlier traditions of painting, Cindy Sherman and a group of young artists who had come to New York from Buffalo or Los Angeles (where they had been taught by John Baldessari) looked instead to television, advertising and other mass media. These were the things that, as Americans, they had grown up with. Generally, Sherman and her fellow artists lacked the idealism of the 1968 generation, and were far more playful and irreverent. But the work they made was also based on a rejection of modernism, which by the late 1970s seemed if not dead then certainly geriatric and infirm. Wary of old romantic notions of the artist's genius and originality, they were happy to borrow and adapt images from elsewhere. They came to New York when it seemed in decline; in the mid-1970s, it had nearly gone bankrupt. In fact, following the resignation of Richard Nixon as president in 1974 and defeat in the Vietnam War the following year, the prestige and self-esteem of the United States at large was at a very low point. These were artists at the end of the American century.

Sherman, being a shy person in her youth, had often gone out dressed up as someone else – a nurse or a pregnant woman. It was a way of being in disguise but also an act of role-play. Sherman's 'Untitled Film Stills', a collection of sixty-nine black-and-white photographs made between 1977 and 1980, turned this act of self-effacement and role-playing into both art and critique. According to Sherman, the idea for the series came to her when she and her then artist boyfriend were visiting another male artist in New York, 'who had been working for some sleazy detective magazine. Bored as I was, waiting for them to get their "art talk" over with, I noticed all these 8 by 10 glossies from the magazine which triggered something in me. (I was never one to discuss issues – after all, at that time I was "the girlfriend".)'[2]

Each of these 'film stills' is a photograph of Sherman adopting a different female persona: vamp, librarian, housewife, lonely woman in nature. By the late 1970s, there was a greater recognition that stereotypes in the media play a major part in

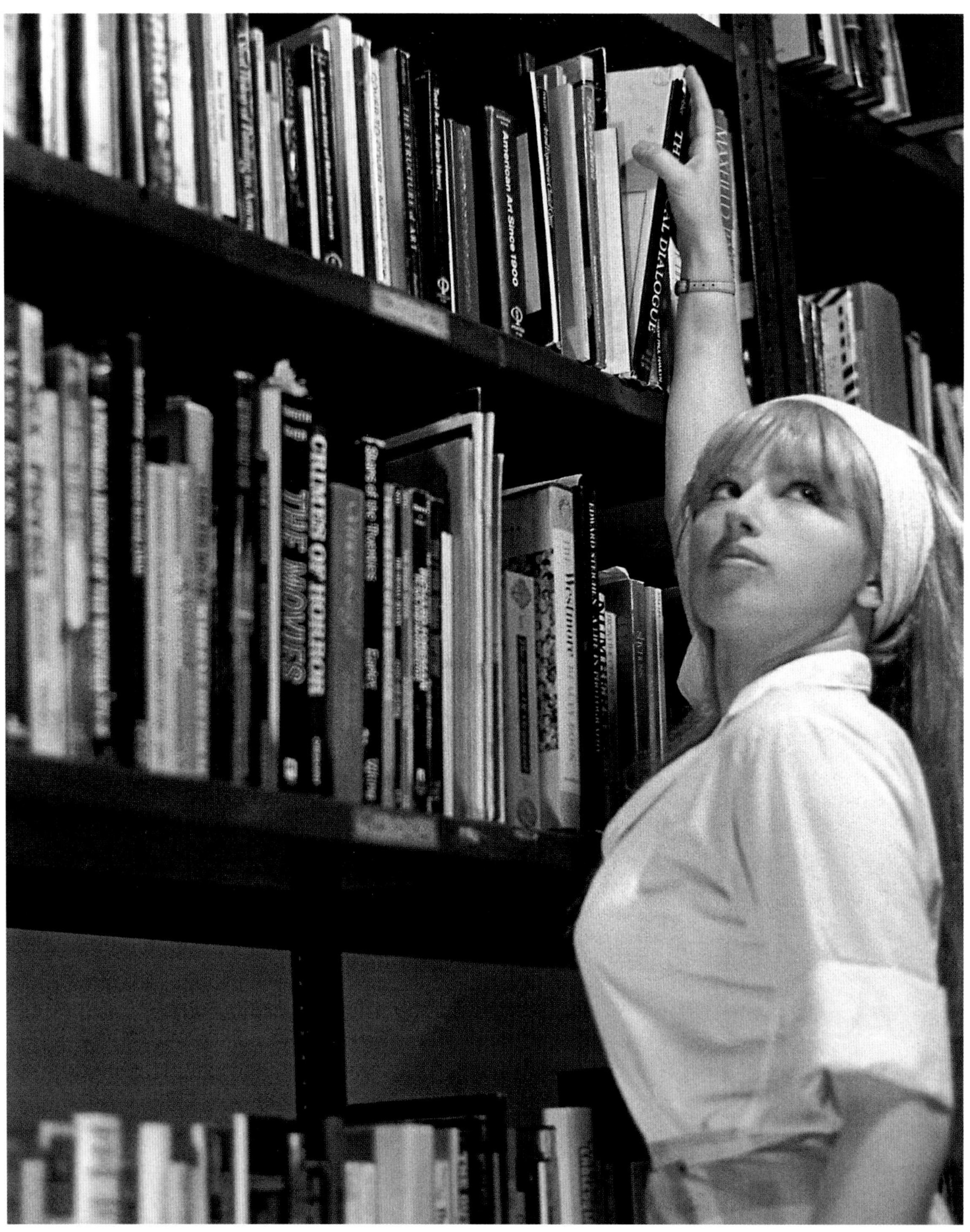

Cindy Sherman, *Untitled Film Still #13*, 1978
Gelatin silver print, 25.4 × 20.3 cm (10 × 8 in.)

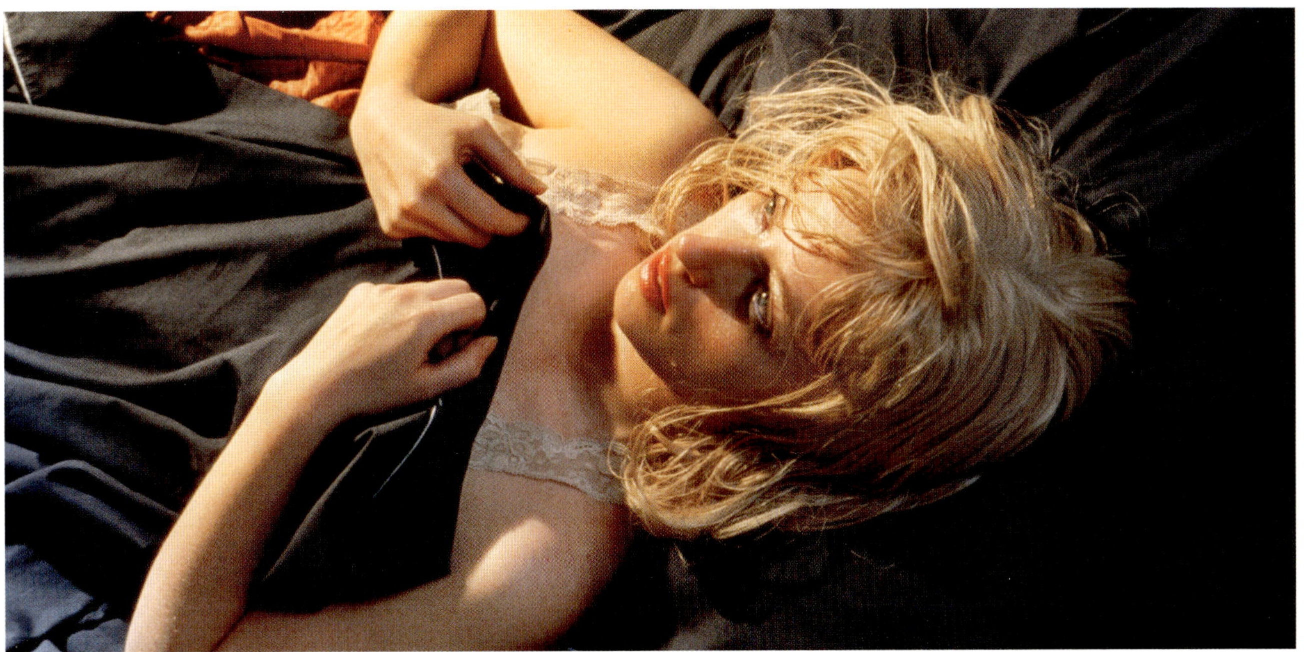

Cindy Sherman, *Untitled #93*, 1981
Chromogenic colour print, 61 × 121.9 cm (24 × 48 in.)

constructing our personalities: we act and look as we have seen people act and look in films and on television. In 'Visual Pleasure and Narrative Cinema' (1975), the feminist film theorist Laura Mulvey argued that classical Hollywood cinema had intrinsically made women objects of desire – by means of the male gaze – and had trained them to perform as such.[3] In her 'film stills', Sherman, who had grown up with and loved such movies, presents Mulvey's argument in a more accessible way: the photographs are not a tirade against the way women are portrayed in the media, but rather a knowing and self-aware masquerade of it. There is no red puritan denial of pleasure. In 1981, when Sherman was commissioned by the then leading art magazine, *Artforum*, to make a set of colour photographs collectively known as the 'Centerfolds', including *Untitled #93* (above), the magazine rejected them as being too close to pornography. In these early years of feminism, the intelligentsia were becoming hyper-sensitive about sexualized imagery.

Sherman's art may have been intellectually savvy but it wasn't cold. 'I want that choked-up feeling in your throat which maybe comes from despair or teary-eyed sentimentality: conveying intangible emotions', she wrote in 1982.[4] Although her work has inspired some exceptionally complex theoretical writing, Sherman described what she was doing in 'Untitled Film Stills' in relatively simple terms: 'My "stills" were about the fakeness of role-playing as well as contempt for the domineering "male" who would mistakenly read the images as sexy.' Whereas earlier feminist art had been wary of anything that smacked of femininity, Sherman showed other artists how it was possible to play with notions of femininity and be critical at the same time.

When looking at Sherman's photographs, it is never quite clear if you are meant to be looking as a woman or a man. Sherman's one-time boyfriend Richard Prince, however, dealt explicitly with male fantasy – or the gap between male fantasy and reality. His *Spiritual America* piece of 1983 is perhaps one of the most outrageous examples of 'appropriation': the act of taking an image by someone else and, by putting it in a different context, changing the viewer's experience and understanding of it entirely. Such a strategy seemed as essential to Prince as it did to most critics of the time, who had been much influenced by the French theorist Roland Barthes' concept of the 'death of the author', which stated that it was the reader's experience that mattered, not the author's. This was also a period when it was felt that direct statement was impossibly naive; Umberto Eco joked that one could say 'I love you' only indirectly or ironically: 'As Barbara Cartland would say, "I love you".' Helene Winer, the gallery owner who in 1980 set up the Metro Pictures gallery to represent the likes of Sherman and Prince, once snarled that, 'to originate an innocent, expressive, personal one-shot statement is an anachronism. Expressionism embarrasses me.'[5]

Having found an image of a naked, ten-year-old Brooke Shields posed seductively, the rights to which Shields – now seventeen – was trying to reclaim through law from the photographer, Gary Gross, Prince opened a gallery called 'Spiritual America' and showed as the only work a slightly cropped, enlarged version of this image in a gold frame, which he titled *Spiritual America*. No other information was provided. Prince had taken the title from a 1923 work by Alfred Stieglitz: a formally beautiful photograph of a castrated horse. It had been Stieglitz's subtle way of suggesting that the United States was the land of repressed desire. Was Prince implying that the country was now turned on by child pornography and money? Put simply, Prince's act of appropriation (some would say theft) was intended to make one think about what the image – and our complex responses to it – mean. As Prince blogged in 2014, 'This was a "complicated" photograph. This no longer had anything to do with money or censorship or even embarrassment. For me this photograph had to do with the medium and how the medium can get out of hand.'[6]

The work has continued to provoke. In 2009, when Prince showed it at Tate Modern, London, the Obscene Publications Unit of the Metropolitan Police Service said that the image might be in breach of the Child Protection Act 1978, and that it couldn't be exhibited publicly.[7] Prince replaced it with *Spiritual America IV* (2005), a much less contentious photo of the then forty-year-old actress in a bikini, taken by Prince in collaboration with Shields. In 2014 Prince found that his Instagram account had been shut down because he had uploaded images of *Spiritual America*.[8] In the same year, the original work came up for sale at Christie's, New York; however, to see it on the auction house's website, you had to click on a panel warning of

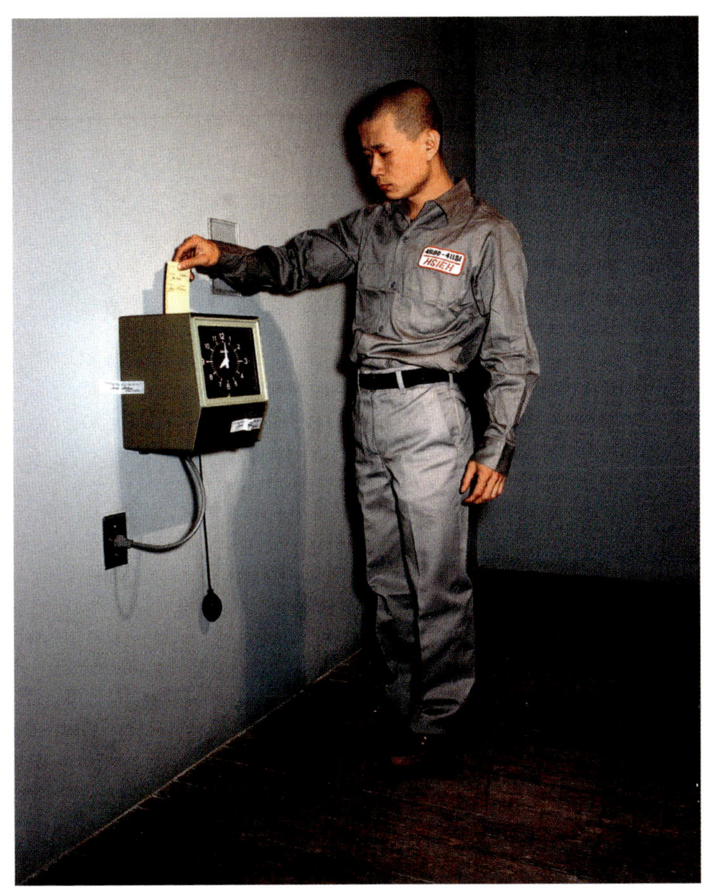

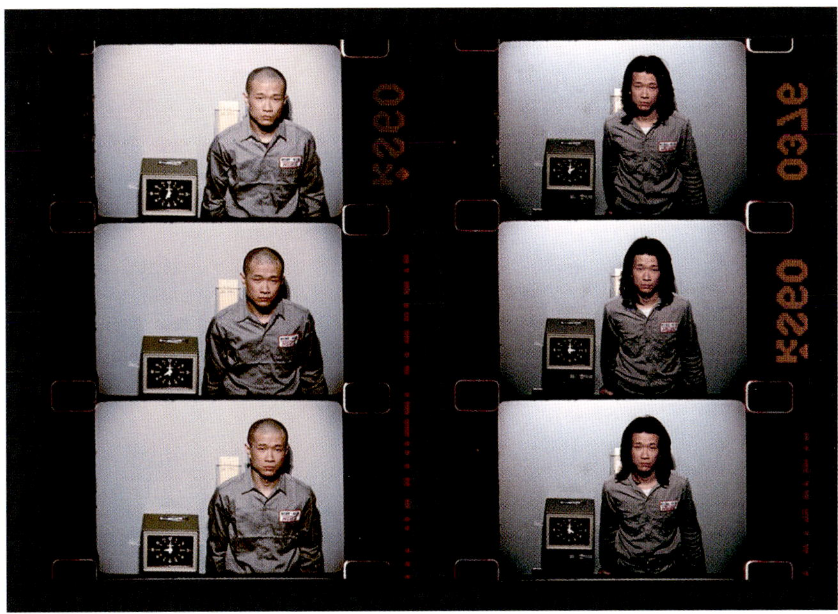

Tehching Hsieh, *One Year Performance 1980–1981*
Top: 'Punching the Time Clock'; bottom: still from 16mm film

'explicit content', confirming you were over eighteen. The work, which exists in an edition of ten, sold for $3,973,000.[9]

Some artists continued to use photographs as mere documentation. Perhaps the most ruthless and thorough use of the camera as an anonymous recorder came at the start of the 1980s: *One Year Performance 1980–1981 (Time Clock Piece)* (page 93) by the Taiwanese performance artist Tehching Hsieh. For one whole year, from 11 April 1980 to 11 April 1981, Hsieh punched a time clock every hour on the hour. Each time he did so, he took a single photo of himself; later, when spliced together, these photos yielded a six-minute film. Hsieh shaved his head before the piece, so that his growing hair would also document the passage of time. Apart from the few occasions when he overslept, he carried out the project rigorously, getting up, clocking in and photographing himself more than eight and a half thousand times. When he made the work, Hsieh was living in the United States illegally, leading some to interpret it as an ironic comment on the job he could not take. However, Hsieh himself has always insisted it is about the experience of time: 'I'm also talking about life. It's not a 9–5 job: I lived in it, 24 hours a day for a year – it is life. Your heartbeat continues. Art and life become one. My work shows different perspectives of thinking about life. For me, life is a life sentence; life is passing time, life is free thinking.'[10]

Time Clock Piece was the second of five one-year performances by Hsieh: in the first, he had locked himself in a cage and not spoken, read or watched television for twelve months; in the third, he spent a whole year in New York without going inside a building (a huge challenge in the bitter winter months!); in the fourth, he was attached to a fellow performance artist, Linda Montana, by a 2.5-metre (8 ft) rope; and in the fifth, he made no art. 'I can only say that I have kept myself alive', explained Hsieh. 'More details are unnecessary, survival is all. What I have done in those years remains in my mind ... This kind of work is not about suffering, it is about existence ... My idea is that time becomes the main thing, how I pass the time is my main concern. It doesn't matter what I do, I pass time.'[11]

Equally systematic are the photographs of industrial architecture made by the German couple Bernd and Hilla Becher. Their project, however, lasted their entire lifetimes. Bernd Becher's initial interest was in documenting all the nineteenth-century industrial buildings – water towers, pitheads – that were being demolished in Siegerland, the region of his birth. Bernd felt they had a unique aesthetic of their own that should be remembered. He drew them meticulously, but it took too long: the buildings were being knocked down before Bernd could finish his work. Thus, in 1959, he enlisted the help of Hilla, an experienced photographer whom he had first met two years earlier. They married in 1961.

The research and photographs produced by the Bechers could be described as industrial archaeology; indeed, a selection of their work was published under that title in 1971.[12] So why was it also being exhibited with the work of minimal and conceptual artists? The answer lies partly in the fact that the Bechers had become

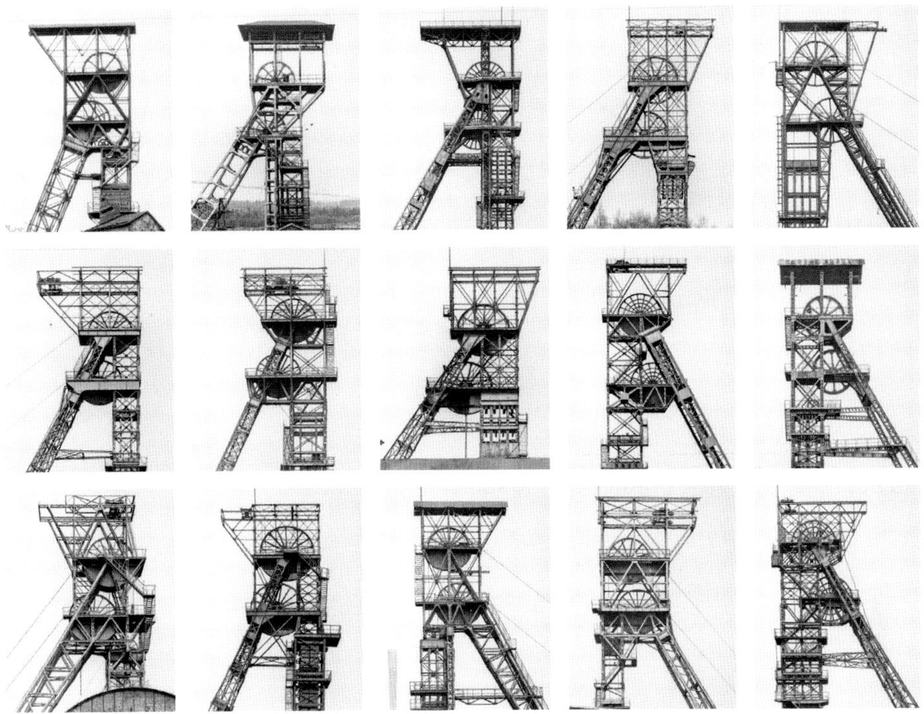

Bernd and Hilla Becher, *Winding Towers*, 1963–1982

good friends with such artists, with whom they shared an aesthetic preference for grids and objectivity. Also, traditional photography, with its emphasis on romantic landscapes and beautiful prints, was alien to them; as Bernd put it, 'If anything, the leap into the art context via the Concept Artists succeeded because we did not fit into photography. Concept Art was not just a direction in art but the experimental attempt to change the form of museum exhibitions.'[13]

True to their origins as documentary archaeologists, the Bechers tried to make their work appear as unmediated as possible, using ladders to raise themselves above foreground clutter, and to be closer to the level of the buildings. Published in 1970, their debut book was called – not entirely facetiously – *Anonymous Sculptures*, one reason for the couple being awarded, to their embarrassment, the sculpture prize at the 1990 Venice Biennale.

The Bechers' emphasis on letting the subject speak for itself, as well as their interest in typologies – often showing nine or twelve photographs of similar structures together – harked back to nineteenth-century photography and the objective photography of August Sander, who, starting in 1910, had attempted a typology of the German people. Speaking in 1989, Hilla Becher said: 'We admire the photographers of the last century because they really used photography

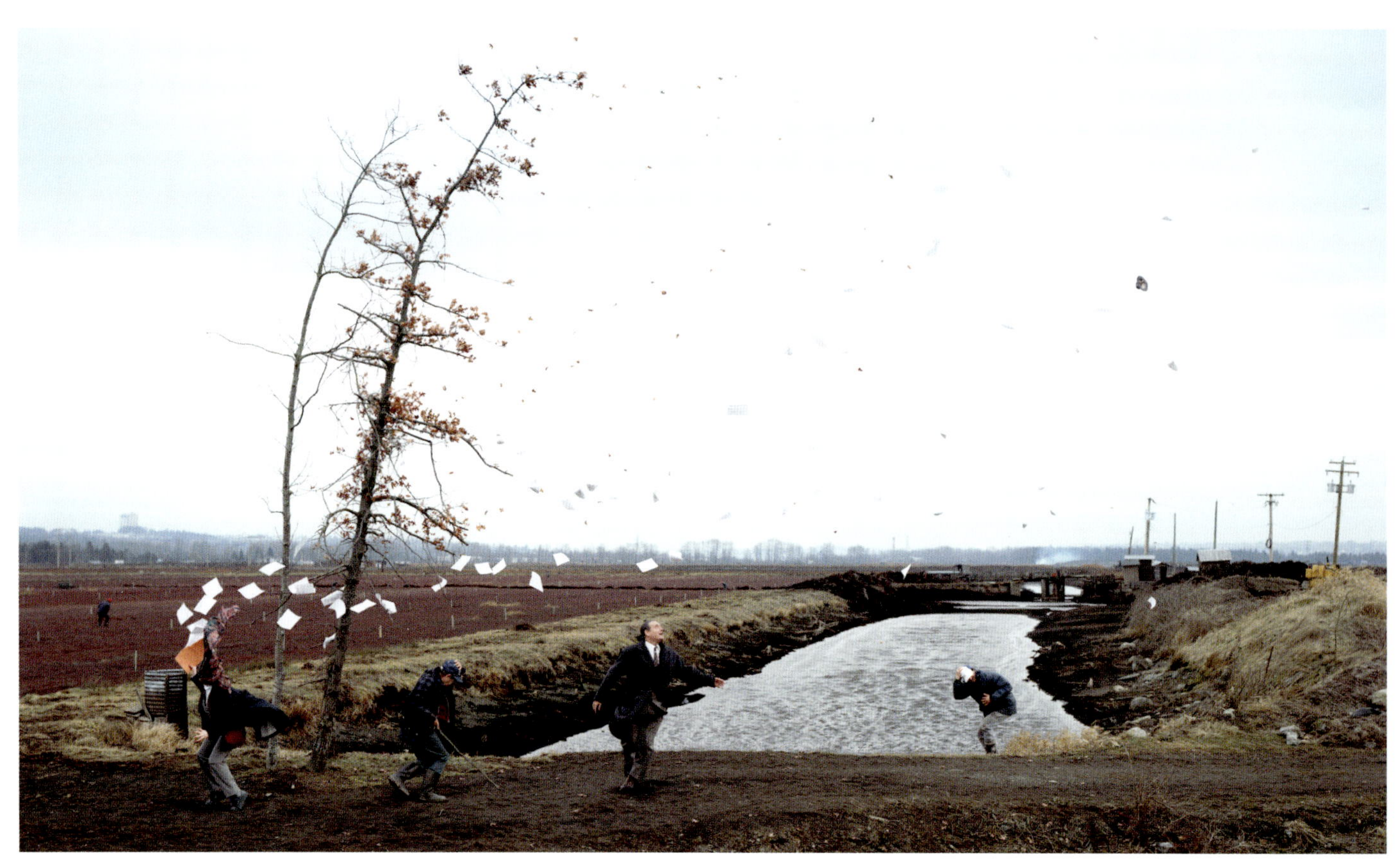

Jeff Wall, *A Sudden Gust of Wind (after Hokusai)*, 1993
Transparency in lightbox, 229 × 377 cm (90¼ × 148½ in.)

in the best way, whilst we had the impression that, in our century, photography had been misused ... In the 19th century, you have both the object and the metaphor and if you use them in the right way it becomes so fascinating that in the end you can really say, but it also stands for a particular historical condition. This is a matter of choice, of course; you cannot photograph everything, you choose typical objects ... [Photography] is very much about remembering things. This is one of the main functions of photography, to transfer things into the form of images, whilst always retaining the connection with the real object ... If you get very involved in something, you have to find a way of distancing yourself. You have to be honest with your object and to make sure that you do not destroy it with your subjectivity, and yet remain involved at the same time.'[14]

But to return to where we began ... In 2007 I took a group of photography students to see Jeff Wall's retrospective at MoMA. They were unimpressed. 'Boring photos', they said. How do we account for such a reaction? Wall had come to photography via cinema and an understanding of painting, and, like the Bechers, he saw the history of twentieth-century art photography as less useful. As we noted earlier, he did not subscribe to such concepts as Cartier-Bresson's 'decisive moment' – being at the right place at the right moment to capture the essence of a scene. Nor did he create his images in a flash of empathy or inspiration; instead, he would carefully construct each photograph, sometimes taking six months to stage and produce a single work. For *A Sudden Gust of Wind (after Hokusai)* (opposite), for example, Wall had to find the right location and then stage it piece by piece – eventually blending fifty photographs together as one.

Wall did not create eye-catching, iconic images; rather, he made images to be read or decoded slowly, as if they had the complexity of a Velázquez or a Manet, or of the work of a film-maker like Robert Bresson. And contrary to what my students felt, Wall wanted his work to be enjoyed as well as thought about. The period of reflection he had taken in the 1970s, after his involvement with conceptual art, had allowed him to stand back and think more widely; remaining liberal in outlook, he had resisted the puritanism that denounced visual pleasure as idealogically unsound. He also felt no need to dissolve the art object or make it seem fragmented: 'Art can be a commodity (which it really has to be in capitalism) and still be taken seriously. The idea that the commodity status of art prevents people from taking it seriously and developing profound relations with it is simply another sacred cow of the progressive consensus ... the commodity status exhausts no object's whole existence, and art makes that visible as its beauty.'[15]

Wall has talked about 'staging' social issues in his work, but also of wanting to show joy, as well as hardship, saying: 'I always try and make beautiful pictures.'[16] Asked some years later whether this was a political statement, he replied that he saw it as 'ethical': 'The experience of beauty is always associated with hope, and art, as Stendhal said, is "a promise of happiness". Things don't have to stay as they are, change for the better is possible. This is the basis of the democratic, and the bourgeois, tradition ... My life without the experience of art would be very different than it is. Aesthetic pleasure changes you. It may not change the world, but it changes you and the way you relate to the world.'[17]

By the time he came to make *A Sudden Gust of Wind*, Wall could affirm that 'photography has now become an art, or a medium with status equal to that of the older ones'.[18] Echoing the composition of a woodcut by the Japanese artist Hokusai, the work shows people on the margins of a city – in reality Vancouver, but it could be anywhere. The shacks indicate that people have settled here, making their own community, but the capitalist city will inevitably expand and drive them out. The better-dressed man to the left is, we assume, a landlord or developer whose property deeds, to the excitement of the squatters, have been swept away by the wind. Through staging and post-production, Wall has made a photograph with the same scale and density as the history paintings of Poussin or Delacroix – and which is also, like the works of Manet, of contemporary life.

Chapter 4

SCULPTURE, INSTALLATIONS OR COMMODITIES?

Around 1987

As we noted in the introduction, few sculptors today see themselves as part of the Western sculpture tradition that ran from the ancient Greeks to Rodin via Michelangelo. Minimalism seemed to represent a complete break with this tradition. How could artists return to sculpture in the traditional sense of the word? How could they reintroduce complexity – even references to the human body – into their practice? In this chapter we begin by looking at five sculptors who sought, in different ways, to do just that.

Although the Welsh-born Richard Deacon sometimes refers to himself as a fabricator, the act of *making* is at the core of his beliefs. His career has been an investigation of materials, including metals, woods, clay, fabric, paper, etc., and of processes: bending, riveting, glazing, marbling – Richard Serra's list of verbs (page 47) enlarged to include more complex, cultural techniques. 'Sculptures', said Deacon in 1986, 'are made both by the hand of man and for it, by man and apropos of him.'[1] As if to emphasize this, the signs of making are always left visible or accentuated in his work; often, there is an excess of marks, or screws, or rivets.

For Deacon, form comes from materials and processes: 'The activity of making sculptures has to do with making objects – with being able to make objects that have meaning.'[2] His sculptures of the 1980s were often open or hollow, encouraging you to imagine meaning, or even yourself inside them. The surface acted as a skin, although it also formed the structure. Deacon preferred material he could manipulate: beech he could steam and bend, clay he could push and cut and shape. 'My idea about sculpture', he has explained, 'was that it was composed of matter but wasn't subject to gravity. This is metaphorical, obviously, but I thought of sculpture as being between me and the world, rather than sitting on the world ... I wanted to make sculpture that showed that aspect of belonging to the human more than belonging to the world.'[3] He was interested in both how materials behaved and the imaginative responses we have to them.

Like many of his generation, Deacon liked working in response to specific contexts. But making his series of smaller sculptures, 'Art For Other People',

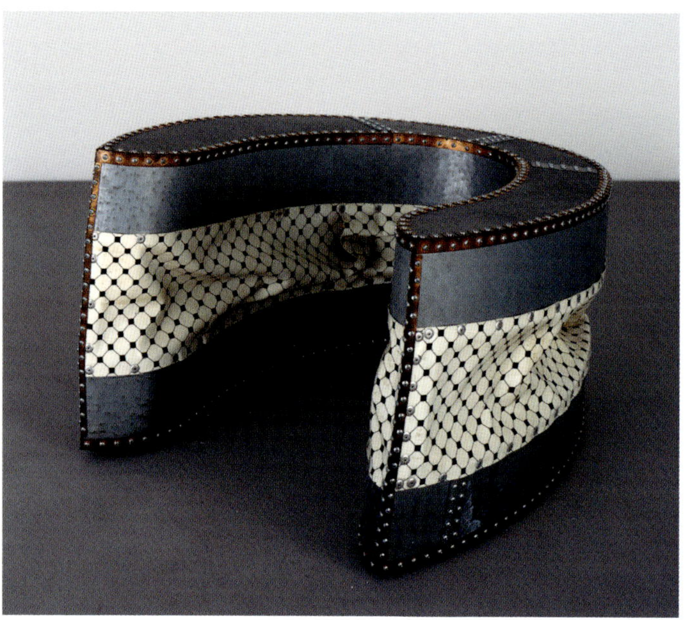

Richard Deacon, *Art For Other People #24*, 1987
Galvanized steel and vinyl, 35 × 92 × 75 cm (13¾ × 36¼ × 29½ in.)

was, he said, more 'like writing letters to people. [The sculptures] were intended to work non-contextually, so that you could take them anywhere.'[4] At first glance, Deacon's objects tend to look familiar, intentionally so. And even when his work has the symmetry of minimalism, he calls on or implies metaphor: *Art For Other People #24* (above) always reminds me of my grannie's false teeth, which would fall out periodically. We all bring our own memories and associations.

Talking of the minimalists, the German artist Thomas Schütte said: 'I respect them a lot. It was this generation that established the grammar, the training and the language. They address the fundamental problems – of lighting, material, meaning and space.'[5] But Schütte is also interested in other forms, in decoration and models. People understand what a model is: as children, they made them with Lego or Play-Doh. In one early work, Schütte presented a brick wall that, when viewed close up, turned out to be made of painted wooden slats, each propped on a pair of nails banged into the wall. Here, the model was not something ideal but something provisional. Other works looked like models of buildings. Miniature people started to appear. Those miniatures then expanded, becoming giant, overbearing figures, yet always incomplete or flawed. 'Many of my works', he once explained, 'have to do with power and are intended as parodies.'[6]

In 1990, discussing his practice, Schütte said: 'The installation of my work is as important as its production. It's a separate work in itself.'[7] He was thinking, no doubt, of the piece he had made for the second Skulptur Projekte Münster, organized by Kasper König three years earlier. While wandering through the city, Schütte had come acress a square that was being used as a car park. It was also full of clutter: bicycle racks, telephone booths, garbage bins and a dead cherry tree waiting to be chopped down. What sculpture would be appropriate for such a messy, mundane place? Not a heroic figure on a plinth! Schütte made a column from the same sandstone used to construct the historic buildings of the town – and then placed two giant cherries on the top (below).

Three years later, Schütte was extremely pissed off, never wanting to make a public work again. Münster City Council had removed the car park, tidied up the square, and added a sub-grade modernist fountain. The cherries had lost their context. 'I've lost interest,' he said. 'Nobody cares. The people who order these works don't care about the artist or the work; for them it is a kind of city advertisement. The sculpture simply becomes a logo … I placed a kitsch sculpture in the middle of a car park. But it's not a car park anymore. Now there's an interesting sculpture in the middle of a kitsch place.'[8]

Later, when a department store commissioned from Schütte a sculpture for the exterior of their premises, they expected cherries or something equally jolly. Instead, they got toy-like yet life-size clay sculptures of refugees and their baggage. This was 1992, when, following the collapse of the communist bloc, many people had travelled to the West looking for work – often to be met with hatred. 'If I have a commission or show,' explained Schütte, 'I always ask myself, what could be

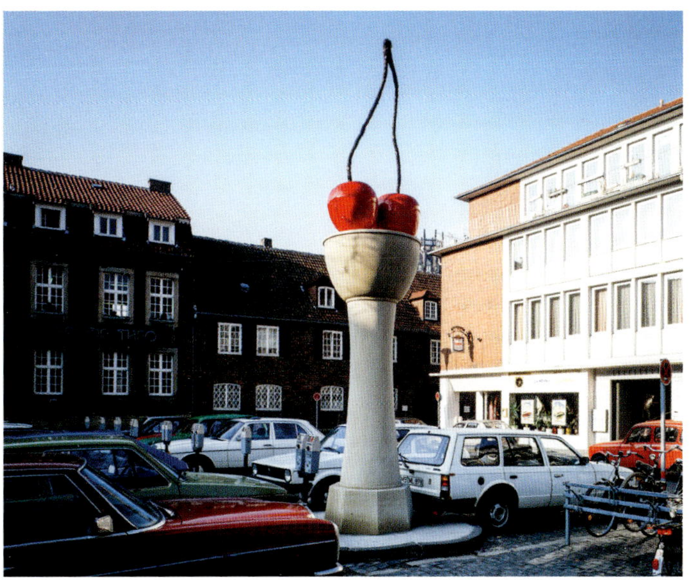

Thomas Schütte, *Kirschensaule* (Cherry column), 1987
Painted cast aluminium, sandstone, 6 m (236¼ in.) high, Münster, Germany

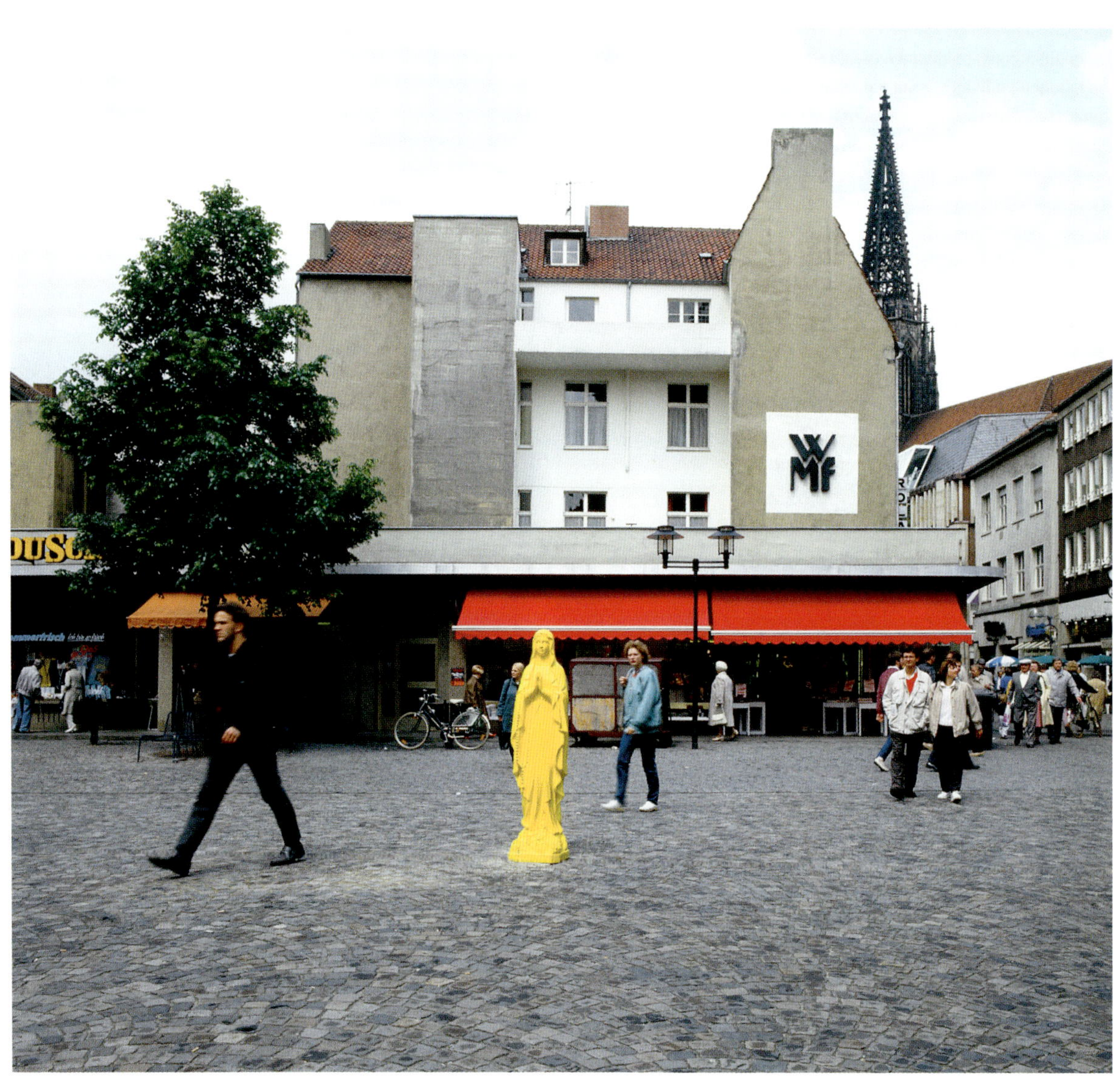

Katharina Fritsch, *Madonna*, 1987
Duroplast, 170 × 40 × 34 cm (67 × 15¾ × 13½ in.), Münster, Germany

necessary? I don't ask myself what I want to do: I ask myself what really is the problem? What could be necessary, what could be useful, what is missing?'[9] Is this the role of the artist today? The awkward conscience?

The German sculptor Katharina Fritsch initially studied as an art historian, and her work has been an investigation of that traditional subject of art history: iconography – what objects can mean. Is it possible to reinvent stereotypes? Fritsch makes very few works, but they are always conceptualized and manufactured with great precision. She first came to notice by making a life-size replica of an elephant, but coated a dull green. Something very familiar, but wrong, or strange. 'Strange', that is, in the sense of 'estranged': it is no longer part of our familiar world. Fritsch is very particular, too, about how her work is displayed; the elephant, for example, was elevated on a large oval plinth.

In 1987, for the second Skulptur Projekte Münster, Fritsch made a life-size version of the Madonna from Lourdes (opposite). Life-size, but a lurid yellow. Placed in one of Münster's main squares, it was meant to get under people's skin. Given that Münster is a staunchly catholic city, it succeeded. The sculpture was vandalized to such an extent it had to be replaced. (Fritsch, of course, had kept the moulds so she could make it again – and again, if necessary.)

Soon after, Fritsch made miniature versions of the yellow Madonna and sold them as part of an unlimited edition at a set price. The work played not only with stereotypes but also with that slippery border between art and commodity. In part, it was a riposte to the contrived rarity of the limited edition – a run of twenty-five prints, say, or nine bronze statuettes. It also referred back to the origins of the 'multiple': the lead badges or woodcuts of the Virgin or saints sold at pilgrimage sites from the fifteenth century onwards. There was no notion of such editions being limited, any more than for a plastic replica of the Madonna you might buy in Lourdes itself.[10]

The 1987 Skulptur Projekte Münster was one of a number of exhibitions in the late 1980s that celebrated the revivification of sculpture in Europe. At the inaugural project in 1977, eight artists had been shown: five Americans and three Europeans, all men. In 1987, the number of participating artists was sixty-four: nineteen from the US, forty-five from Western Europe, with six women among them. None of the sixty-four came from anywhere else in the world – an omission that, at the time, no one seemed to remark on. True, three of the artists had been born in Asia, Nam June Paik included, but they all now lived in the West.[11] (On an island in a lake in the town, in front of an old Bakelite TV, Paik placed a bronze Buddha, apparently engrossed in what he was watching.) This myopic focus on the West was not the result of any conscious prejudice on the curator's part; rather, it was just how the art world then perceived things.

Jeff Koons showed at Münster too. But wasn't the sort of neo-Pop he epitomized, with his yen – like Richard Prince's – for appropriating others' images, the exact opposite of the kind of work produced by Deacon and Schütte? Whereas they were fascinated by making, Koons disdained using his own hands: he was interested in commodities.

In the early 1980s, Koons had become famous, first of all, for presenting ready-mades not as Duchamp had, as everyday objects, but as glossy icons of consumerism – hoovers encased in Perspex with fluorescent lights, basketballs suspended miraculously in the centre of a liquid-filled tank – and, secondly, for casting ordinary things in highly polished stainless steel (which Koons described as the 'luxurious material of the proletariat'), most famously an inflatable bunny. This was the banal turned into the spectacular.

Koons's bunny became an icon for the materialist 1980s. This was the decade, after all, of Thatcher and Reagan, when capitalism seemed rosy, when the stock market boomed, when getting rich seemed possible, when the brand became such a key element in promoting sales. Artists like Koons, taking their cue from Warhol, therefore promoted themselves as brands.

On 19 October 1987 – Black Monday – the stock market crashed, wiping billions of dollars off the Dow Jones. Recession followed. Yet, in the following year, 1988, the art market was still on the up. Indeed, it seemed a safer place to speculate than the stock market. On 11 November, Sotheby's New York was able to report, with undisguised glee, not only that it had sold a Jasper Johns painting, *False Start*, for a record $17 million, but also that its sales of contemporary art for the year amounted to more than $124 million – over ten times the figure just four years earlier. All seemed well with the art world.

As Koons later acknowledged, the second Münster sculpture project marked an important stage in his career. It was the first time he had been commissioned to make a public work – something that had made him think. Also, he had had to change his practice. His intention had been to make an exact, stainless-steel cast of the kitsch yet popular statue in Münster of a man going to market with a wicker basket on his back. When that proved impossible, he had had to make his own version of the sculpture. From then on, rather than presenting ready-mades, he would make things that looked like ideal versions of banal objects. But perhaps we should say 'fabricate' rather than 'make'. When giving a talk at the ICA in London that year, someone in the audience had asked him if he made anything. 'Oh no!' he'd replied, as if shocked at the mere suggestion. 'That would be like masturbating.'[12] However, he has always ensured that his works are made by the best possible woodcarvers, ceramicists or glass-blowers. He is a perfectionist.

For his 1988 'Banality' exhibition, Koons spliced together appropriated images and converted them into three dimensions – in wood, mirror or highly glazed ceramic. Michael Jackson and Bubbles, cherubs with a pig (a work entitled *Ushering in Banality*). Describing another of the works, *Saint John the Baptist*, Koons said: 'I had St John the Baptist there as an authority figure so people would feel open and secure to be baptised in banality. He's holding a pig and a penguin, a take-off on Leonardo's St John ... I was telling the bourgeois to embrace the things that it likes, the things it responds to.'[13] To promote the exhibition, which was staged simultaneously in Cologne, New York and Chicago – not a problem, since each work was in an edition of three – Koons went to the extent of placing four full-page advertisements, designed by him, in various art magazines (he later editioned the adverts as artworks). Why not? As he said in 1989, 'I just present things really the way they are ... I'm interested in advertising, I'm interested in the entertainment industry and media itself, and I respond to it.'[14] Koons believed that, because film and advertising were so much better than art at 'manipulating and seducing and educating an audience', art had to compete with them or disappear.[15]

Appropriating images by other artists is problematic, however, and Koons has faced several lawsuits. In 2017 a French court ruled that *Naked*, a sculpture of two innocent children from the 'Banality' show, had been copied from the work of a French photographer. Koons and the Centre Pompidou, which had recently exhibited *Naked*, were ordered to jointly pay the late photographer's estate €40,000 in fines.[16] As this particular work had just sold at auction for more than $5 million, the fine does not seem unduly harsh!

At the end of the 1980s, such cultural capitals as New York and London were traumatized by the ravages of AIDS. Sex became something that could kill you, not a source of pleasure or love, while the body appeared vulnerable, a site of illness and collapse. The two life-size figures made out of wax by Kiki Smith in 1990 (page 17) seemed to crystallize people's fears and fascination with wounds, illness and decay. Smith herself emerged as an artist in New York in the midst of the AIDS epidemic (one of her sisters died from an AIDS-related illness in 1988). Around this time, she presented twelve silver-coated jars, each supposedly filled with a different bodily secretion – blood, snot, pus, semen, etc. She also made a womb in bronze, a stomach in glass, a tongue in plaster, a torso in paper. For Smith, the body was important because it is something that we all have.

Making is important too, for that is what hands and the body can do. Smith has said that she always has something in her hands, that she is always making, even when watching television. 'Where's the pleasure in making art if it's not in this physical, haptic act of making something?' she once asked.[17] Different materials all called out to be handled and transformed: 'Each medium affords you a different experience. The physical manifestation of it is how meaning is constructed.'[18] Like other artists, Smith was fascinated by all sorts of craftwork – African, Asian, Western. Craft for her is 'a celebration of being physical and an investigation for the different properties of materials'.[19]

Subsequently, Smith became more interested in the life we share with animals, in myth and dreams. 'Most of last year,' she said in 1990, 'I dreamt my artwork, then I got up and did it. That's about letting go, letting things enter you, not trying to hold them. It's about trusting yourself or maybe trusting intuition. You can't control things, you just have to be present for life. You have to put yourself there.'[20] Like Deacon and Schütte, she also took drawing very seriously. For all three artists, drawing – where you can imagine and then form shapes and relationships – is a key site of invention. Unlike hardcore modernists, they felt there was much to learn from tradition, with Deacon travelling the world to look at all kinds of sculpture, and Smith urging people to visit museums. 'The thing I love about going to museums', she explained in 1994, 'is that it is a confirmation. Your ancestors tell you that there's a reason for doing a particular activity, or that they liked doing it too.'[21]

It was also in the 1980s that installation emerged as an art form in its own right, a different way of thinking about objects and space. But how do we define 'installation art', a term used so sloppily? For me, it is best thought of as an art of the room. An art where, above all else, as Christian Boltanski put it, 'the spectator's body is inside the work'.[22] Artists such as Boltanski, Ann Hamilton and Ilya Kabakov wanted viewers not only to have a deeper physical relationship with the material world, phenomenologically, but also to become more aware of the historical and cultural associations that places and things carry with them.

Koons may have looked to Warhol as a model, but these artists were closer in sensibility to a Beuysian way of thinking. They had a heightened sense of place, of how the context always becomes part of the meaning. In a world in which people were moving around more and more, the need for a deeper sense of a particular place – home or otherwise – was becoming a craving. 'An installation', said Hamilton, 'surrounds you, absorbs you into it. You are part of it the minute you step into it.' You, the visitor, or any object in an installation, cannot help but become part of what she refers to as the skin. 'It's like the interior/exterior condition we live within our bodies – the skin creates illusions of separation, but it's a permeable membrane that goes both ways.'[23]

In 1991 Hamilton took part in 'Places with a Past', an exhibition of site-specific works in Charleston, South Carolina – a city of beautiful eighteenth-century houses, often described as the capital of the old South. Hamilton, however, chose to make her installation in a disused garage; and rather than research the kind of 'nostalgic' history liked by tourists, she read about labour conditions. Discovering that the dark-blue dye indigo had been crucial to the city's manufacturers, she ordered more than six tons of used blue work clothes – some 48,000 trousers or shirts. These clothes, she realized, had all been worn by people who had been laid off, or whose employers had gone bust.

As always in Hamilton's installations, everything was touched by hand. She and her assistants carefully folded the clothes before placing them on a large metal platform, creating a stack 5.4 metres (18 ft) tall (opposite). If you had visited the old garage during her installation, you would have found behind this mound of clothes a person sitting at a desk, rubbing out the words in books with blue covers.

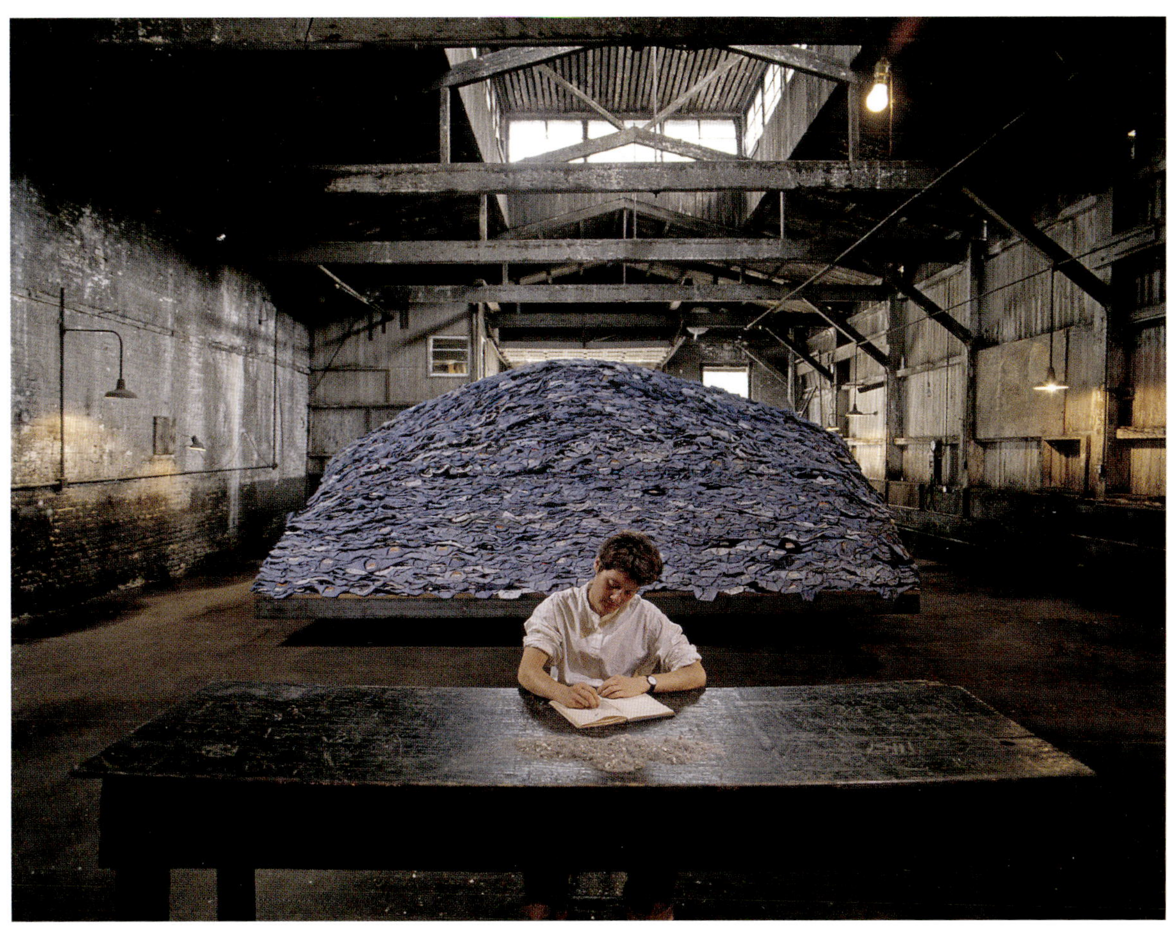

Ann Hamilton, *Indigo Blue*, 1991
14,000 lbs used blue work clothes, folded and piled, c. 5.2 × 7.3 × 5.5 m (17 × 24 × 18 ft), person erasing text from ten blue covered books, 60 sacks of soybeans

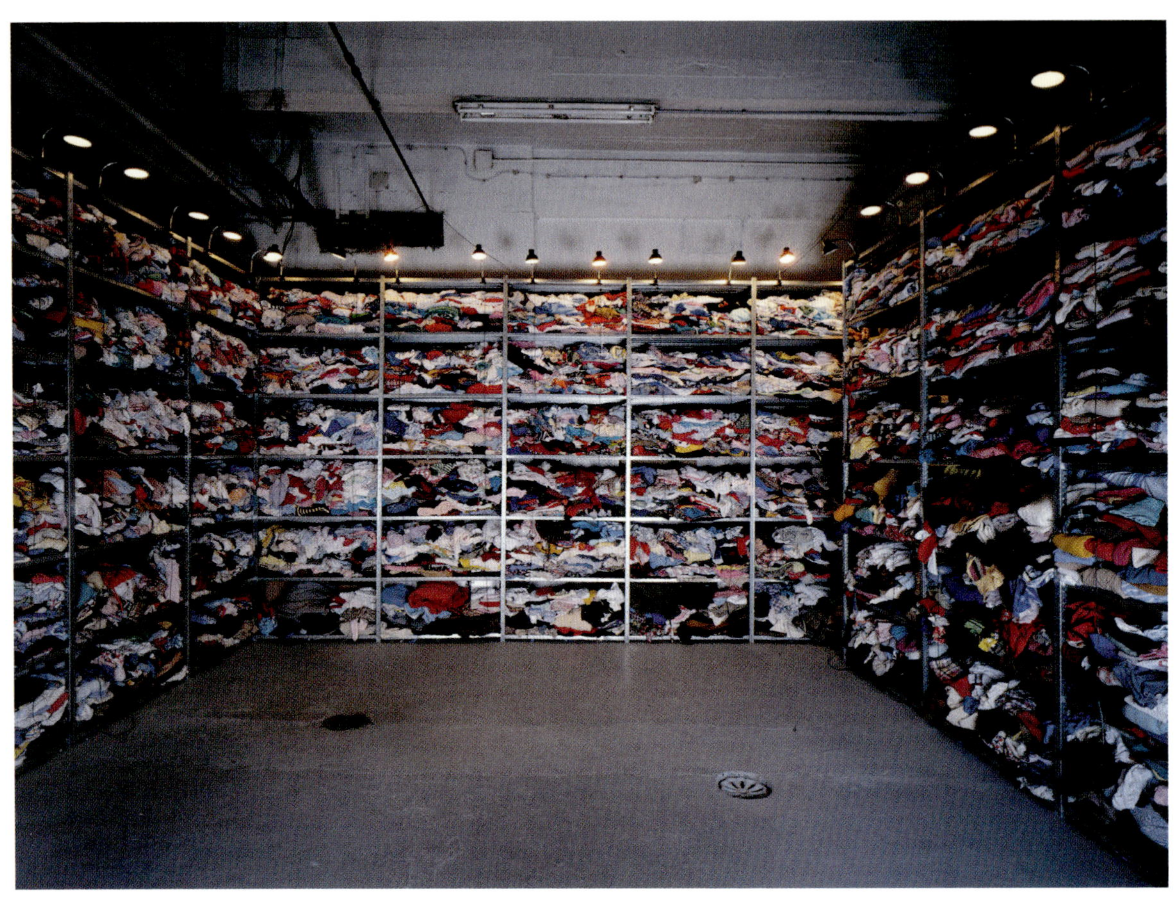

Christian Boltanski, *Rèserve du musée des enfants*, 1989
Used children's clothes, lights

(Hamilton often gets someone to perform some such task, giving her work motion and life.) You would also have been able to look down on the installation from an office. Inside this office were hung 'udder-sized net bags of soybeans which sprouted and later rotted in the leakage of summer rains. With the humid weather, the space was filled with the musty smell of the damp clothes and the organic decomposition of the soybeans.'[24]

Why did installation emerge as a major practice in the 1980s?[25] Artists were becoming increasingly concerned with how and where their work was installed. Minimal sculpture especially made you intensely aware of the environment the object inhabited, so it was inevitable that Donald Judd and others would start to focus on the space, the room. Judd exemplified this approach, using, as we saw in the introduction, a military base in Marfa, Texas, as a site for art. But installation art such as Hamilton's was often very far from minimal.

Above all else, as I said earlier, installation art is an art of the room or interior; it is no coincidence that the rise of such art came at the same time as the success of such magazines as *World of Interiors*. Most installations, though, were ceremonial

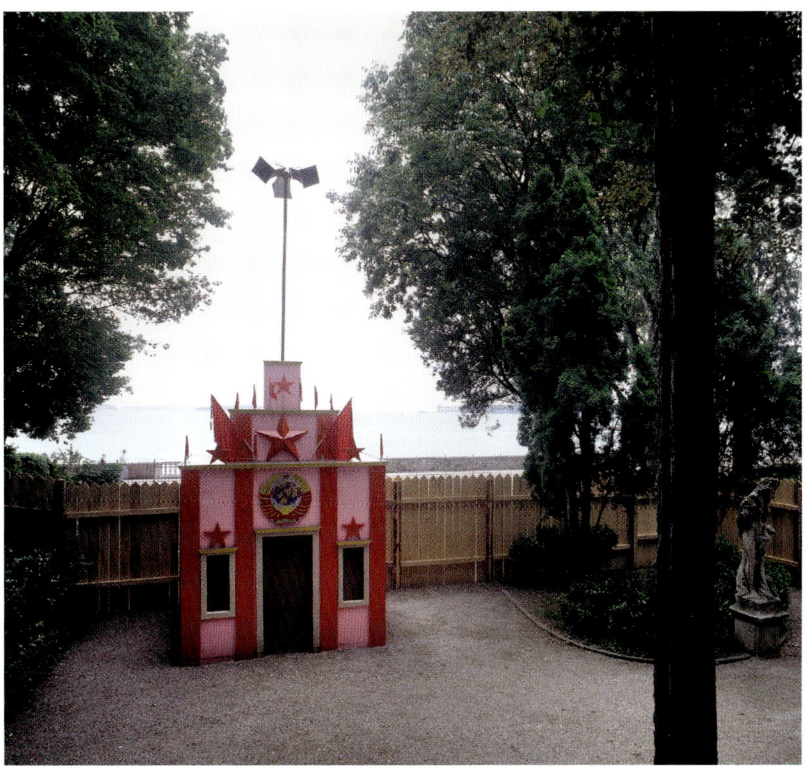

Ilya Kabakov, *The Red Pavilion*, 1993
Wood, board, paint, flags, builder's materials, loudspeakers, music; Russian Pavilion, Venice Biennale, 1993

rather than domestic. They were places where your emotions were engaged, where something might happen – a site or rite of passage. The experience, as Hamilton always emphasized, was rooted in your body moving in an environment and *experiencing* with all your senses: sight, hearing, touch (often), smell (frequently), taste (occasionally) and always that almost unconscious sixth sense of your body moving through space – what neurologists call proprioception, and which can also be called kinaesthesia.[26] You had to physically be there to have this experience. Like so much contemporary art, installations are an attack on the ubiquity of reproduction, especially photographic reproduction. Neither my words nor the pictures on the page can replicate the experience of being there. All they can do is give a faint, distorted echo.

Among the early work of Christian Boltanski – all supposedly made in response to memories of childhood traumas – were hundreds of tiny handmade objects, balls of dirt or small knives, arranged in the sort of glass vitrines one sees in museums, or else collections of banal photographs of people who were not famous, arranged across walls or in photo albums. It was only in the 1980s, when the artist was in his forties, that he began to take over whole rooms, often darkening them to heighten the mood.

In 1989, for example, when asked to make a work in the Musée d'Art Moderne de la Ville de Paris, Boltanski chose to show not in one of the galleries but in two forgotten and rather dilapidated basement rooms.[27] Entering these windowless spaces, you initially came across a grid of fifty-five enlarged but blurred photographs of children who had died, illuminated only by small lamps above. Then you encountered, first with your nose and then with your eyes, a room filled with metal shelves piled high with clothes. (It was vital for Boltanski that these clothes were second-hand and that they smelt, smelt of people who were no longer there.) Clearly, this was about memory, death and the archive.

It is difficult for anyone familiar with European history not to be reminded of the rooms filled with discarded clothes found at Auschwitz and the death camps. Indeed, by the end of the 1980s, Boltanski would admit that the Holocaust was always on his mind: his father had been Jewish, and was apparently hunted by the Nazis, although Boltanski saw himself as more Christian than Jewish. 'My work is not about the camps, it is after the camps,' he explained. 'The reality of the Occident was changed by the Holocaust. We can no longer see anything without seeing that. But my work is really not about the Holocaust, it's about death in general, about all of our deaths.'[28]

What does a museum get when it buys an installation by Boltanski? Maybe some shelves, some lamps, some old clothes; maybe some photographs of dead people. But what happens if the shelves do not fit the room? Or the lamps die? Or the clothes rot? Or the photographs fade? Just get new ones, suggests Boltanski; it is the idea that matters, not the objects *per se*. They are not holy relics. Boltanski believes that what he is doing is providing a musical score, as composers do, which needs to be reinterpreted each time the piece is staged.

If, as I did, you had visited the old pavilion of the Soviet Union at the 1993 Venice Biennale, you might have thought it was closed up. It was surrounded by a rough wooden fence. 'Oh well', you might have said to yourself, 'the USSR has disintegrated so nothing will be happening here.' But if you had noticed an arrow pointing to a gap in the fence, you might have gone through that gap and into the pavilion. There was no exhibition to see, just scaffolding, piles of wood and the smell of construction – dust, paint and newly sawn timber. Ha, you would have thought, this could be a metaphor for Russia itself: fallen apart, but not yet reconstructed. Then you would have heard some tinny music in the distance, and decided to go to the back of the pavilion, where there is a good view of Venice and its lagoon. Once there, you would have realized that, yes, I have been in an exhibition, and yes, it was a metaphor! For there in the garden you would have seen a small building festooned with red flags and Soviet emblems, the three loudspeakers suspended above its roof blaring out the songs and marches once heard at the May Day parades on Red Square (page 109).

Maybe it would have made you nostalgic for a more optimistic time, one now lost. Or perhaps you would have had the same thoughts as Ilya Kabakov, who had set this up: 'This "little pavilion" is the territory of a world which has not disappeared anywhere, but is only hidden, concealing itself behind the back of another. Standing in the depths of the courtyard, it is merely waiting for its own hour so that it may return to the place from which it was recently expelled.'[29] Expectation, walking, smell, music, the light on the waves, surprise, memories, reflection were all part of both the experience and the work. As Kabakov said in 1994: 'If an installation is properly made, you can't leave without going through a whole cycle of emotions. You lose your sense of time.'[30]

Before 1989, Kabakov had been an 'unofficial' artist, making a living in his native Soviet Union as an illustrator of children's books. 'In Russia,' he insisted, 'being involved in art was for me a vital, existential thing, not a professional endeavour.'[31] But after leaving Russia in 1992 and moving to New York, he became a 'professional' artist, albeit one whose subject was always the USSR, its institutions and communal apartments. Sometimes he would describe it as hell, but would recreate it with apparent nostalgia. The many objects that went into what he called his 'total installations' were not important; it was the atmosphere that mattered.

At its best, installation was a way not only of embedding the visitor's body and mind in the actual artwork, and in the material world, but also of engaging with history – not in the sense of dry facts noted in a book, but as lived, or remembered, experience.

Chapter 5

NATIONAL ART OR GLOBAL ART?

1989

The year 1989 is remembered above all for the fall of the Berlin Wall and the collapse of the Soviet Union and the communist regimes of Eastern Europe. But for art, an event of equal importance that year was the staging of the exhibition 'Magiciens de la Terre' in Paris. It was not, as it claimed to be, the first global exhibition of contemporary art[1] – that distinction properly belongs to the Havana Biennale of 1986 – but it was much publicized and, because so problematic, much discussed. It was problematic in that, while choosing fifty well-known artists from the West, the curators chose fifty mainly unknown, 'outsider' artists from the so-called Third World, rather than those Third World artists who worked in the idioms of the West.

The Nigerian artist Meschac Gaba complained that the curators had chosen 'the path of anthropology', and 'had visited artists whom I had always regarded more as artisans'.[2] Others accused the curators of primitivizing or exoticizing African or Asian artists by insisting they be naïfs. To all those artists who had tried to learn from Western art and adapt it for their own culture, it seemed a painful rejection. As one African artist told me: 'I spent twenty years studying to make modern or post-modern art. I resent being told I should have studied traditional mask-making instead.' Indicatively, the only artist in the exhibition from South East Asia, an area with several sophisticated art scenes, was Nera Jambruk, who painted traditional tribal huts in Papua New Guinea.[3]

The installation of a large wall drawing by Richard Long above an earth painting by members of the Yuendumu Community from the central desert of Australia (page 114) provoked especial ire. (Long's practice had extended by now to making large wall drawings with mud from the River Avon, close to where he was born and still lived.) Such ire was expressed most forcibly by the critic Jean Fisher, who described Long's drawing as 'a giant "solar anus" that oversaw everything including the horizontal Yuendumu earth painting below it ... Far from reflecting a dialogue between the two, the relationship replicated the juxtaposition of the colonized and the colonizer, between the West's manipulative relation to the earth and others' bodily association with it.'[4] Long, who certainly didn't intend his work to function like that,

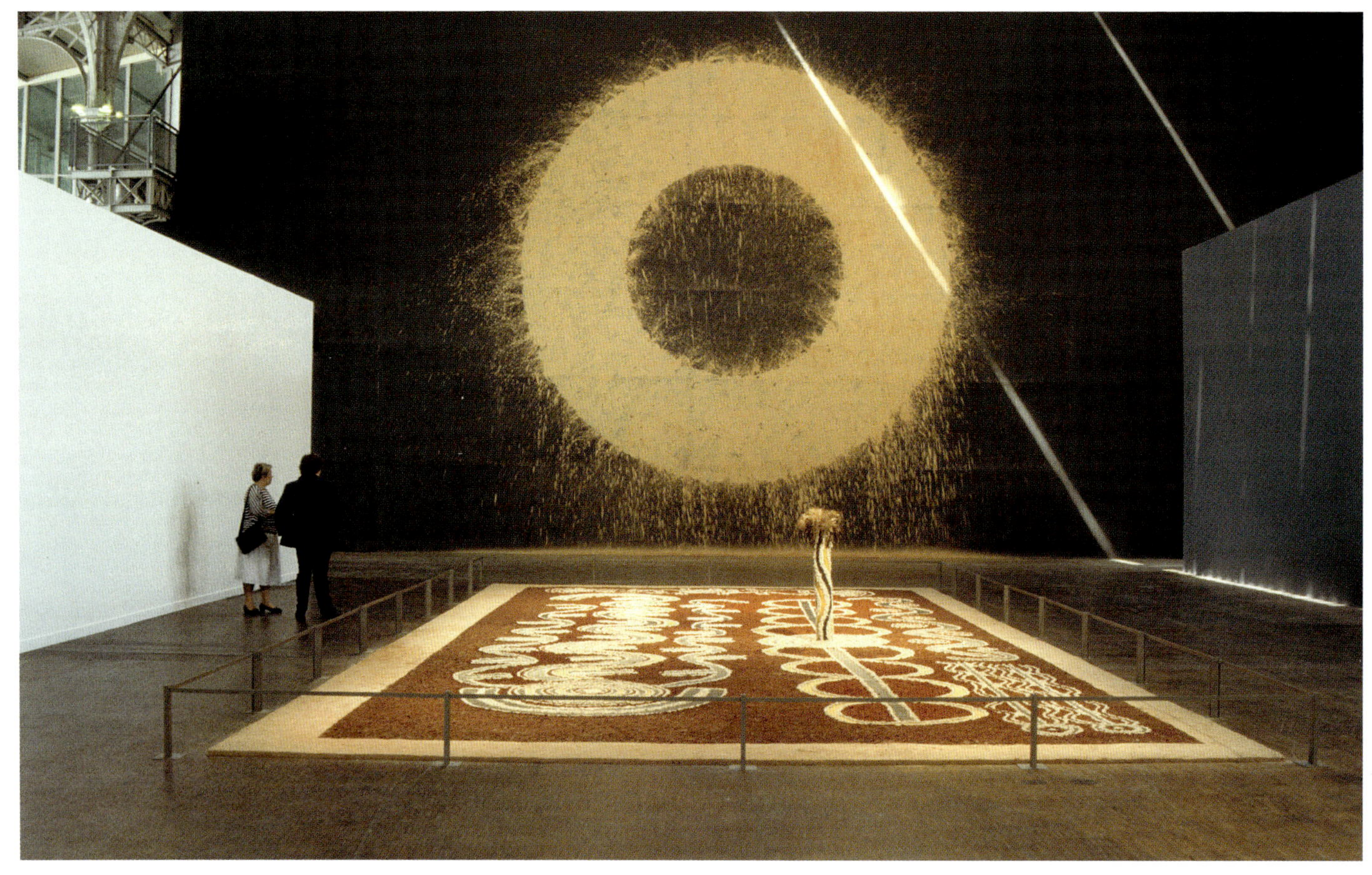

Richard Long, *Red Earth Circle*, 1989
Avon river mud, 12 × 20 m (472½ × 787½ in.), with (on the floor) *Yam Dreaming*, 1989, by seven members of the Yuendumu community, paint, earth, herbs and other objects, 5 × 10 m (196⅞ × 393¾ in.); installation view at the exhibition 'Magiciens de la terre' at the Centre Pompidou, Paris, 1989

saw the exhibition rather differently, writing twenty-four years later that, 'In my view, "Magiciens de la Terre" was one of the rare big ideas of the curatorial art world. It was an honour and pleasure to take part, and the days of installation, working alongside artists from many different contemporary cultures, was fantastic and inspiring.'[5]

Not all the non-Western artists were unknown outsiders. Cildo Meireles, whom we have already met as a conceptual artist, exhibited his installation *Mission/Missions (How to Build Cathedrals)* (below), in which ox bones hang over a 'pond' of coins surrounded by paving stones; between bones and coins runs a thin column of communion wafers. Like Christian Boltanski, Meireles had moved from creating small or conceptual works to installations one could enter. Missing from most photographs of *Mission/Missions* is the black veil that surrounds the piece, through which one has to pass. This act of passing through gives one's experience of the work a sense of both the private and the ceremonial. Physically, it is a shocking but also beautiful piece, especially if we are allowed to walk on the glittering coins, with the bones looming above our heads. If we want to untangle what the work might mean, we should start to think about colonization, which in Brazil was led by the Jesuits (hence the communion wafers), followed by cattle ranchers (the bones), cities (paving stones) and capitalism (coins).

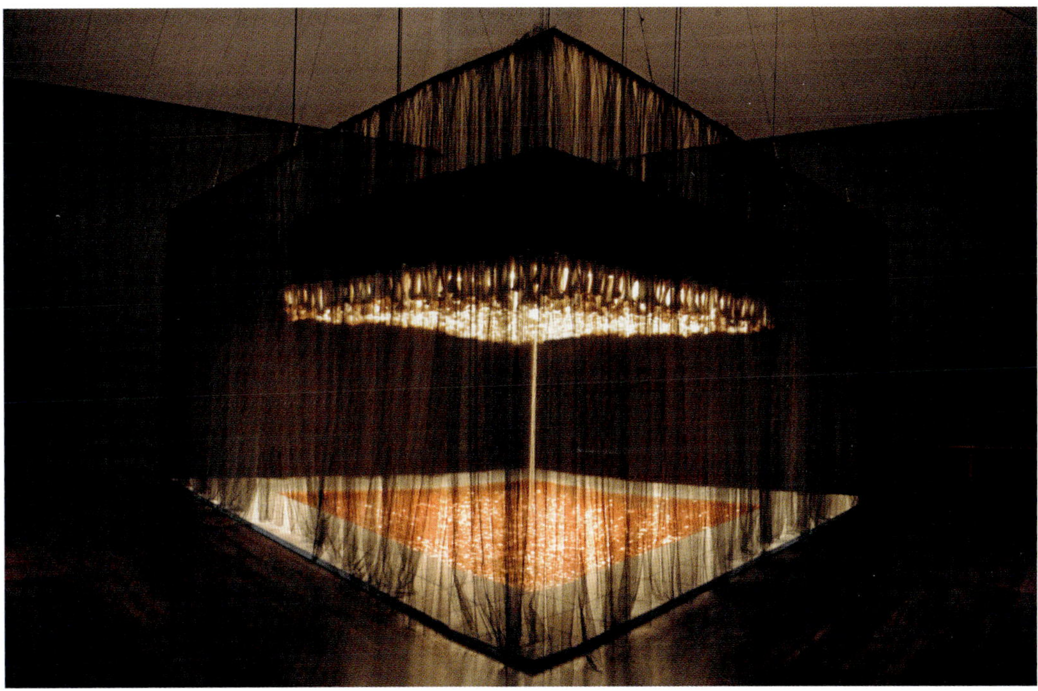

Cildo Meireles, *Mission/Missions (How to Build Cathedrals)*, 1987
600,000 coins, 800 communion wafers, 2,000 cattle bones, 80 paving stones, black cloth, 3 × 6 × 6 m (118⅛ × 236¼ × 236¼ in.)

How many viewers got this? It is a consistent problem with art that has a strong ideological purpose: can it be understood as a political statement without first reading some curatorial text? Or will the viewer just be wowed by the excess of materials? Installations such as this one, rich in materials and associations – baroque, even – are typical of artists from the tropics, where nature is so fertile, as is the desire to make art also from poor materials (the coins in *Mission/Missions* are very low denominations).

For all its faults, and in some ways because of them, 'Magiciens de la Terre' *did* make people think. Moreover, the exhibition marked, as the French curator Nicolas Bourriaud later noted, 'the symbolic inauguration of planetary art'.[6] From then on, artists from outside the West began to be shown more internationally. Important questions were discussed too, such as should artists exhibit only in the context of their particular nation, as had been the norm, or should they be thrown, willy-nilly, into dialogue with artists from other cultures?

Another controversial exhibition also opened in 1989: 'China/Avant-Garde', at the National Art Museum of China, Beijing. Following the death of Mao Zedong in 1976, the People's Republic of China had begun opening up; by the mid-1980s, enough information about art in other parts of the world had filtered through to give Chinese artists a sense of what they had missed during the years of war, socialist realism and the Cultural Revolution. Across China, artists were experimenting with performance, installation and works that satirized establishment art. Opened on 5 February 1989, the exhibition was meant to show ten years of experimental art in China. A total of 186 artists were included, but some of their work, particularly the performances and an action in which an artist fired a gun at her own installation,[7] so scandalized the authorities that they twice closed it down. Eventually, it was open only for nine days.

One of the 186 artists was Xu Bing. The child of academics, Xu had seen his parents imprisoned as reactionaries and sent for 're-education' during the Cultural Revolution. Although there was no art teacher at Xu's school, he worked for the school's propaganda department – which is how many Chinese artists of his generation began making visual communications, if not art. Sent to live with peasants in Yanqing District, Xu laboured in the fields but continued making art. In 1977 he was admitted to the Central Academy of Fine Arts in Beijing, where he soon became an expert printmaker – mainly woodcuts of rural life.

In 1986 Xu began a project to invent 4,000 Chinese characters (4,000 being the number of such characters known by the average Chinese person), each cut in wood for printing. As a child, he had started school just as the Chinese state had begun to reform the writing system with the controversial First Chinese Character Simplification Scheme, in which old characters were simplified or replaced.[8] But Xu's new characters, beautifully cut though they were, meant nothing. Xu printed the characters on long sheets of paper, hung the sheets from the ceiling, and exhibited them under the title *A Mirror to Analyse the World: The Final Volume of the Century*.

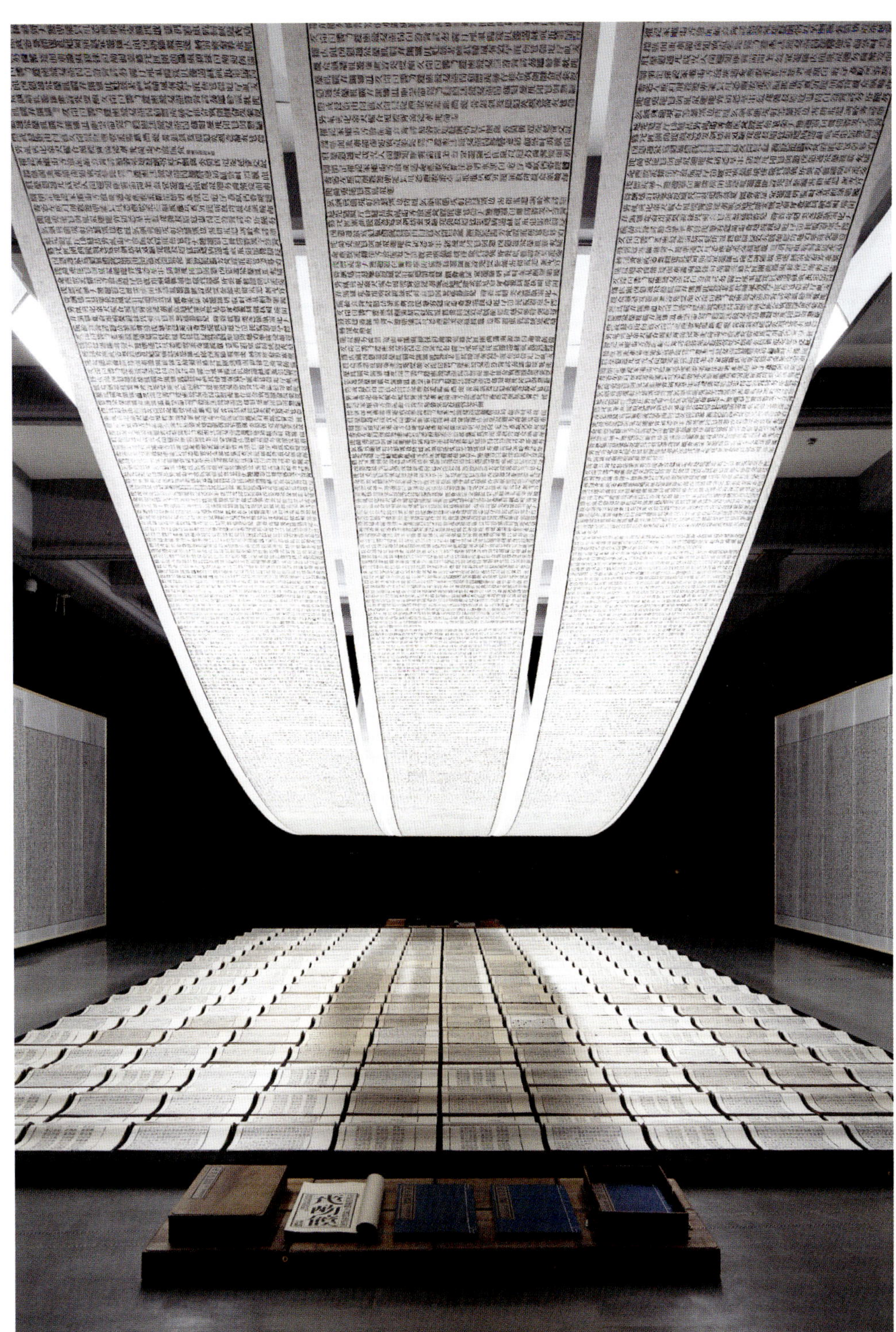

Xu Bing, *Book from the Sky*, 1987–91
Mixed media installation/hand-printed books and scrolls printed from blocks inscribed with 'false' Chinese characters, installation view at Taipei Fine Arts Museum, 2014

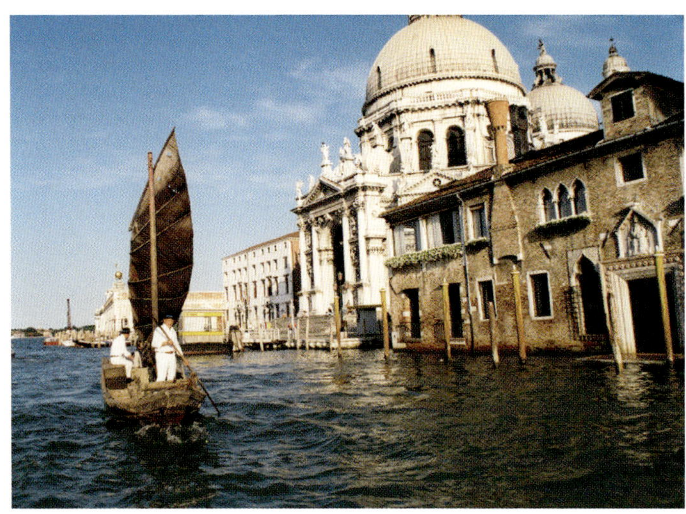

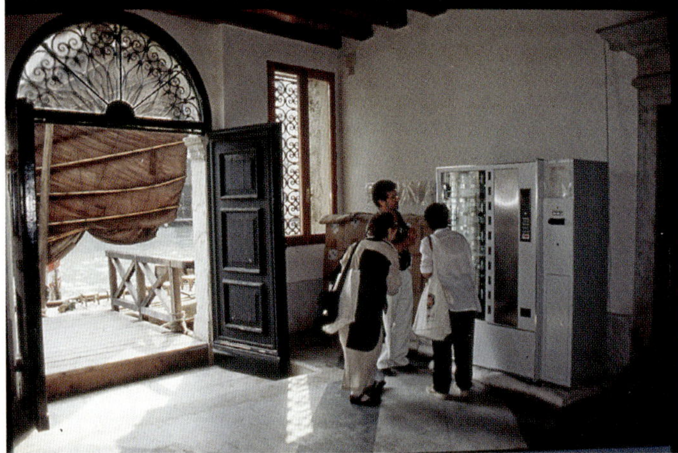

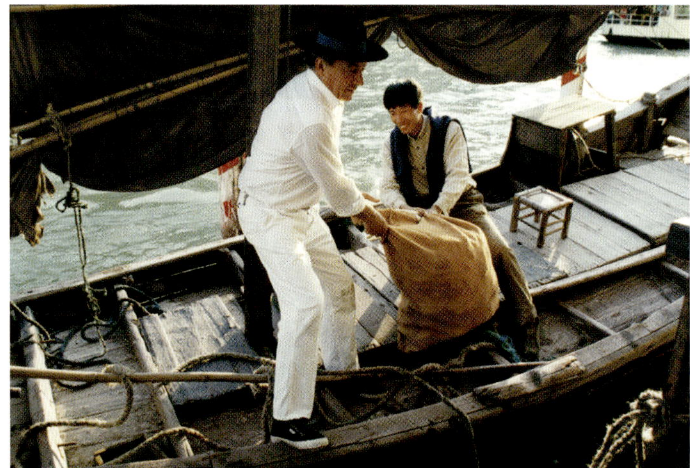

Cai Guo-Qiang, *Bringing to Venice what Marco Polo Forgot*, 1995
Wooden fishing boat from Quanzhou, Chinese herbs, ginseng (100 kg), utensils to prepare and drink herbal beverages, and other artworks by the artist as components; commissioned by the 46th Venice Biennale, 1995

Visually impressive and impeccably made, the work was nonetheless still a tease, devoid of meaning. Chinese viewers, struggling to make sense of the work, would frequently mutter '*tianshu*' (book from the sky), the Chinese equivalent of the English phrase for bewilderment, 'It's all Greek to me!'. Hearing this, Xu decided that *Book from the Sky* would in fact make a better title (page 117).

Four months after the closure of the 'China/Avant-Garde' exhibition, student protesters demanding more freedom were driven from Tiananmen Square, and a period of repression set in. For several years, there was little opportunity to show experimental art.

Xu Bing's work was singled out for criticism, accused of formalism, irrationality, of being anti-art, anti-tradition, etc. Offered a residency in the United States, Xu left China in 1990 and lived away from his home country for the next seventeen years. His work and teaching continued to be about language and communication; among other things, he invented a language that looked like it was made up of Chinese characters, but which was in fact formed from English words. In 2012 he published a 112-page novel 'written' entirely in the sort of pictograms one finds in airports. In Chapter 2, for example, we see the hero go to work: 🕘 ⌂→🚆→🏢 But later at night, after various failed attempts to interest a lady in romance in Chapter 16, he gets very drunk and falls asleep: 🕘 🧍🍺🍺🍺 🛏️ᶻᶻᶻ Chinese artists are often wittier and funnier than people realize.

Xu's fellow artist Cai Guo-Qiang had already left China, having moved to Japan in 1986, and was therefore not included in 'China/Avant-Garde'. In Japan, he had become friends with Lee Ufan and been impressed by the *Mono-ha* quasi-ceremonial way of placing simple things in chosen sites. Like Xu Bing, Cai was both fascinated by Chinese culture and wanted to make it an element within global thinking.

In 1995, the year he moved to New York, Cai was asked to participate in an exhibition entitled 'Transculture', held during the 46th Venice Biennale. Cai arranged for an old fishing junk from his home town of Quanzhou to be sent to Venice, where he employed gondoliers to sail it up the Grand Canal, loaded with medicinal herbs, to the seventeenth-century Palazzo Giustinian Lolin – where 'Transculture' was being staged – and moor it outside. Inside, Cai installed vending machines selling bottles of traditional Chinese medicine and a transparent acupuncture chart (opposite). Visitors could also sit on the junk outside and watch the world go by.

Quanzhou was also the town from which Marco Polo had set off on his return journey to Venice, arriving in the city in 1295 – exactly 700 years before Cai. The artist intended the title of his work, *Bringing to Venice what Marco Polo Forgot*, to be taken literally, pointing out the therapeutic elements of Chinese culture that the explorer had ignored, preferring exotic tales of wonder instead. Or, as Cai put it: 'While Marco Polo brought back many new and rare things and interesting stories, he did not bring back the important spirit, the Eastern view of the Cosmos.'[9] Herbal medicines exemplified that spirit.

It is Cai's use of gunpowder – invented in China – for which he is most famous, initially to make paintings but then to stage events. In 1993 he added 10,000 metres (32,800 ft) of exploding fireworks in the shape of a dragon to the Great Wall of China, and in 2008 he fired rockets to form a black mushroom cloud above Hiroshima, the first town to be hit by an atomic bomb. 'The idea', he insisted, 'was always to derive energy from nature.'[10] Destruction, he believed, could be an act of construction, and re-enacting destruction aesthetically could be an act of healing.

In parallel to this quite sudden prominence of artists from outside the West was the growing prominence within it of identity politics, with artists who were gay or from ethnic minorities in particular demanding attention. (It was also the time when the art world was being ravaged by AIDS.) This development would come to a head in the highly controversial Whitney Biennial of 1993. Felix Gonzalez-Torres, brought up in Cuba and Puerto Rico, naturalized as an American, and strangely not included in the biennial, was both transnational and avowedly gay. A graduate of the Whitney Museum's theoretically savvy Independent Study Program, Gonzalez-Torres took the forms and processes used by earlier minimal and conceptual artists but presented them as having political or ideological power; he described himself as being like a virus in the institution. Crucially, unlike that previous generation of conceptual artists, he also wanted his works to be beautiful.

Like Jeff Koons and Richard Prince, Gonzalez-Torres was reacting against the 1980s' boom in the kind of painting he derided as 'expensive home decorations ... just a massive excessive production of splatters of paint that meant nothing'.[11] His work would often consist of stacks of posters or piles of wrapped candies; viewers could help themselves to one of the posters or candies. A New York friend told me about visiting, in 1990, Gonzalez-Torres's first exhibition at a commercial gallery. 'It was great,' he said. 'There were stacks of posters in the middle of a room. I took one.' 'Have you still got it?' I asked. 'No,' he replied. 'I didn't actually like the poster. But I liked the idea that I could take something for free from a top-end commercial gallery. That was the artwork for me. I put the poster in a bin once I was on the street.'

Talking of one such 'stack piece', Gonzalez-Torres insisted that, 'Without a viewer, without a public, this work has no meaning; it's just another fucking boring sculpture sitting on the floor, and that is not what this work is about. This work is about an interaction with the public ... I tell the viewer, "You are responsible for the final meaning of this piece of paper that is part of this stack."'[12] 'I need the viewer,' he explained on a separate occasion. 'I need the public interaction. Without a public these works are nothing, nothing. I need the public to complete the work. I ask the public to help me, to take responsibility, to become part of my work, to join in.'[13]

Gonzalez-Torres wanted his work to be available to all, although it often had a profoundly personal meaning. Asked in 1991 to make a work for the project space at MoMA, his initial plan was to leave the room empty and put up a series of large-scale posters on the streets of New York. Eventually, however, he gave in to the museum's

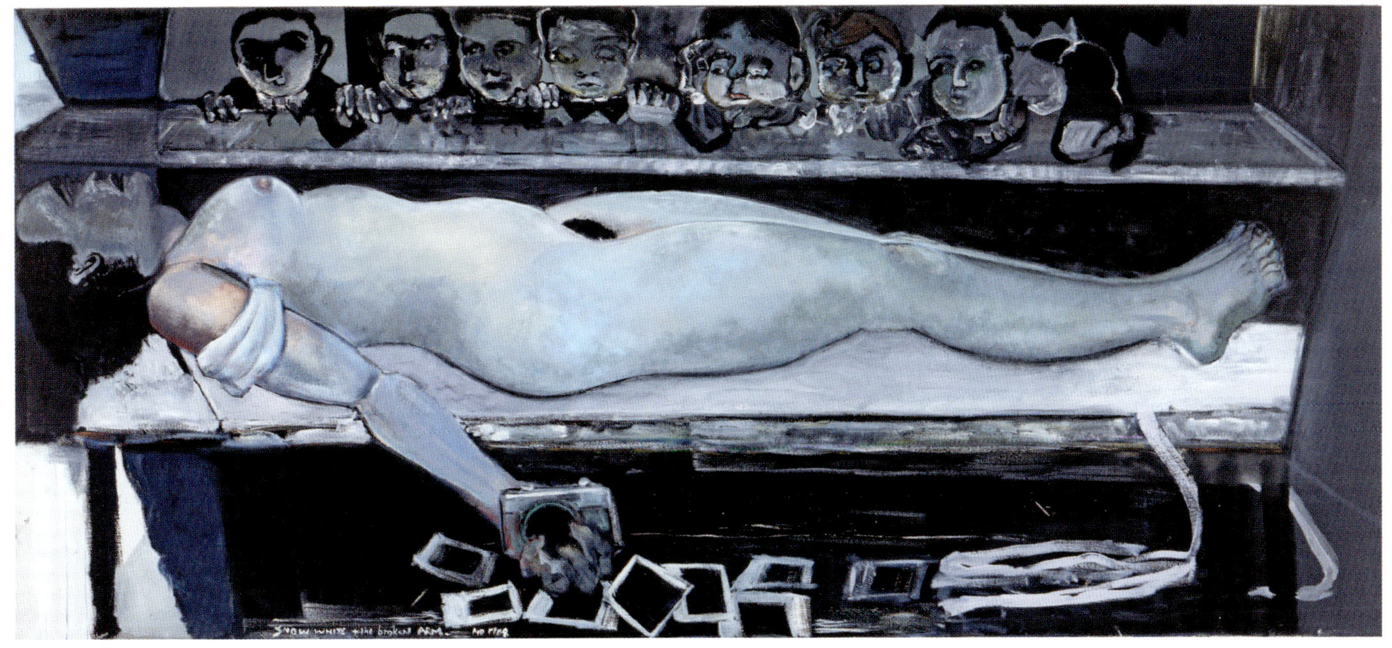

Marlene Dumas, *Snow White and the Broken Arm*, 1988
Oil on canvas, 140 × 300 cm (55⅛ × 118⅛ in.)

desperate craving for an object and placed an unmade bed in the room. But on twenty-four billboards elsewhere in New York, he pasted a large poster of an unmade bed, where the imprint of two heads could be seen on two pillows nestled against each other. To Gonzalez-Torres, this was the bed he had shared with his partner, Ross Laycock, who had died of AIDS; but, as Gonzalez-Torres acknowledged, it could induce different thoughts in different people – although hopefully sympathetic ones. It was a gentle image: he did not want to be confrontational; he wanted to be accepted.

While all this was going on, the world economy went into recession and art sales peaked and then slumped. In his preface to Sotheby's large and glossy 1989/90 annual for collectors, the then owner of the auction house, Alfred Taubman, purred with satisfaction: 'The season marks the culmination of a remarkable decade in the development of the art market, one characterized by tremendous growth and international expansion. During this period, auction sales increased more than five-fold from $573 million in 1979/80 to the record $3.2 billion reported this season.'[14] In the 1990/91 annual, which was neither as large nor as glossy, Taubman was less cheerful. The recession was biting, and confidence had been further eroded by the Gulf War. The art market staggered; contemporary art seemed especially affected. In 1991 I wandered into Sotheby's and commiserated with a friend who worked there. 'Is it grim?' I asked. 'What is nice,' she replied, 'is that the collectors have come back, the prices have come down and the speculators have disappeared.'

It is important to note that, although the focus of critics at this time was very much on such neo-conceptual artists as Gonzalez-Torres – and even though, as the German artist Neo Rauch later noted, 'At the start of the 1990s ... anyone who kept on painting was the fat boy no one wanted to play with. It was just not sexy'[15] – painters did not actually disappear. In fact, during this period some rather important painters emerged, proving that – if such a thing needed proving – paintings could be more than expensive home decorations. They too could 'speak'.

Whether shown on museum walls or reproduced in magazines, the work of Marlene Dumas has reached as big an audience as that of Gonzalez-Torres – or even bigger. She might not be as academic as he was, but she has been equally articulate and equally engaged with the problems of her time. Born in South Africa, Dumas moved to the Netherlands in 1975, aged twenty-two. It was only in 1983, however, that she concentrated on painting, before then producing mainly collages and drawings.

Dumas was angered by apartheid, racism and sexism; but she was also very concerned with how images convey or construct meaning. She was particularly bothered by the phrases 'this is about' and 'this means'. Paintings, she believed, don't disclose information or opinions; they are more complex, more devious than that. Like her paintings, the texts she often wrote to accompany them were freewheeling: sometimes poetic, sometimes jokey, sometimes passionate and argumentative. In 1988, when she made three large paintings with Snow White as a central character, she wrote:

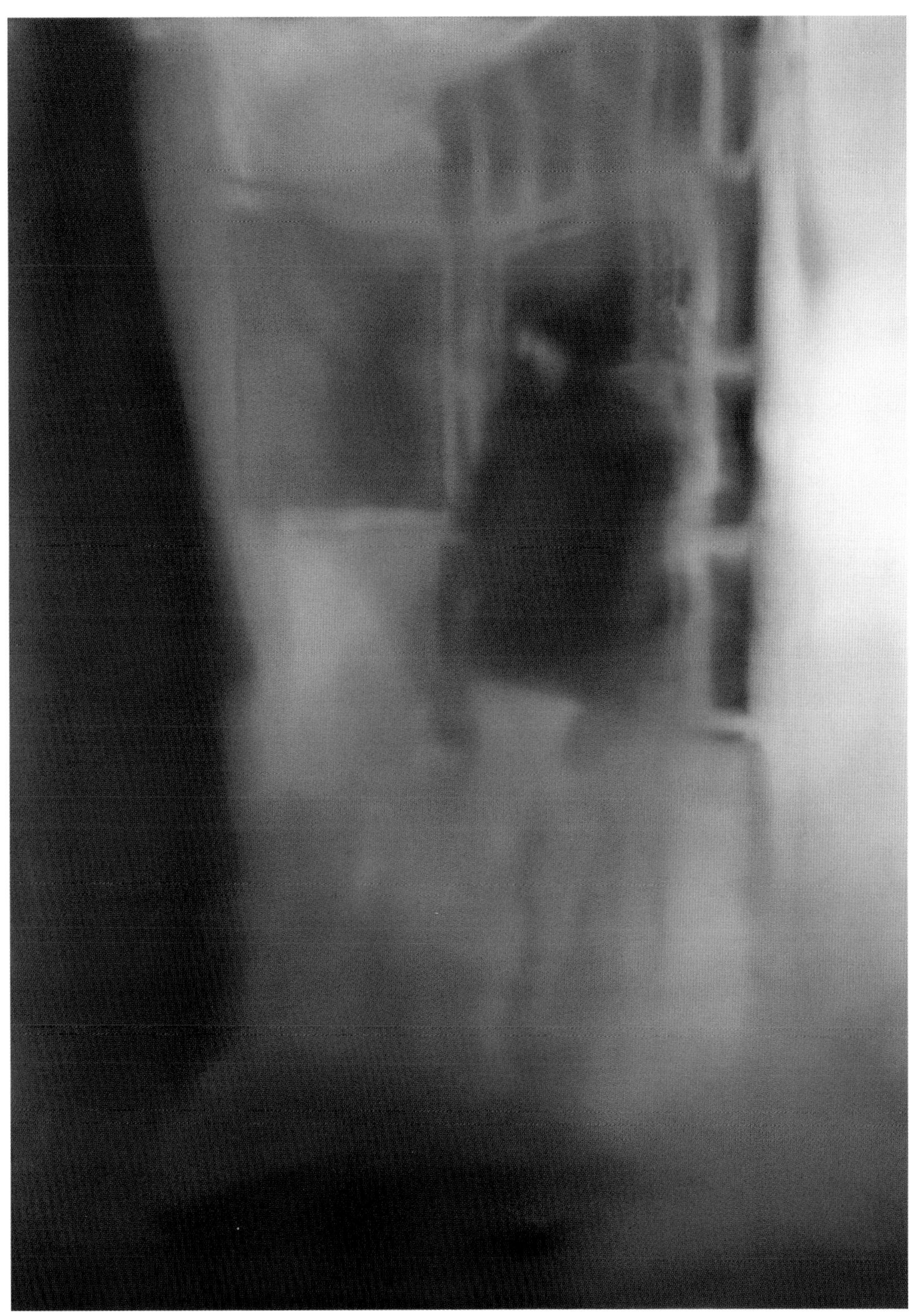

Gerhard Richter, *Erhaengte* (Hanged), 1988
Oil on canvas, 201 × 140 cm (79¼ × 55⅛ in.)

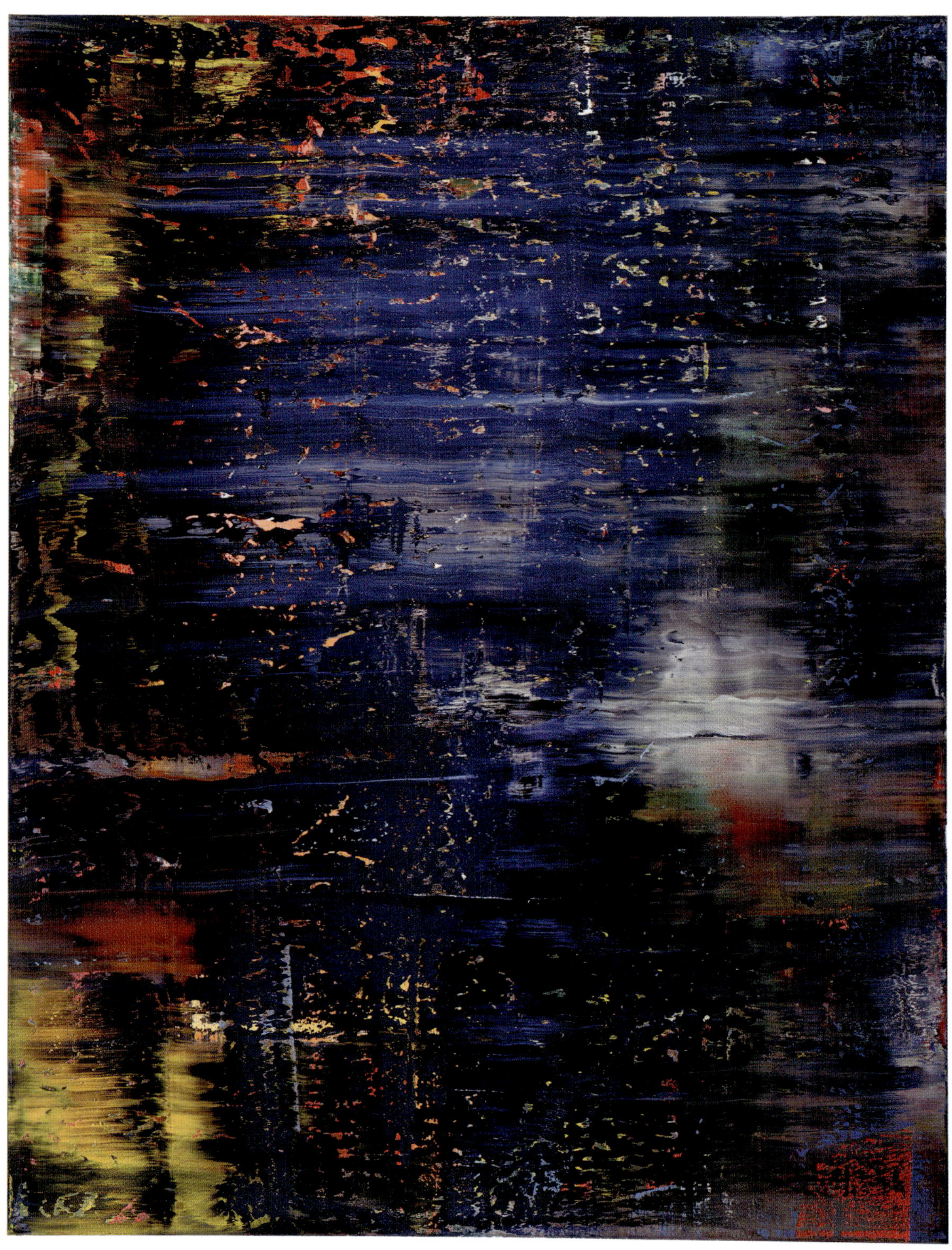

Gerhard Richter, *Forest (731)*, 1990
Oil on canvas, 340 × 260 cm (133⅞ × 102⅜ in.)

The Return of the Non-Dead
Paintings tell stories like zombies walk the earth.
I moved slowly from the face to the bodies.
From the eyes to the skin. From the word to the flesh.
Snow-White wants to compete with the Man of Sorrow.
Snow-White had to compete with the Man of Sorrows.[16]

The meaning of such a painting as *Snow White and the Broken Arm* (page 121) is not immediately apparent. Are we supposed to identify with Snow White? Is the painting a projection of Dumas's own desires and fears? Who has broken her arm? Why is she holding a camera? And why is she now a voluptuous adult, and the Seven Dwarfs peeking children? We have to create our own story and meaning. Dumas uses recognizable figures not only from fairy tales but also from religion – Mary Magdalen, for example – giving her viewers an easy starting point for their own responses.

Photographs, too, have often provided Dumas with a beginning: 'I am an artist who uses second-hand images and first-hand experiences,' she once remarked.[17] Her work was and continues to be figurative, but it is also very much about the sensuality of paint, its colour and textures, or, in her drawings, the flow of ink. Although radically opposed to the alienating voyeurism of pornography, she has always seen her art as raunchy and erotic: 'I'd love to make paintings that have the same kind of sex appeal as soul music. Aretha Franklin with R.E.S.P.E.C.T.'[18] Why can painting not be about love, just as the movies often are?

By the late 1980s, Gerhard Richter – despite not having been as visible as his fellow German artists Georg Baselitz and Anselm Kiefer – was seen as far more important; indeed, perhaps the most important artist in the world. He had never been a neo-expressionist; back in the 1960s, he had been far more affected by Pop, minimal and conceptual art, making monochrome paintings or copying photographs or working with mirrors. His methodical approach appealed to those who were otherwise uninterested in painting.

In 1989 Richter exhibited fifteen paintings based on photographs of the Red Army Faction, the West German left-wing terrorist organization also known as the Baader-Meinhof Group, three of whose members had committed suicide in prison in October 1977. The faction was still a sensitive subject in Germany: it had carried out assassinations, bombed shops, and many believed that the imprisoned members had been murdered by prison guards. As an ensemble, Richter's paintings – known as the 'October 18, 1977' series – were haunting and beautiful, but what did they mean? What was the artist's political position? He had none, it seems. He hated all ideology, admired the terrorists' energy and determination, but could not condemn the state for fighting back. He would give no clear reason as to why he had been stockpiling photos of the faction, or why he had felt impelled to make these subtly modulated black-and-white, or rather grey, paintings derived from them (page 123).

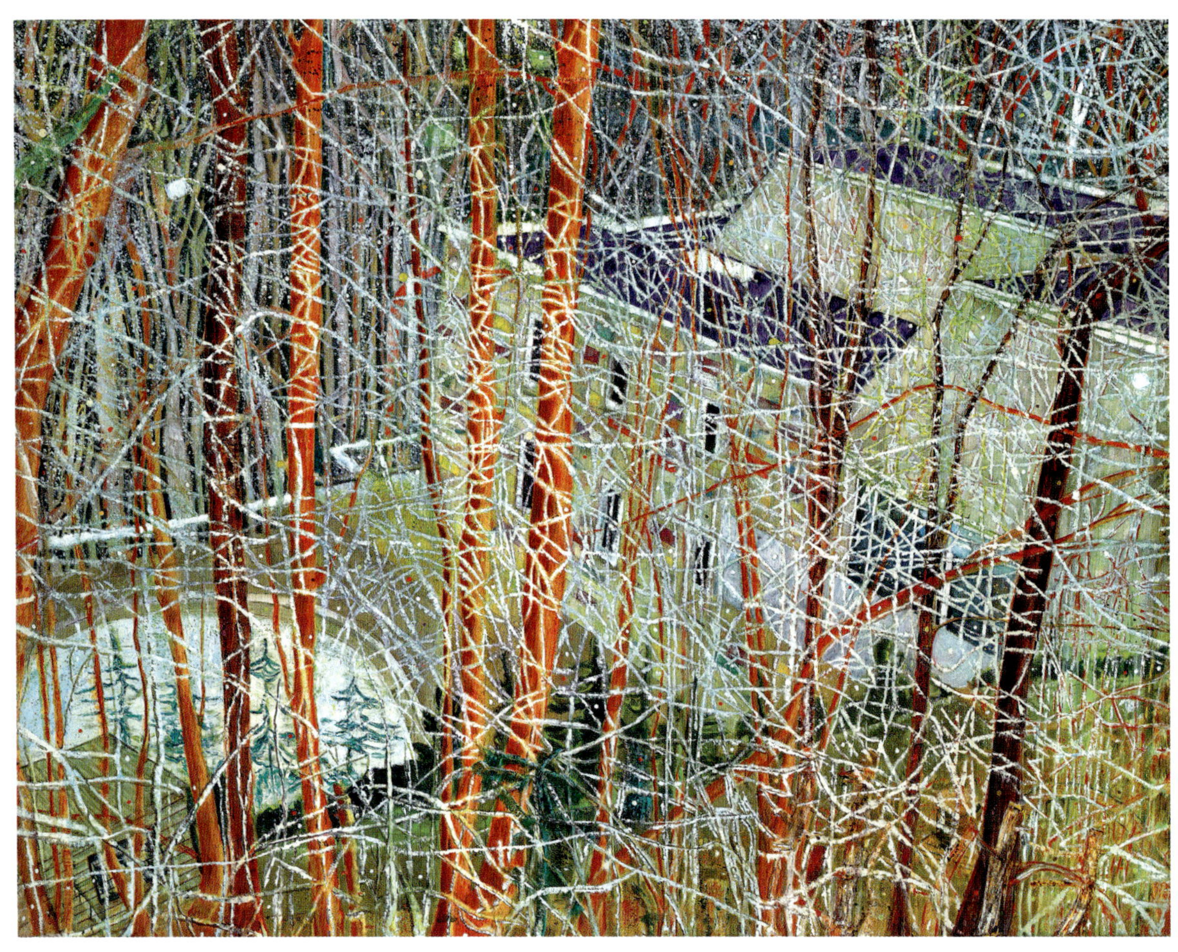

Peter Doig, *The Architect's Home in the Ravine*, 1991
Oil on canvas, 200 × 275 cm (78¾ × 108¼ in.)

To many, they seemed to be history paintings, once the highest form of art, but something rarely seen since the nineteenth century – Picasso's *Guernica* being a notable exception. Others, including myself, were saddened when, after exhibiting the paintings in Frankfurt for ten years, Richter sold them to MoMA. As a result, they lost the edginess of being in a city where the faction had killed, and the country in which they had died. They became just paintings.

In notes made before the series was first exhibited, Richter wrote: 'Deadly reality, inhuman reality. Our rebellion. Impotence. Failure. Death. – That is why I paint these pictures.'[19] Not long afterwards, when asked how the paintings differed from the police photos he had based them on, he added: 'In this particular case, I'd say the photograph provokes horror, and the painting – with the same motif – something more like grief. That comes very close to what I intended.'[20] For him they are about art; art is always about art, but also about death and mourning.

In the many interviews Richter has given, he has always resisted making political statements or grand claims for art – either his or that of others – talking rather of art's 'helplessness', as well as the necessity of art and of painting. Most of the paintings he was making in the 1980s, as well as those made subsequently, were abstract. That

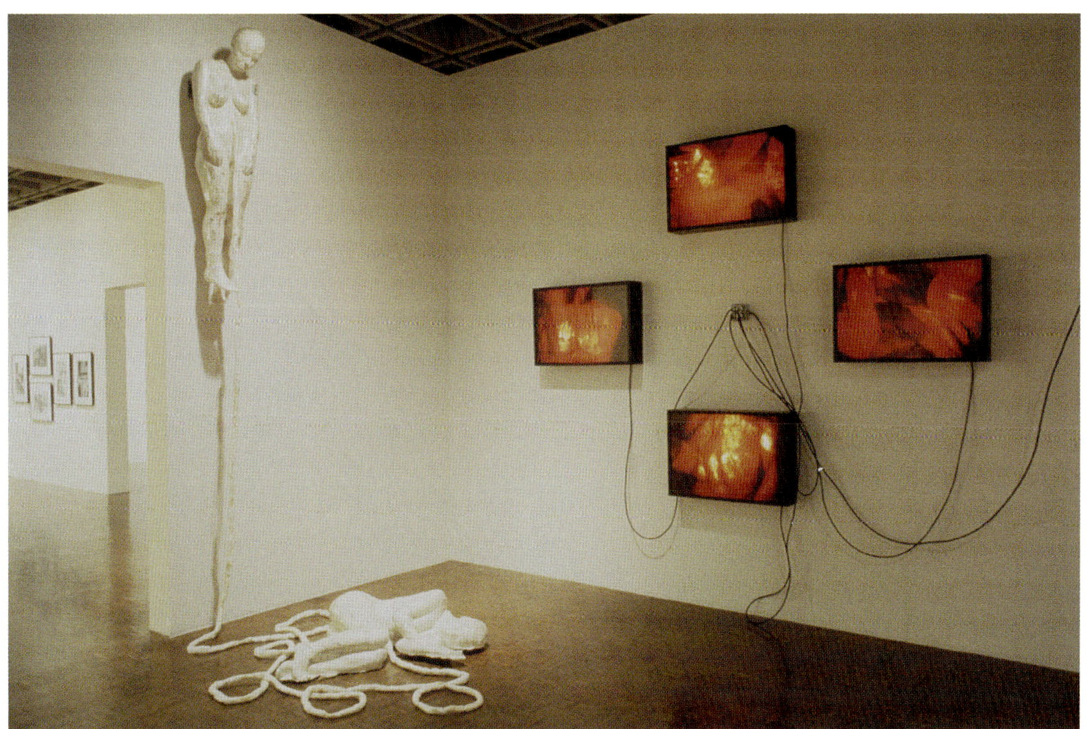

Kiki Smith, *Untitled*, 1992–93 (left); Kiki Smith and David Wojnarowicz, *Untitled*, 1980–92 (right)
Installation view, Whitney Biennial, Whitney Museum of American Art, New York, 1993

he gave a set of four such paintings the title *Forest* was not meant ironically: 'There seemed to me a romantic mood in these four paintings that reminded me of a forest. In the blue, there is the sensation of a diffuse light which is why I came upon this title. I applied the paint across the canvas in two separate movements; across the middle one can see a caesura.'[21]

What was Richter's relationship to those earlier paragons of contemporary art making and thinking, Joseph Beuys and Andy Warhol? Of Beuys, whom Richter knew from his student days, he said: 'I liked him a lot and, sometimes, I even loved him, but I also tried to stay away from him and not get involved.'[22] On another occasion he said: '[Roy] Lichtenstein and Warhol I can take in at a glance; they never had the dangerous quality that Beuys had.'[23] Although admitting the influence Warhol had on him, in giving him 'permission' to 'copy' photographs, Richter was ultimately dismissive: 'Andy Warhol is not so much an artist as a symptom of a cultural situation, created by that situation and used as a substitute for an artist ... though some of his works are amongst the most impressive things done over the last thirty years, and though his oeuvre as a whole holds a decisive and outstanding importance for our age – he was still only a mediocre artist.'[24]

As always, interesting things were happening offstage. Around 1990 the Scottish-born artist Peter Doig, then a postgraduate student, began making landscapes, or landscapes occupied by people or houses (page 126). 'The kind of art that was being exhibited at that time', he later related, 'mostly had a clean, contemporary, slick look. It was highly polished or manufactured to specification. I didn't want to become a part of that world. I purposely made work that was hand-made and homely looking.'[25] He started to move the paint about a lot more, building up the surface. Frequently based on memories of his teenage years in Canada, the paintings were strangely dreamlike, and people often felt that the places he painted seemed oddly familiar. 'Perhaps', he observed, 'my treatment of landscape represents a longing for something outside of my grasp.'[26]

Doig's paintings have been described as seeming fragile, even as bordering on the sentimental. When, in 1994, he exhibited some large paintings of skiers in snowy landscapes, more than one person was heard to say, 'I do wish they didn't look so like Christmas cards!' (or words to that effect). But that was the point: like Marlene Dumas wanting to paint love and eroticism, Doig wanted to paint scenes that intrigued him, even if they felt nostalgic or fey. Years later, he said: '[My paintings] are basically pieced together from things that I've seen, things I've remembered, even wallpaper I've seen, bits of things I've seen in other people's paintings. At the same time, I don't want my work to look like collage; I want it to look like something whole.'[27] His paintings are often multilayered, but harmonious and avowedly evocative – the very opposite of what Richter was doing.

In the early 1980s there was still a consensus regarding which artists were important: those who had appeared at 'Zeitgeist' then appeared at documenta 7 of the same year, and so on. By the early 1990s, however, this was no longer the case. In 1989 the door had been opened not just to globalism but also to a greater diversity. The art world became more varied and diffuse, even fissiparous. From this point on, it thus becomes more difficult to chart art history: after the 1980s and the emergence of neo-expressionism and neo-conceptualism, there would be no more shifts or groups that one could term 'movements'.

The early 1990s was also the time when curators became more prominent. This was particularly apparent at the 1993 Whitney Biennial. Prior to 1993, the biennial had been a survey of what was considered the most important art made in the United States during the previous years. It was often criticized, however, not just for choosing the wrong artists, but also for looking as organized as a vegetable market or jumble sale. The curator Elisabeth Sussman was therefore asked to make the 1993 edition look like a coherent exhibition, not a mishmash. She and her assistant curators produced something not only more coherent but also more contentious: an exhibition that privileged black, Hispanic, gay and feminist artists. The people who funded the Whitney hated it (like almost all museums in America, it depends on donations from the wealthy), as did those who prefer their art to stay unpolluted by anything political.

The exhibition captured the mood of the time. Kiki Smith, for example, showed a fragile work composed of two adults joined together by an umbilical cord. In collaboration with David Wojnarowicz, an artist who had just died of AIDS, she also exhibited a series of light boxes showing photographs of parts of their bodies covered in blood (page 127). George Holliday, who was not known as an artist, was represented by the video he had made of four LA policeman beating up a black man, Rodney King.

I first visited the exhibition one evening when admission was free. The museum was filled with the black and Hispanic people you rarely saw in such a place; in fact, the attendance was double that of any previous Whitney Biennial. Because it was so crowded, however, it was difficult to see the art; and as I wanted to write about the show, I requested a second visit the next day, when the museum would be closed to the public. It was a revelation. There were more videos and audio-visual works than in any exhibition I had seen before. (As the museum wasn't officially open, none of them were running: it felt like going to a fairground after it had closed for the day, silent.) Another journalist, a lady from Texas, did the tour with me. I was surprised at the directness of the junior curator who escorted us: 'This means this, that means that.' After the nice lady from Texas had left, horrified, the curator told me that, the day before, she had shown some established museum patrons round. 'This means the end of collecting,' one of them had told her.

The art museum had become the site of a culture war, not just a repository of objects.

Chapter 6

FOR A COMMUNITY, ONESELF OR ONE'S SOUL?

The Late 1990s

Who do you make art for? Everyone, your own community or just yourself? And why? To entertain, criticize or as a spiritual experience?

Relational aesthetics – art as a shared activity, rather than an object or a concept – was much discussed in the late 1990s. The term 'relational art' was first used by Nicolas Bourriaud in the catalogue for the 1996 exhibition 'Traffic', which he curated at CAPC Musée d'Art Contemporain de Bordeaux. Included in that show were Carsten Höller, the Italian Maurizio Cattelan, and the artist who, above all, represented the moment, Rirkrit Tiravanija, born in Argentina to Thai parents. Famously, as his work, Tiravanija would serve green curry in a gallery, or exhibit the contents of his apartment.

'Cities on the Move' was the exhibition that presented this way of art-making most cogently, focusing on Asian artists and the growth of the new megacities in Asia. First held in Vienna in 1997, it was restaged several times, including in Bangkok; and at each location it was very different. Exhibition-making was being mooted as an art form in itself, the curator its author. 'The entire exhibition is an open system,' explained Hans Ulrich Obrist, who co-curated the show with Hou Hanru from China. 'An exhibition such as this is always a challenge to the institution, the curators, the artists, and the audience, even to the media. We want to create a living event in which the viewer can participate, and embark on an adventure into the unknown – we do not want to exhibit nice works and clever ideas.'[1] Hou explained further: 'In reality art equates to art event. Or to be more precise, if the art is to be effectively presented, it needs to be part of an art event. We are now living in the society of communication. Spectacle is the form. The spectacle, or the event, is the very horizon and bottom line of "Reality".'[2] Which institution such an 'event' happens in is crucial, 'because the institution is the central element in the power system or mechanism that defines the notion and the boundary of art itself. "Where do you show your art?" has become a more telling question than "What kind of work do you make?"'[3]

An innocent visitor to 'Cities on the Move' might have felt that this was a new and energizing approach to art; or wondered if this was not art at all, but rather an anthropology of city life. For many, the standout objects were by Tiravanija and his fellow Thai artist Navin Rawanchaikul: a decorated tuk-tuk, together with a billboard advertising a fictitious film about a tuk-tuk driver who travels to Vienna and falls in love with a Viennese girl (below).

When the South Korean artist Kimsooja was invited to take part in 'Cites on the Move', she recalled how, because of her father's job in the army, her family had lived in many different towns and villages. 'The title [of the exhibition] reminded me of our family's nomadic life and inspired me to do *Cities on the Move – 2727 Kilometres Bottari Truck* performance, revisiting all of the villages and cities of my youth in an eleven-day trip across Korea.'[4] The video of her sitting upright on a pile of *bottari* as the truck drives around Korea is mesmeric (pages 134–35). But what is a bottari? Like the Hyundai truck on which the artist travelled, it is a specifically Korean thing: when women move house, they wrap all their clothes in a large cloth that has been made by sewing old, used cloths together. This gathering is called a *bottari* (bundle). Kim makes hers with the used clothes that belonged to unknown people, whose imprint and smell have been preserved by the fabric.[5]

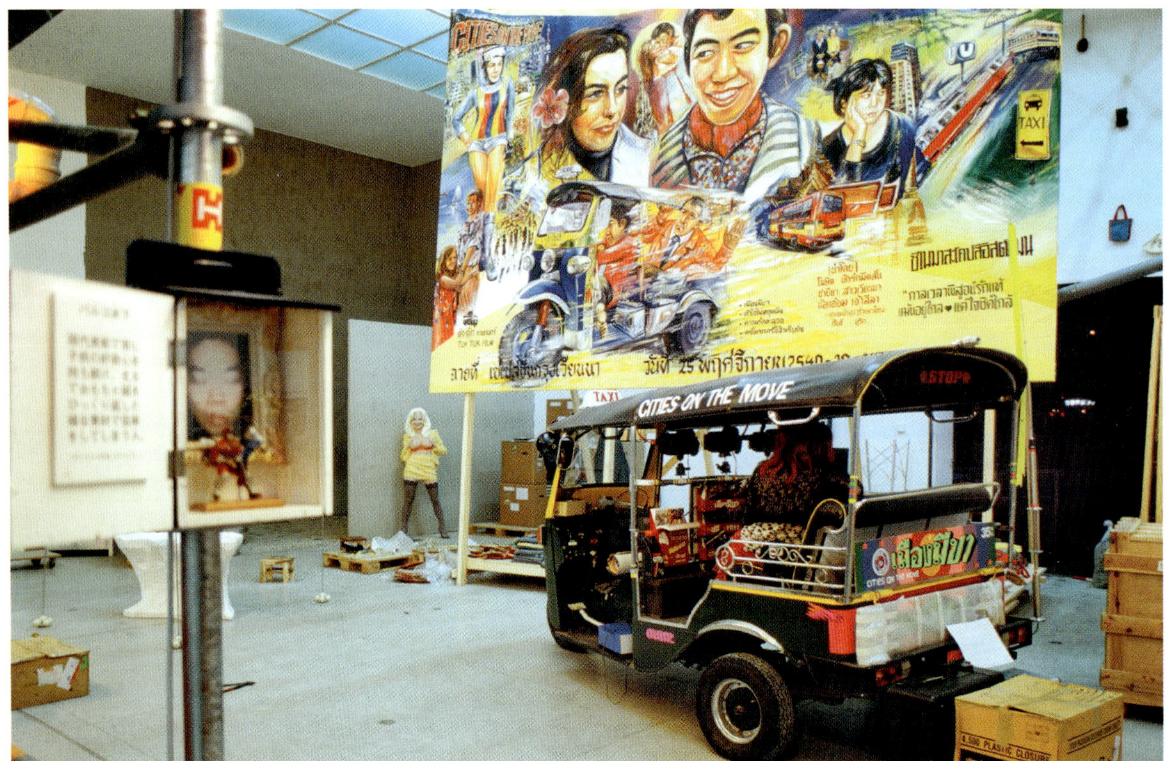

Rirkrit Tiravanija and Navin Rawanchaikul, cinema poster and tuk-tuk
Installation view, 'Cities on the Move', Vienna Secession, 1997–98

'When I ask myself, what in the world did I sew and wrap for over twenty years, I can say now it was the scars, pain, longing, love, passion, parts of my psychology and body as well as my loneliness, which needed to be attached.'[6]

Kimsooja's work has always been to do with travel and displacement. Her approach changed when, after a fellowship in New York, she returned to Korea in 1993: 'I looked at my own culture through completely different eyes.' Later, after participating in 'Cities on the Move', she lived in New York and France. Although she continued to use Korean fabrics, with their national and feminine associations, she insisted she was not a feminist in any 'campaigning' sense of the word. Neither did she see her work as nationalistic: her concern was with universal experiences, a sense of wholeness.

From 1999 onwards Kimsooja staged frequent 'Needle Woman' performances, in which she would stand perfectly still in the middle of a crowded street. Unlike artists such as Marina Abramović, Kimsooja wanted her performance to be passive, not aggressive. 'While I was standing still and remained centre I experienced an incredible transition in my mind from vulnerability to a focused, meditative and enlightened state of mind.'[7] In exhibitions, several 'Needle Woman' performances, filmed in different cities, are often shown together. Always she is shown from behind, absolutely motionless – 'At the still point of the turning world'.[8] To watch her so unmoved as people mill around her can be a meditative experience for the viewer too.

Generally, this was art that wanted to be anything but pompous or tragic. And no one eschewed pomposity more than Maurizio Cattelan – or skewered it more ruthlessly. 'I don't consider myself an artist,' he claimed. 'I make art, but it's a job. I fell into this by chance. Someone once told me that it was a profitable profession, that you could travel a lot and meet a lot of girls. But this is all false: there is no money, no travel, no girls.'[9]

In 1996 Cattelan agreed to show his work at De Appel gallery in Amsterdam. Under the pretext that he had no new ideas, he broke into another gallery, stole all the contents and exhibited them in De Appel as *Another Fucking Readymade*. Asked to participate in the 1997 Venice Biennale, and being aware that many of Italy's most famous, senior artists were also exhibiting, he decided to intervene in their space and mock them. He had a flock of pigeons caught and stuffed, then placed the birds on the dividing walls and rafters of the exhibition space, staring down at the older artists' work. 'We have to kill the father,' he cheerfully declared, 'otherwise we have to lick his feet.'[10] In 1998, after being invited to do a project at MoMA, he arranged for someone dressed as Picasso, complete with a gigantic papier mâché head like Picasso's, to wander round the museum. It may have mocked the cult of genius, but people loved it and, entering into the spirit of things, asked 'Picasso' for his autograph.

Cattelan is probably the greatest tease the art world has ever known. When, in 1999, he organized the '6th Caribbean Biennial', the only thing that happened was that he and the invited artists had a holiday on the island of St Kitts. Just how the sponsors of this effectively fictitious exhibition felt can only be imagined. If this type

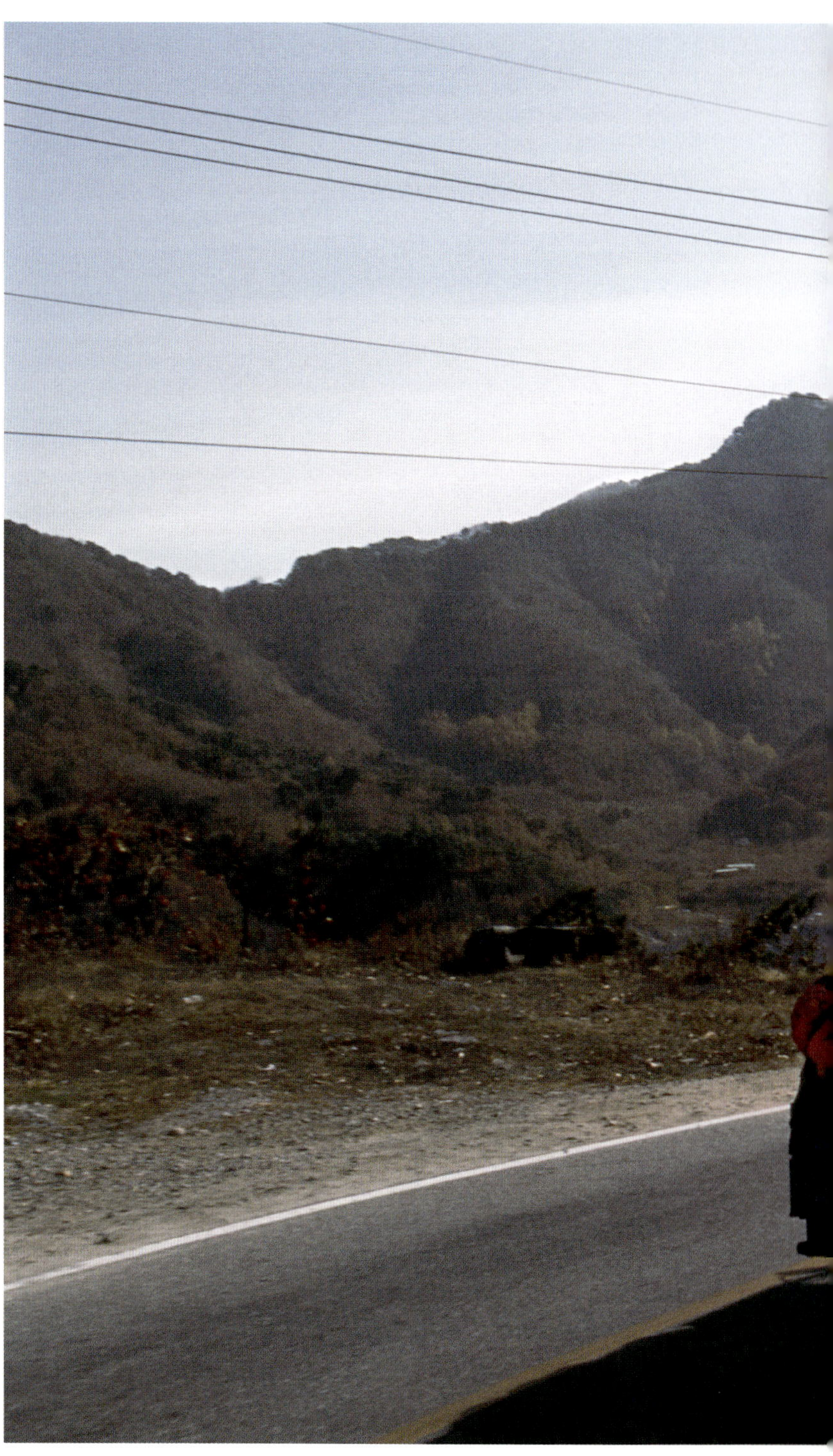

Kimsooja, *Cities on the Move: 2,727 Kilometers Bottari Truck, Korea*, 1997
Still from the performance with 1-ton pickup truck, bottaris made with used Korean bedcovers and clothes, and bungee cord

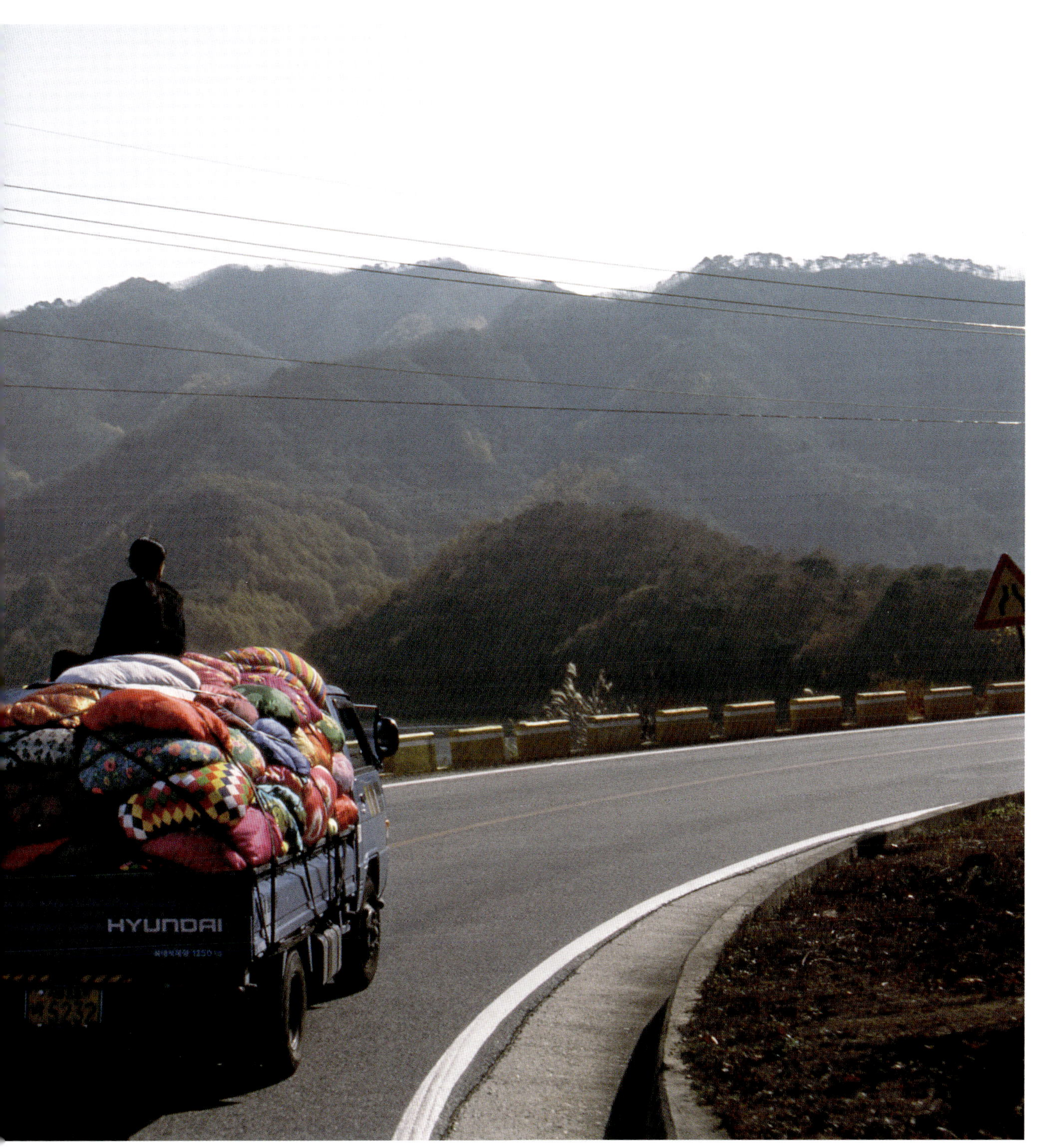
HYUNDAI

of art event was for the community, it was only for the cool art-world community. It also became known that Cattelan had often got one of his friends, the Italian curator Massimiliano Gioni, to pretend to be him for interviews. It was funny at the time, but now, in the age of Trump and fake news, when we read Cattelan (or Gioni) saying, 'The truth is not out there. It's just the moment that you claim something as your own. This is my truth; that is yours,' it becomes difficult to laugh.[11]

Cattelan may mock pomposity, but melancholy, even the tragic, tends to seep into his work. *Bidibidobidiboo* (opposite), for example, is funny but also sad. On the floor, in a model of a poor person's kitchen (supposedly based on that of his parents), a stuffed squirrel is slumped over a table; the gun with which it has apparently shot itself is by its feet. Do we laugh or cry? Or both? Death is the one constant in Cattelan's work. For *Out of the Blue*, created for the 1997 Skulptur Projekte Münster, he placed a mannequin of a blonde-haired woman just below the surface of a lake so it looked like a murder victim. However, in a provocation on provocation, the mannequin sank, so viewers (myself included) wasted time walking round the lake looking for it.

Tania Bruguera deals in confrontation, not irony or wit. She began her career by remaking the performances of Ana Mendieta. As a fellow Cuban artist, albeit one who lived in exile, Mendieta was an obvious role model. 'I discovered that I really enjoyed doing her performances,' Bruguera explained. 'What I liked was that it was just like life. Up until that point, making art had made me feel uneasy because it felt somehow artificial, in that it involved isolating something from its context. With performance, it was just like living life, but in a meaningful way.'[12]

Bruguera soon began to stage her own performances. Of *El Peso de la Culpa* (The Burden of Guilt; page 138), a work inspired by the refusal of the indigenous inhabitants of Cuba to submit to the Spanish invaders, she said: 'In this piece I take on issues of guilt and responsibility in a conscious way for the first time … The only way that some of [the indigenous Cuban people] could rebel – as they didn't have any weapons and they weren't warriors by nature – was to eat dirt until they died … The performance manifests as a solemn ritual which also involves salt water, which engages with the earth as a symbol of tears, and a headless lamb hung from my neck which functions as a protective shield which, in turn, because of its weight, functions as a symbol of submission … I think more than religious activity, what my work approaches is the spiritual and mystical … The lamb, salt water, nails – all those elements have a symbolic weight well beyond any one religion, they're part of a universal iconographic vocabulary.'[13] Bruguera's concern with responsibility would lead her to make art that engaged with social issues: homelessness, unfair treatment of immigrants, a sense of community. She has also proposed an *art util*, or 'useful art', which could include teaching, advising on legal issues, or giving people a platform to speak freely. As we shall see, such actions have not endeared her to the Cuban government.

Unlike Cattelan, the Thai sculptor Montien Boonma had no interest in subverting the art world. Instead, like Kimsooja, he was concerned with a spiritual sense

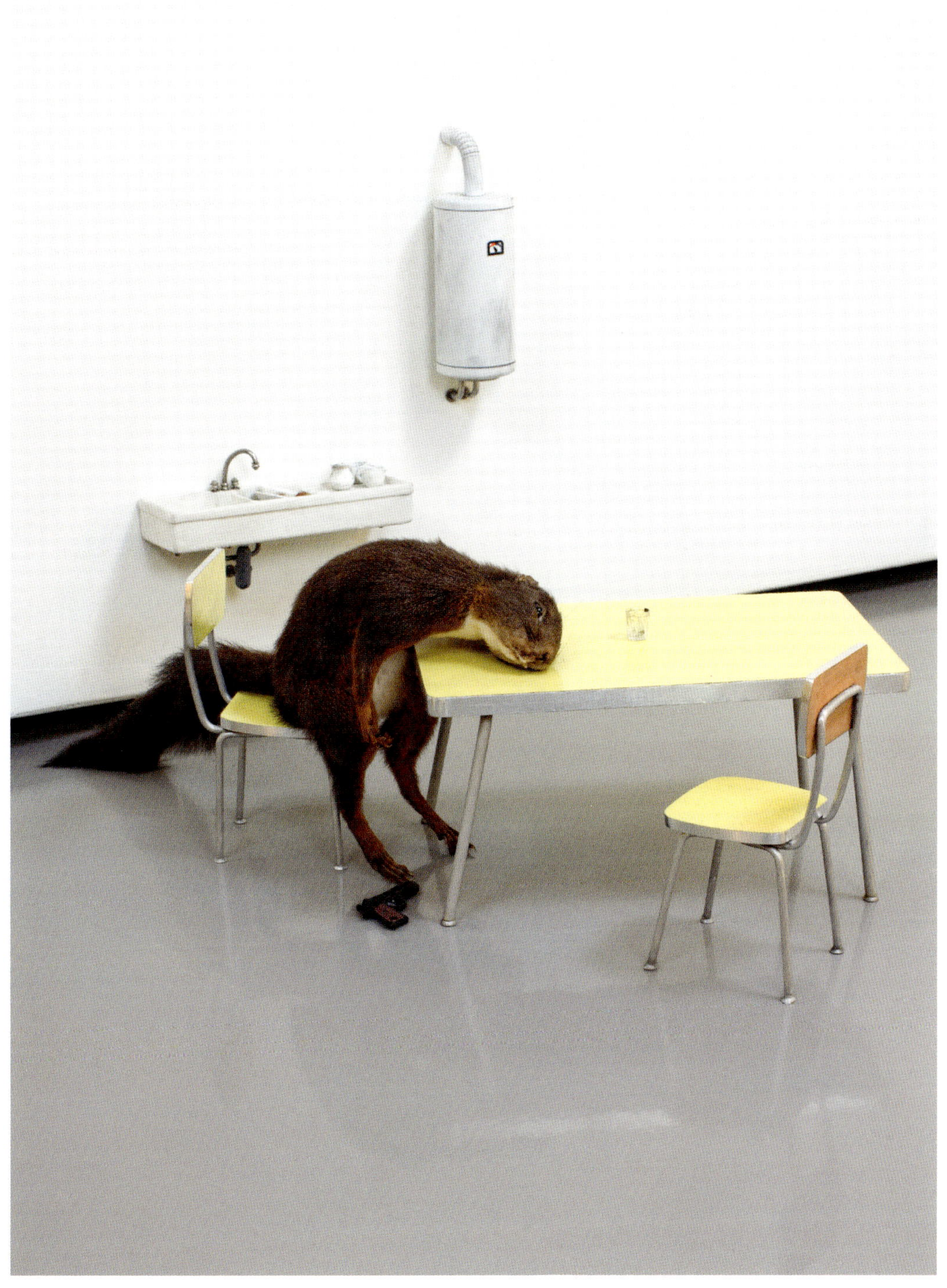

Maurizio Cattelan, *Bidibidobidiboo*, 1996
Taxidermed squirrel, ceramic, Formica, wood, paint and steel, 45 × 60 × 48 cm (17¾ × 23⅝ × 19 in.)

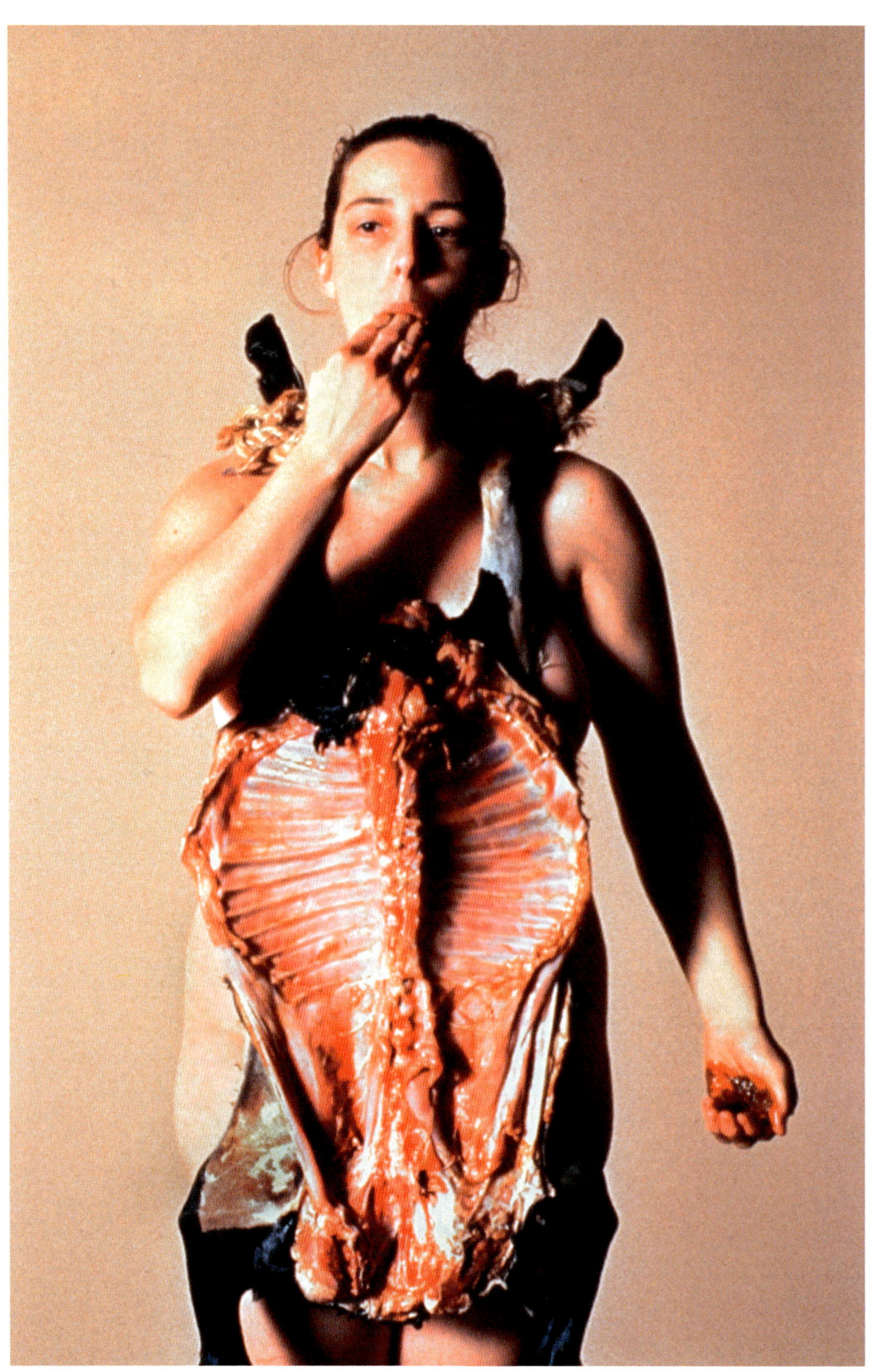

Tania Bruguera, *El Peso de la Culpa* (The Burden of Guilt), 1997–99
Performance with Cuban soil, dead lamb, rope, water, salt

of being. As many Thai men do, Boonma had spent time as a monk. His encounter with the work of Joseph Beuys in 1989, and then thinking about Beuys's shamanism and the way he had humanized the rectangular boxes of minimalism by adding fat and felt, suggested some links between Eastern and Western ways. Teaching afterwards in the northern Thai city of Chiang Mai, away from the metropolis of Bangkok, Boonma also started to learn from rural life, about the connections to nature and to others: 'The artist has to feel and sense what is happening and what could help the individual and the society. Artists have to have quicker response and finer sensitivity. We do not have to think so much about advancement and progress. The more important thing is the quality of life.'[14]

As he nursed his young wife, who had cancer, Boonma began to question the purpose of life. Ultimately, however, her illness and death, and the onset of his own cancer, led him to a more profound involvement with Buddhist teachings. He began to make sculptures with the bells and begging bowls used by monks – two forms that can stand for both fullness and emptiness. From 3 to 6 in the morning, he would draw begging bowls as a meditational exercise: 'Like the alms bowl, the mind needs equilibrium ... [Boonma's] quest was to be inside the black space of the vessels, the realm of nothingness where the mind and consciousness of selflessness and ego-lessness could be realised.'[15]

In the last years of his life, Boonma focused on making installations where others could become involved and absorbed in such experiences. His *Zodiac Houses* (page 140) may look like gothic towers and cathedral spires – he made them during a residency in Stuttgart, Germany, where he also became interested in astrology – but they are very much about a search for spiritual consolation following his wife's death and the decline of his own health. To enter each house you must first bow down – a sign of respect – and then raise your head inside the structure, where you can imagine the tiny apertures above you as stars, or else just sense the light filtering through them into the darkness. If you look long enough, you might begin to recognize the patterns of astrological signs, marked by the apertures. And if you have a decent sense of smell, you might be able to identify the traditional medicinal herbs contained within each sculpture.

In his use of such herbs, Boonma, unlike Cai Guo-Qiang, was not making a point about the differences between East and West. He was happy to be embedded in Thai Buddhism and its traditions, but believed that his art could be understood by all. To reference German cathedrals in *Zodiac Houses* was, for Boonma, to acknowledge the universality of religious experience. 'For me,' he wrote of his preparatory sketch, 'churches are like stars. Sometimes we think that there are things on earth that are related to heaven. My work speaks from between our beliefs. It is about the linkage to heaven. I have imagined the ringing of the church bells and marked the reverberating of these sounds.'[16] Boonma died from cancer in 2000, aged forty-seven. His ashes were scattered on the Chao Phraya River, Bangkok.

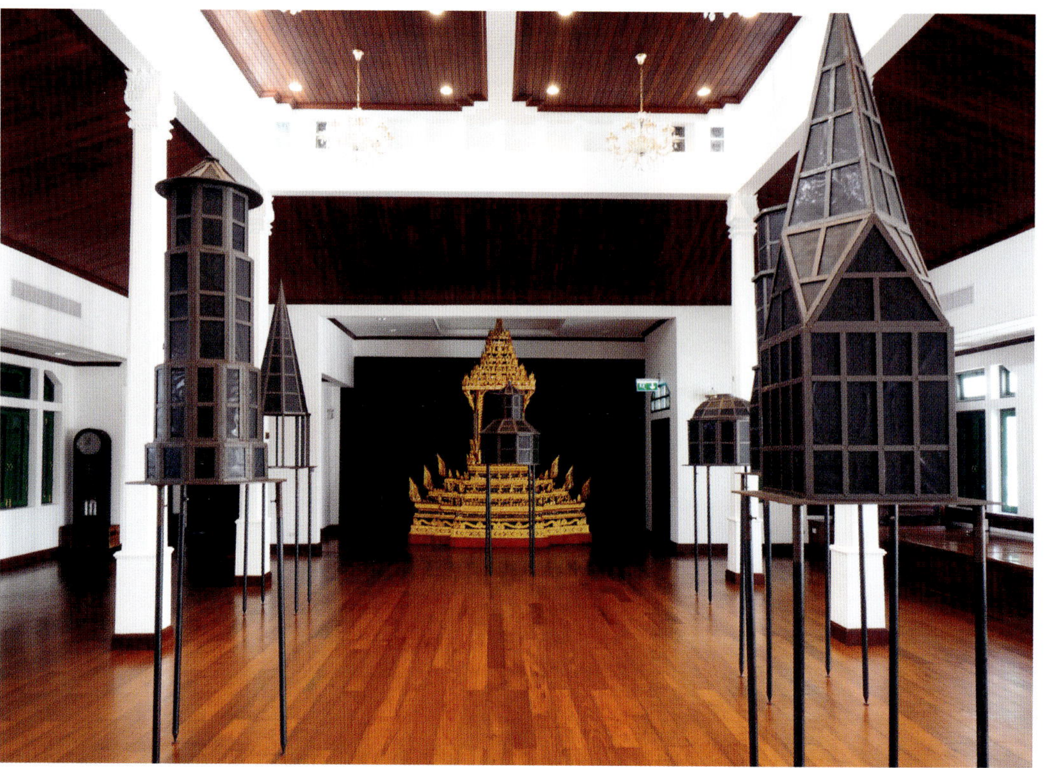

Montien Boonma, *Zodiac Houses*, 1998–99
Steel, transparency sheet, wood, medicinal herbs, cinnabar, 6 elements, each *c.* 300 × 90 cm (118⅛ x 35½ in.)

Bill Viola would agree with Boonma that all religions are connected and compatible; he likewise would hope that his works can be as readily understood by a Muslim or a Buddhist as a Christian. One consistent message in contemporary art is that spiritual experience is ecumenical, not sectarian.

Of course, the spiritual is often most profoundly experienced in the context of a particular religion. Viola's *The Messenger* (opposite) is a case in point. Commissioned by and first shown in Durham Cathedral – a monumental space in which people have worshipped for nine centuries, thought by many to be the most beautiful building in England – Viola's video was projected on to a screen mounted to the door at the cathedral's west end. One watched a small pale blob in darkness slowly growing larger until it was recognizable as a man, and the darkness as the deep water he was emerging from. The man broke the surface of the water, opened his eyes and inhaled. Then he sank down into the depths once more. Four more times the man sank and rose to the surface again before the tape looped back to the beginning. Each submersion and emergence took about five and a half minutes. It was mesmeric, and, in this cathedral setting, tremendously evocative.

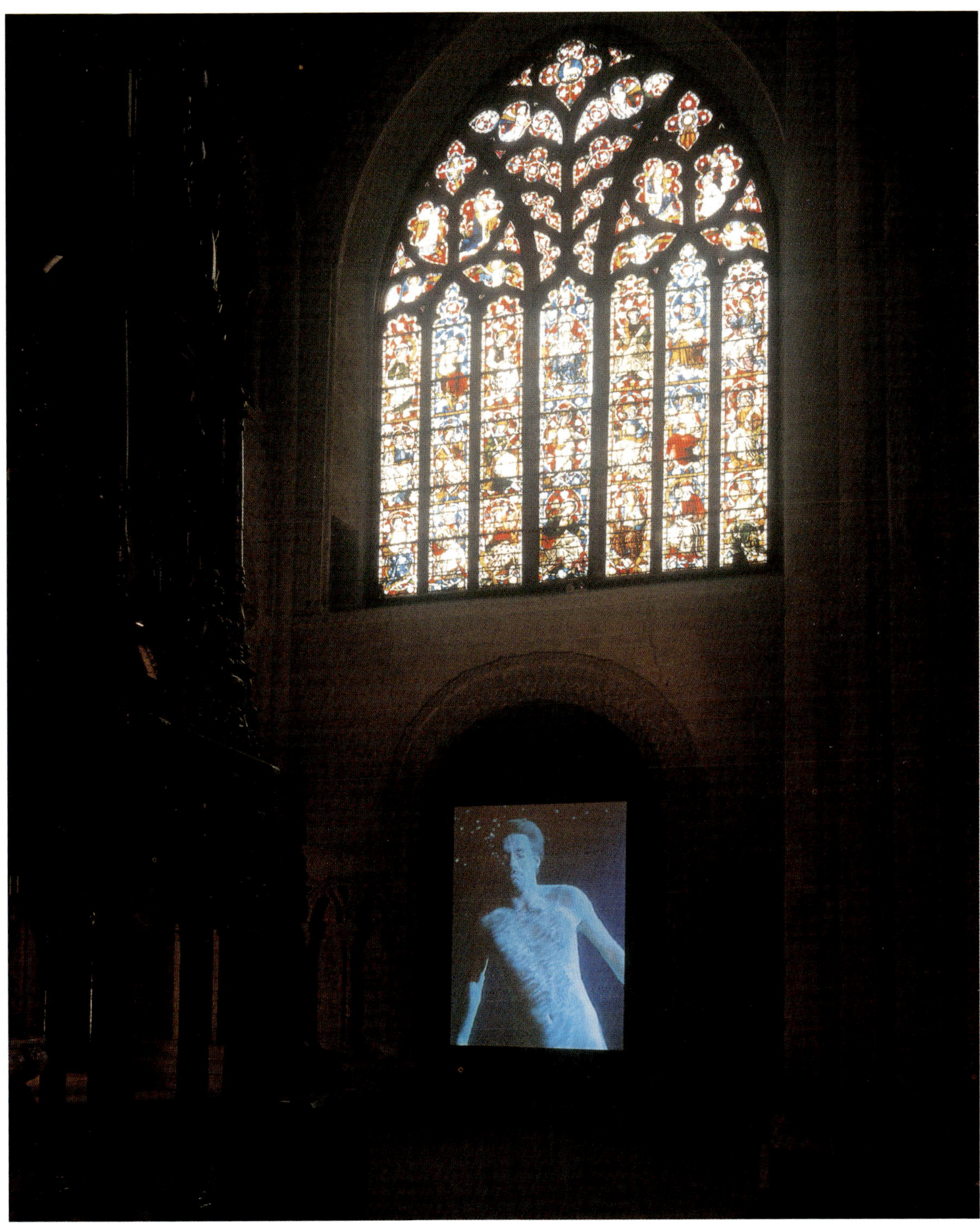

Bill Viola, *The Messenger*, 1996, Durham Cathedral
Colour video projection on large vertical screen mounted on wall in darkened space; amplified stereo sound, 28 minutes

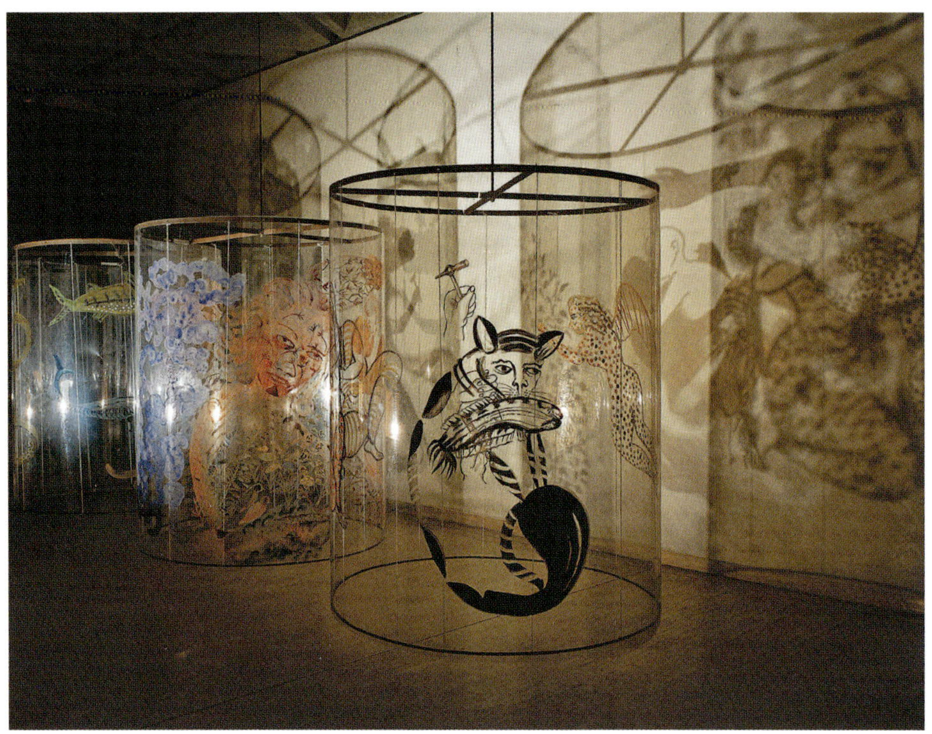

Nalini Malani, *Stories retold: the sacred and the profane*, 1998
Shadowplay, four rotating acrylic reverse-painted mylar cylinders

Of course, compared to when he made *The Reflecting Pool* some twenty years earlier (page 61), Viola had much more advanced technology at his disposal, a bigger team of assistants, a bigger budget and, in Chad Walker, an expert diver. But otherwise *The Messenger* is not so different from the earlier work: a simple, strong image that could be seen as a metaphor for some inner state. The cathedral gave each visitor a handout containing quotes from the Psalms, and from the books of Jonah and Job. 'Naked I came from my mother's womb, and naked I shall return ... Have you entered into the springs of the sea, or walked in the recesses of the deep? Have the gates of death been revealed to you, or have you seen the gates of the deep darkness?'[17] Viola would probably have preferred you to free-associate or have a more wordless experience. Birth, death, an angel, a message from God ... After the opening, the installation was slightly marred by a screen covering the lower part of the projection: the more prudish element of the congregation had protested the diver's exposed genitals.

Viola's work has continued in this vein, trying to deal with the big themes in a way that is both spectacular and easy to understand. The devotional art of the Renaissance has become an important influence: several of his videos are re-enactments of scenes from paintings by Giotto and his contemporaries. Accused by some of making emotionally manipulative works, or simply of being an old hippy, Viola is undoubtedly one of the most popular artists working today.

Until 1992 the Indian artist Nalini Malani had seen herself as a painter, but, as she herself later observed, 'After the demolition of the Babri Masjid mosque in Ayodhya, India, by Hindu extremists in that year and the riots that followed, many women artists in India felt a need to embrace new forms.'[18] How to protest the appalling violence of those riots? And before them, the massacres that accompanied the partition of India and Pakistan – violence that was all too often directed at women? How to reach a wider audience? To only paint was not enough. Video was one solution, because it is seductive and draws people in. The traditional shadow plays so popular in India were another. 'They are mesmerizing,' said Malani; 'you can watch the different images – painted, projected, shadows – overlap and combine.'[19] She sought ways to make her own, contemporary shadow plays.

In the first of these, *The sacred and the profane* (opposite), Malani modernized and complicated the medium: high and low art were blended, with figures from classical Indian sculptures mixing with those from popular paintings – specifically examples of Kalighat painting, a form that began in Kolkata (Calcutta) in the nineteenth century. Malani painted these figures on to four transparent cylinders, which slowly revolved while lights projected and entangled together various shadows on the walls behind. Her focus was on 'erotic tales about demons, gods, and their consorts. This was in reaction to the right-wing party which was trying with force to sanitize Hinduism and erase the erotic aspect of it.'[20] She gave centre stage to the heroines from the popular epic *Ramayana*, showing them as positive, sensual, disruptive presences.

Although Malani had spent time in Paris in the early 1970s, the model for much of her work was what had happened in Mexico with Diego Rivera and Frida Kahlo, who had made political art that was both personal and filled with symbolic imagery. Meeting women artists in New York, including Ana Mendieta, in 1979 was also 'a real eye opener'.[21] 'Being a woman in India is not easy,' observed Malani recently. 'As [the writer] Vrinda Nabar said, being a woman is a caste in itself ... My own art was from the very start female-oriented. I believe this is natural, a given, as women have a completely different relationship to the body than men. And women also hold a different position in society, anywhere in the world compared to men ... understanding the world from a feminist perspective is an essential device for a more hopeful future.'[22]

Since 1992, Malani's work has involved painting, projection, video and performance, in various combinations. Avowedly political, her pieces are not easily read. As she herself says: 'My work is not a slogan but a physical experience that might lead to an internal experience that goes beyond transmittance of knowledge.'[23] She does not see her work as relating only to India: sectarian violence and violence against women can be found all over the world. 'As a global society we partake of a lexicon of images through history and civilizations ... In the flux of change it is important that we cull from this and re-vitalize it in the new global context. Unfortunately, when Western artists do this it [is] considered innovative, but if an Indian or a non-Western artist does it [it] is thought of as derivative. Now in the age of the Internet, all artists inherit a veritable lexicon of images. Now all will partake.'[24]

The Swiss artist Pipilotti Rist may appear to lack Malani's seriousness, but what the two women share is a commitment to pleasure and sensuousness in art. For them it is akin to female eroticism. Rist's statement from 2000 – 'I am grateful for feminism. But women did it once so I don't have to go back and do what they did'[25] – might grate on some ears, seeming to mark her as uncaring. But others might reply: 'Why should she be a feminist just because she makes videos? We don't have that expectation of painters, and, in many ways, Pipilotti uses video rather like painting – blurring, heightening or distorting colours and shapes.' As she herself has said, 'Video is like a painting on glass that moves; video also has a rough, imperfect quality that looks like painting. I do not want to copy reality on my work. "Reality" is always much sharper and more contrasted than anything that can be created with video. Video has its own ... lousy, nervous, inner world quality, and I work with that.'[26]

In Rist's *Ever Is Over All* (opposite), a woman in red shoes and a pale-blue dress walks slowly down the street – we soon deduce that the video is being played in slow motion – holding a flower, one known in English as a 'red-hot poker'. The soundtrack is a wordless and lugubrious pop song. Suddenly, the woman swings the flower and smashes the window of a parked car; clearly, the flower is made of metal. She smiles and skips and swings and smashes another car window. A policewoman walks by and salutes her. The woman in pale blue walks on, ecstatically happy, and swings her flower again ... Is this a feminist work or just teenage naughtiness? Certainly, the woman is a subject here, not just an object. It is funny, sexy and ravishingly beautiful. Even if we focus on the woman, we are subliminally aware that another projection on the right, which periodically bleeds into the street scene, is of a landscape and flowers shot in saturated colours. If we sit or stand in front of the work for long enough, we realize that the projection of the woman is 4 minutes long, while that of the landscape lasts for 9 minutes. They are not synchronized; they blend by chance.

'My subjects are amorphous and overlapping,' Rist has said.[27] Implicitly, she asks the viewer to let go and be immersed in this shower of colours and images, so they too can realize a heightened sense of their own body as 'amorphous and overlapping'. Often in her work the camera, like an inquisitive eye, roams over naked bodies. Likewise, her videos are projected on many surfaces: refrigerators, hanging underwear, floors, ceilings, all four walls and, of course, the bodies of people walking through her installations.

By this point in the decade it was possible to visit at least some exhibitions where half the participants were women. (Half the artists talked about in this chapter are women, and in subsequent chapters close on half or more of the artists discussed are female.) But it was more than female artists just getting to exhibit their work: many now had substantial careers and profiles, among them Kimsooja and Nalini Malani.

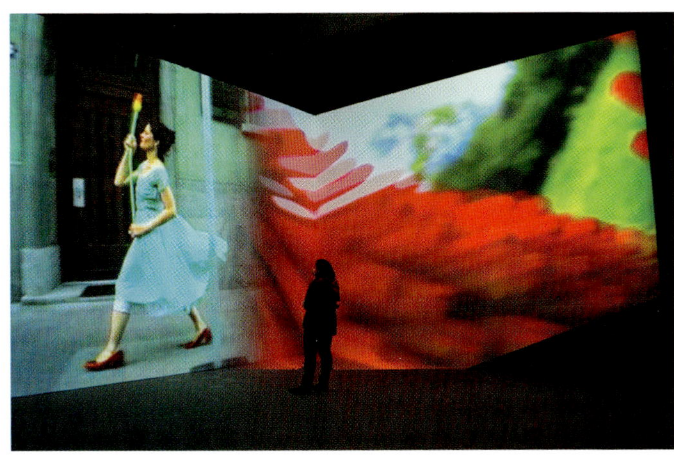

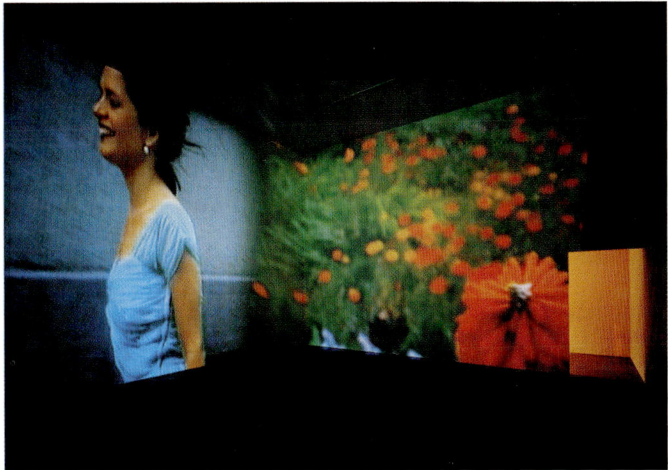

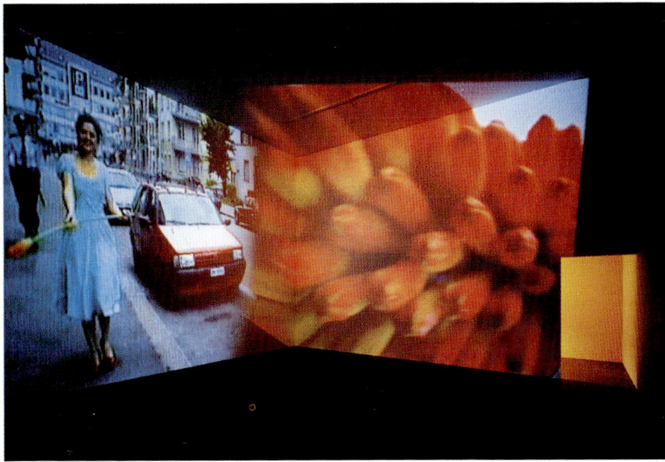

Pipilotti Rist, *Ever Is Over All*, 1997
Two-channel video installation with sound
by Anders Guggisberg and Pipilotti Rist

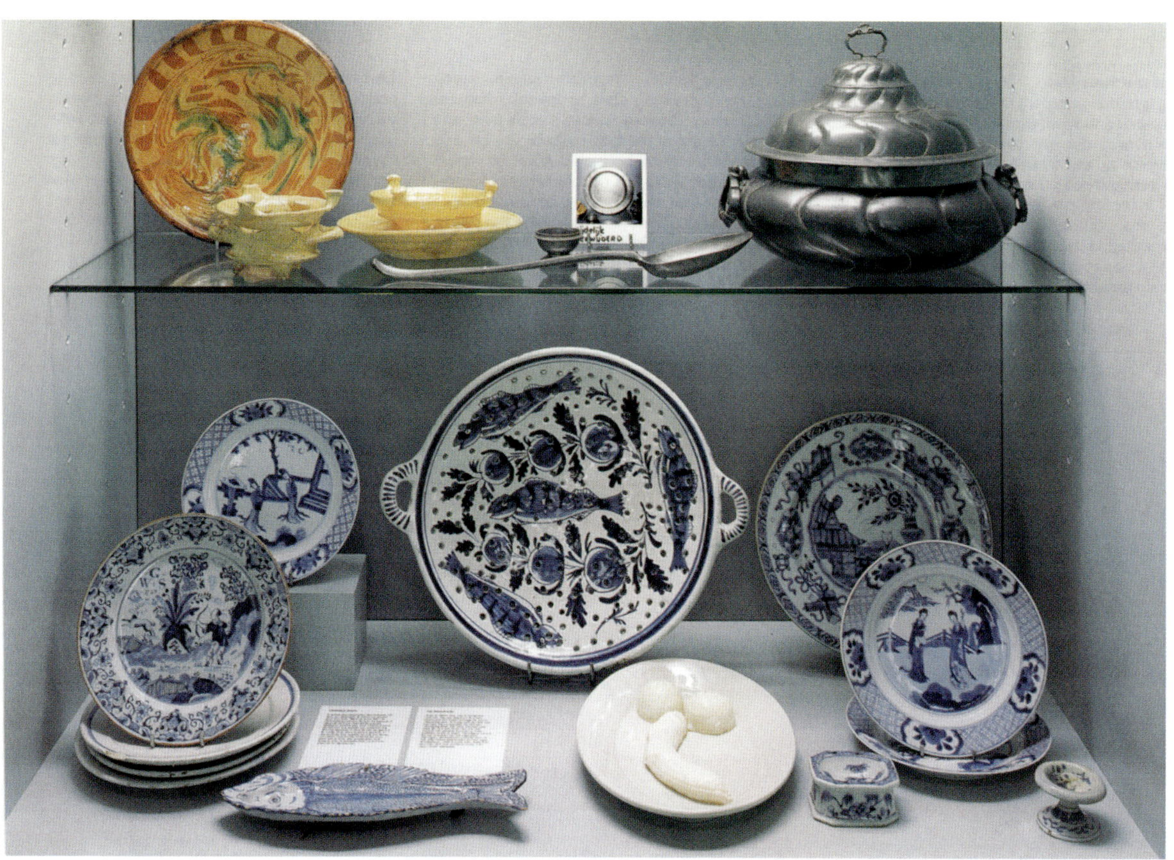

Sophie Calle, *La Visite guidée*, from the exhibition 'Absent', 1994, Museum Boymans-van Beuningen, Rotterdam, 'The Dessert'
Audioguide with spoken commentary and music by Laurie Anderson, objects dispersed in Museum Boijmans Van Beuningen, Rotterdam

Another was the French artist Sophie Calle. As an artist she was like a diarist recounting experiences past. Invited to exhibit or make a project at the Museum Boijmans Van Beuningen, Rotterdam, Calle placed various objects from her life – photographs, fragments of an old bed, a red bucket, a sheet embroidered by her aunt, a red shoe, an old TV guide – in among the existing objects arranged in display cabinets in the design department (above). One went around the collection listening to an audio guide in which Calle, accompanied by music by Laurie Anderson, told a story about each of her objects. At the cabinet in which she had installed a plain white plate with a plaster banana on it among much older plates and bowls, we heard: 'When I was fifteen I was afraid of men. One day, in a restaurant, I chose a dessert because of its name: "Young Girl's Dream". I asked the waiter what it was, and he answered: "It's a surprise." A few minutes later he returned with a dish featuring two scoops of vanilla ice cream and a peeled banana. He said one word: "Enjoy." Then he laughed. I closed my eyes the same way I closed them years later when I saw my

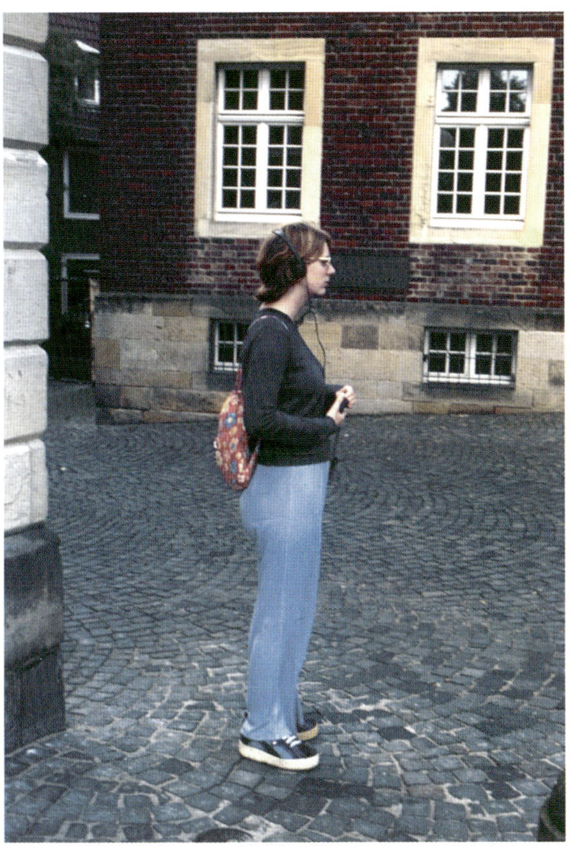

Janet Cardiff, *Münster walk*, 1997
Audio walk with mixed media props, 17 minutes

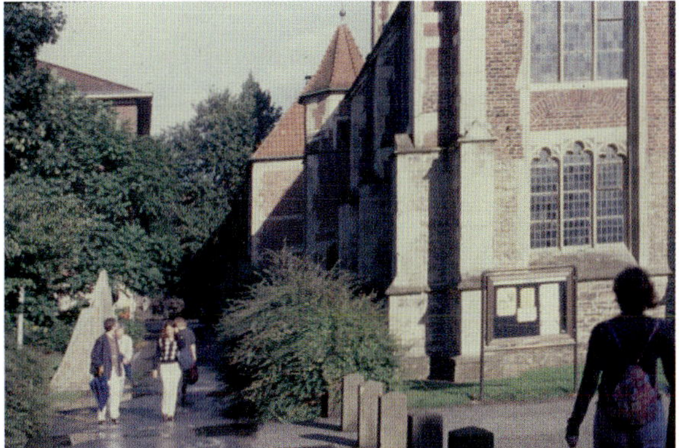

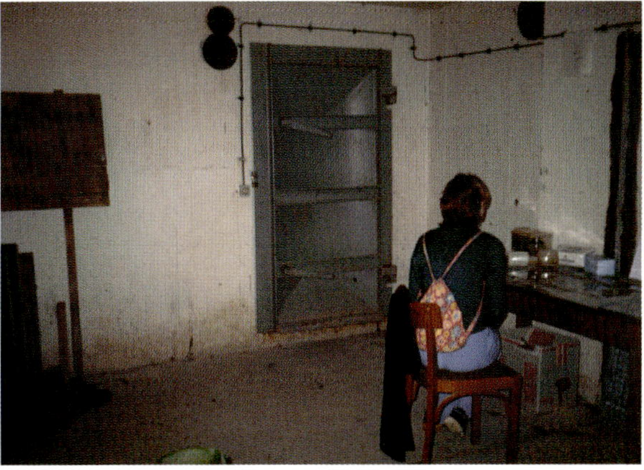

first naked man.' One was entering into her life. But also, it brought the other objects to life: one was reminded that the old plates and bowls had also once belonged to other people and witnessed their lives. When the project was restaged at London's Freud Museum in 1999, Calle draped her wedding dress on Freud's famous couch.

When not acting like a diarist, Calle has acted like a detective in search of other people's secrets: following a man obsessively, taking a job at a hotel and examining what people keep in their suitcases. In 2007 her partner sent her an email dumping her. She decided to ask more than a hundred professional women to analyse the email, and then created an exhibition at the Venice Biennale from their responses. What started as therapy soon became art. 'After [a] month I felt better. There was no suffering. It worked. The project had replaced the man.'[28]

Because the walks being made by the Canadian artist Janet Cardiff moved one through space, Kasper König believed they could be understood as sculpture, and so commissioned her to make a walk for the third Skulptur Projekte Münster in 1997 (page 147). She records with binaural equipment, meaning that, when played back on the Walkman we are provided with, the sounds are incredibly lifelike. 'Come walk with me', we hear her say, and we walk through Münster's city centre with her voice and the sounds she has chosen. We hear an old man, his voice always in our left ear, talking of his search for a lost daughter. We also hear Cardiff talking of walking through Münster, and giving us instructions: 'Stop here, turn left, count ten steps ...' We walk through the city, listening, imagining and remembering:

> Janet Cardiff's voice [a Canadian accent]: It's daytime now. I love the sounds in this street ... There's a window open above us, someone's getting some fresh air.
> *Sound of dog barking, car roaring up the street.*
> Older man [German accent]: 'If you close your eyes you can go back in time ... *sound of large horses pulling a wagon come up from behind, dogs barking, then fades away.*'[29]

Sounds from the city, contemporary and historic, interrupt the flow of words. Sometimes clips of old films are heard, and there are hints of a crime having been committed. Sometimes we seem to go far away:

> Janet Cardiff's voice: You're listening to me in Germany but I'm at home right now in Canada walking beside the river with my dog. There are five deer on the other side of the river. Their white tails are up in the air. Something must have startled them ... His image is like a dream now. Disappearing more with every second.[30]

We end up in an old, disused bomb shelter (80 per cent of Münster was damaged or destroyed by bombs in the war), where Cardiff has placed photographs and maps.

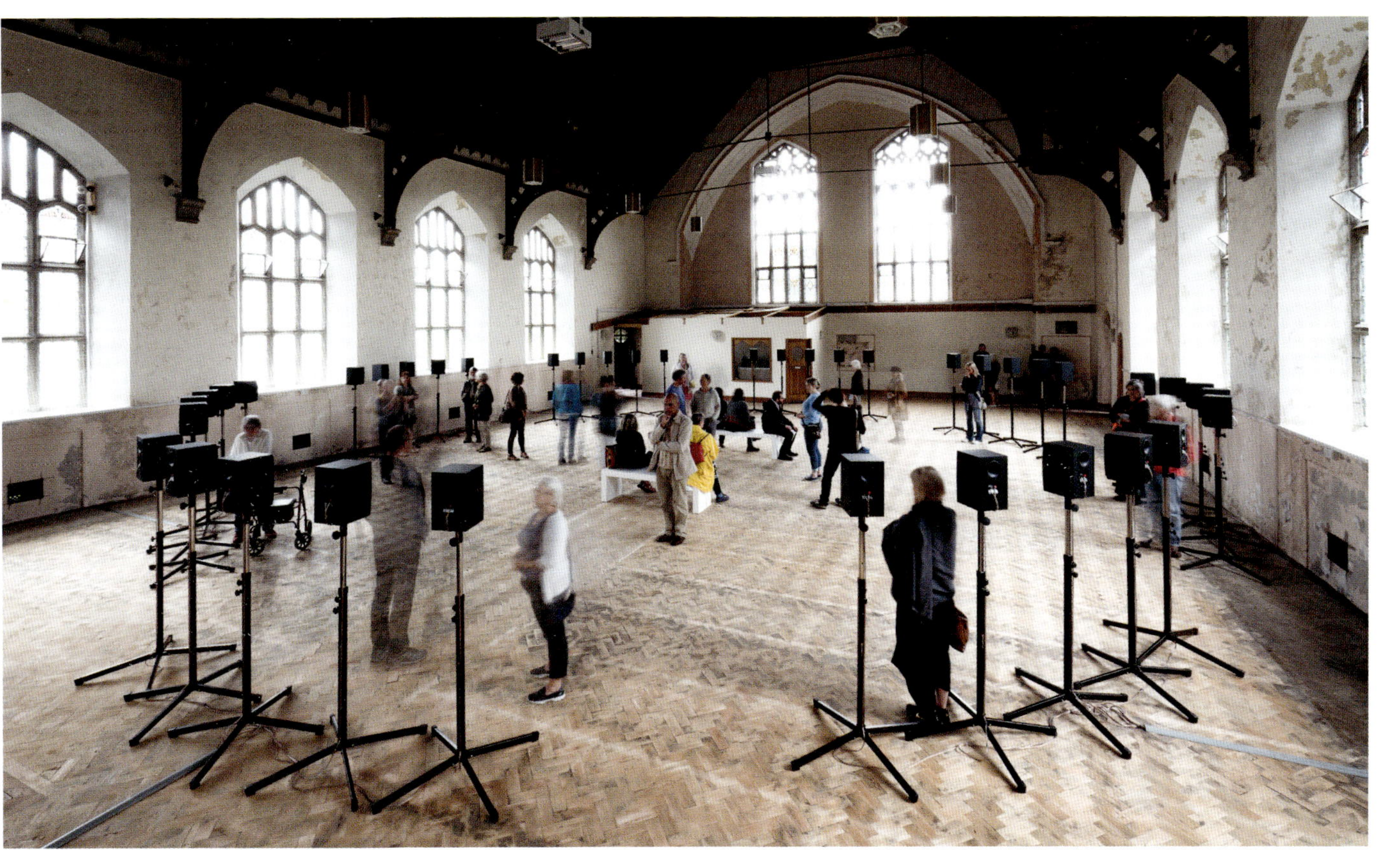

Janet Cardiff, *Forty Part Motet*, 2001
40-track audio installation, 14:7 minutes, sung by Salisbury Cathedral Choir, shown here installed at Richmond Chapel, Penzance, 2018

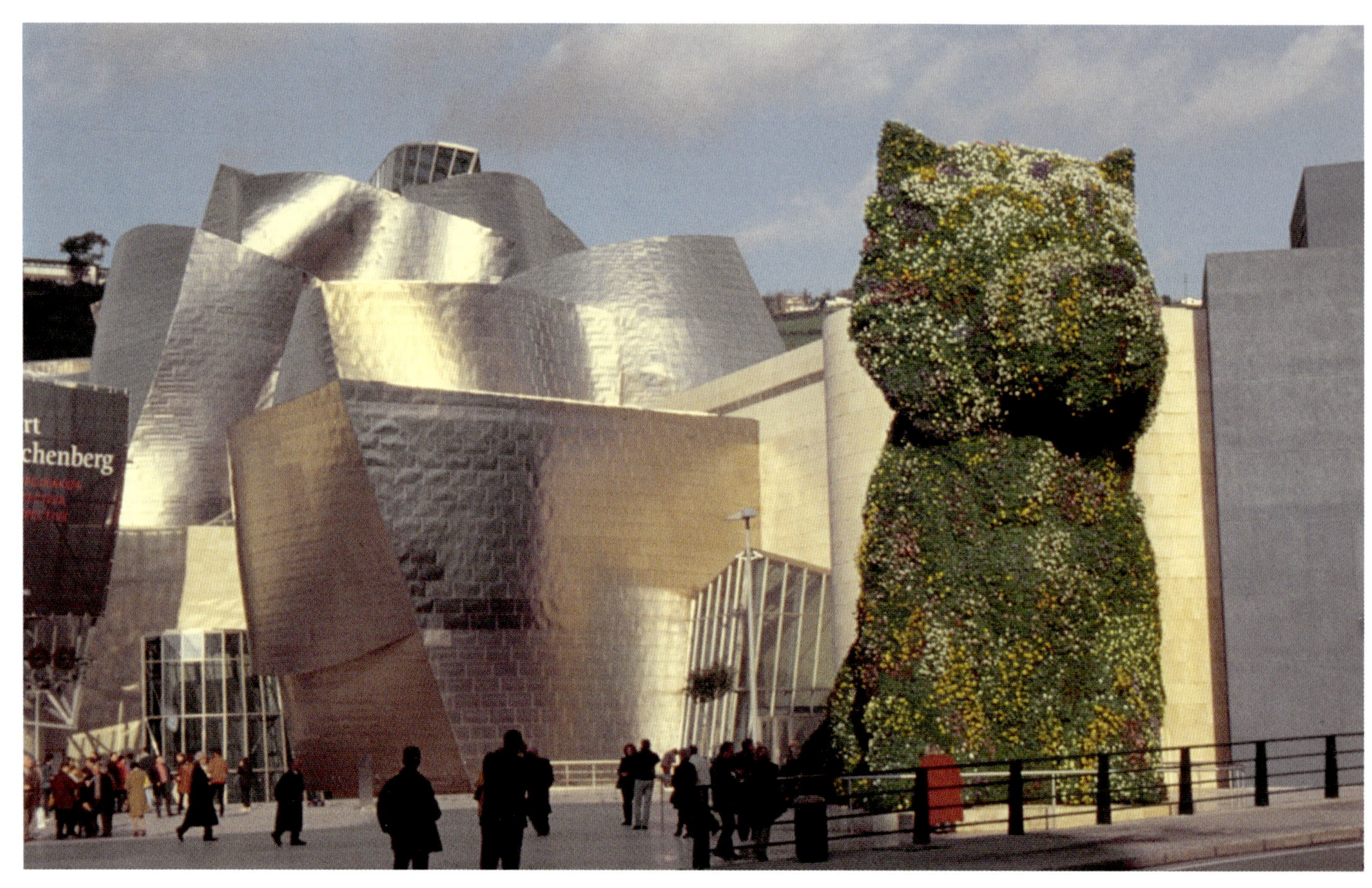

Jeff Koons, *Puppy*, 1992
Flowering plants, steel, wood and earth,
11.5 × 4.8 × 6 m ($452\frac{7}{8}$ × 189 × $236\frac{1}{4}$ in.)

We sit, as she asks, at an old table and imagine the old man's ruminations and her fears. As an experience, it was far more complex, compelling and challenging than any museum audio guide. It was like sharing another person's consciousness.

Among the other artists taking part in the third Skulptur Projekte Münster was the Turkish artist Ayşe Erkmen, who made three proposals for interventions in, or 'alterations' to, the city's cathedral: a large clock on the rose window; red covers over some of the windows, changed on festival days; and a cluster of street lamps where the old entrance to the cathedral (destroyed by bombing) had been. But each proposal was rejected. Undeterred, Erkmen hired a helicopter to fly old sculptures from the local museum through the air space above the cathedral – which the cathedral authorities had no jurisdiction over. The event had effectively replaced the object.

Although the organizers of the 1997 Skulptur Projekte Münster boasted that the exhibition now featured more than seventy artists from twenty-five countries, all the artists born in Asia, Latin America or the old Eastern Bloc – with the exception of two from Tokyo – now lived in the West. The art world might have been getting more global, but it was a definite advantage to work in New York, London or Berlin. Fifteen of the artists, however, were female, as against none in 1977 and six in 1987. The world was changing.

Four years after making her Münster walk, Janet Cardiff made a work that many have found profoundly moving (page 149). She asked Salisbury Cathedral Choir (the first cathedral choir to include girls) to sing the famous forty-part motet by Thomas Tallis, *Spem in alium* (1556–70) – a prayer for forgiveness, and a work of great beauty but testing complexity. She recorded each voice separately so that, when played back on forty speakers, one can wander from one to another as if wandering among the choir, listening to each individual voice. As with the words that introduce Cardiff's walks – 'Come walk with me' – it is a strangely intimate experience, especially because, before the singers start singing, we hear them chatting: the men about great recordings, the girls about what they will have for supper.

Was art for the community at large, oneself or one's soul? Some believed it was all for the market, which, at the end of the 1990s, was booming again. In May 1998, a 1964 Warhol painting of Marilyn Monroe sold for $17,327,500, the second highest price ever paid for a contemporary work of art. 'In this climate,' purred Tobias Meyer, Sotheby's then director of contemporary art, 'clients are recognizing that the value of a key Warhol, for example, is equivalent to that of a key Picasso. High calibre artists of this century are beginning to be appreciated and priced on a similar level.'[31]

If there was a landmark work of art for this period, it was the glittering and spectacular Guggenheim museum in Bilbao designed by Frank Gehry (opposite), with its trademark Jeff Koons sculpture of a giant puppy covered by flowers, outside. Once cities had built grand cathedrals or town halls to show their civic pride and ambition (and wealth); now they built museums.

Chapter 7

THE SPECTACULAR OR THE EVERYDAY?

2000–2004

There have always been artists who are attentive to the ordinary things of everyday life. There have also always been artists who yearn to make something spectacular; and sometimes there have been patrons wealthy enough to commission and house such works. The Guggenheim Museum in Bilbao – not, many people thought, actually a very good space to show art in – epitomized this desire for the spectacular work or landmark building. Perhaps never before had so many large and spectacular works been made as at this time: Antony Gormley's *Angel of the North*, Olafur Eliasson's *Weather Project*, Matthew Barney's extraordinary *Cremaster* film cycle. However, at the same time, many artists were instead concerned with everyday things and experience: Doris Salcedo's worn and domestically sized sculptures, Meschac Gaba's libraries, Thomas Hirschhorn's cheaply made structures.

Which best represented the time? And would it be artists who would speak for it? For this was also the zenith of the curator as major protagonist, or as author in their own right. Indicatively, before the 1990s there had been scarcely any postgraduate courses on curating; now there were several, and more opening

The destruction of the Twin Towers in New York on 11 September 2001 was such a shocking and spectacular event that it seemed it must be the landmark for a new era. Inevitably, as documenta 11 opened in the following year, its curator, the Nigerian Okwui Enwezor, had to respond. The opening pages of the catalogue are given over to colour photographs of people in South Africa demanding HIV medication, Iranians protesting against press censorship, Slobodan Milošević facing a war-crimes tribunal at The Hague, a child making chalk drawings of passenger jets on the pavement following 9/11, and so on. The reproductions were deliberately low-grade, as though printed in a cheap newspaper or sent over the wire.

This was a very different documenta from any previous edition. Curated for the first time by someone neither white nor European, it was both more avowedly global and more political. It featured far more documentary films (one estimate was that it would have taken 600 hours to see them all) and photographs than ever before. It was also very concerned about connecting with people outside Kassel via the Internet.

The exhibition did not just consist of artworks: in four conferences, or 'platforms', staged around the world before the exhibition opened, current critical issues were discussed – democracy, truth, reconciliation, creolization, income inequality, etc. In the long and dense essay with which Enwezor opened the text element of the catalogue, he insisted that art was not autonomous; it was always about societal change.

If you had wandered into one of the exhibition buildings, the documenta Halle, you might have been unsure as to whether what you saw was a somewhat chaotic library or an artwork. It was in fact both. Odd things gave it away: a computer with a bike attached to it, as if one might need to recharge the batteries in the event of a power cut by pedalling; burnt books attached to candelabra hanging above the tables (opposite). Speaking before the exhibition, Meschac Gaba, maker of this work, talked both about the lack of contemporary art museums in Africa and about how museums or galleries were not enough in themselves: 'There is a sort of museum in my own imagination. And I also wonder what my role would be if this museum existed. My museum of contemporary African art has no walls. I want to show artists that you can show work everywhere, you can do it on your own. Have the courage to decide for yourself who you are. I've done the *Draft Room*, the *Museum Architecture*, the *Museum Shop*, the *Summer Collection*, the *Game Room*, the *Art and Religion Room*, the *Music Room*, the *Restaurant* and the *Marriage Room*. I am now doing the *Library*.' Asked why there was no room for a collection, he laughed. 'It's an empty museum, but rich in philosophy. My museum doesn't exist. It's only a question.'[1]

In 2012, for an exhibition in Paris, Gaba added a salon to the museum, filling it with bric-a-brac he had found in France. 'An individual's culture truly begins with everything he has seen and experienced,' he explained. 'So, when I refer to culture, I am thinking of my own experience. I am mobile, I travel, from Benin to Rotterdam, from New York to Japan ... My culture is everything I experience, everything I see.'[2] Like other African artists, Gaba doesn't want to be constrained by tradition; he is not a *magicien de la terre*. Spending half the year in Rotterdam, half in Benin, his experience, like that of so many other artists today, is transnational, polyglot.

Works such as Gaba's library at documenta also epitomize a major problem in contemporary exhibitions: to fully appreciate or understand the work, one should sit down and read for, say, two hours. But how can you devote so much time to one work when, at the likes of documenta, there are other sites and perhaps two hundred other artists to discover? Very few people can spend more than three days at such an event.

Before the opening of Tate Modern in 2000, a number of seminars were held in which curators and architects discussed their vision for the gallery. Some of the Tate's staff talked of the 'Wow!' effect they wanted visitors to have when they walked into the old power station and were confronted by an enormous void, some 35 metres (115 ft) high and 155 metres (500 ft) long. This vast space, the former power station's turbine hall, has since become the venue every year for a specially commissioned work of art.

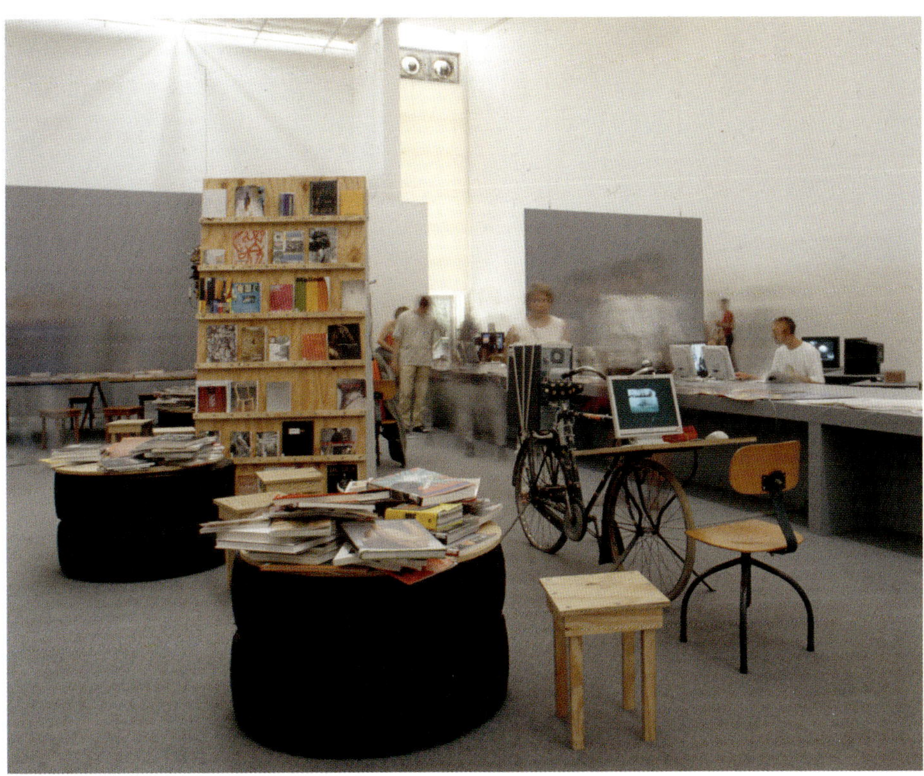

Meschac Gaba, *Museum of Contemporary African Art*, Library, 2002
Installation view, documenta 11, Kassel, Germany, 2002

Did the Danish-Icelandic artist Olafur Eliasson want people to go 'Wow!' when they saw his *Weather Project* in the turbine hall in 2003 (page 157)? Probably not. What mattered to him was a more complicated and conscious reaction.

What people saw first was a giant sun at the far end of the hall; a welcome sight in London during the winter! Indeed, many of the 2 million people who came to see the work opted to lie down in front of it, as if they were at the beach – a sort of comfortable New Age experience, perhaps? 'What interests me,' Eliasson has said, 'is that I think there is often a discrepancy between the experience of seeing and the knowledge or expectation of what we are seeing ... If the installation is working well it supports not only the immediate experience – the experience of the spectator with the installation – but also the spectator's ability to see her or himself in that particular situation. And that means you will have the opportunity to see yourself seeing. And this is where you can see this discrepancy.'[3]

If you and the sunbathers had looked up, you would have seen yourselves reflected, for the ceiling had been covered in reflective foil. And if you had looked harder at the 'sun', you would have seen that the top half of it was actually its reflection in the foil, that its light came from sodium street lights, and that the haze drifting around the hall was artificial fog. The installation was not just an illusion, but an illusion about illusion – a 'device for the experience of reality', as Eliasson once described it.[4] You could enjoy the installation simply as spectacle, or begin to think about how and why it was made, and why it was called *The Weather Project*.

In a text given to visitors at one of his earlier installations, Eliasson asked: 'Before entering the exhibition, did you notice the weather outside?'[5] The artist's work, which is increasingly about ecology, is intended to challenge our consciousness, to make us aware of our ability to look and, indeed, act. As he said of a later work that had you looking out of a museum at the city outside through glass tinted with the full spectrum of colours: 'A city is a cosmos, a site for social encounters and cohabitations. A museum is a vision machine that challenges our senses, thoughts and felt opinions. The public, you, is a barometer of the world. You mould as much as you create.'[6]

The *Cremaster Cycle* (1994–2002; page 158) of the American artist Matthew Barney is indeed spectacular. A set of five, consecutive feature-length films with a total running time of seven hours but only ten lines of dialogue, it is also painfully slow. When it was shown at the Guggenheim Museum, New York – complete with giant screens hanging from the ceiling and installations (live birds *et al.*) from the films, drawings, photographs and sculptures – it certainly had the 'Wow!' factor. To some people, these additional elements are too much like the merchandise you might buy when taking your child to see a *Star Wars* film – albeit much larger and far more expensive. Barney claims that the sculptures are what the work is all about, and that the film cycle is a sculpture too. I would go along with those who see the sculptures and installations as like film sets: best seen from a distance. The films themselves are the thing. The plot – a kind of extended parable on (a) how the cremaster muscle raises and lowers the testicles, and (b) how gender is determined in the foetus – is complicated. As Norman Mailer, who starred in one of the films, said: 'For people who want to follow the story, it's hopeless, they'll hate the work. But there's an intensity of perception, and a visceral experience you have when you watch this stuff which is extraordinary.'[7]

However, the exhibition as a whole was also seductively glamorous, especially as part of the third film in the sequence had been shot at the Guggenheim. In the film, Barney himself, who once aspired to be an athlete, climbs up the inside of the museum while wearing a kilt and a preposterous pink bearskin hat. Like a knight on a quest, he encounters obstacles on his journey: a chorus line of girls dressed as lambs, two heavy-metal rock bands playing loud, an amputee fashion model who transforms into a cheetah, an architect (played by Richard Serra) whom he, Barney the apprentice, must for some reason kill.

If you happen to be in England, driving north along the A1 towards Newcastle, you will probably spot Antony Gormley's *Angel of the North* (page 159) well before you get there. You may decide to stop and take a closer look. Having parked your

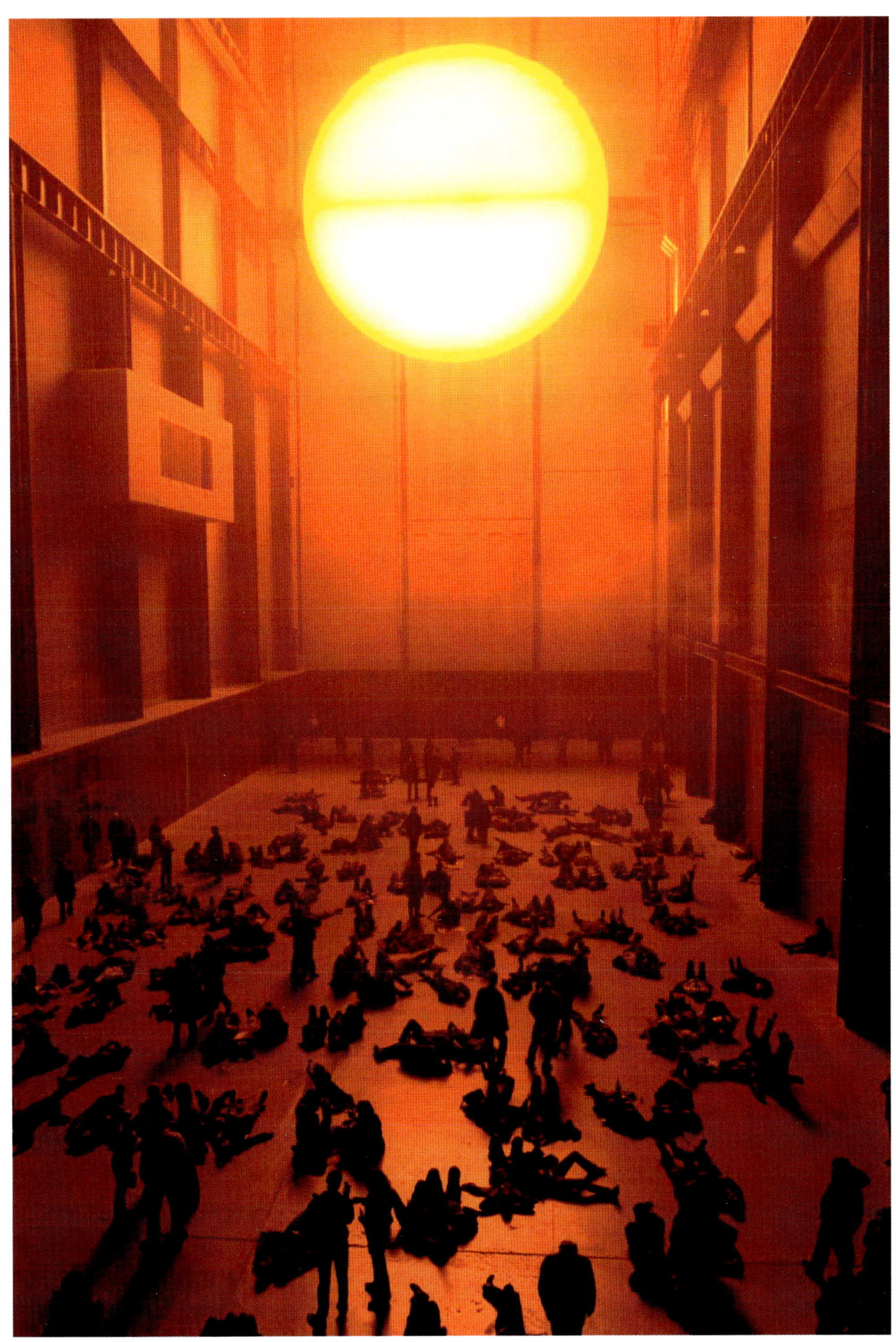

Olafur Eliasson, *The Weather Project*, 2003
Monofrequency lights, projection foil, haze machine, mirror foil, aluminium, scaffolding; installation in Turbine Hall, Tate Modern, London

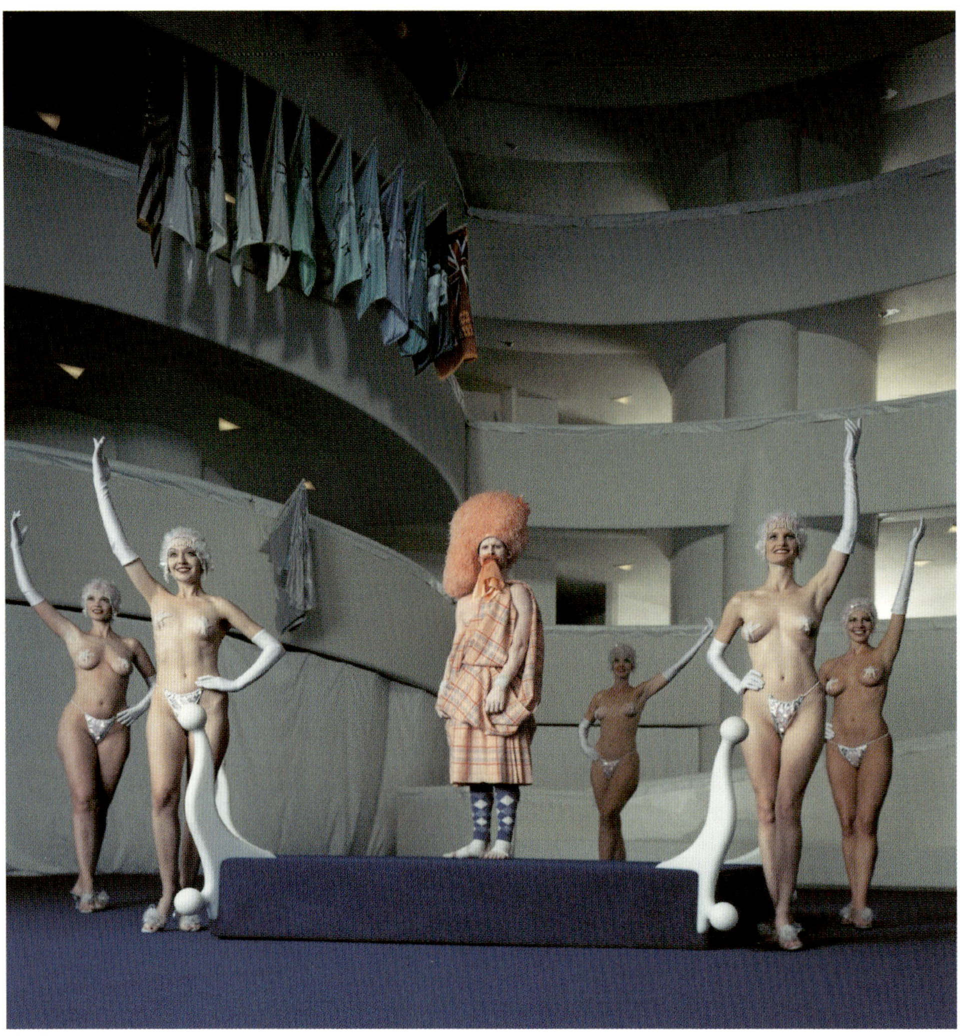

Matthew Barney, *Cremaster 3*, 2002
Filmed at the Guggenheim Museum, New York; production still

car, you will find other people there. Many of them will be carefully examining the plaque that tells how the sculpture was built: 500 tons of concrete as a foundation, anchored to the rock 21 metres (69 ft) below the surface, the sculpture itself made with 200 tons of Corten steel. Chances are that they will then walk down the slope in front of the sculpture, stand up straight, extend their arms like the angel's wings, and be photographed.

When it was being built, the angel was condemned by many as an expensive folly (it cost £800,000) in an area blighted by post-industrial unemployment (it is built on the site of a former coal mine), but the local community has taken to it. As a sign of its acceptance, a number of Newcastle United fans managed to put

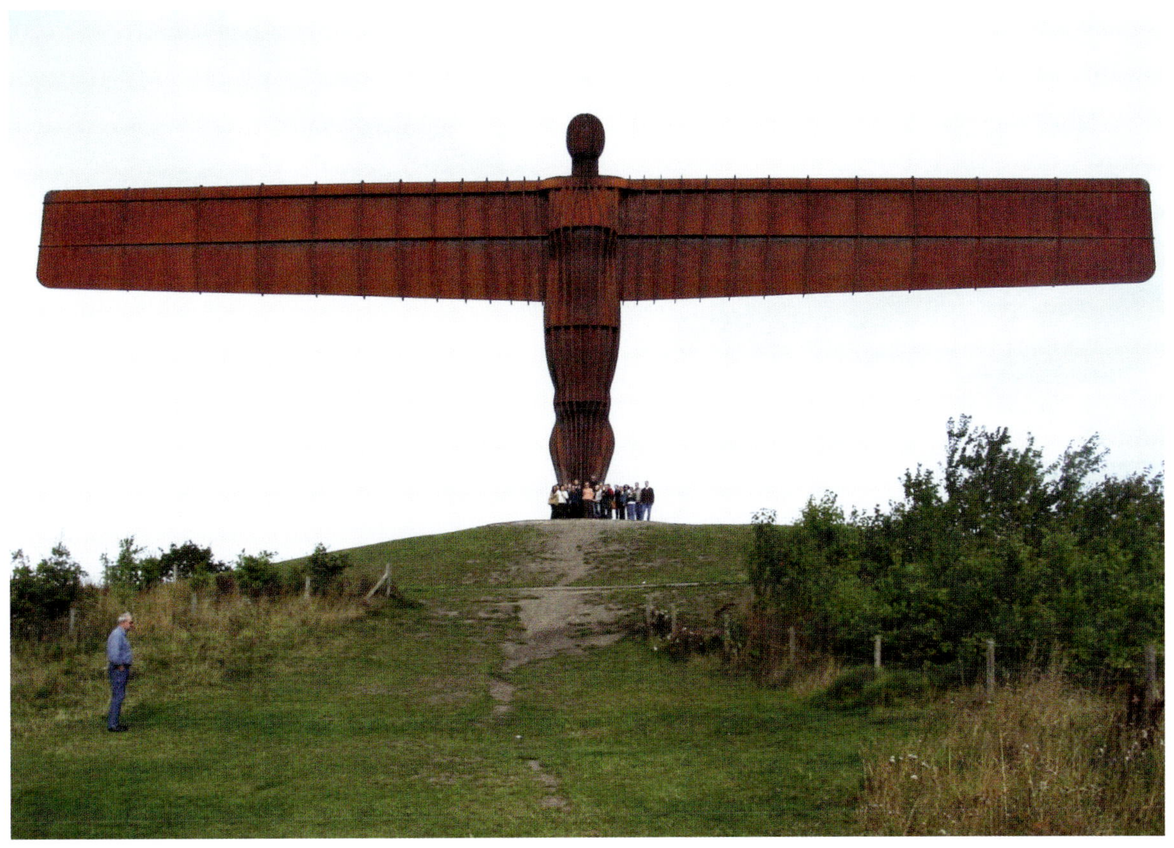

Anthony Gormley, *Angel of the North*, 1998
Reinforced steel, 20 × 54 m (787½ x 2,126 in.)

a giant football shirt on it, emblazoned with the name and number of the local sporting hero, Alan Shearer. Perhaps not quite the reflective response Gormley was looking for. 'We need sculpture more now than at any other time,' he said a few years later, 'simply because it is a still moment in a moving world that asks the question, "What are you doing here?"'[8]

Gormley's work has always been about the body: how we understand space through the body; how the body is, in effect, a place. Although *Angel of the North* is large, Gormley does not want it to be monumental. As he has said: 'Playing on scale (which is not the same as size) makes us feel our bodies-in-the-world.'[9] On other occasions he has made figures small enough to hold in your hand, such as the thousands of terracotta figures deployed in his 'Field' works. In another project, variously titled *Another Place* (1997), *Time Horizon* (2006) and *Horizon Field* (2010–12), he took 100 life-size upright iron figures and placed them, respectively, on a beach where the incoming and outgoing tide conceals and reveals them; in an olive grove, some half-buried, some on plinths; and spread across slopes of the Austrian Alps. On each occasion he wanted to make us more aware of the space they, and we, are standing in.

Apart from shrinking, enlarging and multiplying the human figure, Gormley casts it, reduces it to rectangular blocks and turns it into negative space in concrete blocks – all for much the same reason: 'I suppose all these projects are trying to make the everyday strange, so that you see it again in a new way.'[10] The stillness of Gormley's figures is crucial: they sit, lie or stand, but never walk. In this respect his work is akin to Buddhist and Jain sculptors, who rarely portray the Buddha or saints in motion. Although Richard Serra's work is always abstract, Gormley admires it; they have an equal obsession with stasis and absolute weight (Gormley's life-size iron figures each weigh 750 kilograms/1,653 lbs).

It may seem as though Gormley, who has peppered the world with very large and very heavy objects, and Susan Philipsz, who leaves no trace on the landscape save the sound of her voice and perhaps some carefully concealed audio equipment, have little in common, but they are both concerned with a sense of place. What they do with place, however, is very different. To a certain degree, every work by Gormley has the same focus: one's sense of being a body in space, and stillness as a spiritual or quasi-spiritual experience. It is the stories and histories of a particular place that interest Philipsz.

Although Philipsz uses sound in her work, she is not a 'sound artist': the audio she adds to a particular context is to be experienced simultaneously with being in that context. So the work we discussed in the introduction (page 22) was as much about the derelict industrial space it was installed in as 'The Internationale'. Originally, that work had been made for Manifesta 3 (2000), held in Ljubljana, Slovenia, where it played under a public walkway in the city centre. Philipsz chose the song because, when delivered in her voice, its meaning became ambiguous: was it a rallying call to political action or a lament to the past? Only a few years previously, Slovenia had gained independence from communist Yugoslavia. 'One of my enduring memories [of Slovenia]', said Philipsz, 'was seeing a group of elderly women standing stock still silhouetted in the underpass, humming along to it. One of them was crying. It was amazing.'[11] That could not have happened in Sydney: the work changes with a new context.

Philipsz's work for the fourth Skulptur Projekte Münster in 2007, *The Lost Reflection* (opposite), was made in response to a footpath that wound its way around a romantic lake and beneath a bridge. Like many works for the Skulptur Projekte, it has become a permanent fixture. 'Lovely night, oh night of love, smile upon our

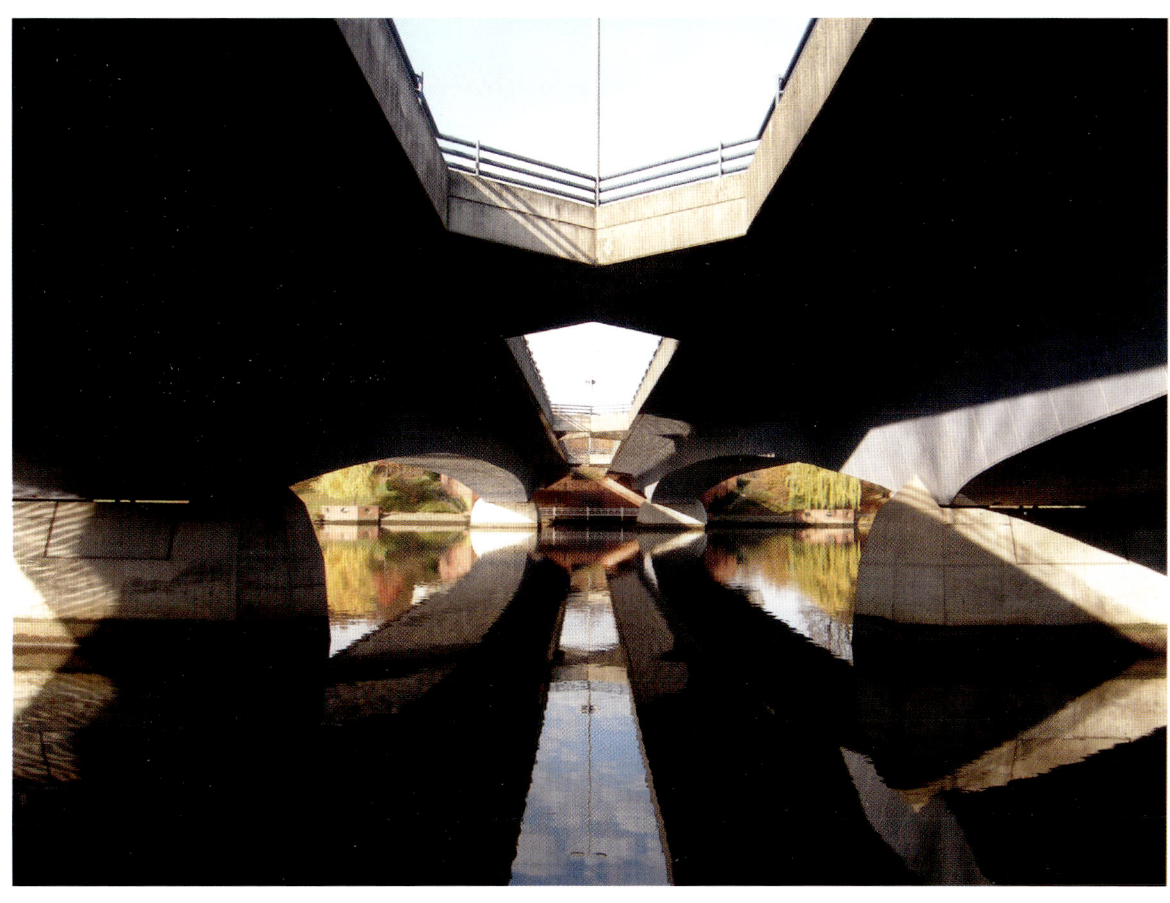

Susan Philipsz, *The Lost Reflection*, 2007
Two-channel sound installation, 2:05 minutes

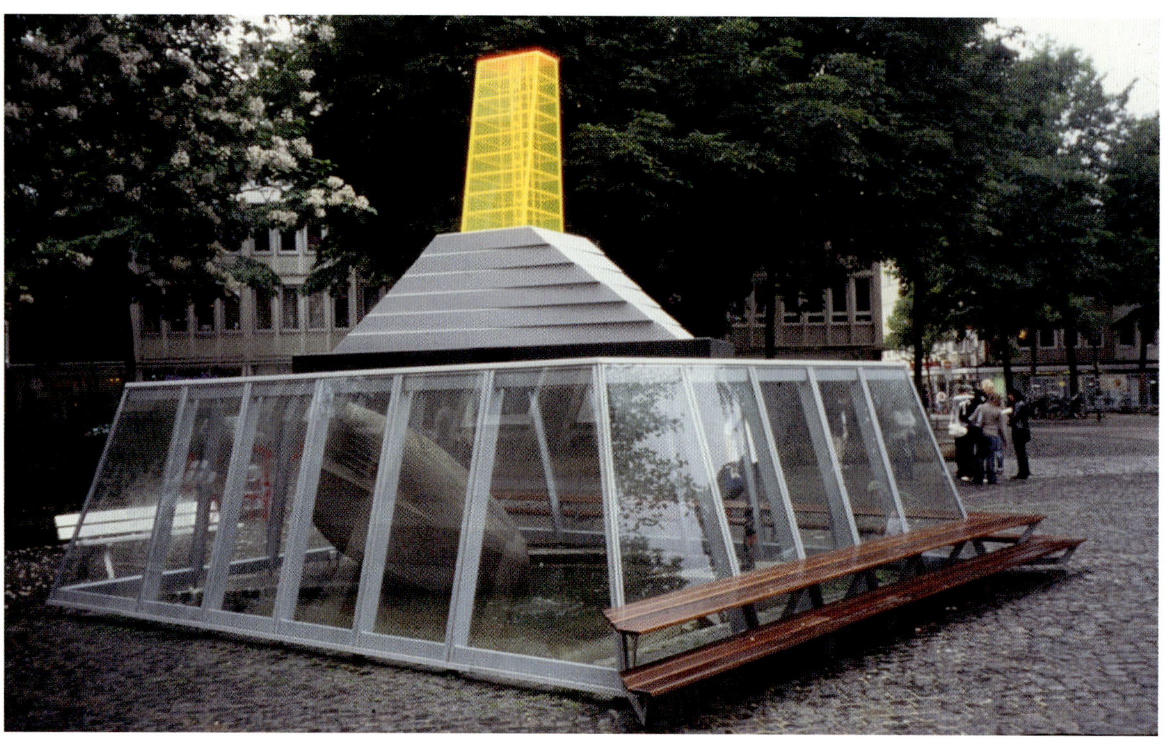

Thomas Schütte, *Model for a Museum*, 1980–2007
Installed at Skulptur Projekte Münster, 2007

joys', a soprano seems to sing (it is in fact a recording) under the bridge on one side of the lake. 'Time flies by, and carries away our tender caresses for ever! Time flies far from this happy oasis and does not return', the voice of a mezzo-soprano replies from the other side. If you are an opera or film buff, you might recognize this as the famous duet in Offenbach's opera *The Tales of Hoffmann* – as filmed by Powell and Pressburger in 1951 – in which Giulietta, a Venetian woman standing in a gondola, sings a duet with her mirror image. But even if you aren't, you will pause, listen and look at the reflections on the water. 'It's all about how the emotive and psychological effects of sound can heighten your awareness of the space you are in,' Philipsz tells us.[12] She has a decent voice, able to sing both parts, but it is not at a professional level: she doesn't want to impress us with her virtuosity, and would rather we relate to it as we would to a friend or neighbour singing.[13]

As we saw in Chapter 4, in 1987 Thomas Schütte had made a sculpture for a car park, and had then been infuriated when the context for the work was radically altered. Twenty years later he was allowed some revenge. Part of the municipal facelift of the square had been the addition of a fountain. Described by the Skulptur Projekte Münster's curators as 'misconceived' and a 'banal design element', they invited Schütte to cover it up. He turned to a project he had been working on since

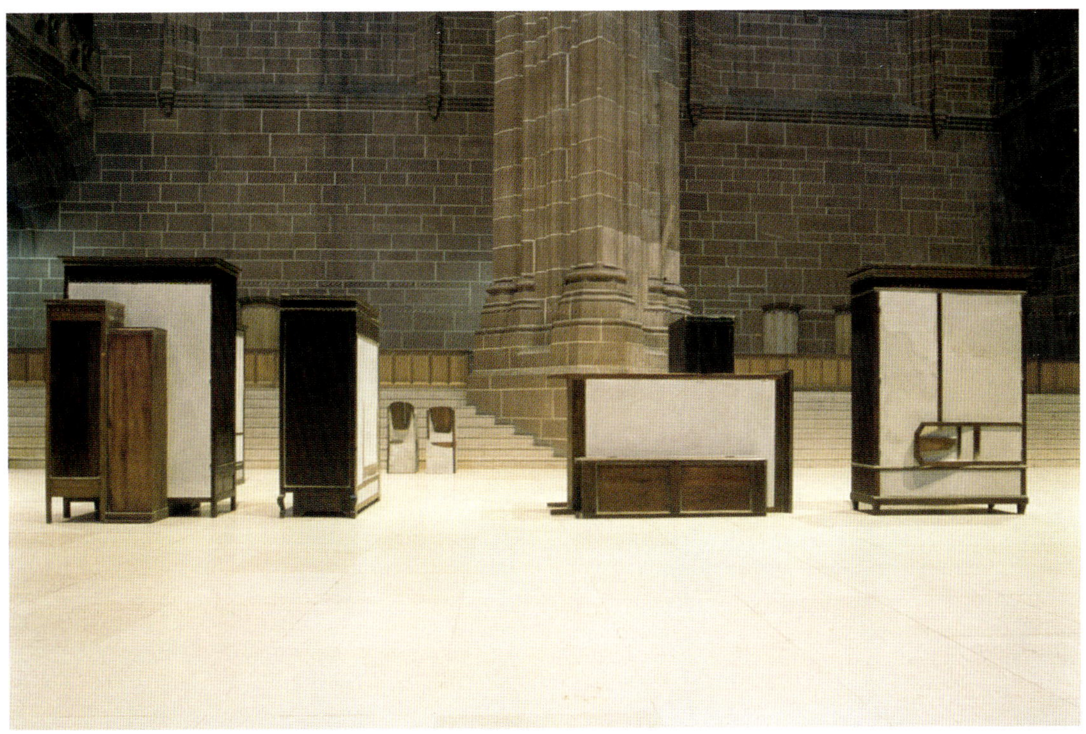

Doris Salcedo, untitled series, 1989–98
Installation view, Liverpool Anglican Cathedral, for Liverpool Biennial 1999

the early 1980s: *Model for a Museum* (opposite). When first exhibited as a miniature model, it had been shown alongside paintings of Auschwitz-like furnaces, suggesting that the 'museum' was perhaps dedicated to the destruction rather than preservation of artworks. Whether we should see the yellow Plexiglas tower as an administrative block or a chimney is uncertain. Such ambiguity or uncomfortableness is typical of Schütte.

Installed over the fountain for the duration of the sculpture exhibition, this new *Model for a Museum* was both useful – it had seats attached – and puzzling. Was the little bronze figure inside the structure contemplating the big stone element of the fountain or mocking it? The work was deliberately problematic, and without the witty charm of Schütte's original cherries: it sat awkwardly in the square, challenging its complacency.

If Schütte's sculpture sat in the square like an uninvited heckler, the untitled sculptures installed in the cavernous space of Liverpool's Anglican cathedral in 1999 by Doris Salcedo (above) seemed more like homeless people invited in and given succour. Old beds, chairs and wardrobes stuck together, filled with concrete, sometimes with fabric embedded in them, as though old clothes had become trapped there. The domesticity of the objects, their signs of use, their silence, were accentuated by space. (The organ was also playing when I visited, which probably contributed to my profound emotional response – a sense of loss, mourning but also solace.)

Salcedo's work always begins with her talking to the victims of violence, in this case of the ongoing civil war in her own country, Colombia. Objects that once belonged to victims – clothes, hair, shoes, furniture – are often integrated into her sculptures: 'When a beloved person disappears, everything becomes impregnated with that person's presence. Every single object but also every space is a reminder of his or her absence, as if absence were stronger than presence.'[14] Even if you didn't know the specific context, these sculptures still conveyed a sense of loss, of furniture turned into gravestones, everyday materials made monumental. The beauty of the work also becomes part of the act of mourning.

Salcedo's art is political but non-sectarian. Talking in 2018, in this instance about works relating to victims of rape and migrants who died crossing the Mediterranean, she said: 'I am an artist and I believe in art. I don't think art will save a life nor give consolation to the survivors, nor solve the economic crisis in any country. Art cannot do that but it gives us dignity. It restores to us some sense of humanity, of brotherhood.'[15] It had been important to Salcedo, when she first left Colombia, to research Joseph Beuys and his notions of 'social sculpture'; it was also important to her to experience being a 'foreigner' and, on returning to Colombia, to continue to feel displaced.

In 2001, in the central space of the Belgian pavilion at the Venice Biennale, Luc Tuymans exhibited ten paintings. Initially, they seemed to be unconnected. Next to a painting of a white man in a white uniform (opposite) was a painting of a church; on other walls were paintings of a leopard skin, two black people looking down from an apartment block, a black man wearing glasses, four black men in discussion, large cars stopped under trees. If you had just wandered in and looked around cursorily, you might have enjoyed the rather faded colours – he has a very low-key palette – and found the painting evocative, but enigmatic. But if you had paused for just a moment and noted the title of Tuymans' show, 'Mwana Kitoko – Beautiful White Man', and then realized this was also the title of the painting of the man in white, you would probably have deduced this was all about Africa, or more specifically the Congo.

If you were already aware that Tuymans's work is always about memory, but where any sense of nostalgia is quickly displaced by that of trauma, you probably wanted to know more. Tuymans has talked of how, 'From the beginning, I had this idea about painting as a sort of antique.'[16] He has also talked of how impossible it is to make something wholly original: 'All you can do is make an authentic forgery. I wanted the paintings to look old from the start, which is important because they are about memory.'[17] Tuymans's paintings are often derived from old photographs or reproductions, usually in a degraded state; he used to work from Polaroids, as they carried less information and gave him more freedom. To some extent, the 'Mwana Kitoko' series was also a response to Gerhard Richter's series 'October 18,

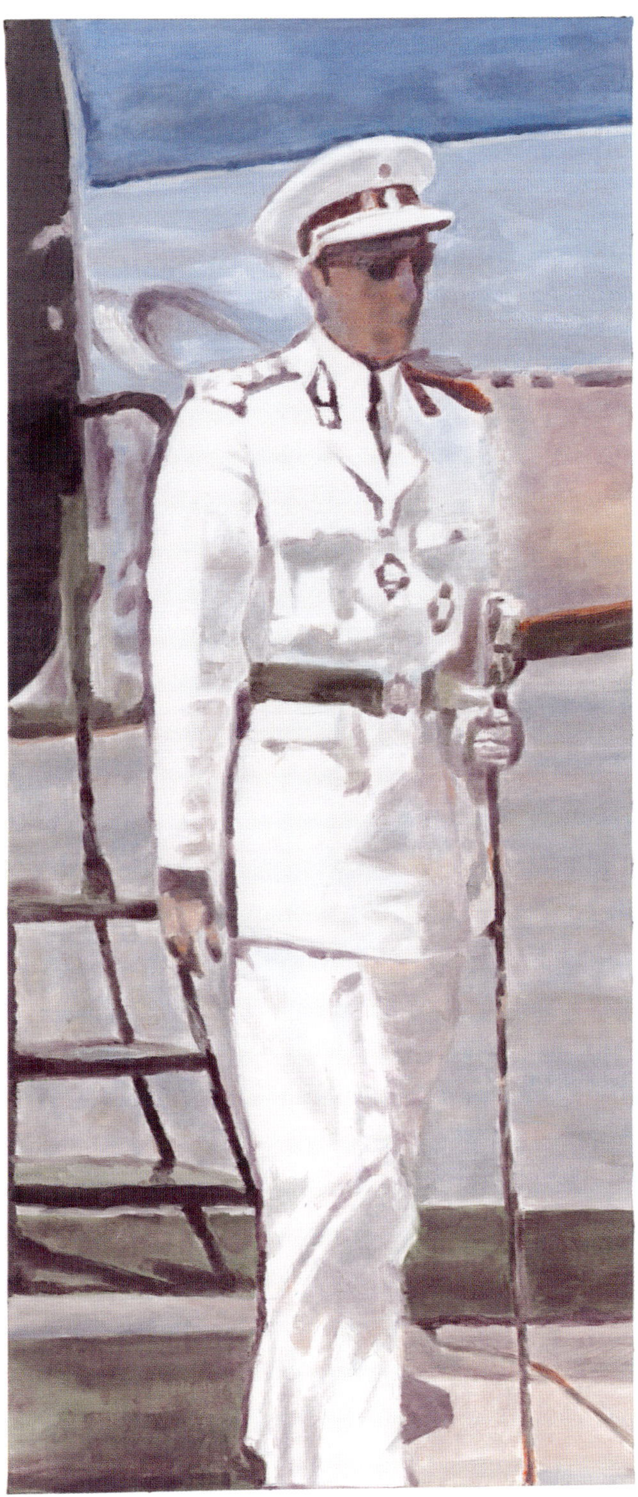

Luc Tuymans, *Mwana Kitoko*, 2000
Oil on canvas, 208 × 88 cm (82 × 34¾ in.)

1977' (page 125). But Tuymans's images never look like photographs; they are very clearly painted by hand. If Richter's series exudes the chill of a memorial chapel, Tuymans's sets up something more like a seminar room.

The 'Mwana Kitoko' paintings are composed of scenes from the history of the Belgian Congo, presented like antiques. The man in white is a young Baudouin I, king of the Belgians, shown arriving in the Congo in 1955 and presenting himself as *bwana kitoko*, 'beautiful master'. In the other paintings, the church is a mission, the tower block an apartment building in Leopoldville, a town named after the nineteenth-century king of Belgium who saw the Congo as his personal property to be exploited. The black man with glasses is the charismatic but erratic Patrice Lumumba, who in 1960 became the first prime minister of the independent Democratic Republic of the Congo, but who was captured with Belgian assistance by a rival faction, tortured and eventually shot.

Tuymans's paintings do not constitute a history lesson, but – understated though they are – they do lead you to one. They were effectively part of an official debate in Belgium about the country's role in the Congo, especially its connivance in the murder of Lumumba. More generally, they are about colonial bad conscience.

Whereas Salcedo uses everyday materials to enact mourning, Tuymans uses banal or everyday images to register trauma: in one of the paintings from the 'Mwana

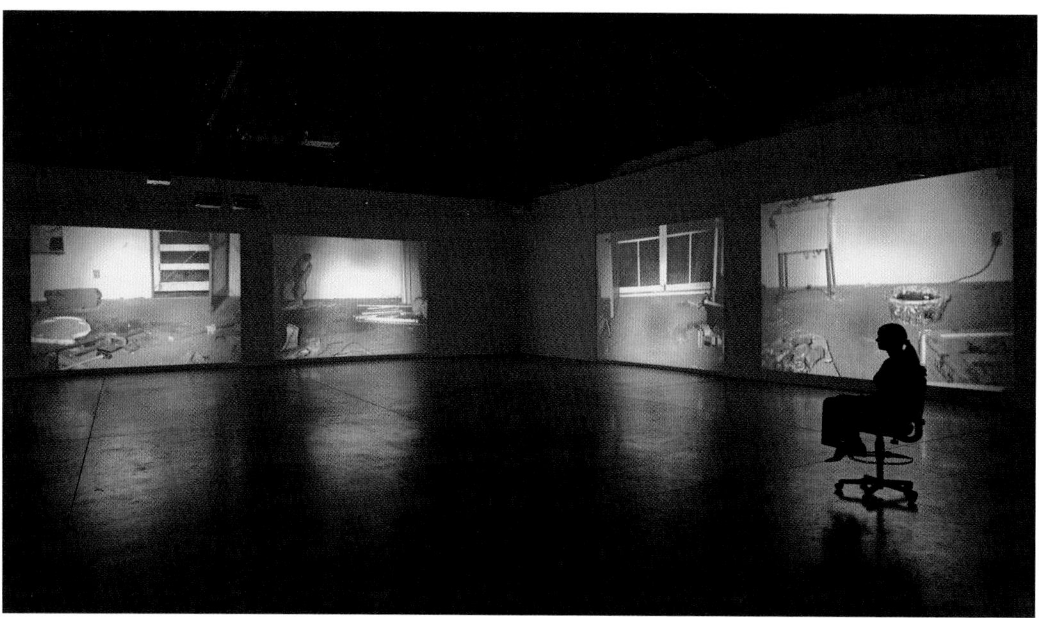

Bruce Nauman, *Mapping the Studio I (Fat Chance John Cage)*, 2001
Video installation with 7 DVDs, 7 DVD players, 7 projectors, 7 pairs of speakers, as installed at Dia:Chelsea, New York, 2002

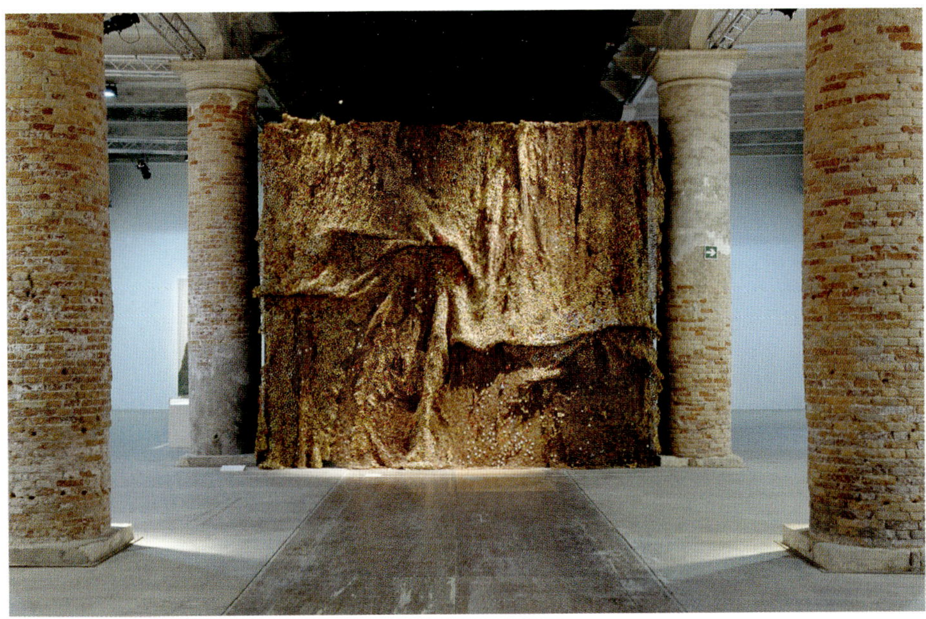

El Anatsui, *Dusasa II*, 2007
Found aluminium and copper wire, 546.1 × 655.3 cm (215 × 258 in.), installation view, Venice Biennale

Kitoko' series, *Chalk*, we see two white objects in a man's outstretched hands. In fact, they are probably the two teeth with gold fillings that were reputedly extracted from Lumumba's corpse before it was dropped in an acid bath.

The Ghanaian sculptor El Anatsui, with the help of up to twenty assistants, will flatten aluminium bottle tops and string them together with wire. These are then formed into large – often very large – sculptures. Perhaps we can call them metal tapestries. They are very attractive, and much sought after by collectors; indeed, Anatsui may now be the best-selling African artist. There is surprisingly little interest in his career before 2000, which is when he started working with bottle tops, but from the 1960s he had been working with wood or broken pots in ways that took from both traditional African modes and modernism.

Speaking in 2006, Anatsui said: 'People at times see my works without any knowledge of their context or even their titles, and they create their own meanings out of them. Some interpretations reveal how close we are as humans. I would agree that context is both an aid and a hindrance. In certain ways, it helps to anchor a message, and depending on the viewer's capacity and experience, he could go from there to expand or simply stop. I don't think that I define myself strictly in a locational context.'[18] He is relaxed about these differing interpretations, often titling his pieces in his own language, Ewe, knowing few people will understand it.

Much of Anatsui's work has been about using everyday things: 'I look for things that are immediately available, thereby sustaining my practice. I am drawn more to materials that have been subjected to considerable human use: mortars, trays, graters, tins, and, of late, liquor bottle tops.'[19] Their history is important to him: 'I wanted to work with materials that had been used, that people had put their hands on ... When working with materials that have such history, the process has some kind of connective energy: the energy of all the people who have interacted with them.'[20] But he wants to make them new again: 'In my practice, I transform the media; I give them a new lease on life ... My processes are rather basic too, very much a part of everyday life. Working with bottle caps requires the most rudimentary of means.'[21] Behind everything Anatsui does is an appeal to materials, to things he can find and, as he notes, transform.

In 1973 Bruce Nauman stopped making films and videos. Fifteen years later, he started making them again, but not of himself. Instead, he filmed actors in staged, often cruel or repetitive scenarios. In *Mapping the Studio* (page 166), the 'actors' are, in theory, some mice and Nauman's cat. In practice, when the work is installed properly, the viewer is the actor.

In 2001 Nauman had a problem: field mice were getting into his studio and his cat was not dealing with them. He had no new idea for a work, so he acted as he had done before and began working with whatever was in the studio: the mice. Over the course of seven evenings, Nauman placed his video camera in a different position in the studio, set it to infra-red, and let it record what happened in the darkness. He then exhibited the resulting videos, projected large and simultaneously. Each projection is almost six hours long.

Mapping the Studio was first exhibited in the largest space of the Dia Center for the Arts in New York; office chairs on wheels were provided for people to sit on. Even though almost nothing happens in the work, save for mosquitoes flickering across the screens periodically, I stayed watching for a very long time, every so often moving my chair to a different spot to watch a different set of videos. I, like the other people there, who also kept moving about, had become as much the actor as any mouse – perhaps more so. When the work has been restaged in smaller spaces, without such chairs, it has seemed less riveting. But what is it about? What is the viewer's experience? Nauman has often said that his work is about frustration.[22] Frustration and fascination, which are two major aspects of daily life. The work is a structured compendium of everyday experiences: waiting, watching and, at least at Dia, sitting on an office chair.

For Thomas Hirschhorn, engagement with the everyday means not only using everyday objects – newspapers, aluminium foil, packing tape – but also engaging with everyday people. His artworks, such as *Bataille Monument* (opposite), can be spectacularly big, but in a shambolic way. They are often described as installations; he prefers the term 'kiosk' or 'display'. Like Warhol, Hirschhorn was trained in graphic

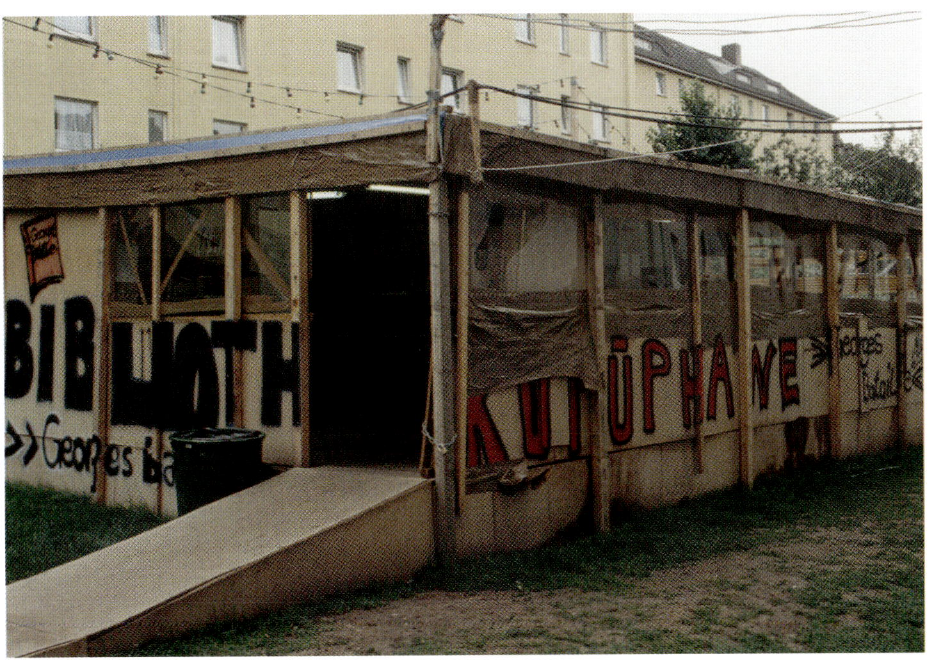

Thomas Hirschhorn, *Bataille Monument*, 2002
Installation view, documenta 11, Kassel, Germany, 2002

design but did not want to work either in advertising or for clients, but for himself. (He often refers to both Warhol and Joseph Beuys as models for his practice. What he makes can be seen as 'social sculpture', but his language owes much to Warhol's emphasis on reproducibility.) Eventually, Hirschhorn realized that being an artist does not require being trained as one, but deciding to be one: 'The decision to be an artist is the decision to be free. Freedom is the condition of responsibility. I realized that to be an artist is not a question of form or content, it's a question of responsibility.'[23]

Hirschhorn often collaborates with writers, printing or photocopying their texts and placing them in his displays, where people can read them or, sometimes, take them away to read at home or on the bus. He objects to the way exhibition catalogues have become so expensive that few can afford them; he wants to reach the broadest audience possible. Beautiful design and colour plates are not, he believes, necessary: 'What is important is the distribution of ideas, positions and manifestos, not the form and the design ... For me, Art is a tool to learn about the world, a tool to engage with reality, and a tool to experience the time I live in.'[24]

Having made monuments to the thinkers Spinoza and Gilles Deleuze, Hirschhorn decided to create one to Georges Bataille (above). He was, he said, simply a fan of these philosophers' work. Apart from a large sculpture of tree roots, made with the artist's trademark tape, foil and cardboard, the monument consisted of four improvised buildings. It was installed in a poor residential district of Kassel for

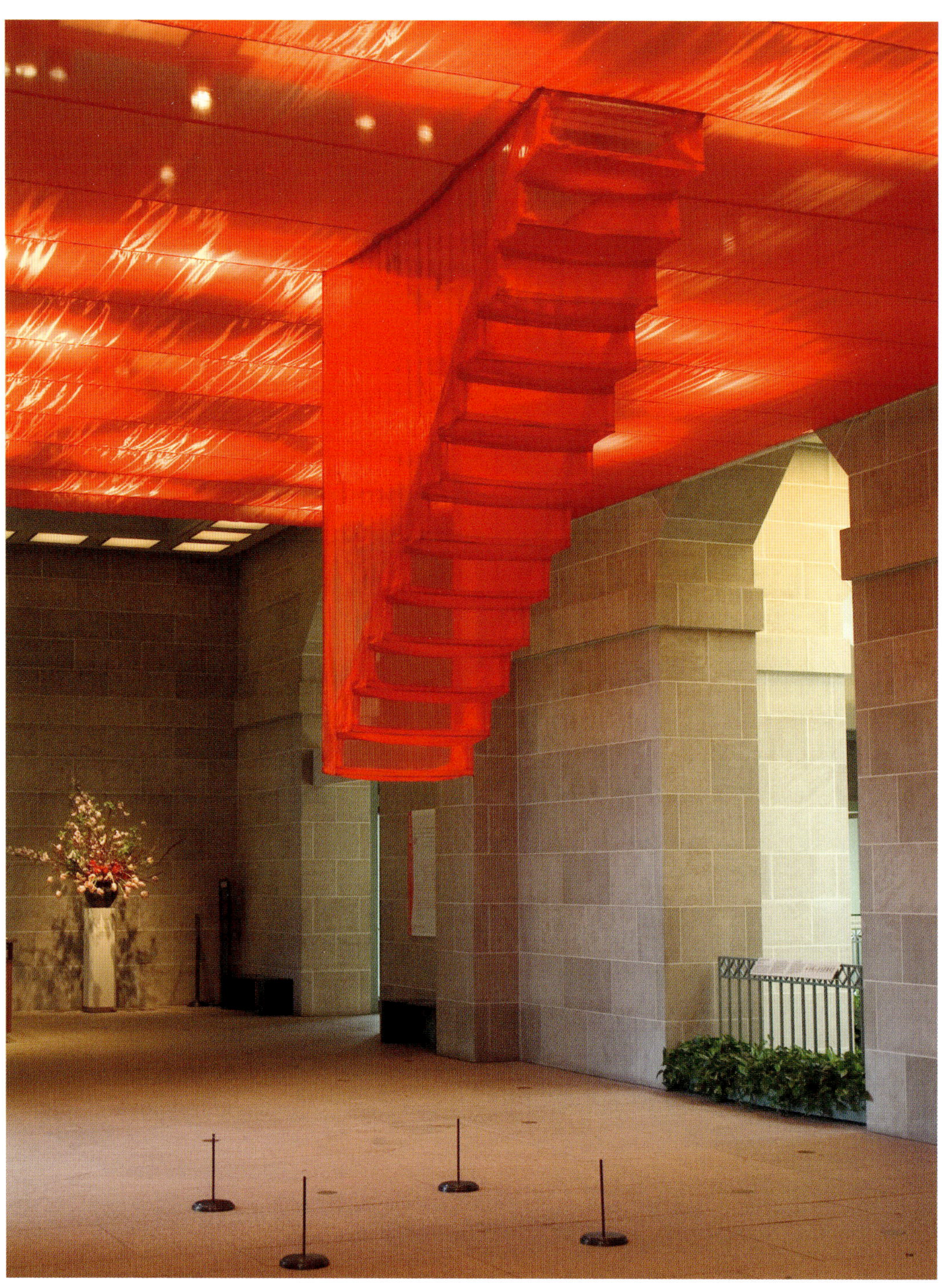

Do Ho Suh, *Staircase-IV*, 2004
Translucent nylon and stainless steel tubes, dimensions variable, installation view, Arthur M. Sackler Gallery, Washington DC, 2004

documenta 11 – with a library of Bataille's writings that Hirschhorn had provided, a snack bar, an exhibition space and a TV studio, where each day a programme was recorded to be broadcast locally – and local inhabitants were encouraged to get involved. Hirschhorn acted as 'caretaker' for the monument for the entire 100-day duration of documenta, keeping the monument open twenty-four hours a day.

In a world in which we change where we live more and more often, our home and our notion of home become both more precarious and more important. Do Ho Suh was born and raised in South Korea; in 1993, however, aged thirty-one, he moved to the United States. Since then, he has travelled back and forth between Korea and America. 'It puts you', he remarks, 'in a very alert position about your surroundings ... travelling, living in different places, is an essential component in my work.'[25] When Do moved to a very noisy neighbourhood of New York City in 1996, he began to wonder: '"When was my last time to have a really good sleep?" And that was in a small room, back in Korea. And I wanted to bring the house, somehow, to my New York apartment.' But his apartment was smaller than the house in Korea, so when he finally remade his original Korean home in 1999, he did so with fabric so it could fit inside his New York apartment. In fact, he could fold it into a suitcase and carry it with him: 'Home is something I carry with me.'[26] Speaking in 2016, Do said: 'The space I'm interested in is not only a physical one, but an intangible, metaphorical and psychological one.'[27]

Do had to measure the Korean house inch by inch because it is the small, intimate things that make a home personal. Next, he made an equivalent fabric version of his New York apartment. After that he made staircases (opposite). When we see these staircases hanging in museums or galleries, we marvel at the detailing and the way they float, as if in a dream. Even though they are not copies of stairs we have ever trod, they seem uncannily familiar. In 2016, when Do had to leave his New York apartment, he decided to 'capture the information of the space that was lacking from my fabric version ... to remember the space, and also somehow memorialise the space'.[28] To do so, he first of all covered every surface with white paper, and then rubbed the paper with coloured pencils to get an impression of the surface beneath. 'I'm trying to show the layers of time,' he explained. 'If I wrote "rubbing" in Korean, people could read it as "loving" because there's no distinction between "r" and "l" in the Korean alphabet. I think the gesture of rubbing is a very loving gesture.'[29]

We started this chapter by talking about 9/11. In fact, in terms of art and culture, 2001 was more significant for an event that was barely noticed: the decision by Google to actively farm all the surplus data it was receiving via its search engine to predict the services and goods people might want. This would soon blur into suggesting what people should both want and do. The ability of corporations and the state (by now obsessed with identifying terrorists) to invade private space and increasingly manipulate people's behaviour would soon become apparent.

Chapter 8

STORYTELLING OR ABSTRACTION?

2005–2009

Why was Victorian and academic painting so detested by modernists? Because, in short, it was slick, sentimental and told stories. Although some famous modernists, Picasso for example, had continued to draw or paint narrative situations, abstraction – pure form – had been seen as the apogee of modernist art. After modernism, could artists return to storytelling? And what of abstract painting, its apparent opposite? Had that come to an end?

Film was the great narrative form of the twentieth century and it had long fascinated artists. Indeed, the dream of many artists was to direct a film of their own, with the likes of Julian Schnabel, Cindy Sherman and Shirin Neshat actually doing so. But the big budgets demanded by film-making were way beyond the reach of most artists. Could they tell stories some other way?

In 1989 the South African artist William Kentridge made the first of what he called his 'Drawings for Projection': animations, each between 3 and 9 minutes long, made from charcoal drawings that had been patiently drawn and redrawn. They were most unlike Disney-type cartoons, with the clearly visible residue of endless drawing and rubbing-out making it obvious they were very much handmade. Each could take up to nine months to make. Kentridge produced the ninth and last of the 'Drawings for Projection' in 2003, and although he would make many other films and drawings, it was this series of works that secured his reputation. Deceptively simple, beautifully drawn and evocative, they have always been popular. In their own way, they are as charming as any cartoon; but, like daydreams, they can – and do – turn nasty.

Kentridge grew up in Johannesburg during the years of apartheid. He still lives there, confessing that, 'In the end, all my work is rooted in this rather desperate provincial town.'[1] His works did not document apartheid, but, as he himself has observed, 'were spawned by and fed off the brutalized society left in its wake'.[2] Neither are the stories that his 'Drawings for Projection' tell diatribes against apartheid; rather, they are poetic works in which the two main characters – Felix Teitlebaum, a poet-dreamer, and Soho Eckstein, a voracious but melancholy industrialist – play out their passions.

According to Kentridge, his main motivation is 'the desire to draw: the drawing does not begin as a moral project; it starts from the pleasure of putting charcoal on paper'.[3] Where Bill Viola has suggested that video can be like human consciousness, Kentridge sees drawing as a metaphor for how we think. Drawing, for him, is like 'thinking aloud'.[4] The 'Drawings for Projection' flow back and forth between dream and consciousness, the private and the public, between the internal desires of Teitlebaum or Eckstein and the history and politics of South Africa.

Kentridge has also had a long association with theatre, and the 'Drawings for Projection' have led him to installations, lectures and stage events, often combining projected film with sculptures, live acting or speaking. Such hybrid events appeal to him because of the energy they both need and unleash. They can, however, seem more cumbersome, provisional and less memorable than the simple films that made him famous.

How else can artists, normally with limited resources, make films or videos that do not seem unprofessional compared to what we can see on television or at the cinema? Alas, go to almost any biennale or art event and you will encounter videos that are painfully clumsy, boring and far, far too long. One way to make video art both totally different from a televisual or cinematic experience and workable in a gallery context is to make video installations – as Viola has and Nam June Paik did – where the video is only part of a larger whole, or where there are several related video screens or projections working together, enabling the viewer to move within the installation and become immersed in it.

The British artist Isaac Julien has said: 'I'm trying deliberately to frustrate the ontological gaze of the spectator.'[5] What does he mean? One of the most compelling video installations I have ever experienced was Julien's *Ten Thousand Waves*, a nine-screen work premiered at the 2010 Sydney Biennale. Key to my experience of the work was its installation in a large, windowless room, the only light coming from the nine projectors. Periodically they paused, and we viewers were immersed in darkness. We could walk around or lounge on beanbags. I was conscious of the many other people in the room, but they were nothing more than shadow-like presences in the dark.

The work begins with news footage of the twenty-three illegal Chinese immigrants working as cockle-pickers in Morecambe Bay, north-west England, who, in 2004, were caught and drowned by the tide. One was unlikely to enter exactly at the beginning of the fifty-minute video loop, but no problem; this was no straightforward, realistic narrative. ('I always think, "Realism – why bother?"' says Julien. 'There are other, more fruitful approaches.')[6] Additional stories were being told at the same time, one merging into another: lost Chinese sailors in the sixteenth century; a film being made in 1930s Shanghai; a woman brooding in a skyscraper in contemporary Shanghai; a calligrapher writing. Recordings of music and of poetry being read aloud combined to make the work extremely immersive. The nine screens were arranged asymmetrically around the room and at angles that meant you couldn't view all

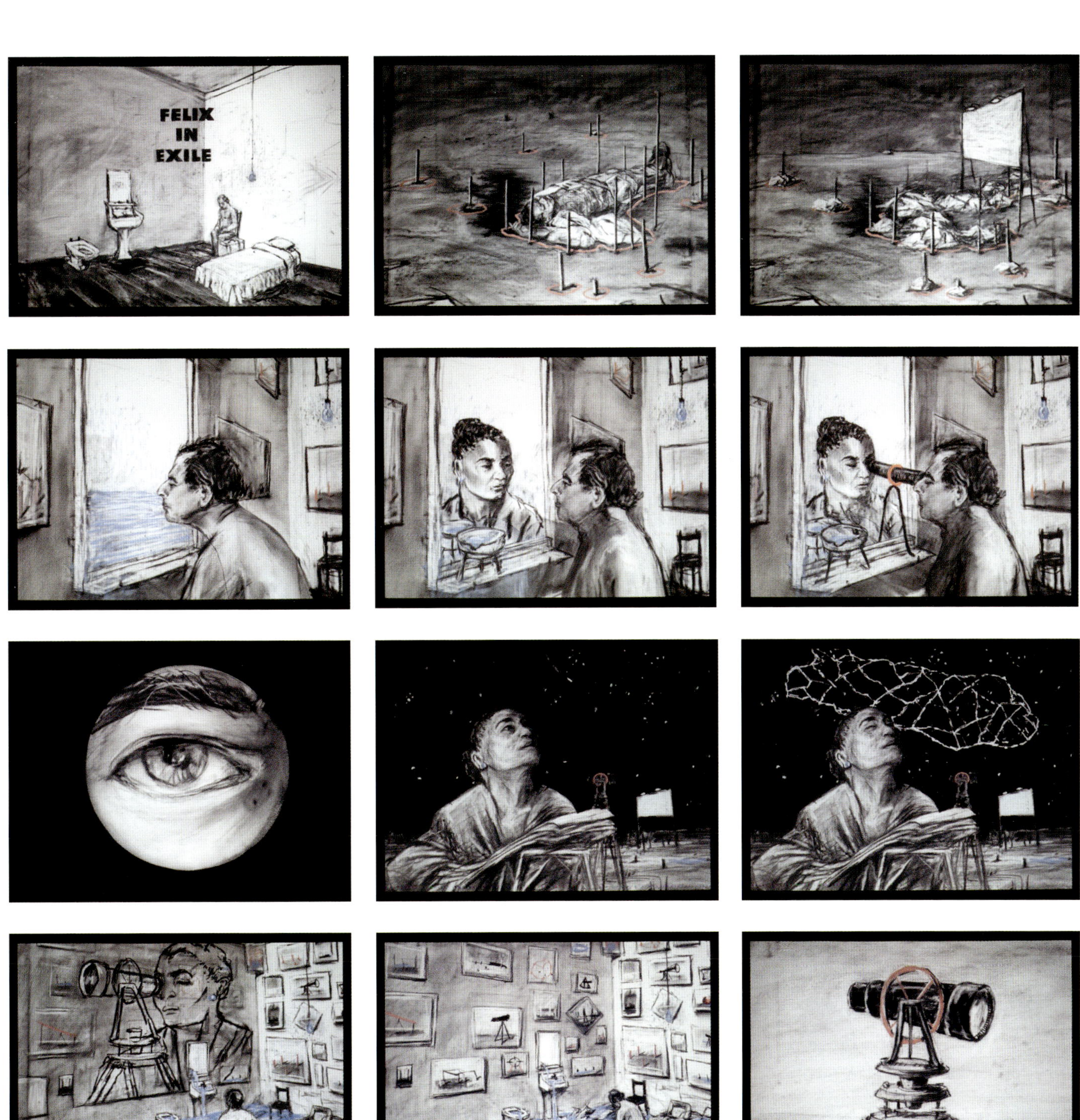

William Kentridge, drawings for the film *Felix in Exile*, 1994
Film: 35mm animated film transferred to video, 8:43 minutes;
drawings: charcoal and pastel on paper, various dimensions

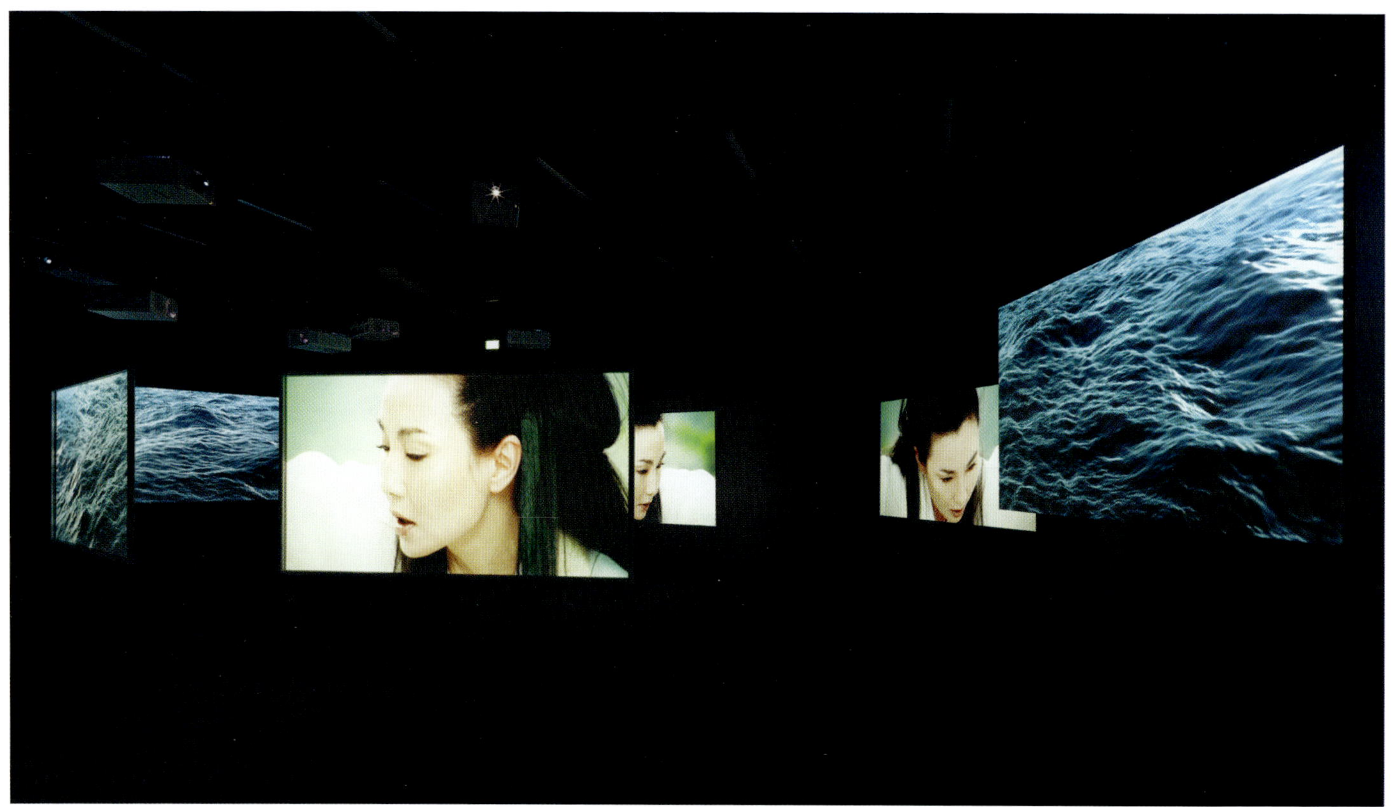

Isaac Julien, *Ten Thousand Waves*, 2010
Nine-video installation view, Museum Brandhorst, Munich

of them from any single vantage point. Different videos appeared on each; at one point, four were showing water in motion, one was blank, and the remaining four were showing images of the famous Hong Kong actress Maggie Cheung as Mazu, a Chinese sea goddess, floating in the sky. You could move around to try to follow the action, or sit in different spots to watch different combinations of screens, but there was no way you could see all the footage at the same time: you had to join up what you *could* see in your head; you had to find your own resolution to the stories.

One critic grumbled that there was no coherent message.[7] But that is to completely misunderstand the work: it is not an advert or party-political broadcast. It is experiential, about making you think, not telling you *what* to think. 'That's what I mean by frustrating the ontological gaze,' explains Julien. 'In the gallery, you won't be able to see the whole work at once, so any narrative you establish is necessarily fragmented.'[8] As an artist, Julien has been much influenced by film theory, but he does not want his pieces to be dry. 'I want to make a work that may have intellectual ideas that are embedded in cultural and artistic theory ... seen by as wide an audience as possible ... The challenge is to make a work that brings spectators to see it and speaks to an audience, and at the same time gets one to think about the issues the work raises.'[9]

Julien, whose parents came to London from St Lucia in the Caribbean in search of a better life (like the cockle-pickers and other migrants), has talked about how worried he is by the growing hostility towards immigrants. Among other things, *Ten Thousand Waves* is about getting to know China better, about how we experience the world – and about how we dream.

Ten Thousand Waves is a complex work that took six years to conceive and make. It also required a lot of financial support. And that, of course, is a problem for most artists – as indeed it was for Julien in his early career, when he too had to survive on a shoestring. Making a video is cheap – you can even do it on your phone – but a successful video installation needs to be produced to a high standard and installed seamlessly.

Migration and exile are also of concern to Shirin Neshat. Born in Qazvin, Iran, in 1957, Neshat moved to the United States in 1975. In 1990, after visiting Iran for first time in more than ten years, she felt the need to explore Iranian culture since the Islamic Revolution; the result was 'Women of Allah' (1993–97), a series of mesmeric black-and-white photos of women posing as martyrs in chador, bearing guns, overwritten with Farsi script. Then and now, much of her work is about being a go-between – between Iranian and American culture and society. 'Once you leave your place of birth, there's never a complete sense of centre: you're always in the state of in between and nowhere completely feels like home.'[10]

As Neshat's work developed, she increasingly turned to film-making, often focused on the condition of womanhood in Iran. In *Rapture* (1999), for example, she contrasts an Iranian man singing to an audience and an Iranian woman singing to an empty theatre – women were then forbidden to sing in public. The man goes silent, and appears to start listening to the woman's singing, which has an ecstatic quality very different from his own. In other films, scenes of black-clad women walking en masse, launching a boat and setting sail are symbolic of women's power and potential freedom. 'I'm always interested in more allegorical, surrealistic ways of storytelling,' Neshat has said.[11] Music is central to her films; she wants, she says, to move her audience: 'I want that intensity from any work of art; I want to be deeply affected, almost like asking to have a religious experience.'[12] In her photographs, the hierarchical poses and the stark but beautiful contrasts of black and white are key.

When first exhibited in 2012, Neshat's series 'The Book of Kings' included 54 large photographic portraits, with each person labelled as belonging to one of three groups: 'masses' (45), 'patriots' (6) or 'villains' (3). Two additional photographs showed a pair of legs hanging in mid-air and a man striking his heart. Texts by contemporary Iranian poets, as well as from *Shahnameh* (Book of Kings) by the tenth-century poet Ferdowsi, were written across them in Farsi. All the subjects had been involved in the Arab Spring, that moment in 2011 when a desire for democracy in the Arab world seemed on the verge of being fulfilled. The figures pose as if they are actors about to declaim their story. Even if we cannot read Farsi, the writing makes us see

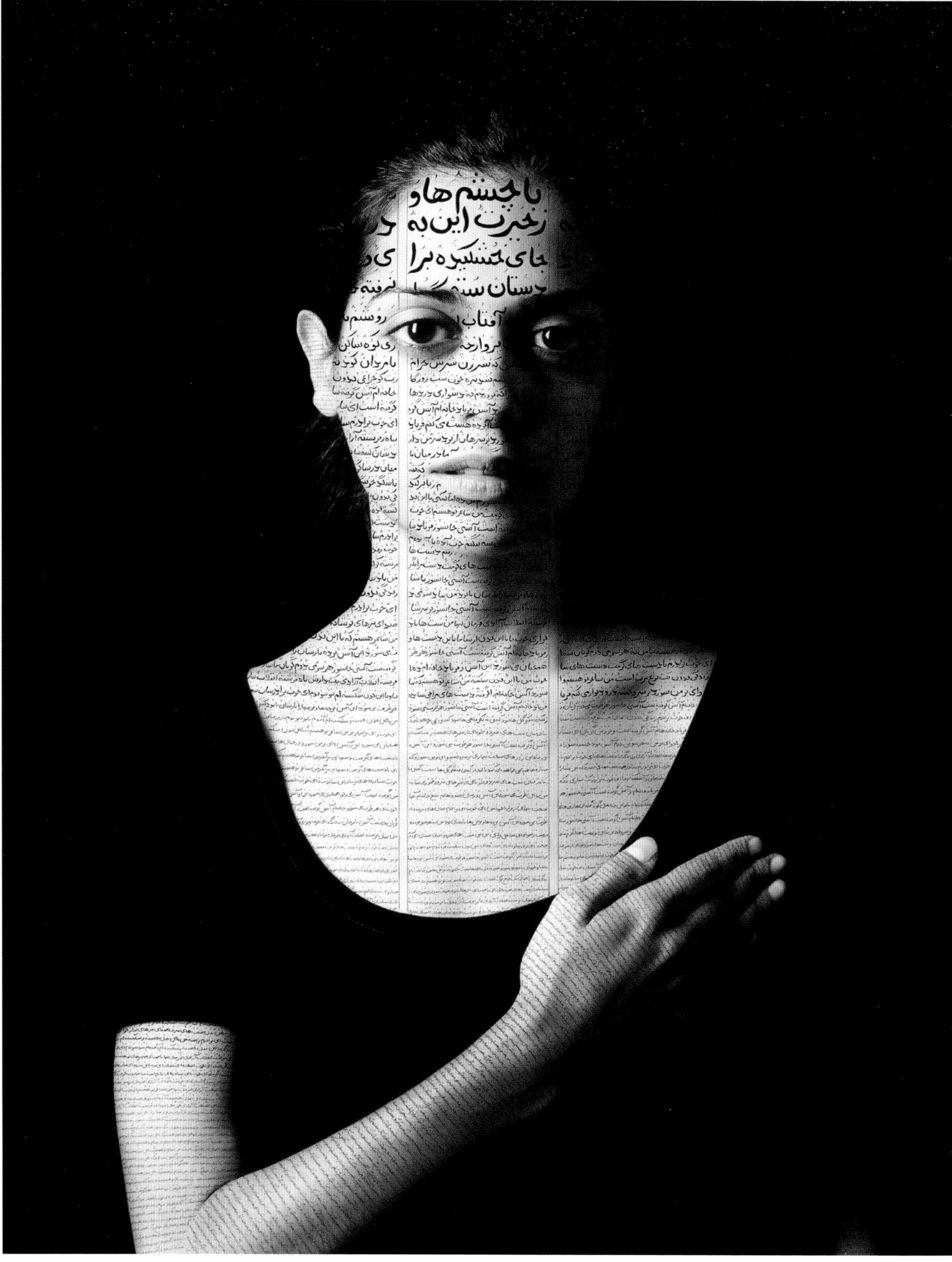

Shirin Neshat, *Roja*, 2012
Ink on LE silver gelatin print, 152.4 × 114.3 cm (60 × 45 in.)

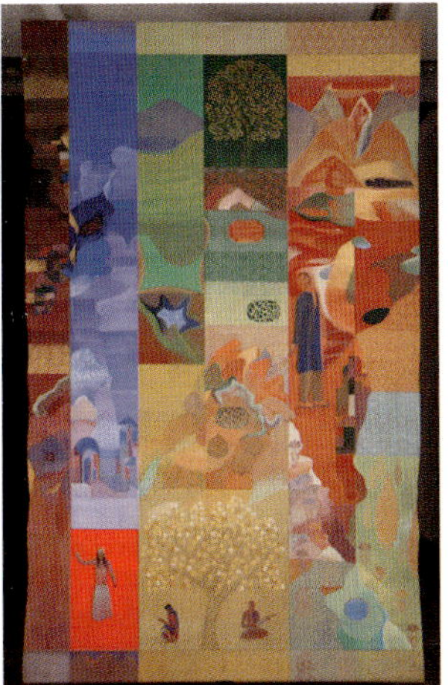

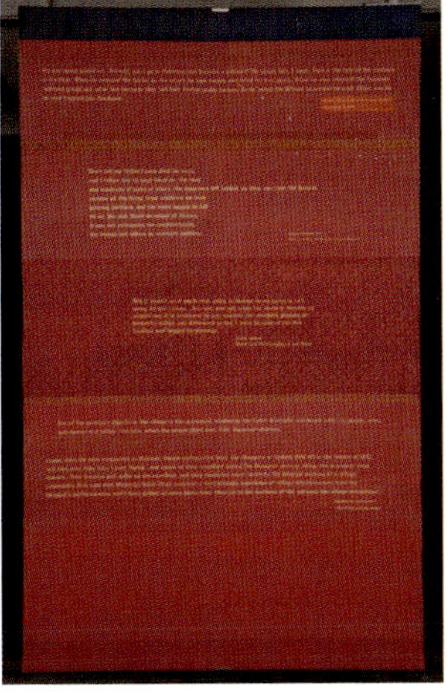

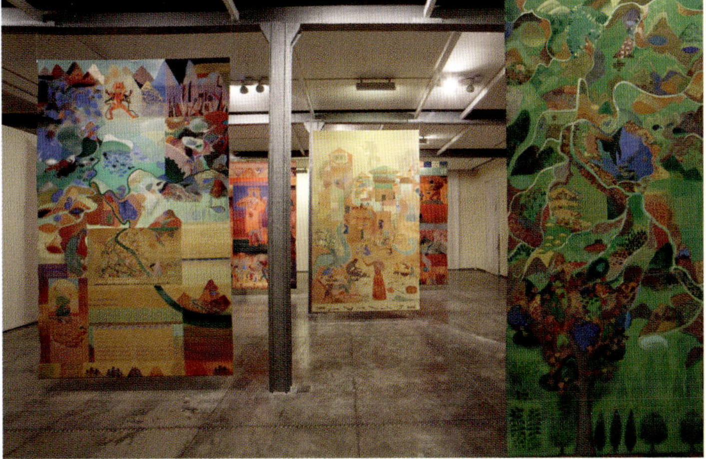

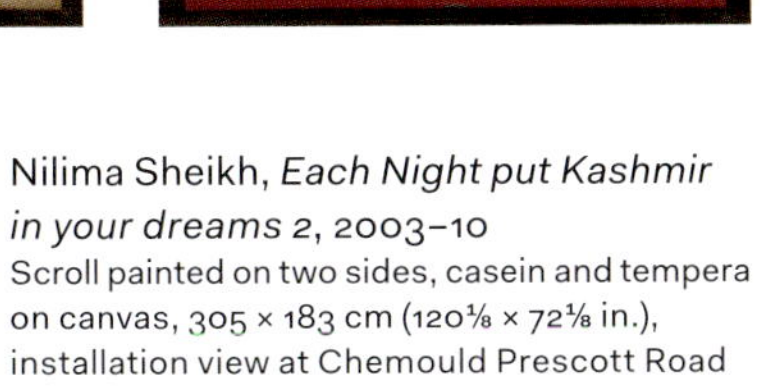

Nilima Sheikh, *Each Night put Kashmir in your dreams 2*, 2003–10
Scroll painted on two sides, casein and tempera on canvas, 305 × 183 cm (120⅛ × 72⅛ in.), installation view at Chemould Prescott Road

them differently, wondering what their story is. 'The calligraphy', Neshat tells us, 'adds a level of aesthetics. To me, this is another added level of beauty.'[13] Previously, she has explained: 'It is particularly important in relation to my subject since in Islam, beauty is critical, as it directly ties to ideas of spirituality and love of God.'[14]

Compared to the series 'When Champa Grew Up' (see Chapter 2), Nilima Sheikh's more recent work does not provide the viewer with such a clear narrative. A constant reference in her work, however, has been Kashmir, where she spent much of her childhood walking with her mother. Sheikh remembers it as a place of great beauty; since then, it has been the scene of much tension and violence between Muslims and Hindus – a paradise lost.

Between 2003 and 2010, Sheikh made nine very large, banner-like paintings combining different images of Kashmir: mythic, historic, personal. They were map-like, but maps of memory, not topography. The memories were of all that Kashmir had been – a meeting place of various cultures, Hindu, Chinese, Muslim, colonial. When Sheikh exhibited all nine together, it was as an immersive installation, with each painting suspended from the ceiling so one had to walk between them. On the reverse of each painting were numerous texts about Kashmir and memory by writers, academics and poets, notably Agha Shahid Ali (a line from one of Ali's poems, 'Each night put Kashmir in your dreams', became the title of the work as a whole). Like Julien, Sheikh wanted the viewer to be involved in a rich and multilayered experience, highly sensual – neither artist is scared of beauty – but also thought-provoking.

As we saw in the introduction, Shahzia Sikander's early career was based on learning the techniques used in the painting of Moghul miniatures and adapting them to depict the contemporary world. Like Sheikh, she would later produce much larger works, first hangings and then projected animations. But whereas Sheikh has always lived in India, taught there and brought her children up there, Sikander left Pakistan and moved to New York, eventually taking US citizenship. The community she makes art for are the people she knows in New York: 'For me, art-making is so much about creating your own world and language, rather than reinventing tradition. Whatever I create, whether it's a miniature or something else, it has to be rooted in a personal connection to art and communication with others. This is what interests me as an artist: how you can create work that somehow transcends place and time.'[15]

Of the work illustrated here (opposite), Sikander wrote: 'The animation *The Last Post* was inspired by my ongoing interest in the colonial history of the subcontinent and the events of the opium trade with respect to Shanghai. The protagonist is the East India Company man who appears in the piece in various guises. In one instance, the exploding man is a metaphor for the departure of the Anglo-Saxon hegemony over China ... In the animation, I have also used subtle references to the "Company School", a style of visual language patronized by the English in nineteenth-century India.'[16] At times burlesque, at times condemnatory, the animation is also very lyrical. Sikander used both traditional miniature-painting techniques and modern image-editing software to combine, elide and transform individual scenes. Transformation, she says, is what her work is always about.[17] When *The Last Post* was shown for the first time in Shanghai, it was accompanied by a projection on the floor and a musical performance by the Chinese-born composer Du Yun, who had created the soundtrack for the animation. Film-based art often calls for collaboration with other types of artist.

The Bodies (III) (page 182), a painting by the Belgian artist Michaël Borremans, is ostensibly of two people asleep in bed. But it seems wrong: charming yet disturbing. 'That's a strange painting,' Borremans has admitted. 'I wanted to refer to death and playing dead. It's kind of sinister. All the actors in the paintings [in his 2006 New York show] are masculine. In the history of painting, it's the men who go to war, who are fighters. Women are softer. Psychologically, the whole show dealt with that. The men in the bed have pillows behind them. This creates a strange interference in the psychology of male figures. Because they're soft again.'[18]

Like many painters, Borremans often uses photographs. He doesn't want his paintings to *look* photographic, however, so, when painting, he displays the image on a monitor that is some distance from where he is working. His scenes have an airless quality: everything is stilled, as though something has not yet happened. There seems to be no story, only a situation that could develop into one. 'With the paintings,' he says, 'at first you expect a narrative, because the figures are familiar.

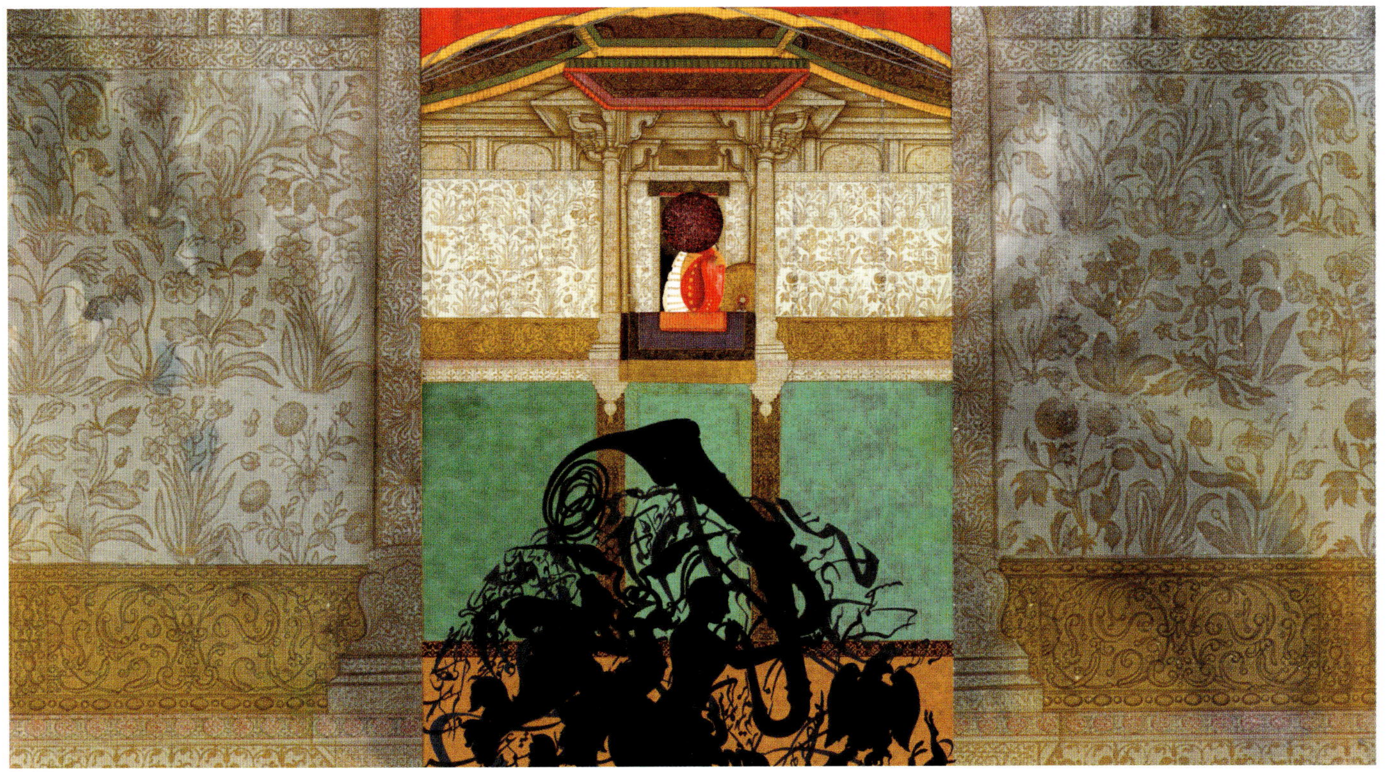

Shahzia Sikander, *The Last Post*, 2010
Single channel HD digital animation with 5.1 surround sound, music by Du Yun, 10 minutes

But then you see that some parts of the paintings don't match, or don't make sense. The works don't come to a conclusion in the way we expect them to. The images are unfinished: they remain open. That makes them durable.'[19]

Although Borremans trained as a printmaker, taking up painting later in life, he has an appealing, soft way of painting. It is the way he paints and the way he leaves things unsaid, as much as his curious subject matter – including such oddities as giant women and a man drawing a windmill on a woman's back – that makes his work feel so strange. Borremans cites, like many of his contemporaries, Manet as an influence; he sees other influences at play, too: 'I think my work actually does have a particular Belgian touch – the ubiquitous absurdity' (think Magritte or Hergé).[20] He also believes it to be universal, 'because I use clichés and other elements that are part of a collective consciousness. These elements are easy to recognize – my work would be perfect on biscuit tins.'[21] It seems as if he drops random objects into his paintings, thus transforming them. He likens this process to sampling in music: 'In all disciplines we see an explicit culture of sampling. That explains the new interest in painting in the visual arts: painting is a clichéd medium that allows the use of a wide range of materials and an almost endless profusion of references.'[22]

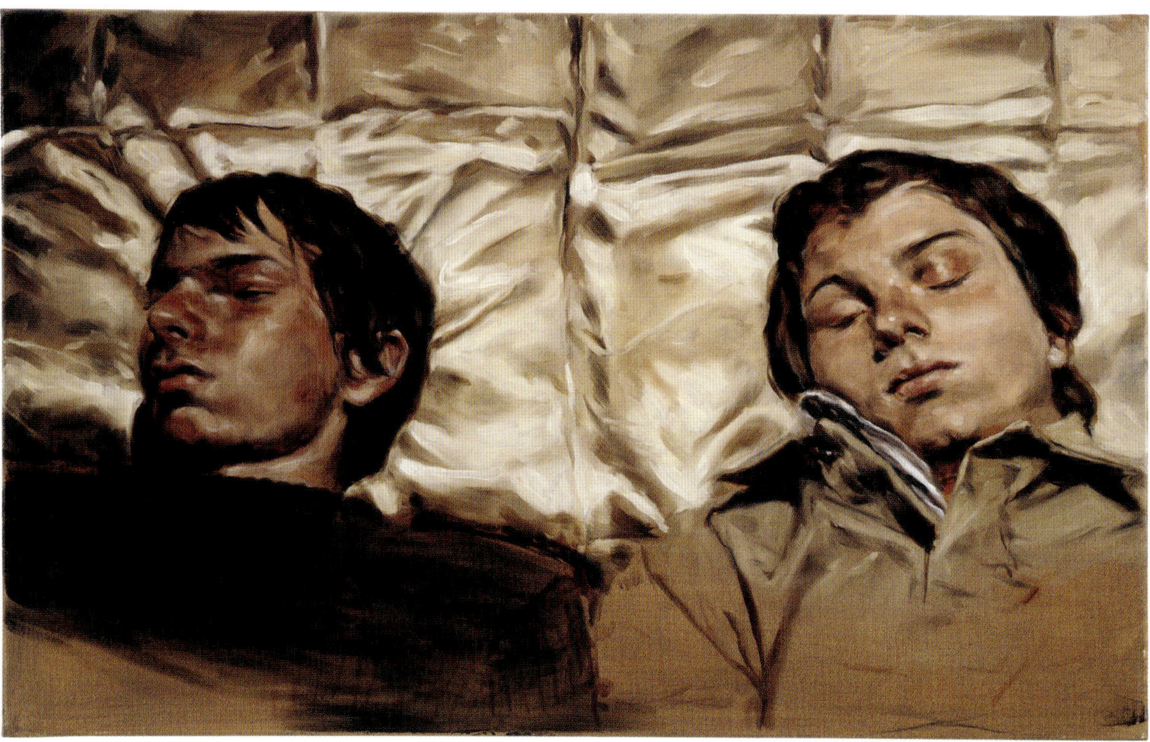

Michael Borremans, *The Bodies (III)*, 2005
Oil on canvas, 70 × 110 cm (27⅝ × 43⅜ in.)

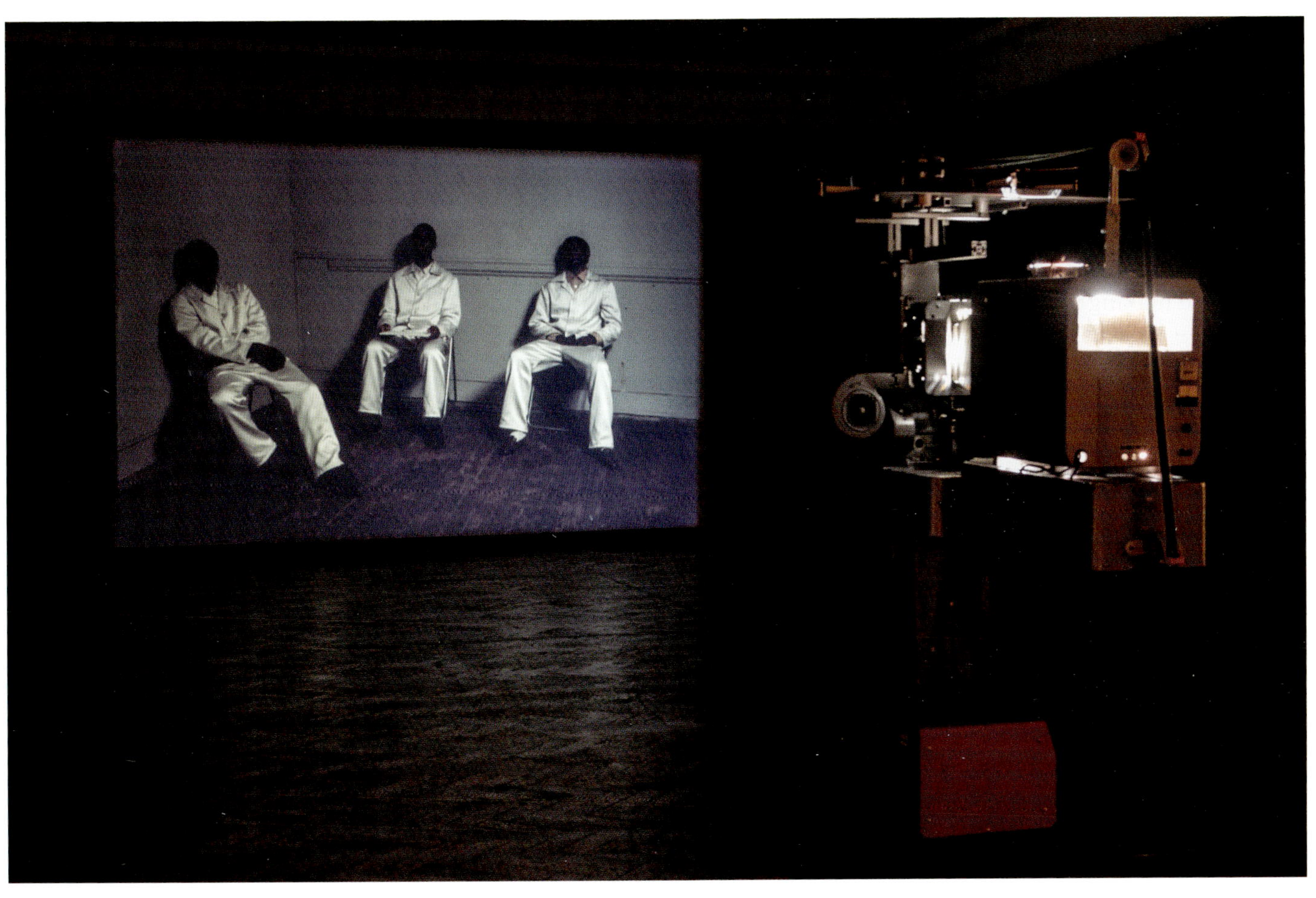

Michael Borremans. *The Storm*, 2006
35mm film, 1:07 minutes (continuous loop), edition 3

Borremans also makes films. Not videos, films – the distinction is crucial. Unlike video or digital media, film has a tactile quality. Likewise, asked why he does not use Photoshop to create his pictures, he insists you need the tactility of paint. Nothing appears to happen in his films, although it seems as though something *has* happened, or is about to happen. In one, *The Storm* (page 183) – a typically short, one-minute loop – all you see are three men sitting. 'They were young guys,' Borremans tells us, 'and they'd been out the night before on drugs and they were just sitting there. I saw them there by accident and told the cameraman, "Please film this!" And it was much better than the film I was working on. I threw away the other film and kept this.'[23]

The German painter Neo Rauch, whom we heard from in Chapter 5, was born and educated in East Germany. People often assume, therefore, that his work is about life in that state and its collapse in 1989–90. It is certainly the case that he got a much better technical training as a painter than he would have got in the West, and that his dry, muted colour sense is related to some extent to the absence in East Germany of the garish advertising typical of a consumer society. However, when asked how he had responded to the Berlin Wall coming down, he replied: 'I was so busy at that time finding myself in my work that the major upheaval caused by the political and social situation could only have been processed in my work as a very mild aftershock. The greatest change in my life came with the birth of my son in 1990. That's when I crossed over into greater responsibility, but at the same time it offered me the chance to embrace child-play once again.'[24] As he has also noted, 'To a small child, the world still seems very magical.'[25]

Again and again, Rauch has emphasized that he has no ideology, that he only wants to paint. 'What is painting, as you define it in your language?' he once was asked. He replied: 'Responsible use of the elementary ingredients of colour, form and composition ... What I want is for the element in the painting – colour, form, the interlocking spaces inside it – all to suggest an impression of tension just about to break. And the figures have a role to play in that, as far as they can.'[26] 'As far as they can': although often of heroic build, Rauch's figures seem strangely inept, unsure whether they are acting in a comedy or a tragedy. The spaces in his paintings often bring to mind an old-fashioned proscenium. Indeed, as he himself has said, 'I understand myself to be a director of plays.'[27]

What should we make of a painting such as *Waiting for the Barbarians* (pages 186–87)? After reading the painting's title and looking at the very German figures it depicts, we might imagine the horrors of 1945, when the Russians invaded Germany, but the carnival atmosphere speaks against that. We're likely to think differently when we learn that the title refers to a poem by the Greek poet C. P. Cavafy in which, after a long wait for the invading horde, a group of townspeople are told that the barbarians no longer exist. They reply, mystified, 'What are we going to do now without the barbarians? In a way, those people were a solution.'[28]

But why is one man having a bull's mask placed on his head, as if for a masquerade, whereas another bull-masked man is tied to a stake ready for execution? And who on earth is the ridiculous figure with the long red nose? Why is he playing pool? Despite all these oddities, we note how beautifully painted the blue-and-white dress is, although it seems not quite finished. Rauch always leaves things precisely composed and poised, but not yet concluded.

So, is Rauch, as has been suggested, 'the Picasso of the twenty-first century'?[29] No; he hasn't the incredible range of Picasso. No one working today has. But when one abstract painter said he was the best artist today,[30] it was an understandable tribute to both his exceptional skilfulness and the uniqueness of his vision.

None of the preceding seven artists produce narratives in the same direct way that Michelangelo or Rembrandt did – incidents from a known or easily deduced story. Why should they? As one artist put it: 'Painters don't have to deal with literal narrative anymore because the movies do it so perfectly.'[31] Rather, they give us an experience about narrative, or an experience like narrative, but with no linear progression. Whereas a nineteenth-century painter would have tried to illustrate a dream, now painters would rather make the painting function like dream-work. We have to find our own way.

If storytelling in art has changed, has its supposed opposite, abstract painting, also changed? As we have seen, painting did not disappear after conceptual art, and neither did abstract painting – despite its pretensions being so derided by conceptualists. A number of artists, Agnes Martin among them, were content to carry on making minimal or pared-down painting, oblivious to fashions. However, several painters who emerged in the late 1970s and 1980s wanted to make abstraction more dynamic. They wanted to both reconnect to the whole rich tradition of abstract painting and paint for the rapidly changing contemporary world.

Inevitably, much of this continuing discourse on abstraction has taken place in New York, where Pollock, Rothko *et al.* once worked. Several strong personalities have emerged, each with distinct positions.[32] One of them, Jonathan Lasker, is typical in wanting to steer a course between the earnestness of the Abstract Expressionists and the irony of the neo-conceptualists. For him, as for many other painters of his generation, studying at a college where conceptual artists had taken control was not easy. Lasker attended Cal Arts, Los Angeles, where John Baldessari taught. 'At Cal Arts,' he recounts, 'to be a painter meant you had to take a stance, because there was a very antagonistic attitude towards painting there. In a way it was good for me, because it forced me to shape my reasons for making paintings. It also forced me to make paintings that had reasons for being paintings. So I think, in a way it pushed me in a good direction, although the experience was alienating.'[33] Lasker, like others, had to develop his own position and argue for it. As do many of his peers, he theorizes about what painting is and how it fits into our consciousness of the world. Asked back in 1989 if it was possible to make abstract

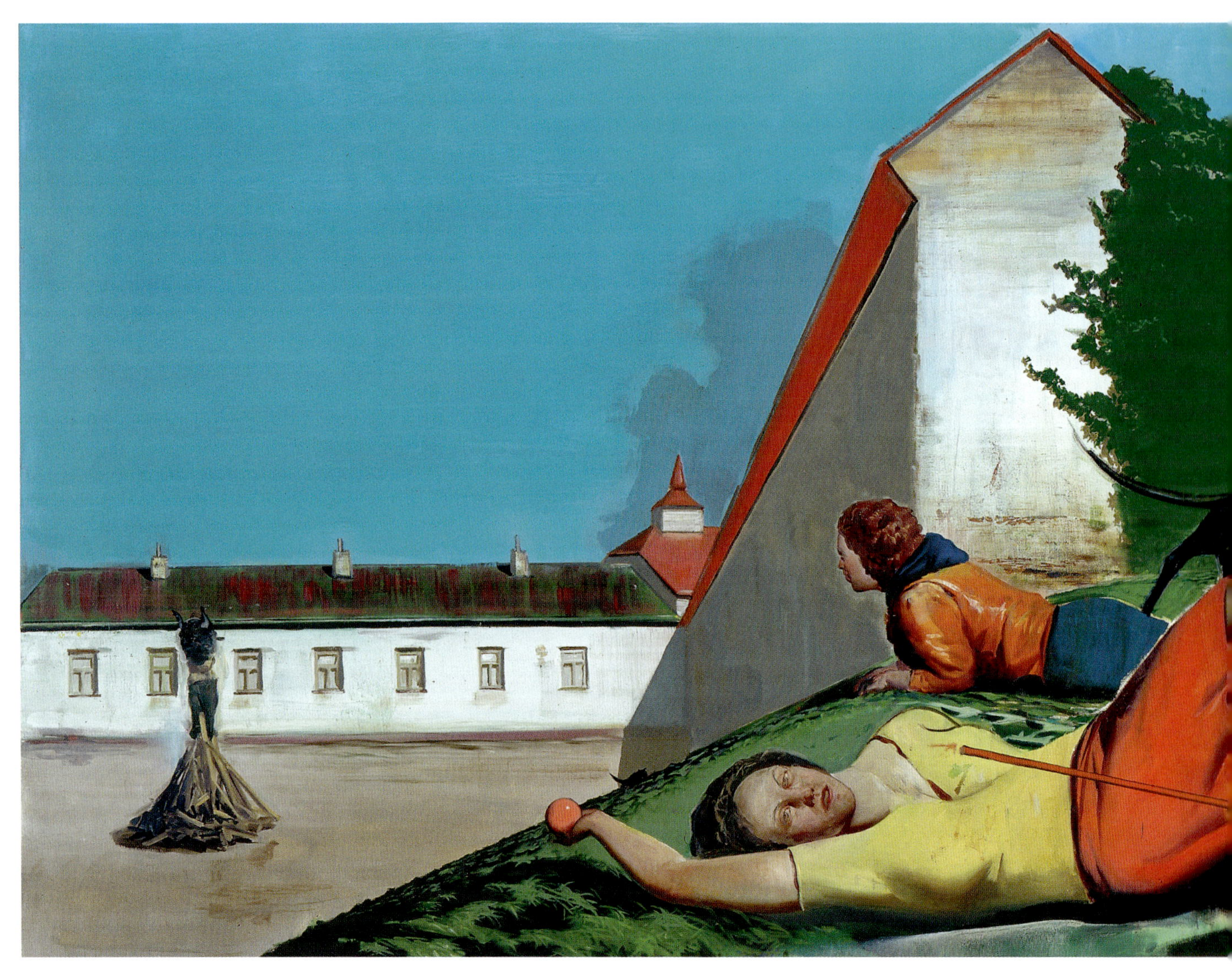

Neo Rauch, *Waiting for the Barbarians*, 2007
Oil on canvas, 150 × 400 cm (59 × 157¾ in.)

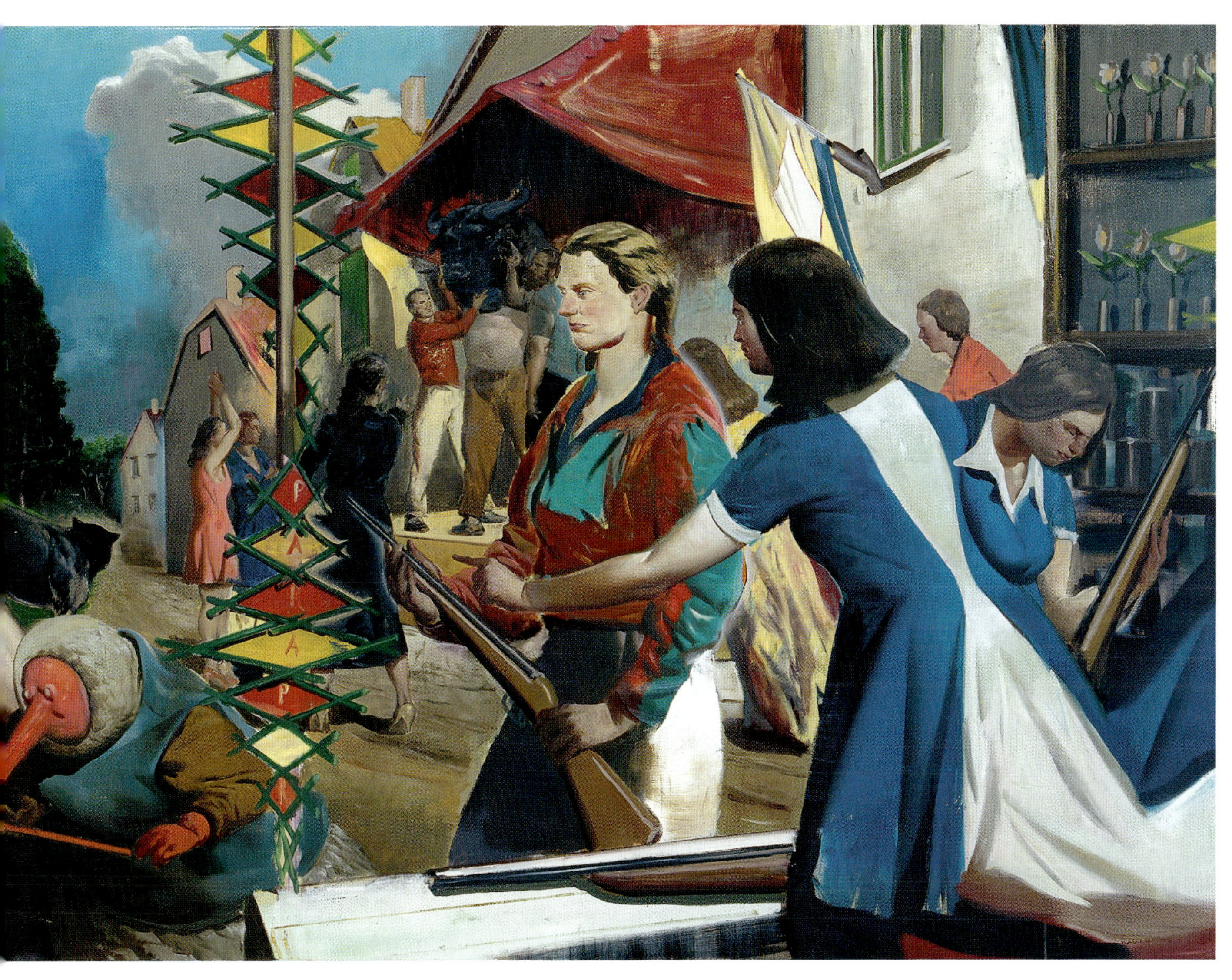

paintings without being cynical, he answered: 'It's very hard to not be somewhat self-conscious in this age. It's very difficult, though I wouldn't say it's impossible ... The issue is a question of belief, really... I believe in the marks that I make ... It's a case of the subconscious becoming conscious of itself.'[34]

Unusually for a painter working today, Lasker makes preparatory sketches for all his paintings, often no larger than 15 by 20 cm (6 by 8 in.). Scribbles made intuitively. These sketches are then enlarged and copied on to a blank canvas. They do not parody the instinctive drawing of the surrealists or Jackson Pollock but, as Lasker claims, reference it – the subconscious becoming conscious of itself.

Above all, Lasker has put figure–ground relations back into abstraction, so that, when we look at his paintings, we can easily imagine his shapes are people moving around a room or within a landscape. When teased about the fact that, in his youth, he played bass guitar in a band, he mused: 'there is something that relates to your basic rock 'n' roll trio in these paintings. The three elements in my paintings – figure, ground and line – are almost like the three elements in a band – bass, drums and lead.'[35] There is also a play between 'lumpiness' and 'flatness' in his work; in the painting illustrated here, for example, it can be seen between the gunged-up yellow area against the meticulously neat scribbles and the loosened knot of thicker lines that seems to float away to the right. Like many of his peers, Lasker could be described as a painter's painter, seemingly dealing with formal issues, with ways of making a painting. But it is always to a purpose, thinking about issues of perception – the difficulty, as he puts it, 'of ascertaining reality'.[36]

New York might remain a test bed for abstract painting, but all around the world one can find abstract painters responding sometimes to local traditions and stimuli, and sometimes to Western practice. For many, the appeal of the Brazilian painter Beatriz Milhazes (whom we met in the introduction) has always been the intensity of her colours and their vibrant rhythms. We almost inevitably relate these to Brazil's tradition of carnival or the country's tropical landscape. Milhazes may not have participated in carnival processions, but she is moved by them and seeks an equivalent intensity in her work. Speaking in 2004, she said: 'I have a compulsive need for physical contact with my paintings. Colour is the core of my work. It's by colour that I begin and finish a painting.'[37] And, a year earlier: 'If the colours do not work, then the seduction fails.'[38] 'Seduction' – the word is telling. Milhazes wants us to have a close, physical relationship with the painting. Indeed, in the paintings she made in the 2000s, there is an added level of physicality. After applying paint directly to a sheet of transparent plastic, she would press the plastic against the canvas. It made for a flat surface, but one with many imperfections and, when the work was seen close up, an added texture and vitality.

If her work has a subject, or, for her at least, an implicit meaning, can we sense it? 'I have stories in my mind,' she has explained, 'and I think they are the sentiments, sounds and smells that guide me. As far as I am concerned, this is transmitted by

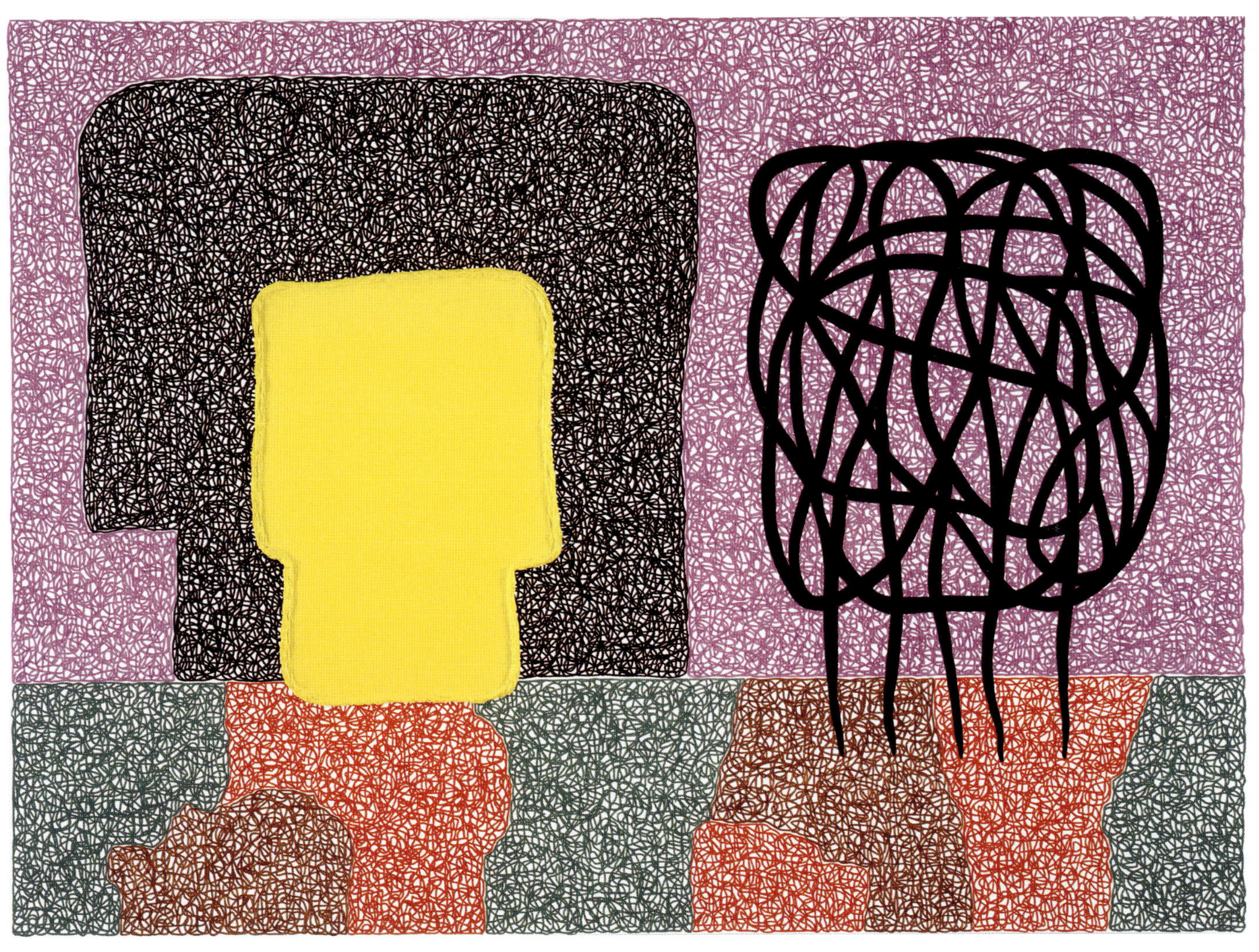

Jonathan Lasker, *The Quotidian and the Question*, 2007
Oil on linen, 229 × 305 cm (90 × 120 in.)

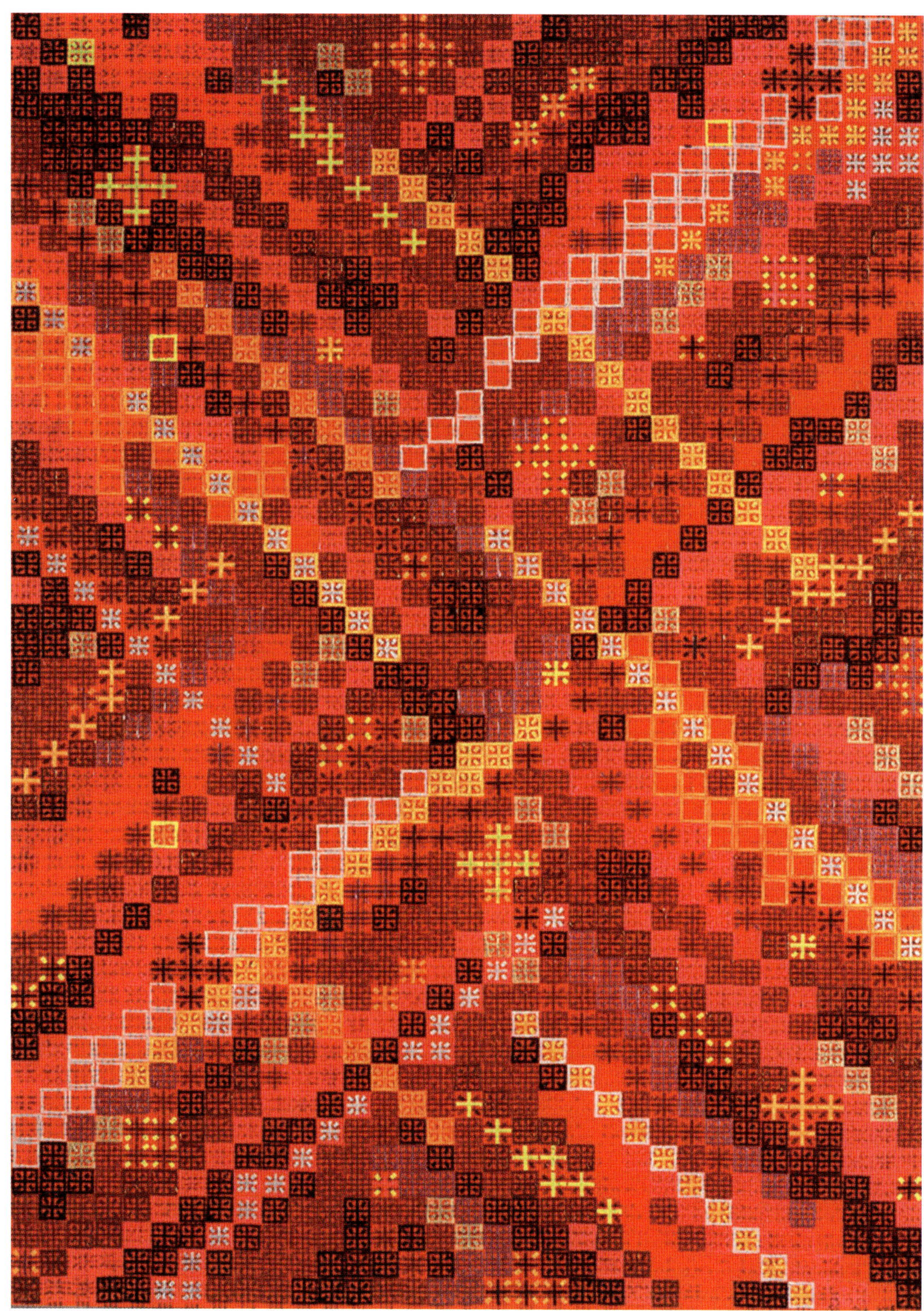

Ding Yi, *Appearance of Crosses*, 2006–14
Acrylic on tartan, 200 × 140 cm (78¾ × 55⅛ in.)

my painting.'[39] She has also talked about her passion for music, both bossa nova and opera. If there is a deeper meaning to her work, it will only be found in the direct experiencing of it. Talking of 9/11 and how artists should respond to such events, she said: 'I believe in life, in the beauty of things that bring a positive energy. It is also up to art to give a certain direction to its time and show an alternative path.'[40]

How come Ding Yi, an artist from Shanghai, became an abstract painter in the late 1980s? For him, 1988 was a kind of 'year zero'. In China at that time anything seemed possible, and Ding wanted to take painting back to its basics. The Cultural Revolution had ended, meaning that Chinese artists were no longer obliged to crank out socialist realist art, and they were finally getting some information about painting in the West. But what about traditional Chinese painting, something Ding Yi had studied? 'I don't think that is part of our genes anymore,' he told me. 'For the last forty years, China is only striving for one thing: development, fast economic growth and wealth accumulation – we are not reflecting upon our culture. Compared with the abstract movements in Korea and Japan, such as *Mono-ha*, we have a totally different background. The true source of Chinese contemporary art is nothing else than the reality of the society, the giant transformation of social changes.'[41]

In 1988 Ding made the most basic painting he could imagine: just the three primary colours and no marks on it save for crosses set out in a grid. The crosses were painted as impersonally as possible – a vertical line on a horizontal. It was as if Ding had re-invented minimalism. For more than thirty years now he has painted nothing but such crosses arranged in a grid formation. But rather than repetition, this has led to a process of constant development: every painting is different. In 1996 Ding started to paint on commercial fabrics with tartan patterns. He liked the idea of using something so ordinary and unlike high art, and enjoyed the challenge of transforming each tartan into something unique and more complex. 'I am not painting in order. Sometimes I put one point here; sometimes I start to put another point on the other side of the painting. I structure my painting like playing Go. Take the centre! Take the corner! I paint the middle part as the first place. This is like a Go strategy, though I don't play the game myself.'[42]

In 1998 the Canadian art historian Serge Guilbaut visited Ding in his studio and asked him why he was not responding to the city he lived in, specifically its striking nightscape of neon signs. Ding answered by creating some exceptionally bright and vivid paintings. But it was the vividness of the signs that influenced him, not the form of any particular example: as always, each painting had to be made with crosses.

Unlike Ding and Milhazes – in fact, unlike most of the artists in this book – Emily Kame Kngwarreye did not go to art school at a young age. Indeed, she did not start making paintings on canvas until she was nearly eighty years old. Yet by the time of her death eight years later, in 1996, she had produced enough work to be judged one of the great artists of the late twentieth century. But even ten years after her death, her importance was little recognized beyond her native Australia.

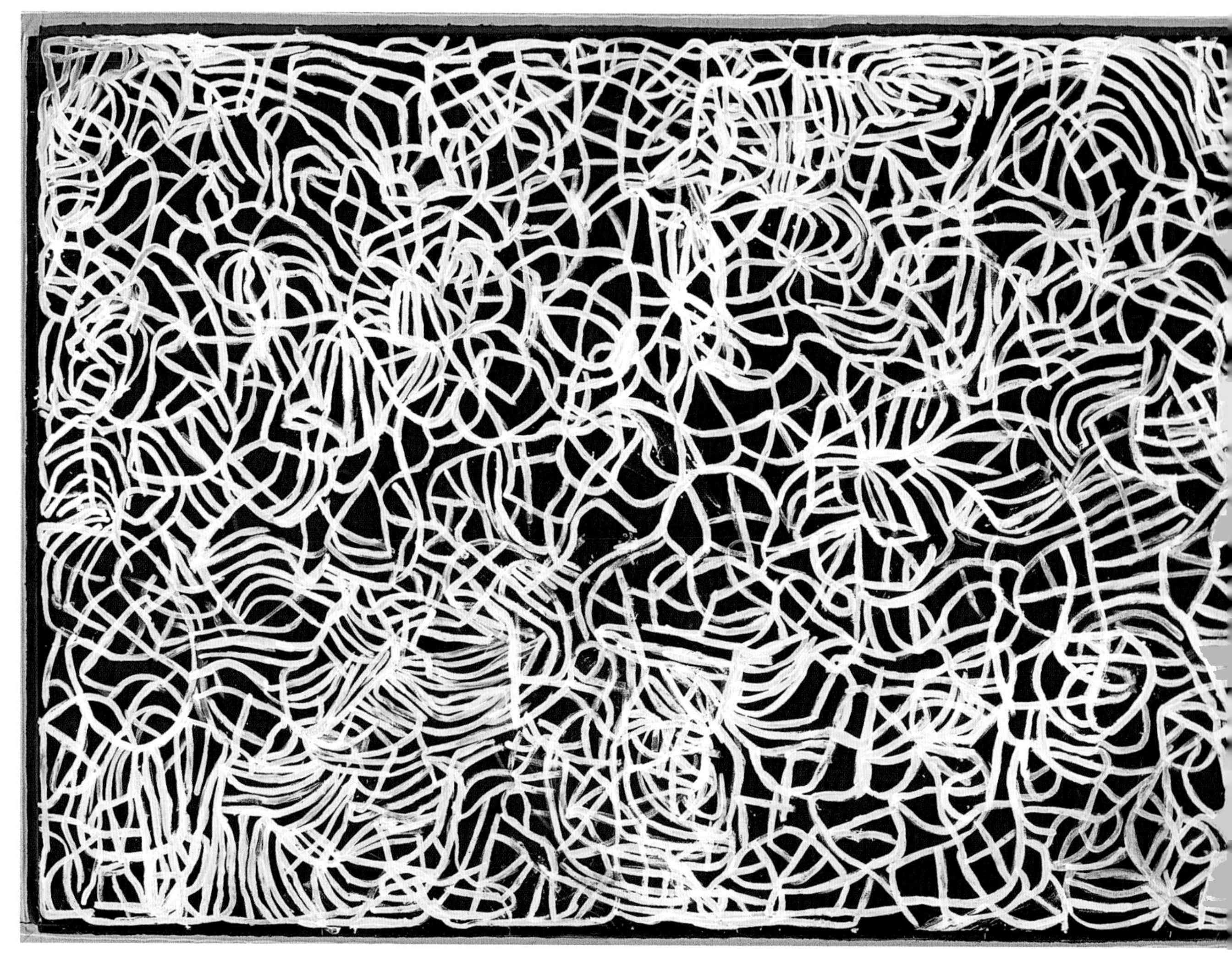

Emily Kame Kngwarraye, *Anwerlarr anganenty (Big yam Dreaming)*, 1995
Synthetic polymer paint on canvas, 291 × 801.8 cm (114⅝ × 315¾ in.)

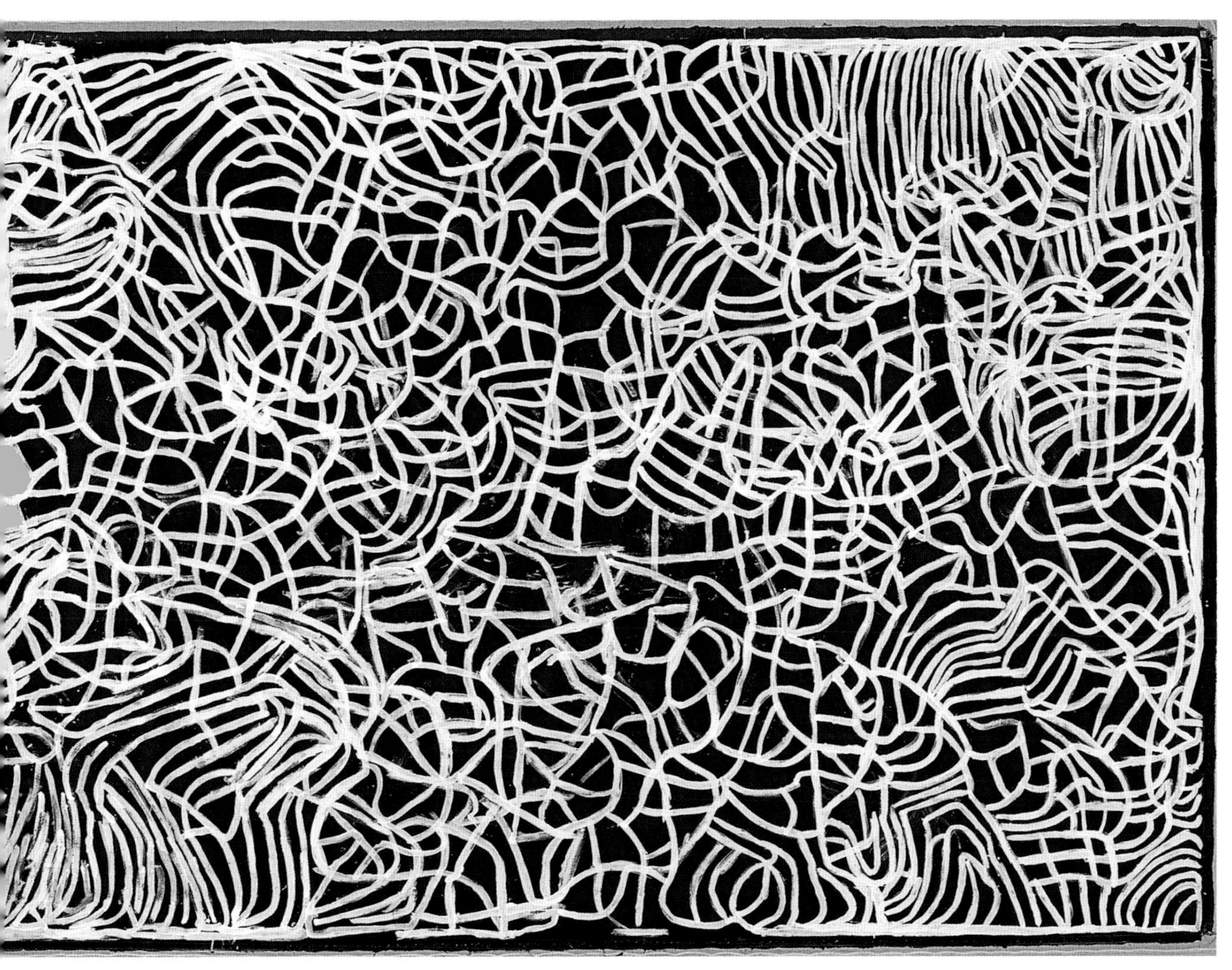

Starting in the early 1970s there had been an extraordinary effervescence of painting by Aboriginal artists in Central Australia. Although much was quickly knocked off for the tourist trade, there were several genuine and outstanding artists at work. But why have none of them been seen in the wider context of abstract painting, rather than being confined to the ghetto-like category of Aboriginal art? Alas, racist attitudes are still ingrained in the art establishment.

Most Aboriginal paintings are based on ancestral dreamings, or myths, although often coded or abstracted to some extent; Emily's paintings were the most avowedly abstract, referring to her dreamings only in the most general or indirect way. She may not have had any formal artistic training, but she had been making batiks for many years; and all through her life, she had painted women's bodies for ceremonies. Her art evolved out of the patterns and marks used for such ceremonies, but in its rapid evolution it dealt with many of the formal problems of modernist and contemporary painting – of which she knew very little.

Measuring more than eight metres in length, *Big yam Dreaming* (pages 192–93) is one of Emily's largest works. It has a tremendous rhythm and energy. We can see the network of white lines as the spreading roots of the finger yam (Emily was the custodian of that particular dreaming). Or we can experience the work much as we would one of Pollock's large drip paintings: a dance of the eye, arm and body. We are told she completed the work in two days – her speed partly explained by her ability to paint with both hands at the same time. The canvas was primed by two assistants, then laid down on the ground; Emily sat cross-legged in the centre and painted her way across it. Everything was improvised; there was no preliminary sketch.

The four preceding artists variously produce a sort of impure abstraction. Each slips external references into their pieces: scribbling (Lasker), carnival (Milhazes), tartan (Ding), dreamings (Emily). Their paintings embrace complexity. In that respect, their effect is not so different from the narrative situations or conundrums of Neo Rauch or Nilima Sheikh.

Perhaps a clearer polarity between storytelling and abstraction can be seen in the case of two British artists working with clay – two artists who make ceramics as art rather than craft. Apart from the mass-produced bowls, plates and cups we use for breakfast each morning, there are two types of ceramics: studio ceramics (handmade objects bought in craft shops), and ceramics made by artists. Studio ceramics had a rich history in the twentieth century, but was normally seen as being in a different category from art, and as a practice deeply committed to the craft tradition. In the 1960s, however, a number of artists began producing ceramics that were experimental, funky and inventive. In the 1980s Grayson Perry, and in the 1990s Edmund de Waal, developed complex but differing relationships with the craft tradition. Unlike Picasso, Richard Deacon or Antony Gormley, these are not artists who sometimes use clay, normally with the help of assistants, but individuals whose central act as artists is making pots. How could they maintain a relationship with the tradition of ceramics and yet remain as artists, as Sheikh and Shahzia Sikander have with traditional miniature painting?

Two very different people making very different things. De Waal, whose father was dean of Canterbury Cathedral, hails from a privileged background. Perry, by contrast, comes from a suburban home, 'a culture-free zone with no books and no meanings',[43] as he described it, with a milkman for a stepfather: 'I never had a conversation with him in fifteen years. I was an alien presence in his house and I couldn't identify with what a man was supposed to be.'[44] When he first started making pots, aged twenty-eight, Perry covered them with rude words and images. It was self-therapy. Famously, he had also become a transvestite, and the emergence of his feminine alter ego would run hand in hand with his development as an artist.

De Waal has been making pots since the age of five. After university he tried to make a living as a potter, producing individual pieces for discerning collectors. Increasingly, however, he became uneasy with that way of life, as well as the philosophy of the humble craftsman he had inherited. On a scholarship to Japan in 1992, he saw how differently ceramics were used in the tea ceremony: 'Tea was revelatory. I discovered how objects work in space, how they have agency.'[45] Such an understanding was akin to that of the minimalists: that sculptures only work with and in a context. Placement, as with the work of Donald Judd or Richard Long, was crucial.

Invited to show with nine other ceramicists for a prize in 2001, De Waal exhibited fifty-five small, slender pots in a carefully considered sequence, like birds sitting on a ledge. The title he gave this work – *A Bad Day for the Sung Dynasty*, a reference to a book of poems by the Scottish poet Frank Kuppner – mystified and irritated the traditional connoisseurs of studio ceramics, as did De Waal's insistence that the pots could only be purchased as a group, at the kind of price more often associated with the art world.

Since then, De Waal has worked site-specifically, or else provided a movable context for his pots by placing them in containers he has designed himself, as in *Predella* (page 196), a reference to the horizontal row of paintings, featuring scenes from the life of Christ or the saints, that was placed under pre-Renaissance altarpieces. De Waal had found a way of belonging to what he had come to understand as the wider global traditions of ceramics while also being open to the possibilities of contemporary art: 'There is this banal break that people insist on making between the contemporary and the past. I am working in the presence of other traditions all the time, endeavouring to be completely new. I don't start from a position of rejection.'[46]

Perry's work is iconoclastic, referencing society as well as history, art history and craft traditions. De Waal has spent his life visiting museums and travelling to Japan and China, trying to obtain a deep understanding of ceramic traditions. Both have turned out to be exceptional writers and curators as well as artists. If De Waal seems a minimalist, Perry delights in excess – 'when in doubt bung it on', he tells us.[47] The power of his earlier pots lay partly in combining banal suburban backgrounds

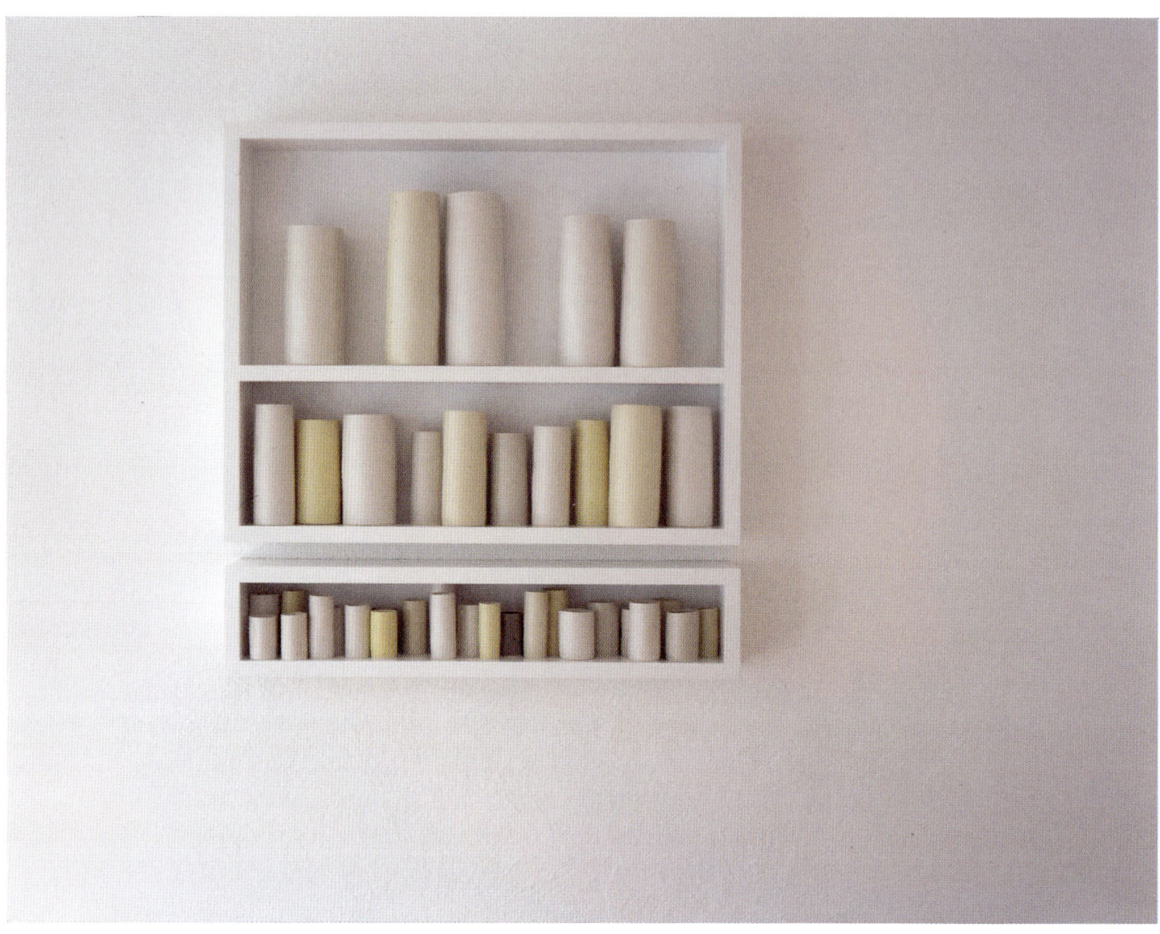

Edmund de Waal, *Predella*, 2007
39 porcelain vessels in 2 wood cabinets, 120 × 130 × 18.5 cm (41½ × 51 × 7¼ in.) overall

with outrageous sexual behaviour, but mainly in his sheer inventiveness. 'I like the whole iconography of pottery,' says Perry. 'It hasn't got any big pretensions to being great public works of art, and no matter how brash a statement I make, on a pot it will always have a certain humility.'[48]

Making is key for both artists. De Waal sits at his wheel and makes pots every day, while Perry can take up to three months over a single pot. If, early in his career, Perry had mocked the idle class-cosiness of the craft tradition, he is now more angered by artists who have their work fabricated; for him, using your hands to make art is key. 'Craftsmanship is often equated with precision but I think there is more to it. I feel it is more important to have a long and sympathetic hands-on relationship with materials. A relaxed, humble, ever-curious love of stuff is central to my idea of being an artist. An important quality of great art of the past was the pure skill in the artists' use of materials.' I am quoting here from the book Perry

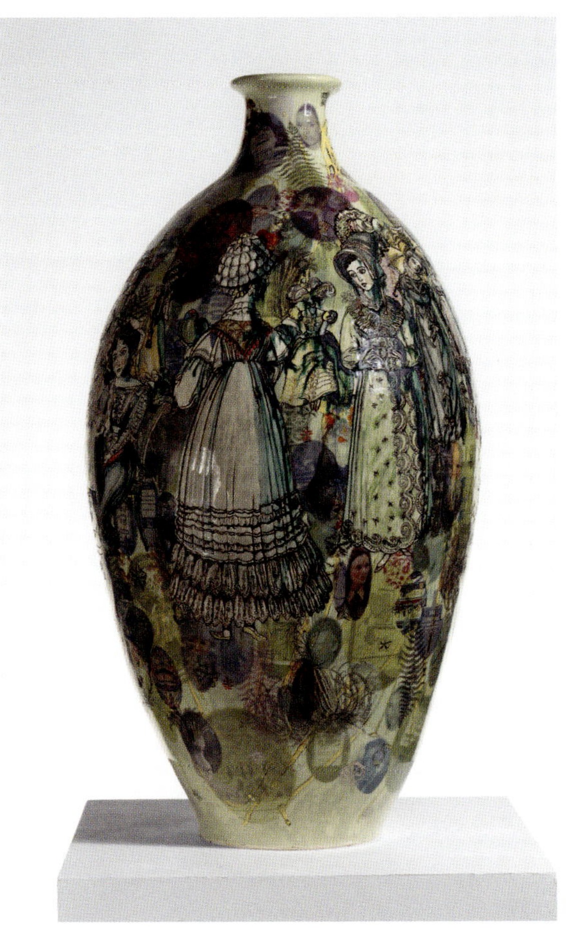

Grayson Perry, *Jane Austen in E17*, 2009
Glazed ceramic, 100 × 51.5 cm (39½ × 20¼ in.)

wrote to accompany an extraordinary exhibition at the British Museum, 'The Tomb of the Unknown Craftsman' (2011–12), which featured Perry's own ceramics, sculptures, embroideries, drawings and customized motorbike alongside the handmade objects from the museum's collections that had inspired them: medieval pilgrimage badges, maps, costumes, Maori carvings, Roman cameos, etc. Often touching, as other recent work of his does, on pilgrimage and our need for religion, it was as much about the triumph of imagination as making. For him, the two come together.

That would be true of all the artists we have looked at in this chapter. They all put an emphasis on making, on a very personal vision and a drive towards complexity. Even the work of De Waal, whose individual pots might seem simple, but which he presents in subtle arrangements, is complex, or multilayered if you like, like that of the other artists, both in composition and in meaning.

Chapter 9

AUCTION ART OR BIENNALE ART?

2010–2014

In 2007 the daughter of the billionaire Pete Peterson told an interviewer: 'There's so much money on the Upper East Side [New York] right now. A lot of people under forty years old are making, like, $20 million or $30 million a year in these hedge funds, and they don't know what to do with it.'[1] Buying expensive contemporary artworks is one way to spend all that money. Artworks are 'positional goods': things that, because of their uniqueness, bring you prestige and make you part of an in-crowd. They might also be a good investment. And who knows – you might even enjoy looking at them. Ivanka Trump, who has collected works by Richard Prince (to his distress) and others, is typical here. No cool multi-millionaire today would be satisfied with framed *Time* pictures of themselves (like Ivanka's father): they want things that are NOW!

There are, of course, many equally rich young people in London, Shanghai, Singapore and elsewhere, all in their protective bubbles. This plutocracy is trans-global: a 'community of peers who have more in common with one another than with their countrymen back home. Whether they maintain primary residences in New York or Hong Kong, Moscow or Mumbai, today's super rich are increasingly a nation unto themselves.'[2] There is no better place to observe them gather than at a top-level art fair: Frieze in London, say, or Art Basel Miami. Watching them rush from booth to booth, from restaurant to hotel, one is astounded by their extraordinary sense of entitlement. But how do the artists who attend such events and deal with such people feel? 'It's like life at the court of the 0.1%,' says the artist Ragnar Kjartansson. 'You really feel like a court jester. Then you go home and take the kids to the kindergarten on the bus.'[3]

This is the age of extreme income disparity. Supposedly, 0.1 per cent of the population has taken over half of the world's wealth since 1980.[4] But although the very rich may be getting even richer, the middle classes are getting poorer while the poor remain desperately poor. This process started some time ago: already in 1993, Felix Gonzalez-Torres (see Chapter 5) was complaining that, 'during the last decade, we saw 1 per cent of American households getting richer. By 1989, the top 1 per cent were worth more than the bottom 90 per cent of Americans ... The average corporate executive, who earned as much as 41 factory workers or 38 teachers in 1960, was earning as much as 93 factory workers or 72 teachers by 1988.'[5]

Such disparities have been mirrored in the art world. Economists have observed that income inequality correlates to art prices: the bigger the difference between top income and no income, the higher the prices paid for works of art.[6] Indeed, the artworld seems to be booming: record price after record price; more art fairs (over 260 in 2018, compared to only 55 in 2000);[7] and ever more biennales (238 at the last count).[8] Is all this money, all these opportunities, enabling for artists, or corrupting?

The pressure on many artists to make yet more works for more fairs and more biennales can become inexorable. All but a few top galleries are struggling too. As an increasingly greater number of sales occur at art fairs rather than exhibitions in galleries, the financial pressure on galleries in the middle market has become extreme: they have to go to fairs to sell, but cannot really afford to do so. The cost of flights, hotels, renting booths at the fairs, advertising, entertaining and shipping artworks overseas can be crippling. When I talk to gallerists around the world, they say the same: that a few mega-galleries – Gagosian, White Cube, David Zwirner, etc. – are making enormous sums, but those in the middle range (i.e. galleries selling works costing between $5,000 and $50,000) are finding it harder to survive.

Is art, then, just a lot of commodities for sale, or is it meant to change the world?

Nowadays, more than ever before, people talk of 'auction art' and 'biennale art', as if they were separate entities. Generally speaking, painting is seen as 'auction art' – perhaps 80 per cent of what is sold at auction is painting. Biennales, by contrast, rarely include paintings. The curators who organize them take their cue from conceptual art's contempt for late modernist painting: they want installations or issue-based art. The art world has therefore become somewhat schizophrenic, although in fact many artists happily produce both paintings and installations. And painting underlies much else; as Kimsooja tells us, 'I began my practice as a painter, and most of my evolution stems from my position as a painter.'[9]

In March 2018 Sotheby's in London sold Peter Doig's *The Architect's Home in the Ravine* (see Chapter 5) for £14,376,400. What is most surprising is that this was the fifth time it had come to auction since it was painted. Sold initially by the artist in 1992 directly to Arthur Andersen & Co., probably for a five-figure sum, it had then gone to Sotheby's in London in June 2002, where it was bought by Charles Saatchi for £314,650. Five years later, Saatchi sent it to Sotheby's in New York, where it sold for $3,624,000. In February 2013 it was back in London at Christie's, where it fetched £7,657,250. In February 2016 it was once again at Christie's in London, selling for £11,282,500. Each of the six vendors made a tidy profit, and the auction houses made good money too.

When I asked a friend at one of the auction houses why Doig's paintings, especially his earlier work, was so sought after, he replied: 'Tony, isn't it obvious? There are so few good Impressionist paintings left to buy, and there are so many very rich people who want to buy one, they have to look elsewhere for something that looks like Impressionism. Doig fits the bill. The Russian billionaires love his work.' This does not, of course, make Doig a bad or corrupted artist. In fact, it is clear that he has *not* become a 'brand', churning out the same old thing time and time again. He has continued to develop, experimenting with forms and materials. Moreover, he isn't just looked at by a few Russian billionaires. When he exhibited his work in an obscure palazzo at the 2015 Venice Biennale, what was striking was how many people, young and old, came to see it.

In the 1990s, before he had become famous, Doig gave a lecture to my students. Unusually, rather than showing slides of his completed paintings, he showed a selection of details, talking about the difficulties he had had in making certain areas work. His paintings are complex, and what happens in and on the surface carries much of the meaning. 'Maybe', he suggested later, 'the surface is an abstraction of the memory of being in a certain frame of mind under certain weather conditions and in uncertain places.'[10] Places and how they affect us matter to Doig: 'In Trinidad [to which he moved in 2002] the landscape is so present and powerful; it's everywhere, even in Port of Spain. I'd experienced this growing up in Canada, and here it hit me again.'[11]

Doig has said that the man on the horse in *Horse and Rider* (page 202), shown at Venice in 2015, is in part a self-portrait, that it also has echoes of Goya's portrait of the Duke of Wellington on a horse, and that he was also thinking of how, during a carnival, people often play at being the bad man, in a dark but also comic way. 'A painting as opposed to a photograph', Doig added, 'is much more cinematic in the sense that it has all these layers of information that go beyond just the imagery that is depicted.'[12] Although he often uses photographs as a source, they are never copied; rather, they are merged in a working and reworking of the paint. What makes his best paintings so satisfying is their complexity.

'Weird' is how the artist Adrian Ghenie describes the experience of seeing paintings he once sold for a few thousand dollars coming to auction and selling for millions. 'The market is so crazy,' he said in 2015. 'It's frustrating to see people make so much money so quickly. I feel I'm being speculated. It's not me. It's the new art world.'[13] Why has an artist from Cluj, Romania, become such a subject of fascination? His works are well painted, very visceral and different. You can sense a strong personality behind them. 'I don't think my work would have been noticed if it hadn't coincided with Europe's opening up to Eastern countries,' he observed, ruefully. 'I came up with this very specific subject and Eastern European atmosphere that perfectly matched expectations. They didn't want a second-hand abstract expressionist piece made by an Eastern European guy – they wanted that basement feeling. For them, that was the feeling of Romania and dictatorship.'[14] Collectors are also happy to know that he was once so poor he shaved his cat to make his brushes.

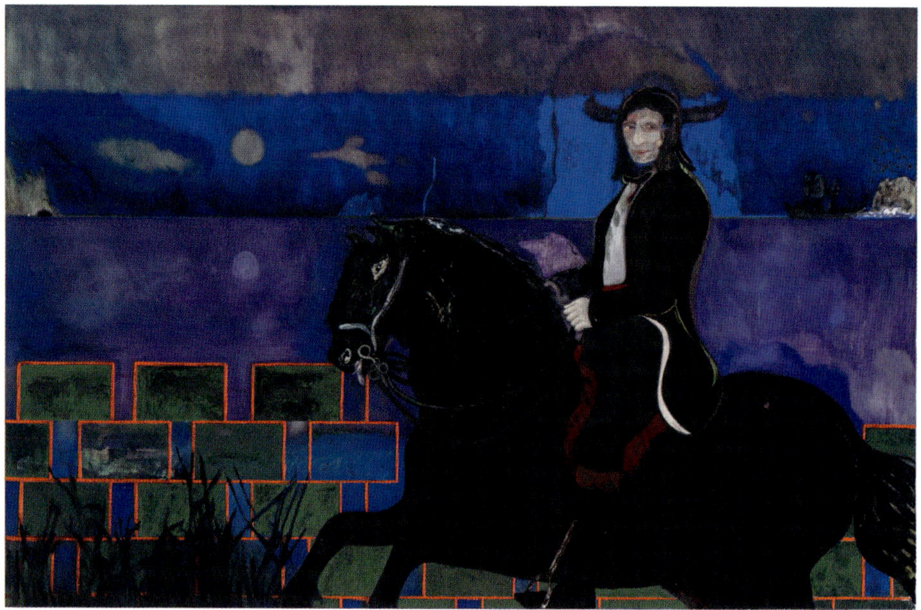

Peter Doig, *Horse and Rider*, 2014
Oil on canvas, 240 × 360 cm (94½ × 142 in.)

Ghenie's 'basement' is one in which recent history – what the artist describes as a 'century of humiliation'[15] – is re-enacted, in which Darwin, Mengele, Ceausescu, Stalin, Lenin and Hitler all reappear, crusted with or deformed by paint. The works are compelling because you can't quite put your finger on exactly what they mean or what their fascination is. 'If an image is not loaded with symbolic meaning on a Jungian level', says Ghenie, 'then it's an empty image. I guess I'm trying to do for arts what [the 'herd' psychologist and advertising innovator] Edward Bernays did for marketing: invent an object not just to resolve a human need, but to resolve a human desire.'[16]

Ghenie's *Persian Miniature* (opposite) has a very misleading title for a large painting of a man – in fact a self-portrait – in a forest. Or a man covered with paint. It wobbles uncomfortably between abstraction and figuration, as if each were a virus trying to infect the other. Like many artists, Ghenie has been inspired in particular by David Lynch. 'As a teenager', recalls Ghenie, 'there was just one series that really touched me, *Twin Peaks* ... I found it absolutely horrifying. In '92 it aired on Romanian TV. As I dove into my painting career David Lynch remained a core inspiration. He's not just making movies ... he's making experiments. He plays with something inside of his audience, and his work is so well executed we don't realize it. I think consciously and unconsciously I want to master in painting what Lynch has done in cinema. It was with Lynch that I started to build the visual language of my paintings.'[17]

Peter Doig has suggested that painting now is outside contemporary art, that it exists on its own.[18] One can see his point: first, that biennale art can seem like

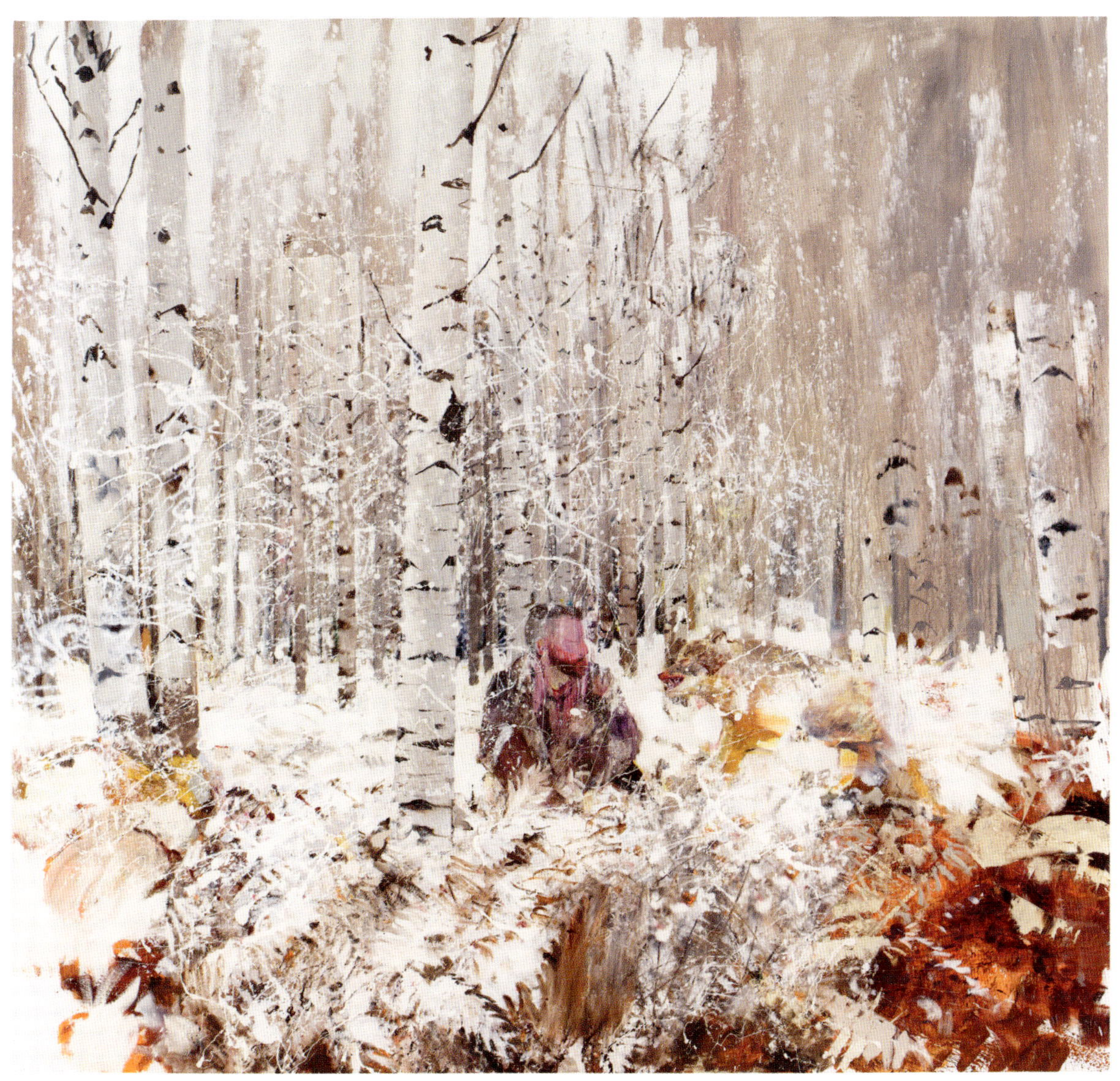

Adrian Ghenie, *Persian Miniature*, 2013
Oil on canvas, 300.4 × 290.2 cm (118¼ × 114¼ in.)

a self-contained system; and secondly, that painting is as much about a conversation with the past as about any notion of progress. Ghenie has said something similar: 'For me, chronology doesn't exist in art. Caravaggio and de Kooning were trying to solve the same problem.'[19] But I can't agree with Doig: even if contemporary art is being pulled and stretched in different directions, it is still one lump of dough, just one story, however complicated.

The rage for new art is a global phenomenon. In Indonesia, for example, the search for the next big thing is just as intense as it is in the West; speculation, too, is just as rife. In a brilliant series of cartoon-like drawings and paintings, Uji Handoko Eko Saputro, better known as Hahan, has parodied this world of speculation and hunger for fame, whether national or global, in which so many artists strive to succeed but only a very few will.

In 2016, at Art Jog in Yogyakarta, Indonesia – an art fair run, unusually, by artists – Hahan showed a vast, 7.5-metre-wide (24½ ft) work called *Speculative Entertainment No. 1* (opposite), part of an ongoing project. Also present were numerous assistants armed with computers and printers and the paddles used to bid in auctions. A grid was projected on to the painting, and one by one each of the resulting squares (there were several hundred of them) were put up for sale, bid for, sold, cut out and given to the successful buyer. What they bought was not so much a painting as a fragment or fetish of a painting. What a brilliant spoof of the system! When enough squares had been sold, one could read the following words on the wall behind: 'The true art is the selling of it'.

Zeng Fanzhi, we are told, 'is considered by many to be China's greatest living artist'.[20] How we long to call artists 'great'! How we enjoy arguing as to who is the 'greatest'! However, let's leave that discussion to the final chapter. We have already noted (in the introduction) how much money Zeng's work sells for. Has that wealth corrupted him as an artist, or has it given him freedom? Certainly, he has not been accused, as so many other Chinese artists have, of using assistants to paint his paintings, hence increasing production and enhancing revenue. Nor has he stuck with his original winning formula: 'I don't just want to be known as an artist who paints masks.'[21]

Those paintings were a response to the loneliness and confusion Zeng felt when he moved to Beijing in 1993. More recently, however, he has concentrated on painting landscapes. 'In 2002,' he tells us, 'I grew a pot of Chinese wisteria in my studio in Yanjiao. After the winter all the leaves had fallen off, exposing the intertwining vines and branches in which I found a special beauty, and I felt inspired to paint a piece with "chaotic brushstrokes".'[22] Zeng paints with a calligraphy brush; he wants to emphasize the Chinese-ness of what he does. Before this, because of an injury to his dominant hand, the right, he had to paint with his left. He liked the mistakes he inevitably made, so, once he had fully recovered, he started to paint with a brush in each hand, one creative, one destructive. He talks of how

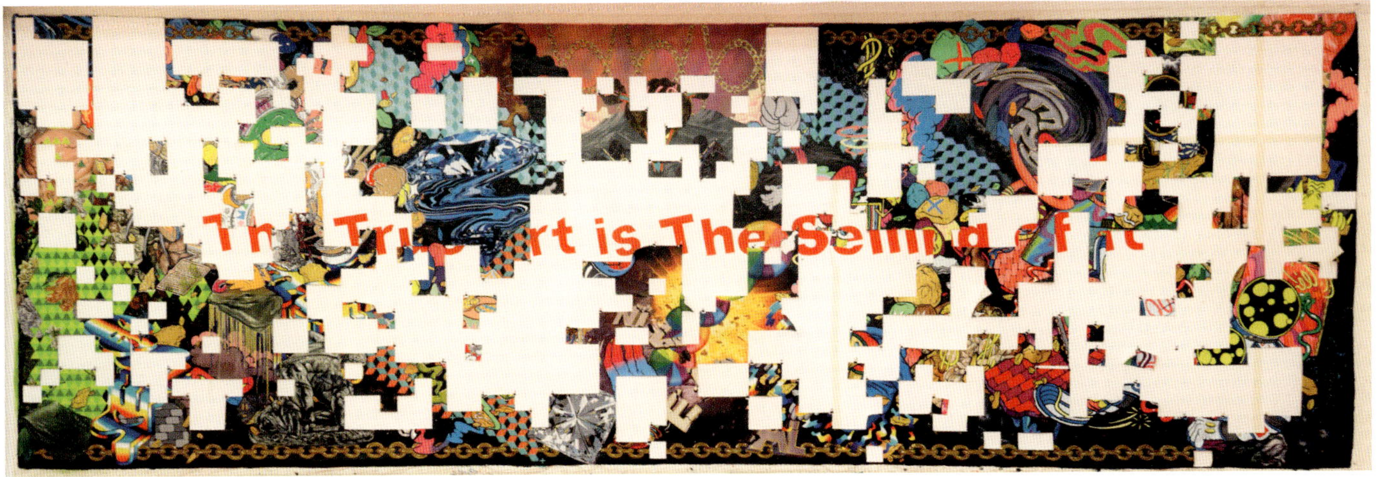

Hahan (Uji Handoko, Eko Saputro), *Speculative Entertainment No. 1*, 2016
Acrylic, ink and spray on canvas, 260 × 750 cm (102⅜ × 295⅜ in.)

lines, although rarely featured in Western oil painting, have always been an aspect of Chinese painting. And apart from becoming a keen gardener and researching the long history of Chinese gardens, Zeng has developed a sympathy for literati culture and Song-dynasty ink paintings. But what we see in his work is not retro Song painting but an unusually harmonious blend of Chinese landscape painting and European expressionism. We are all influenced by each other.

It is apparent to me that Doig, Ghenie and Zeng are unique individuals, each with a large body of strong, wide-ranging work – not just a formula repeated. They have the respect of their fellow artists. But there are other artists whose pieces sell for millions at auction whose work fails to convince me. It seems predictable, it lacks complexity; it doesn't add anything to the story of contemporary art. However, who am to I judge? I have forty years of looking at art, and no vested interests. But I'm aware, too, that there are so many different types of art today, it is difficult to be responsive to all of them. I am sure we have all had the experience of not thinking much about a certain type of art, music or even food, and then eventually developing a taste for and understanding of it. Nevertheless, I look at some much-promoted and much-praised art and think it to be nothing but over-priced decor.

The key question is, who decides? Compared to previous periods, there is little consensus today on what is good and what is not. The art press has become enfeebled: no magazine has the circulation or authority that, for example, *Artforum* had in the 1970s. There is a lot of hype. Judgments are further skewed because few art critics are keen on painting. The Internet has effectively replaced the printed-on-paper magazines, but it is inchoate.

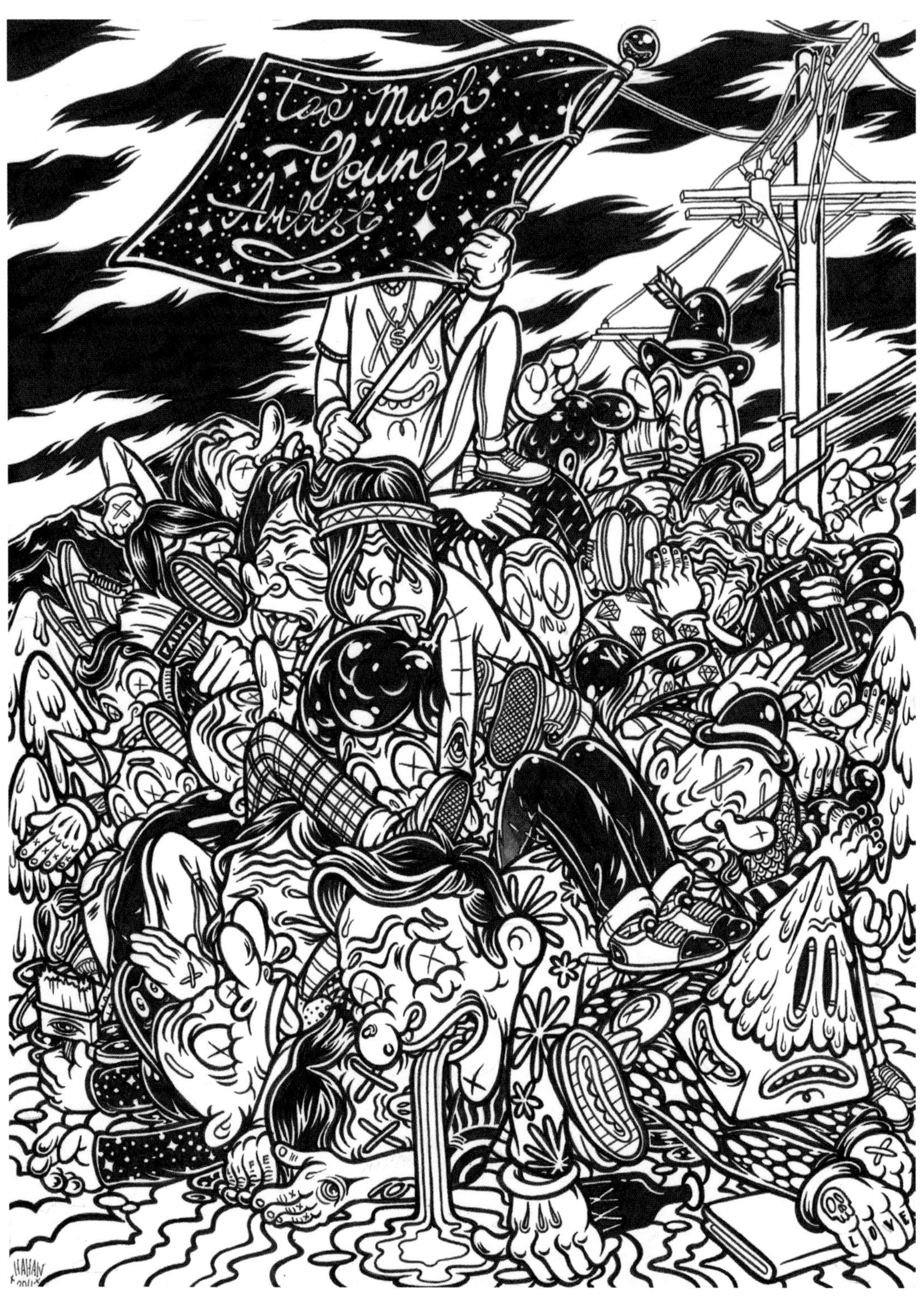

Hahan (Uji Handoko, Eko Saputro), *Letters to The Great Saatchi*, 2011
Indian ink on acid-free paper, 29.7 × 21 cm (11¾ × 8¼ in.)

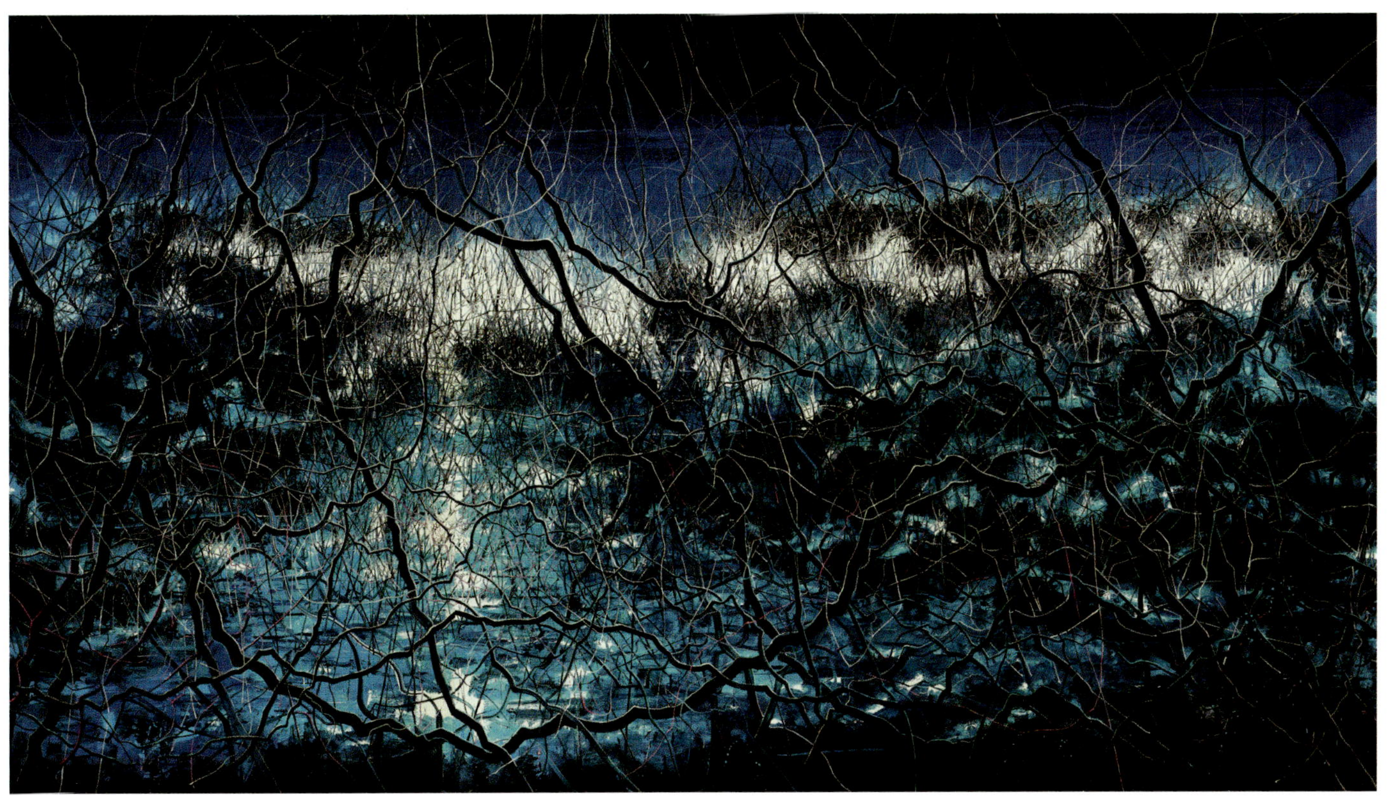

Zeng Fanzhi, *Blue*, 2015
Oil on canvas, 3 panels, 400 × 700 cm (157½ × 275⅝ in.)

There is a plethora of information but very little sign of considered analysis and assessment, save for lists and rankings put up by people you havc never heard of. Auction prices can be a misleading guide to quality. Of course, some collectors are discriminating, but en masse they are compromised by their obvious financial interest. The market is far from an infallible judge: we can point to many examples of artists whose prices have surged, then slumped. So what do we do? Find art that is interesting and challenging, then see if the artist who made it is capable of developing or is just happy to replicate their 'brand'.

The Chinese artist Liu Xiaodong works like an Impressionist, setting up his easel outside and painting what he sees, but he acts like a very twenty-first-century artist. Just as Doris Salcedo does, he wants to talk to the people he portrays, about their lives and problems. The girls in *Out of Beichuan* (page 208) are there to be painted, but also to talk about themselves, and presumably how the avalanche, visible in the background, has destroyed their town. When Liu first exhibited the work, at the 2010 Shanghai Biennale, he showed photographs, sketches and a video alongside it. You could call it a research project, of which the painting is just the largest element.

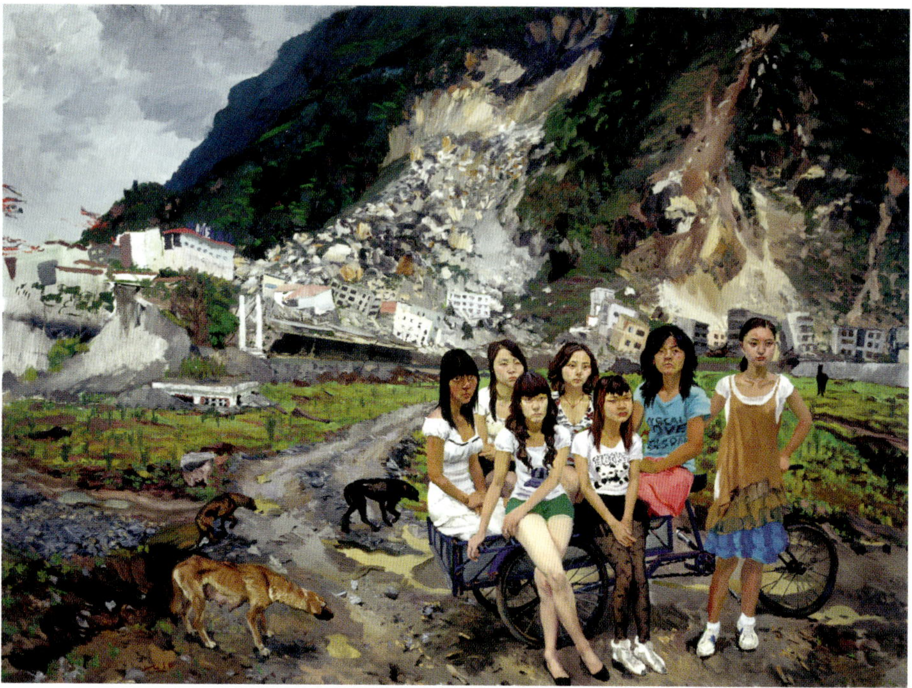

Liu Xiaodong, *Out of Beichuan*, 2010
Oil on canvas, 300 × 400 cm (118⅛ × 157½ in.)

Much of Liu's work deals with the trauma of urbanization and ecological spoliation, both in China and elsewhere. Like many people, he finds himself alienated from his own roots: 'As soon as you begin to talk about your homeland, something starts to happen inside you, something like homesickness. I think in my innermost self, I do not want anything to change in my hometown. You just want your old home to stay as it always used to be. Only if it stays that way can it remain a refuge for us, however much reality is different ... Urbanization is spreading much too quickly, destroying everything that we loved or did not love; forming a new city out of everything.'[23]

The New York-based artist Dana Schutz's recent painting *Mountain Group* (opposite) could be seen as her version of Goya's famous print *The Sleep of Reason Produces Monsters* (1797–99). But her monsters are more jokey, less scary than Goya's, and her protagonist does not fall asleep but persists, painting the mountain as if the monsters were not blocking the view. Perhaps they are only an illusion.

Empathy has always driven Schutz's work: 'I'm interested in how something feels, rather than how it looks,' she says.[24] Her imagined monsters are strangely sympathetic. Often, her paintings have tried to give an equivalent to a physical sensation – sneezing, for example, or working out on a treadmill. The chunkiness of her painting accentuates such physicality. Furthermore, her paintings are always very satisfying from a formal perspective, like complex but perfectly made knots.

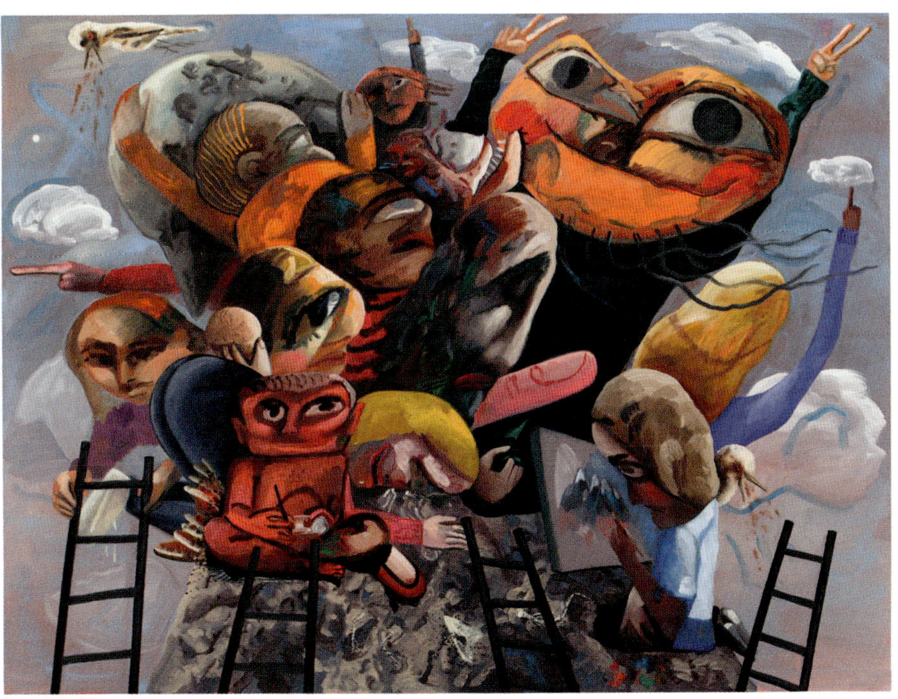

Dana Schutz, *Mountain Group*, 2018
Oil on canvas, 304.8 × 396.2 cm (120 × 156 in.)

Most of Schutz's paintings come from the imagination. But one based on a photograph of the black teenager Emmet Till lying in his coffin after he had been lynched in 1955 caused much controversy when exhibited at the 2018 Whitney Biennial. Black activists, claiming that a white artist had no right to make money from black pain, stood in front of the painting to impede others' view of it and demanded it be destroyed. Although seen as insensitive, Schutz was no doubt trying to empathize. It is a complex issue: in writing about or picturing those who have suffered genocide or slavery, one does not want to be seen as voyeuristic or manipulative, but to say only black people can paint black people is like saying only women can write about women, or men can write about men. If that were the case there would be no more novels.

Bruised by the whole experience, Schutz refused either to take down the painting or to sell it. Her subsequent exhibition, in which *Mountain Group* appeared, was not presented as a justification of what she had done, but rather a display of paintings about doing things and imagining worlds. Paintings that were simultaneously chunky and visionary – a mixture that only she seems capable of. The exhibition was also about persisting. Of the time in which they were made, she said: 'Painting itself kind of actually felt more urgent, after [the Whitney controversy]. It was a relief where you just felt grateful to be able to paint. For me at least, that feels like the only way to get through something.'[25]

Like Shahzia Sikander, the Pakistani artist Imran Qureshi trained on the miniature-painting course in Lahore. If people suggest miniature painting is outmoded, he responds by saying: 'I think it's just a medium. And for me, it's like I'm talking in my mother tongue, instead of talking in a foreign language. I'm so comfortable with it.'[26] And as with Sikander, miniature painting for Qureshi became a way to talk about contemporary events, especially the violent ones.

Although Qureshi enjoys the slow, quiet, meditative process of making a miniature, he also allows the more extrovert aspect of his personality to appear in his installations, filling spaces with scrunched up balls of paper, each enclosing a drawing or lithograph in red ink, or painting on walls and floors. When Qureshi saw a courtyard in Sharjah, UAE, it reminded him of all the courtyards with gardens in Pakistan. He was taken with the idea of filling the courtyard with red flowers. From afar, however, the work looked like a bloodbath; only close up could you see that it consisted of the rather formalized foliate shapes you find in Indian miniatures, specifically Pahari painting. He wanted, he said, 'an element of attraction and repulsion at the same time ... there was so much violence around us at that time.'[27] Later, he added: 'There's the idea of life, beauty and death working together. There is an element of violence in the work. At the same time, when you come close to it and start looking at it carefully, it becomes poetic as well.'[28]

As someone who also makes installations, Qureshi is more likely to be invited to participate in a biennale than someone who only paints. Curiously, such Asian painters as Qureshi, Nilima Sheikh and Geraldine Javier seem more likely to also work in installation: perhaps they feel less constrained by Western expectations of what a painter should be or do.

So far we have looked at seven painters, each very different from the other, each responding to the world around them in a highly personal way. Several of them, although not all, are 'stars' of the auction system. Not all stars of that system are painters, however: sculptures by Jeff Koons or Antony Gormley, as well as photographs by Cindy Sherman, have also become a form of currency. But what about the biennale system? Can that be corrupting too? Could it be another market that has demands? Even if artists receive funding from the state or private sponsorship, many individual projects have to be paid for by dealers, who need sales. You may not find price lists at the Venice Biennale as once you did, but it is still a marketplace. Already in the 1980s, the neo-conservative critic Peter Fuller was sneering at what he called 'Biennale International Club Class Art' (BICCA). Is there such a thing? If so, is it good or bad? Let us look at a further eight artists, each of whom regularly appears in biennales.

Although Sarah Sze (whom we first encountered in the introduction) began as a painter, she sees herself now as a sculptor, albeit one who spreads objects out, rather than pulling them together. She believes in physical things: 'I'm more interested in how we endear ourselves to objects or create meaning from objects or

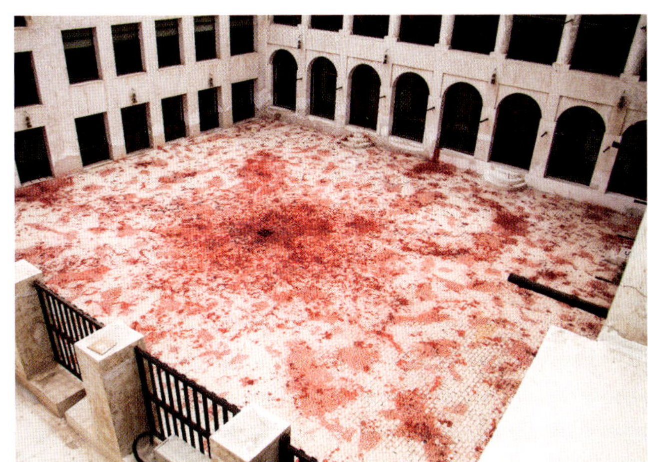

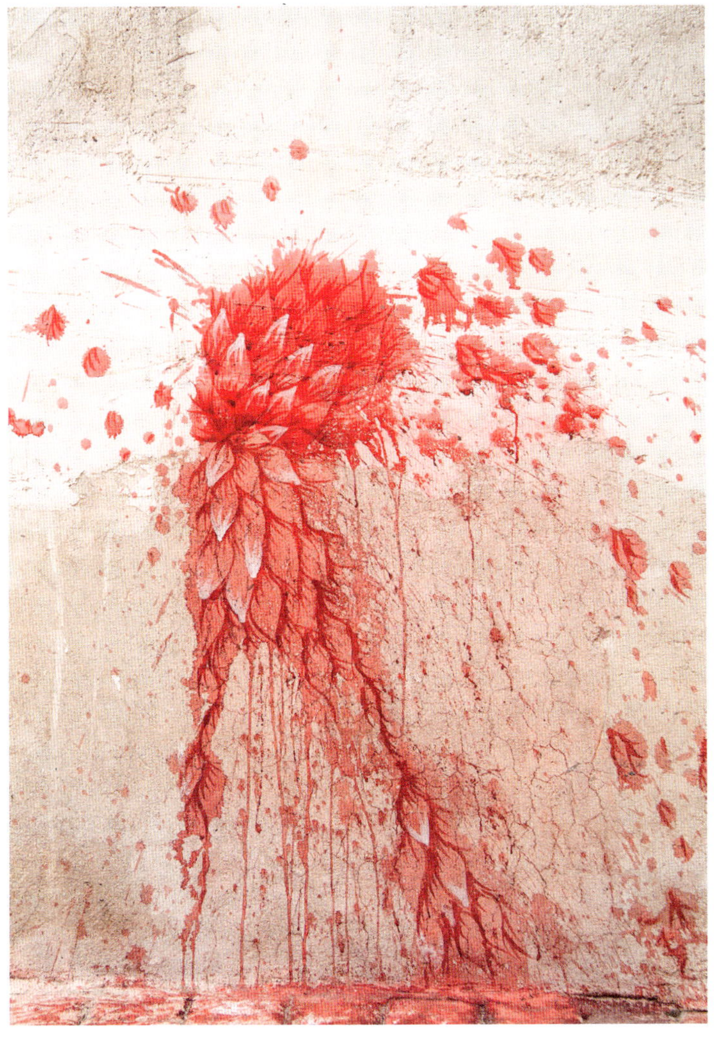

Imran Qureshi, *Blessings upon the Land of my Love*, 2011
Acrylic and emulsion paint on interlocking brick pavement, site-specific installation, commissioned by Sharjah Art Foundation

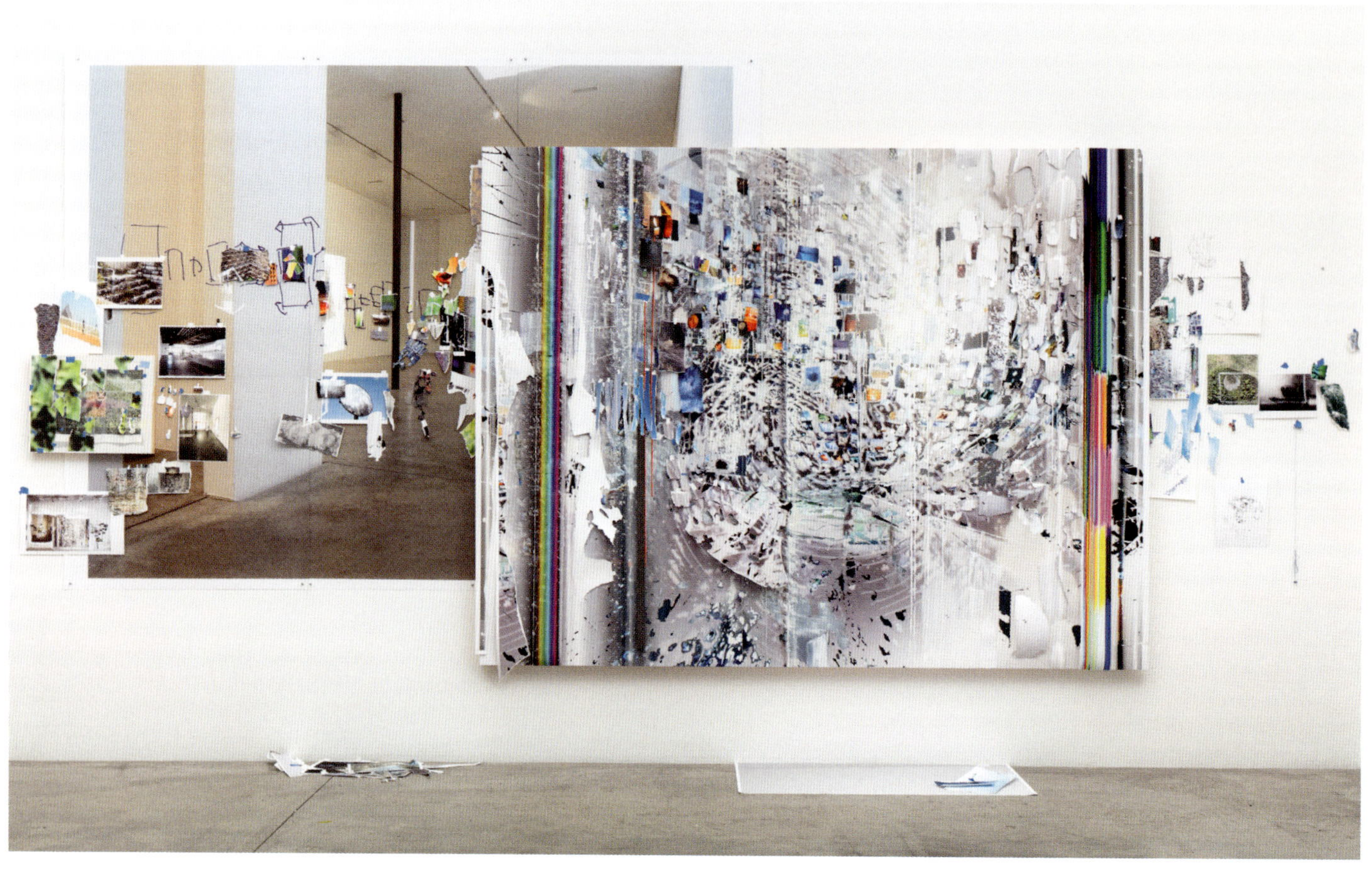

Sarah Sze, *Afterimage, Rainbow Disturbance (Painting in its Archive)*, 2018
Oil paint, acrylic paint, aluminium, archival paper, UV stabilizers, adhesive, tape, ink and acrylic polymers, shellac, water-based primer on wood, 262 × 550 × 12 cm (103⅛ x 216½ x 4¾ in.)

carry conversations through objects'.[29] In 2013 she suggested that 'most artists are ... in some way playing with the way in which people find value in objects and how objects give value to social relations ... It's the language of contemporary living, isn't it?'[30] It is a statement that many, addicted as they are to social media, might not agree with. But should they?

Sze talks of how the restlessness of her work, the multiplicity of images and objects – some still, some moving – has to do with our new way of life, in which, for example, we might be travelling physically on a train or coach while also travelling internally by flicking through images on our smartphone.[31] We seem to be in many places at once. Sculpture, for Sze, 'has to address this volatility of place, because amidst the travelling through time, space and information that has become so facile, sculpture can cultivate what sculpture can do like nothing else: it can cultivate the value of concrete experience in space, in real time.'[32]

On the one hand, Sze's work can look like planetariums or temporary environments, scientific models of complex systems built with whatever comes to hand. Like the mountain that Roy Neary (played by Richard Dreyfuss) builds out of mashed potato in *Close Encounters of the Third Kind*, they are scientific but in an intuitive way. On the other hand, each object seems invested with some potential importance, even if it's just a cotton-wool swab, a fragment of a landscape photograph or a splodge of paint.

Recently, Sze has used an increasing amount of video, such that the work seems more about being in time, or large photographs of her paintings as a basis for making something that spreads across and beyond the wall. There is always a constant play between representation and 'stuff', between actual objects and copies of objects. Her work often looks improvised, even unfinished, and so fragile that a malicious kick could destroy it; but there is an appealing ingenuity and delight in how she forms her pieces. Her work is collectable, too – if you have a big house.

'How', asked the South Korean artist Haegue Yang in 2008, 'can I overcome the somewhat lonesome and disconnected condition of work and move towards reconnecting with worlds? Certain vulnerable sentiments give me a strong empowerment for acknowledging my fragmented social existence as an artist, assuring my desire to get myself engaged in the world.'[33] Two years earlier, she had made an installation inside the derelict house (Sadong 30) in Korea where her grandmother had lived, using mirrors, origami, drying racks and fragments from the building itself. Yang planted chrysanthemums in the old outdoor water basin and put bottles of water in the fridge for any visitors. It was an act of reparation and recovery: turning a broken-down house into a transitional space, somewhere where you might have an experience, have ideas, or change your life in some way.

Yang often makes sculptures from everyday objects – venetian blinds, for example. Yet these sculptures, in a way that is difficult to identify, are about ideas and emotions; they are also satisfying to look at, more than just good design. She has admitted

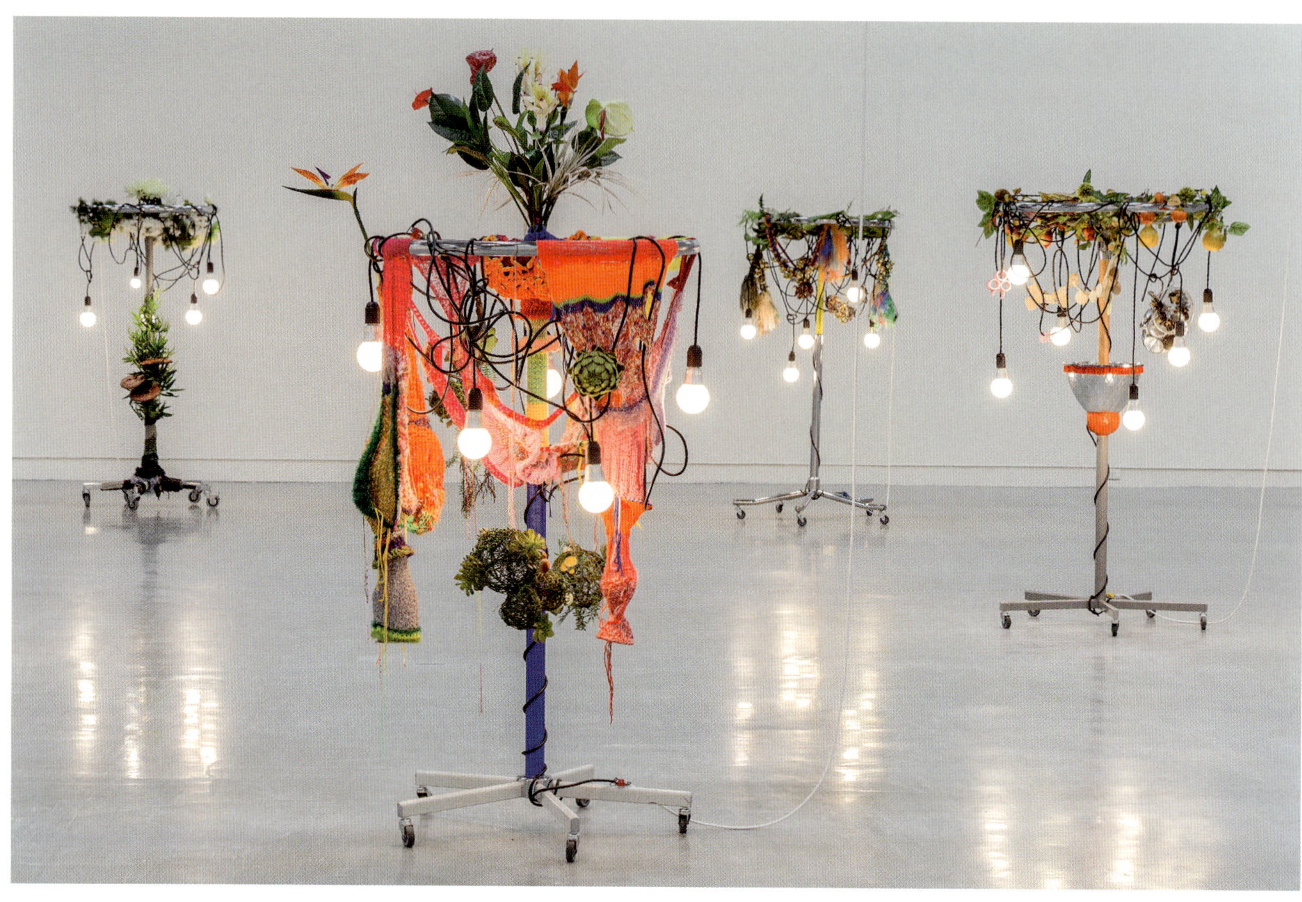

Haegue Yang, *Female Natives* (detail), 2010
Installation view, 'The Great Acceleration', Taipei Biennial 2014, Taiwan, 2014

to sometimes thinking, as many of us do, of objects as people. Her *Female Natives* and *Medicine Men* sculptures (above) are witty and complex enough to suggest each has a personality. But why would she ask for Stravinsky's *Rite of Spring*, a violent evocation of a primitive ritual, to be played alongside these jolly-looking constructions? To help us imagine them coming to life and moving about? To suggest a violence or angst in these kitschy or everyday objects?

Yang's works, or so she has said, deal with 'the topics of migration, displacement, postcolonial diaspora, forced exile'.[34] This might not seem obvious just by looking at the works, unless you also read her discussion of all the things she is researching. 'My driving interests and motivations are often concrete, but my artistic language is one of abstraction,' she notes.[35] What her work clearly embodies is a sense of oddness, of things in the wrong context or combination, while looking aesthetically 'right'. This is a conversation about both belonging and being out of place.

Biennales are important venues for those artists who prefer to make work that is site-specific, that responds to the social, historical or ecological character of a place. One such artist is Ayşe Erkmen, born in Turkey but now living in Berlin. When I first saw Erkmen's *Plan B* at the 2011 Venice Biennale (below), I was struck by how beautiful it was, the brightly coloured tubes making an exquisite contrast with the distressed walls of the old Arsenale building in which it had been installed. Erkmen would probably not have minded such an initial reaction: 'Showing an idea is important,' she notes, 'but it must be done in the most aesthetic way possible. Everything has to have a purpose.'[36] And even if it did look a little like some painted abstract sculpture from the 1960s, *Plan B* did have an idea. It was a water-filtration plant, each colour showing a different function. Moreover, it worked: water was taken from the canal outside, filtered so it was drinkable, and then sent back

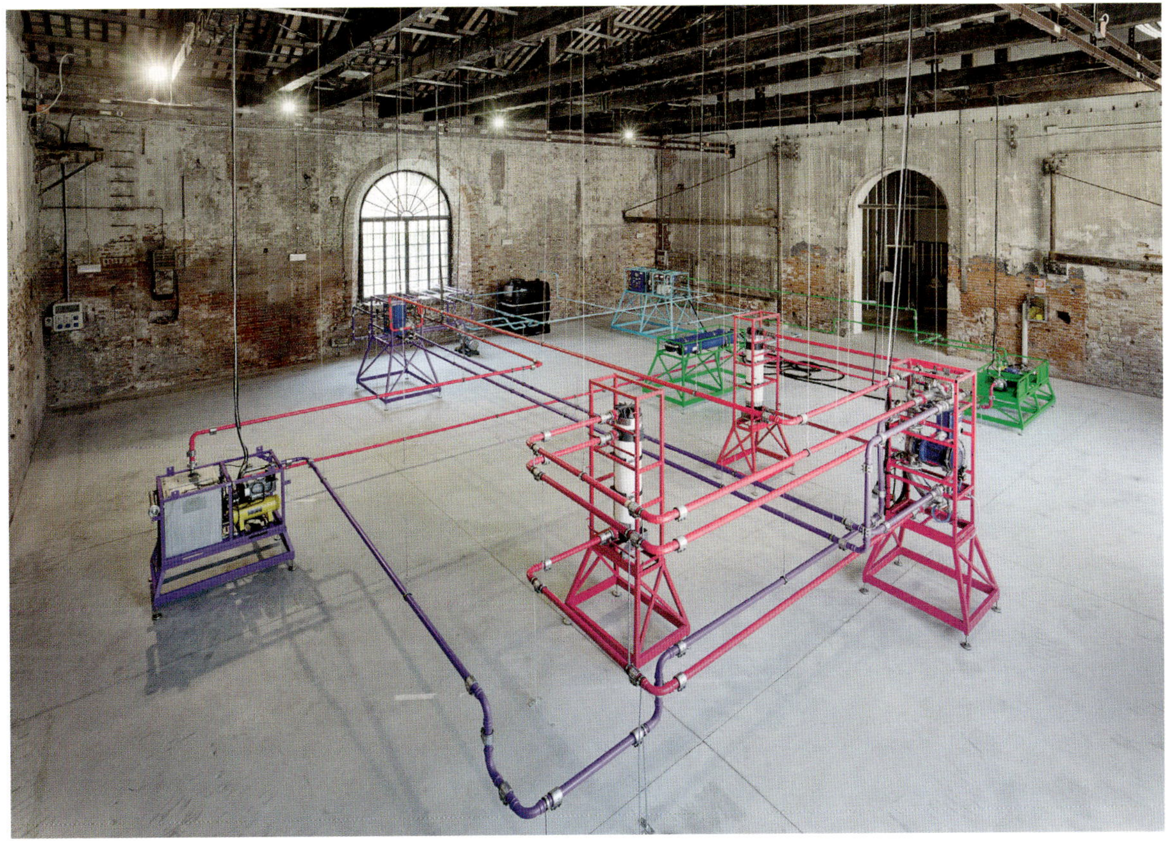

Ayşe Erkmen, *Plan B*, 2011
Water-purification system, pipes, pumps, cleansing machines painted in specific colours according to their function; installation view, Venice Biennale, 2011

to the canal. 'There is nothing to drink, no product – just the fact that the canal gets the water back. I think this works more in line with the idea of art – working with no purpose.'[37]

Like other artists who believe that their works should be site-specific – in and responding to a particular place and context – Erkmen has no studio. She travels to places and, if she needs anything made, relies on fabricators. Not all her work, however, is site-specific: in 2011 she exhibited 1,400 images she'd found by Googling her name, 'Ayşe Erkmen' (most of them were not of her). It told us of Google's compulsion to swamp us with facts, 'alternative facts' and irrelevances.

Video installations are another thing you find at biennales. Often, the organizers can offer production money for such projects. In *Jaonua: The Nothingness* (opposite), an installation by the Thai artist Araya Rasdjarmrearnsook shown at the 2016 Singapore Biennale, five videos are projected on to four fabric screens and a bed. We see a water buffalo tied to a post and then slaughtered; a couple having a romantic meal in a restaurant; a young woman on an elevated chair reading or sleeping in a field filled with horses; sheep on the back of a travelling van, staring out at the world; the artist herself writing, an image double-exposed over footage of the tide coming in, waves breaking and fading away – 'We are talking about the fate of a soul trapped in the endless cycle of birth and death', we see her write. People eat beside a cremation, a violinist plays, people have sex, a dog stands beside the sea. Images and sounds overlap; it's a complex discussion on and confrontation with death, life and animals.

Rasdjarmrearnsook first became known for making videos of herself in a hospital talking or reading to dead people. This may seem ghoulish, but you should remember that art has always been a way for people to contemplate death and mourn. 'Life and death', she tells us, 'should not be understood as opposites. People deal with death by trying to hide it. They hide death behind ritual or hope to prevent it with medicine. I want people to have more imagination and confront reality!'[38]

What would you have seen if you had gone to the 2015 Venice Biennale and entered the Danish pavilion, where Danh Vo (born in Vietnam but brought up in Denmark and now living in Mexico) was exhibiting? A large white room with a few small objects scattered around it (page 218). You might have been so puzzled that you'd tried to find a written guide straight away, or you might have decided to try to work it out for yourself (it's always best to do that; you can read the blurb later). Let's assume you went for the second option ...

At your feet lies a worn wooden box containing a segment of a marble sculpture, perhaps of a face or a torso. The table is the biggest thing in the room so you approach it. You are tempted to ask the young woman sitting at the table what the work is all about, but she seems very preoccupied with her book. You wonder if she is part of the installation (whether intended to or not, gallery attendants always become part of the viewer's experience). The bottle on the table contains not water, as you expected, but sipping tequila; Danh Vo's name and the slogan 'Lick

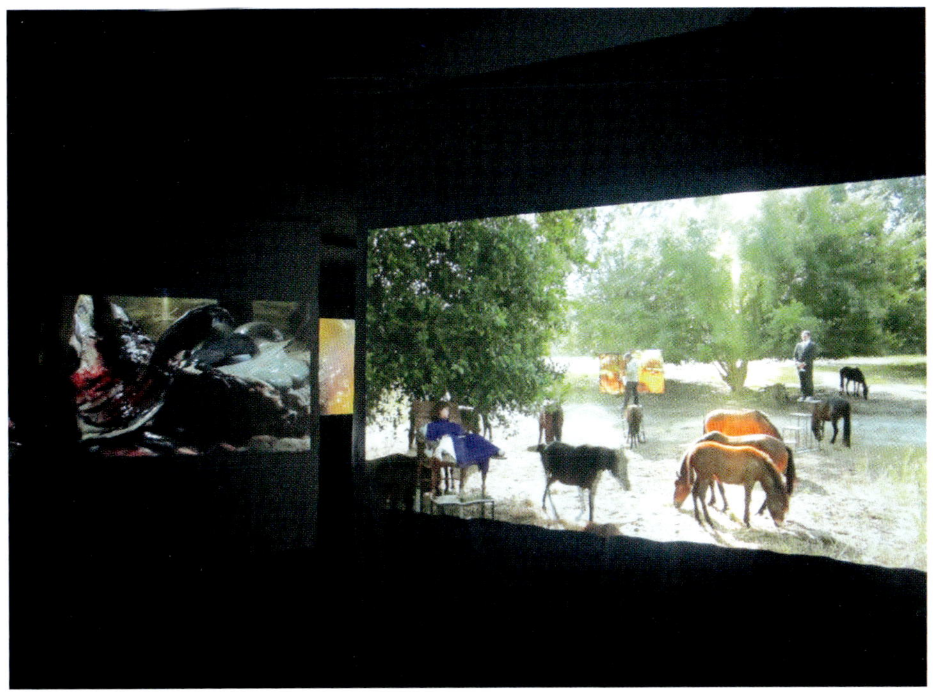

Araya Rasdjarmrearnsook, *Jaonua: The Nothingness*, 2016
Five-channel video installation, 35 minutes

me! Lick me!' can be seen on the label. Embedded in the table's surface are thirty silver coins. When you look closely at the tree trunk on the table, you can see that the gilded faces of angels have been attached to the end of some of the branches. There are more branches on the floor behind the woman, and they too have gilded angels attached to them. On a bench opposite is a mustard-yellow cushion and a paper construction shaped like a wedding cake with a red ribbon and a red candle.

Fallen angels, trees, a sliced-up bit of sculpture – it is hard to make any logical connections. You might feel frustrated and leave, or maybe you think of the poetry of T. S. Eliot, Rainer Maria Rilke or Paul Celan, which is not easy to understand, but which we return to periodically because we like the sound of the words, the imagery, and the way we discover something new each time we read it. It is very unlikely that anyone will recognize many of the references, let alone all of them; the marble torso, for example, is from an ancient roman sculpture of Apollo, while 'Lick me! Lick me!' is a quote from *The Exorcist*. Images of lust, fear and inebriation start to float together, if not quite connect. Everything looks so cool and elegant because Vo has stripped the pavilion of everything added to it since it was built in 1960, including the electric lights, and added a bench and table designed by the Danish designer Finn Juhl in 1949 and 1953 respectively.

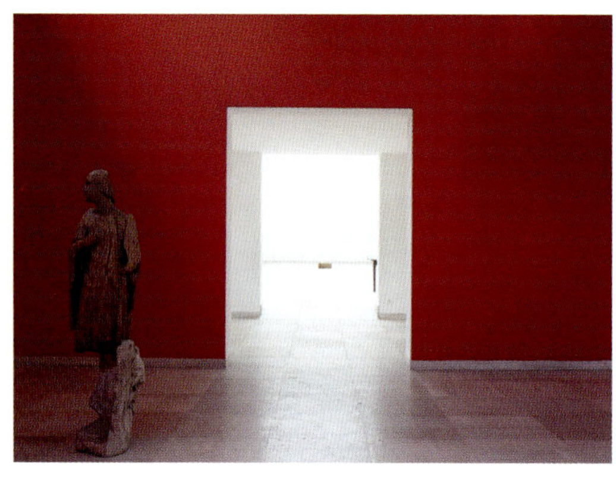

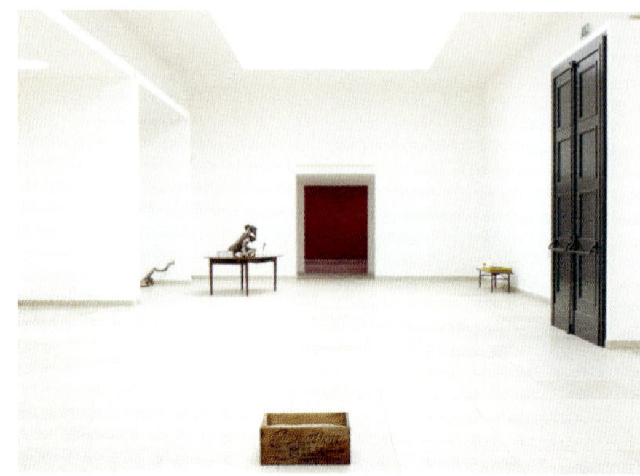

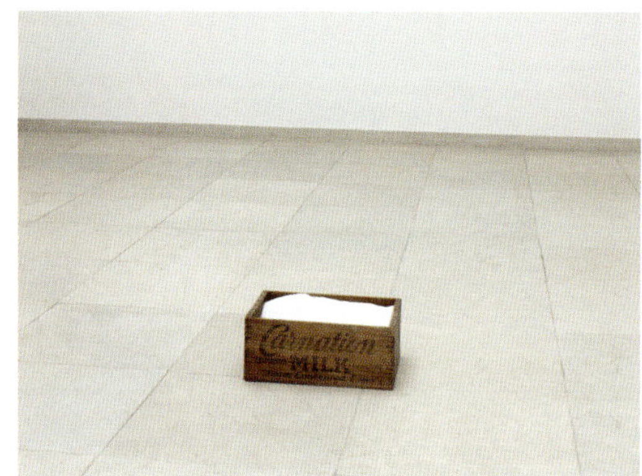

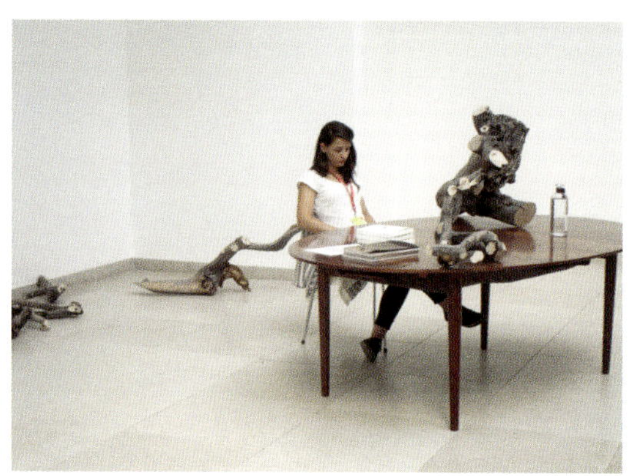

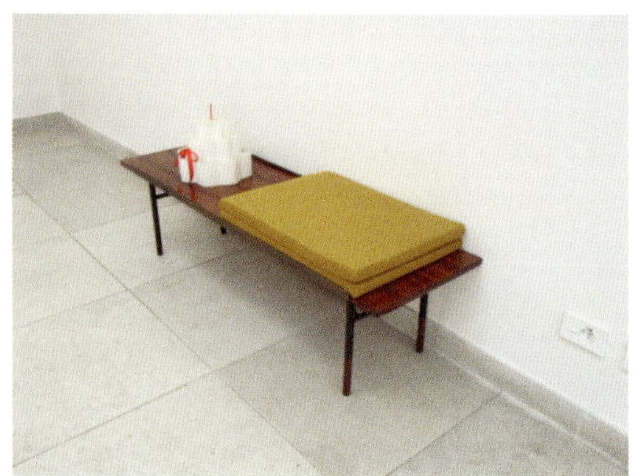

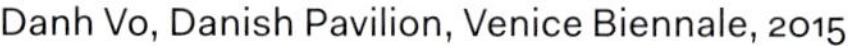
Danh Vo, Danish Pavilion, Venice Biennale, 2015

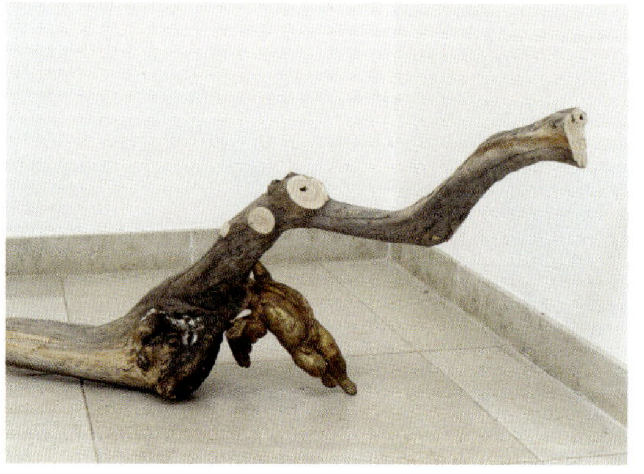

Not everyone was entranced by Vo's installation. The critic Claire Bishop, for instance, while acknowledging the beauty of what Vo does, accused him of failing to synthesize and of allowing an 'information overload' where things were 'gathered and presented, but to aesthetic and ornamental ends'. Moreover, instead of interpretation, Vo offered only the sort of 'captioned sensibility' one finds everywhere on Instagram.[39] Well, I think we have to acknowledge that some art has always been poetic and difficult, and some direct. It depends on the artist and the situation.

If Vo is elusive and allusive, Teresa Margolles, from Mexico, makes work that could be described as 'in your face'. Talking about the first time she saw the work of Joseph Beuys, she said: 'I almost fainted. I felt like vomiting and leaving. I said to myself: Would you dare to do something like this? Would you have the balls to do it? The power of art scares me.'[40]

At the 2006 Liverpool Biennial, Margolles covered the ground underneath a bridge with broken glass from car windows. You could walk on it. It glittered in the sunshine. But once you'd learnt where the glass came from, you saw the work very differently. Speaking in 2006, she said the work, for her, 'represents the loss and the emptiness. The loss, the void and the damage for society when someone is murdered. In the last few years in Mexico there's been a style of murders, "settling scores", where people are murdered in their cars. They shoot them sitting in their cars and they're killed on the spot. The police tow the car away, but the glass remains on the streets. The broken glass becomes part of the city. As it incorporates, it starts to shine.'[41]

What Else Could We Talk About? was the title Margolles gave to her installation at the 2009 Venice Biennale (pages 222, 223). She brought lengths of fabric soaked in the blood found at the scenes of Mexican gang murders and hung them as paintings inside the threadbare palazzo used as the Mexican pavilion; one length she hung outside as a flag, between those of Venice and the European Union. Every day, an assistant would mop the floor of the palazzo with blood, and every day Margolles would stitch into the fabrics with gold thread some of the warnings left by the gangs: 'SO THAT THEY LEARN TO RESPECT'; 'SEE, HEAR AND SILENCE'. Why? 'We're losing a generation that will demand redress for our having remained silent,' Margolles insisted. 'How can you not mop the floor of a Mexican pavilion at the Venice Biennale with the remains of the dead? Are you going to dress it up, or give it a slick design?'[42]

When I lecture in the UK, I sometimes ask the students if they have ever seen a dead body. Usually, only a few of them have, although all of them, of course, have seen thousands of murders and death-bed scenes on television and at the cinema. One aspect of Margolles's projects is about exhibiting death as part of our world – a memento mori, if you like. The Venice project also bore witness to the breakdown of civil society in Mexico, and sought to expose the complicity of those in other nations who buy their drugs, however indirectly, from the narco gangs. At the Venice press view, Margolles handed out thousands of plastic invitations, the same size as a credit card. On one side was the image of a murdered man, and on

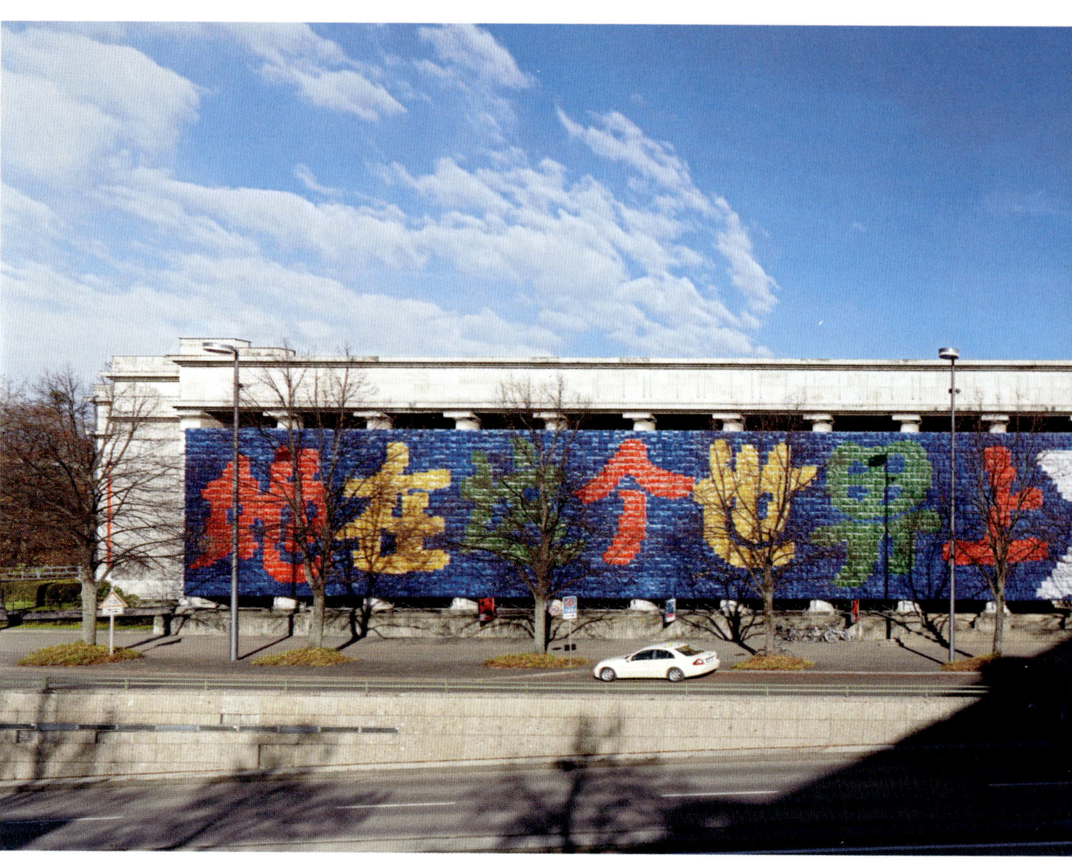

Ai Weiwei, *Remembering*, 2009
8,738 backpacks on metal structure, 9.2 × 106 m
(30¼ × 347¾ ft), Haus der Kunst, Munich

the other the words 'Card to cut cocaine'. One wonders if any of the glitterati used the cards for that purpose. And, if they did, whether they felt any guilt.

In 2000, at the same time as that year's officially approved Shanghai Biennale, Ai Weiwei curated a show entitled, in Chinese, 'Ways of Non-Cooperation', and, in English, 'Fuck Off'. The artist felt that Chinese and Western institutions, dealers and curators had become too similar, always about the deal, always about 'trademarking different interests'.[43] He wanted to provide a place where independent artists could speak freely. 'I never place art,' he said, 'apart from basic human rights – freedom of expression, for example. It's the responsibility of individuals, and artists, to speak out [about] what you believe in ... Art is an individual expression and should encourage private thinking and self-reflection.'[44] Ai's work had always been clever, inventive and provocative: painting ancient pots in bright industrial paint, or smashing two beautiful Qing bowls – a way of questioning both what Chinese culture was and what it means to the Chinese now. His work was always about China, always questioning it, always probing.

On 12 May 2008, a powerful earthquake struck the province of Sichuan in northern China. More than 69,000 people died, a high proportion of them children:

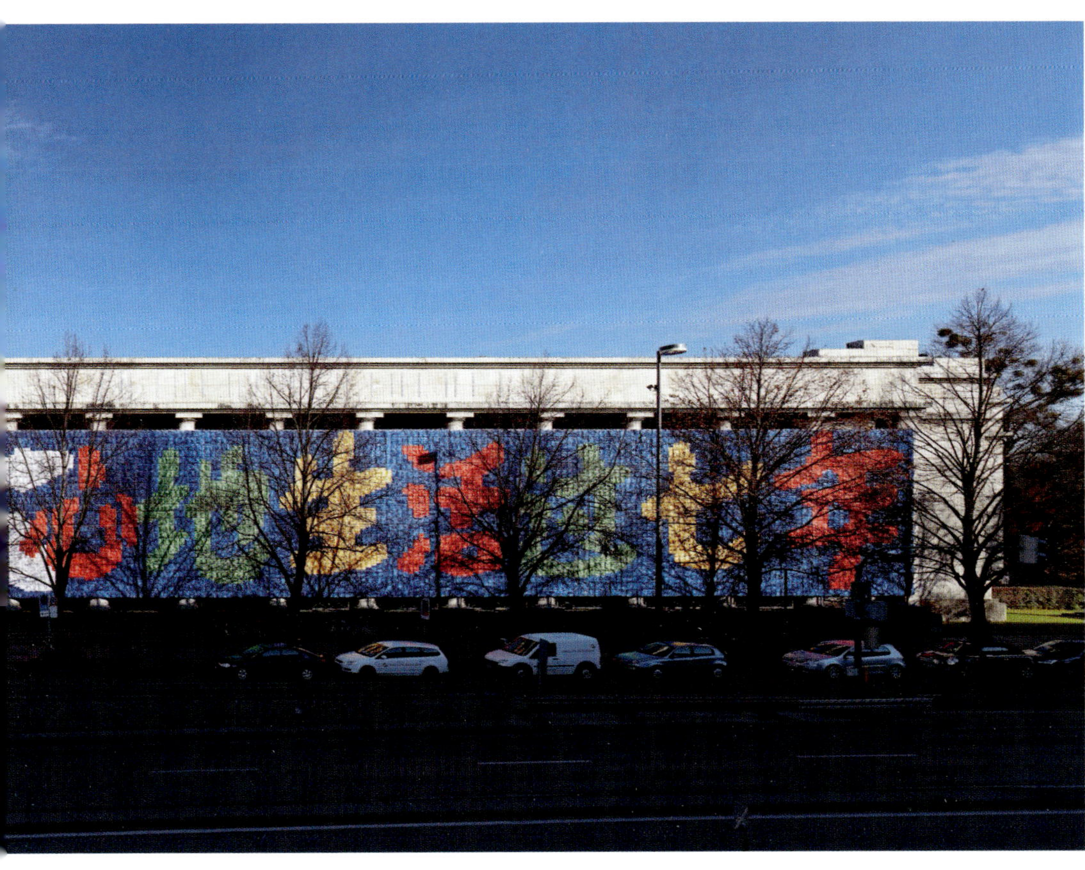

their schools, because of corruption, had been shoddily built, and collapsed. Ai was struck by the images of their rucksacks lying in the ruins. He was also appalled at the refusal of the authorities to provide information about the victims. 'So,' he explained, 'I used the internet to set up a citizen investigation team. On my blog, I said: "This is my question: 'Where are those lives?'" The information we requested was simple: names, dates of birth, the schools the children lost their lives at. Over the months, members of our team were arrested many times. But we stayed determined and sent new people in. After almost a year of research, we had 5,219 names.'[45]

Ai's blog was closed down in 2009. When he travelled to Chengdu in Sichuan to testify on behalf of an activist, he was beaten by police. As a result of this beating, when he arrived in Munich soon afterwards, to install an exhibition at the Haus der Kunst, he was in danger of suffering a cerebral haemorrhage and needed an emergency operation. Part of the exhibition was a work called *Remembering* (above), made especially for the museum's façade. It consisted of 9,000 children's rucksacks arranged to spell out, in Chinese, what one woman had said of her daughter killed in the Sichuan earthquake: 'She lived happily for seven years in this world'. The visual power of the work, its simple, elegiac message, was enhanced by the museum's past:

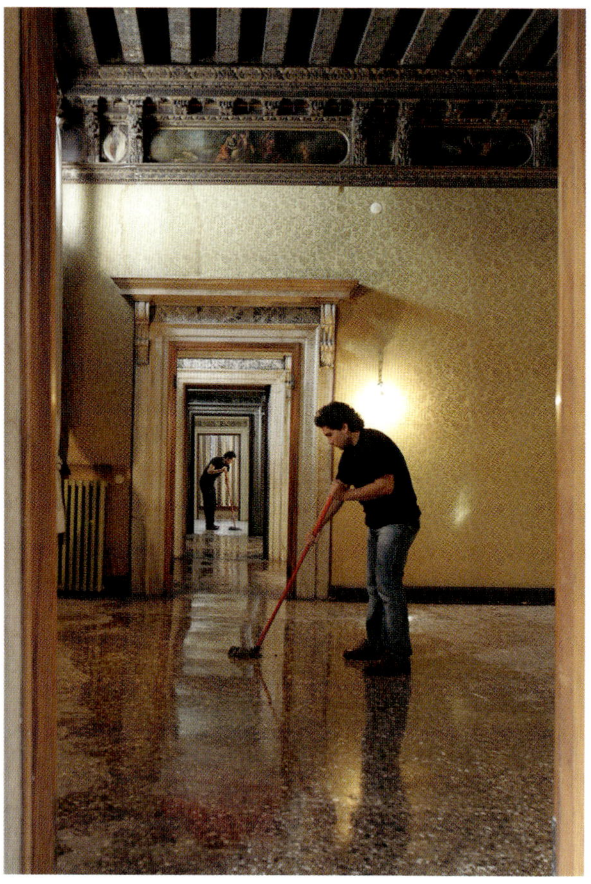

Teresa Margolles, *Cleaning*, 2009
Cleaning of the exhibition floors with a mixture of water and blood from murdered people in Mexico. The action took place at least once a day for the duration of the 53rd Bienale di Venezia. Performance view, 'What Else Could We Talk About?', curated by Cuauhtémoc Medina, 53rd Bienale di Venezia, Italy, June - November 2009

built by the Nazis in 1937 as a grandiose showcase for 'true German art', it still has swastikas embedded in its ceilings.

Like Margolles's Venice installation, *Remembering* was an act of both mourning and protest. Like Margolles herself, Ai was ready to take his country's dirty washing and hang it out, exposed to the rest of the world. After this experience he seems to have accepted that he was not just an artist but also an activist. He began to spend eight hours a day on Twitter and gave frequent interviews. By now he had become an internationally famous artist, and one loved for his wit, humour and frankness – so different from the opaque public face of Chinese politicians.

The Chicago-based artist Theaster Gates does a lot of things. He makes pots. That is how he started, as a ceramicist, and he has never stopped making vessels – not

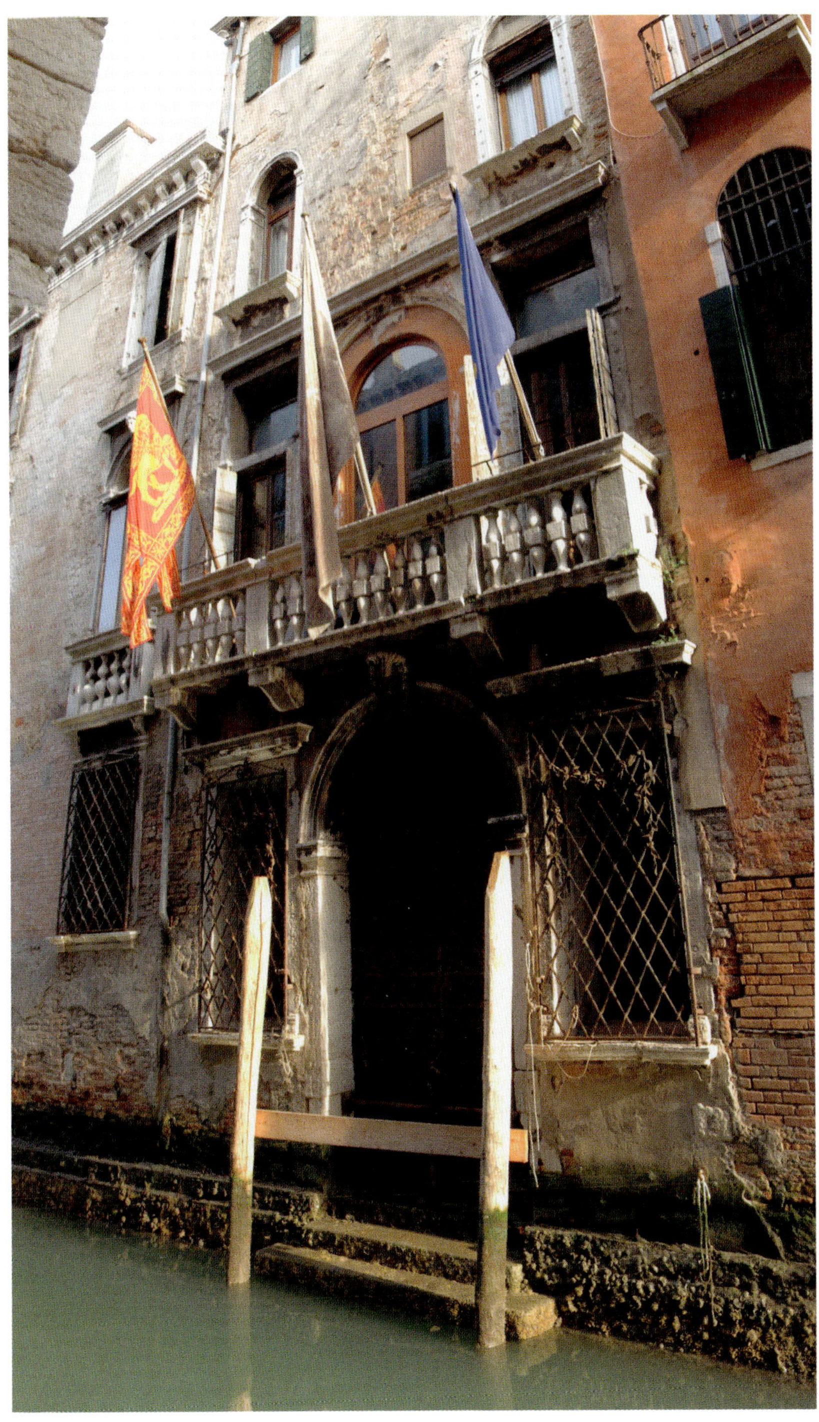

Teresa Margolles, *Bandera (Flag)*, 2009
Fabric, dyed with blood collected from executions on the north border of Mexico. Installation view: exterior of the Rota Ivancich Palace, 'What Else Could We Talk About?', curated by Cuauhtémoc Medina, 53rd Bienale di Venezia, Italy, June - November 2009

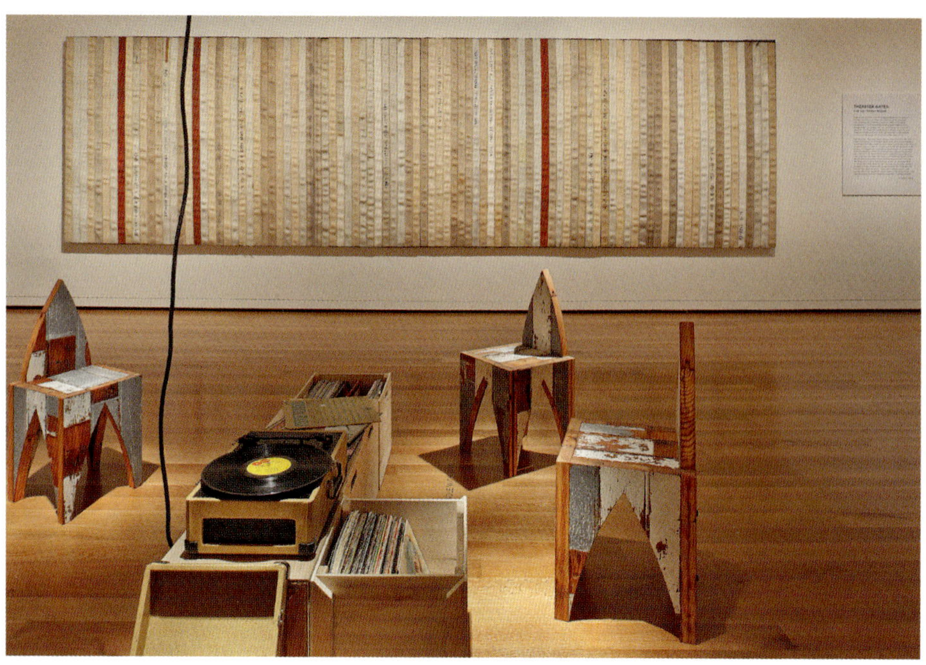

Theaster Gates, *The Listening Room*
Wood, long-playing records, metal; installation view,
Seattle Art Museum, Seattle, 9 December 2011 – 1 July 2012

as a lone practitioner anymore, but communally as part of the Soul Manufacturing Corporation that he helped set up. As a major art project, he has bought abandoned buildings in Chicago's blighted South Side, where he lives. By selling sculptures made with materials salvaged from these buildings, he pays for the renovation. He gives them a new social purpose. The first building, now known as 'Dorchester Projects', which he bought in 2008 when 40 per cent of the properties in his neighbourhood were standing empty, now has a library and a slide collection; suppers and concerts are held there. In another, 'The Listening House', he has set up a music archive with records taken from a defunct music store. He sees this as an artwork, and, entitled *The Listening Room*, it was shown as such at the Seattle Art Museum (above). Nevertheless, he remains, he insists, 'a lover of sculpture and painting and drawing, and I spend a tremendous amount of my time thinking about that stuff and making art in that way. But ... people are also important to the work that I do.'[46]

These activities all fit together. Gates helps people, and they help him make artworks that can be sold. Above all, what he wants is engagement: 'By engagement I am asking someone ... "can we do this together?" Whether it's the Black Monks of Mississippi making music with me – a temporary gospel choir and we're all singing about Dave the slave potter with new music I've produced ... or the creation of a political party by Tania Bruguera. I'm still wrestling with the relationship between the symbolic work that ends up on a wall and the pragmatic work that kind of changes lives or creates new education options, or creates new employment pathways.'[47]

What Gates does is bring the skills or virtues many artists have – empathy, energy, enthusiasm, the ability to improvise, a love of well-made things – to issues that may seem social, but which can be reinvented in an artistic way. He presents us with a model of an artist who gives the sort of inspiring, moral leadership that we seem to see too rarely in our official leaders, politicians and bureaucrats.

Apart from biennales and auctions, there is another place where artists of all kinds meet: art fairs. Art fairs were originally rather sober events for trade and corporate buyers, but they have since transmogrified (especially Art Basel Miami and Frieze London) into glitzy events, with VIP lounges and posh parties for the very rich, all promoting 'the idea of contemporary art as a lifestyle choice'.[48] In 2014, Eric Fischl made his views on art fairs perfectly clear: 'I'd always avoided art fairs like the plague. Now I have been, I still think they are the plague. It's like every single reason for art to exist does not exist in those places. They have just become a celebration of money-making. I went to a fair a few weeks ago and in the middle of this thing was a De Kooning painting. I thought, "Wow!" It turned out it was in a booth for a real estate company. They had this De Kooning for sale as well as the $40m homes. You could buy the house and get the painting for an extra $5m or whatever. The barriers have collapsed between the commercial and the art world. It is not irony – it is just cynicism … And then you've got people who are just there for the social scene. So, you have people texting or not paying any attention at all. It is as if the art is not there, or that they think it has no effect on them. But when you stop the moment you can see this weird world that is taking place. They are being regarded and judged by the work itself in some ways.'[49]

In 2017, conscious that his work usually disappeared into private collections to be seen by few, and not wanting to be perceived as just making 'emblems of discreet luxury for a refined cosmopolitan elite',[50] Edmund de Waal chose to show his work for the year at the immensely popular Frieze art fair. That way, it would be seen by tens of thousands, compared to the hundreds who would have seen it had it been exhibited in his London gallery, White Cube. It was a nice gesture, but could you actually 'see' these subtle, unassuming objects amid the bustle and hubbub of chatter, posing and selfie-taking that an art fair now consists of? Was it possible to calmly meditate on these works when the context, at heart, was a four-day spending spree for the ultra-rich? In such an environment, it may also have been hard to overlook the fact that these rows of simple but beautiful pots might have cost you more than you earned in a year. In 2019 de Waal installed some of his ceramics in the Jewish Musuem of the Venetian ghetto. To see them in that context, so rich and haunted with history, often painful, one's experience and hence the meaning of the work was totally different. Their monetary value became irrelevant; what mattered was their eloquent silence, their elegance and their elegiac reticence.

Chapter 10

ART IN THE AGE OF SURVEILLANCE CAPITALISM

2015 Onwards

'We know where you are. We know where you have been. We can more or less know what you are thinking about.'[1] So the then CEO of Google, Eric Schmidt, told us in 2010. 'All of our minds can be hijacked. Our choices are not as free as we think they are,' a former Google employee told us more recently.[2]

'We are the Google generation,' laughs Hahan, the Indonesian artist we met in the previous chapter. Thanks to the Internet, he knows far more about art outside Indonesia or his home town of Yogyakarta than the preceding generation. It is easy for him to get in touch with artists in Australia or Japan, or anywhere. No one could deny that this is a good thing, but in recent years a profound unease has built up about the ambitions and effects of Google, Facebook and other social-media giants.

The Internet promised so much. Global communication. Freedom of information. A global community in harmony. Any such illusions were shattered by, among other things, the realization that elections and referendums could be corrupted by hostile agents and their trolls working through the Internet, that the Internet was a safe haven for racism and conspiracy theories, and, above all, that Google and Facebook were just fronts for extracting our personal information. We realized, too, that it is not we who are the true customers of Google, but the advertisers.[3] We were being harvested for data just as a field of turnips is cropped by a farmer.

In *The Age of Surveillance Capitalism* (2019), Shoshana Zuboff demonstrates how Google and Facebook extract private information on an unprecedented scale, and how they've become part of what she calls 'surveillance capitalism', a rogue capitalism obsessed with control.[4] If, as she claims, the aim of a state-controlled Internet in China 'is the automation of society through tuning, herding and conditioning people to produce preselected behaviours judged as desirable by the state',[5] the same is happening elsewhere, but as judged desirable by the market. For all Google's and Facebook's utopian babble about freedom and connecting us all, and 'despite their claims of objectivity and neutrality, they are constantly making value-laden, controversial decisions. They help to create the world they claim to merely "show" us.'[6] Surreptitiously, they are using mass behaviour-modification

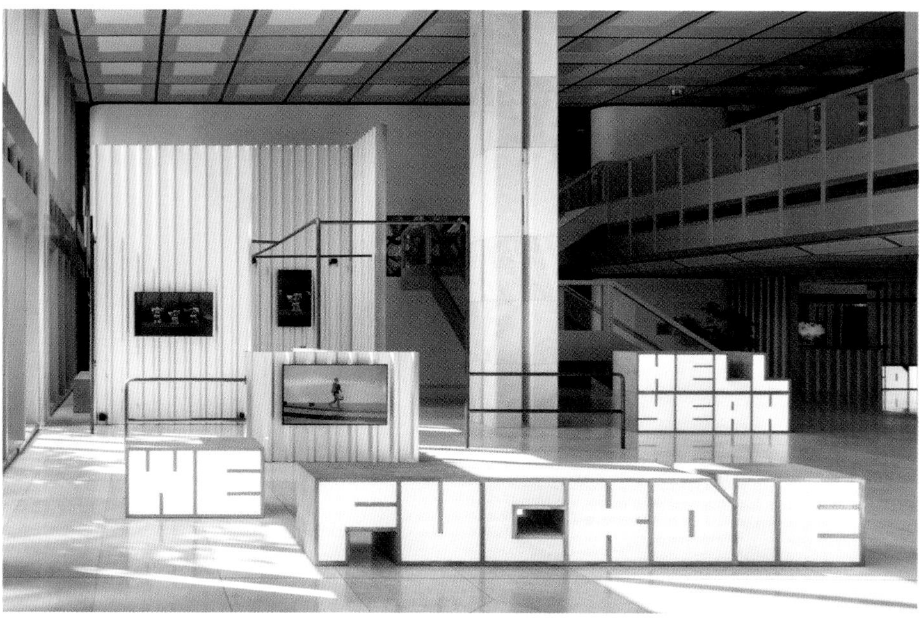

Hito Steyerl, *HellYeahWeFuckDie*, 2016
3-channel HD video file, 4:35 minutes; installation view, Skulpture Projekte Münster, 2017

techniques to work against 'the existential project of the post-war philosophies that planted authenticity, free will, and autonomous action at the heart of second-modernity yearning.'[7]

Authenticity and free will can be elusive things – how authentic do you think Andy Warhol or Joseph Beuys were? But art is an important arena in which individuals and communities can assert themselves, struggle for authenticity and claim some degree of autonomy. And what does Zuboff mean by 'second modernity'? The first, the age of industrialization and collective solutions, ran from the mid-nineteenth century to somewhere around the middle of the twentieth. It was then that a second modernity emerged, an age of jet travel and consumer goods in which many people, not just the elite, could focus on their selves and on self-determination. The Internet, which is probably making a greater change to the nature of consciousness than the invention of printing, has pushed us into a third modernity. The question is, do we gain new freedoms in this new age, or just become more controlled?

The notion of a second and third modernity is, I believe, a better way to think of our situation than the notion of modernism and post-modernism, which was much discussed twenty or thirty years ago. This latest modernity – the period we're living through now – is also plagued by narrow-minded nationalism and populist leaders who appeal to fear and prejudice rather than good will and hope, and by income inequality, overpopulation, climate change and the very real threat of ecological disaster.

How have artists responded to these issues? Can they help us? Artists as diverse as Theaster Gates, Hito Steyerl and Dana Schutz can be seen as calling for a real, non-virtual experience of the world. In doing so, they pick up the distaste for the ubiquity of reproduction shown by such earlier artists as Carl Andre, who, back in 1973, was insisting that 'the photograph is a lie ... art is a direct experience with something in the world and photography is just a rumour, a kind of pornography of art.'[8] Is art a place where we can fight over truth – and individuality, communality, responsibility, freedom? Perhaps a younger generation is not so bothered, having spent so much time on social media that the erosion of private space is the norm they have always known. Moreover, raging against the Internet can be seen as fuddy-duddiness.

How, then, does a tech-savvy artist like Hito Steyerl make art for *now*? In Steyerl's installation for Skulptur Projekte Münster 2017 (opposite), video monitors showed animations of robots created to save people in disaster zones. On another monitor, children in a warzone asked Siri when the robots would come to save them. Light boxes, which you could sit on, showed the five most used words in music at the time: 'HELL', 'YEAH', 'WE', 'FUCK', 'DIE'. It was entertaining but also puzzling: what might the work mean? One clue was the context: the clean, modernist foyer for the head office of a bank, furnished with op and kinetic artworks from the 1960s, when people still believed in progress. This was dystopia masquerading as utopia.

Few artists address more cogently than Steyerl the nature of life in the Internet age – 'the dissolution of distinction between physical reality and the world of digital images'[9] – or how the Internet consumes us: 'Duration cannot be sustained because people are exhausted. They cannot afford it anymore. They don't have time. The time they have has to be artificially boosted or extended. You have to pretend you're basically present on one online channel while you try to catch some sleep, but all the tab browsers are open at the same time.'[10] Her films (extracts of which can be found online) function more like provocative essays, collages of documentary footage, CGI and herself talking. She uses post-production tools to 'complexify', reconfigure and subvert imagery. The films are dense, but leavened with jokes and rude words to keep a non-academic audience interested. Not only, we are told, is Steyerl 'at war with the commodification of art and the corrupting power of the market';[11] she also 'represents a new paradigm of the artist not as solitary genius but as networked thinker'.[12]

Nevertheless, people continue to look for that 'solitary genius'. They still believe 'great artists' will illuminate this age, as they did previous ages. Who, they still ask, are the great artists of today? Who are the Rembrandts, the Hokusais, the Michelangelos of our time? Recently, I have seen Anselm Kiefer, Yayoi Kusama, Richard Serra, Bruce Nauman, Gerhard Richter, Neo Rauch and even the New York painter Mark Grotjahn described as the 'greatest living artist'. I doubt that any of them is as influential as Beuys or Warhol, and none of them has the range or fecundity of Picasso.

With a ravenous market demanding ever more of their products, and such uncertainty as to what good art is, it is a challenge for artists to develop their careers. How many of today's older artists have developed a late style – a new and profound way of making things in their final years, as did Rembrandt, Hokusai and Michelangelo? Cy Twombly certainly had a late style, making vast, loose, wholly abstract gestural paintings in the years before his death. And Richter has remained enormously productive: some find his more recent work fascinating, others clinical and dull.

In comparison, recent paintings by George Baselitz can seem rather scruffy. The paintings he made around 2005 were quite overtly remixes of older ones, as if he lacked new ideas and images. However, they were made very differently from those that came before: their quirky sketchiness was disturbing. Seen en masse, his most recent paintings convey a sombre mood. They seem to be about getting old: images of knobbly bodies floating as in a dream through a colourless world. This, I think, is a late style, work that is uncomfortably candid in facing realities, in looking death in the eye – albeit not without humour. The humour in the last works of Maria Lassnig is even more brutal, in a style pared down even further than Baselitz's. *You or Me* (opposite) must be one of the most unsparing self-portraits ever.

Totally unlike these late paintings of Baselitz or Lassnig are those Srihadi Soedarsono has been making in his eighties. Fascinated by the spirituality of

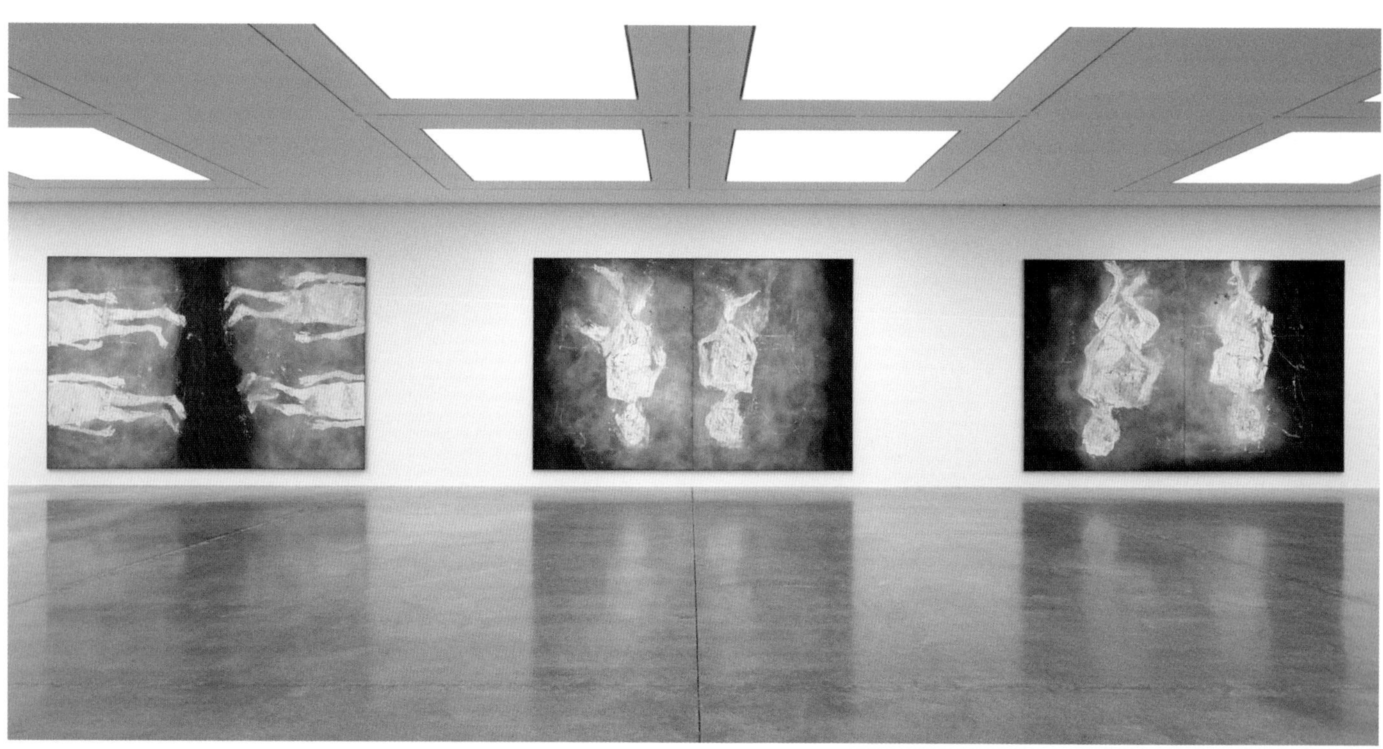

Georg Baselitz, 'Wir fahren aus (We're off)'
Exhibition at White Cube Bermondsey, London, 27 April – 3 July 2016

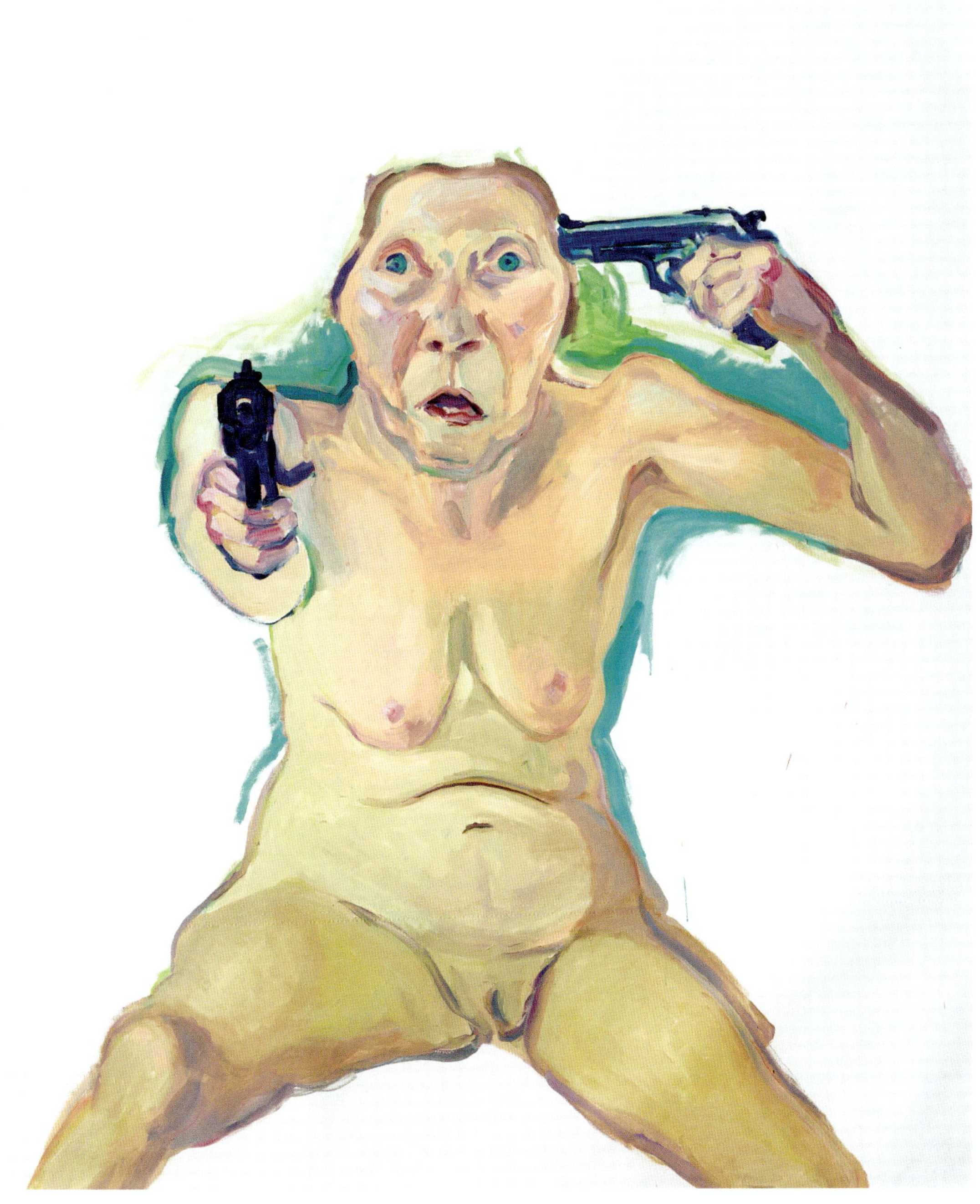

Maria Lassnig, *Du oder Ich* (You or Me), 2005
Oil on canvas, 203 × 155 cm (80 × 61 in.)

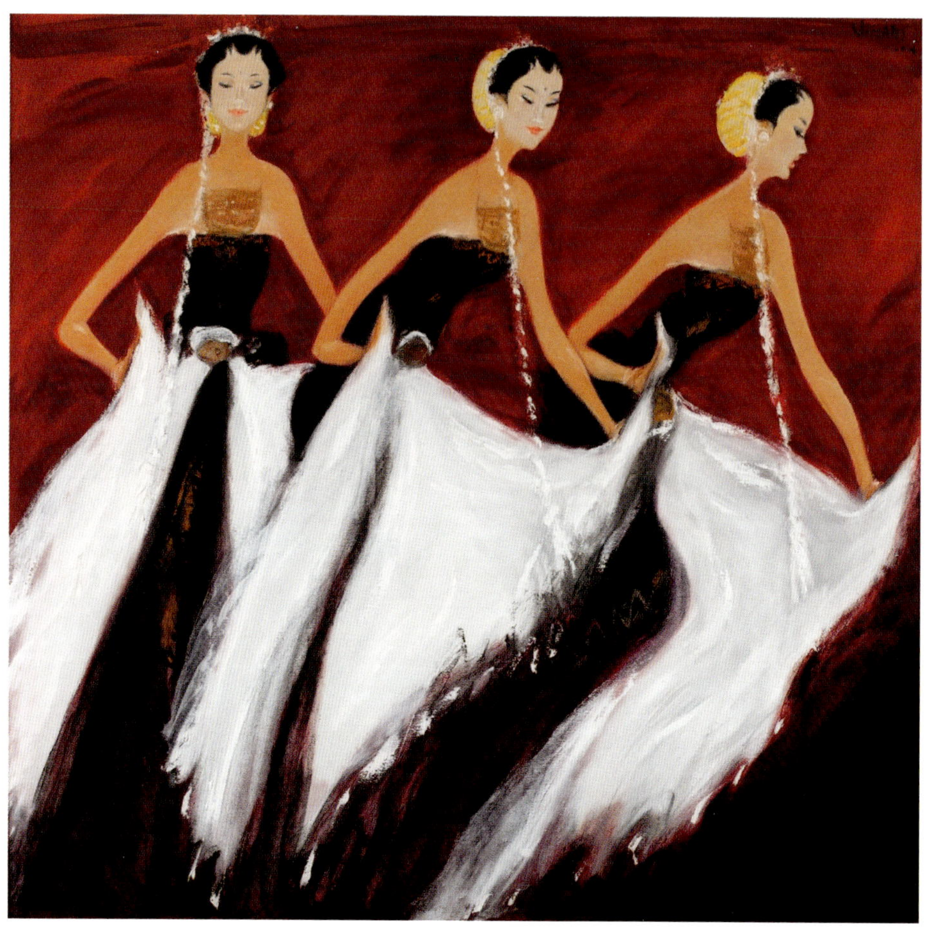

Srihadi Soedarsono, *Bedaya Ketawang – Moment of Contemplation*, 2014
Oil on canvas, 150 × 150 cm (59⅛ × 59⅛ in.)

traditional Javanese dances, he has painted them obsessively. Obsession with one or a few subjects is common in an artist's late work. Although the subject in Srihadi's is always the same, each painting is different, the first few loosely drawn contours leading to a long process of painterly gestures. This is about calm in one's last years. Perhaps, apart from the subject matter, these could have been made by an American painter in the 1950s; but in our world, modernist and traditionalist painting can still be made, can still be authentic. They are options for those it suits. Not all our contemporaries are 'cutting edge', or fixated on how the Internet has changed the world.

In the case of Anselm Kiefer, although his works remain enormously popular (and expensive), he has become, to this writer at least, one of the most disappointing of today's artists. The works have become bigger and bigger, as if, having no new idea, he has just 'biggered' up an old one. The paintings and objects look more and

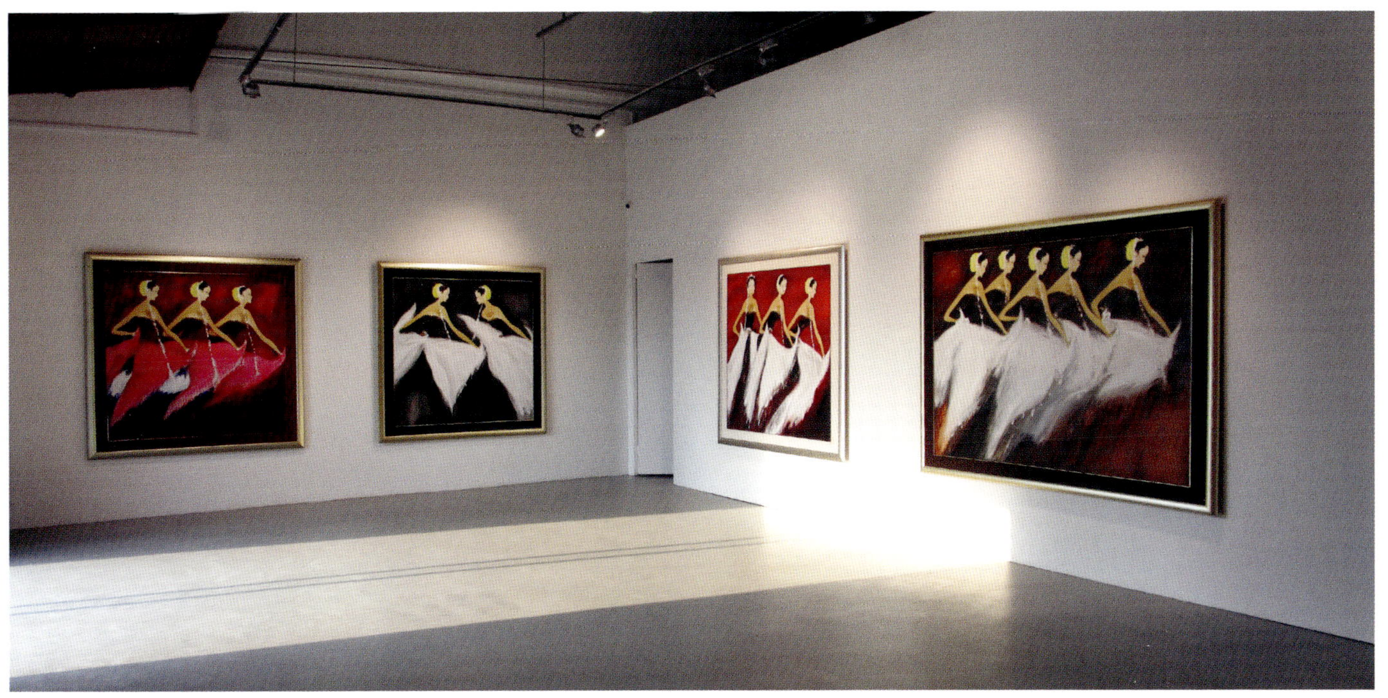

Srihadi Soedarsono, installation of *Bedaya* paintings at Equator Art projects, Singapore, 2014. From left: *Bedaya Ketawang – Moment of Contemplation*, 2014; *Bedaya Ketawang – Moment of Meditation*, 2014; *Bedaya Ketawang – Moment of Contemplation*, 2014; *Bedaya Ketawang – Beauty of Soul*, 2013

more like stage sets, less and less handmade, more and more like special finishes applied by assistants to a pre-arranged formula. There is no interesting detail when seen close up, and all the works look so similar, so brand 'Kiefer'. Of course, some will recoil at me saying this, seeing him as *the* visionary artist.

We all have an idea of what a late style is in a painter: Titian, Rembrandt, Philip Guston and others have all given us exemplars. But what of artists who work in installations, photographs or performance? How do they achieve a late style?

Walking into a shopping centre during the 2017 Bangkok Biennale and seeing an enormous Yayoi Kusama installation (page 234), I wondered if this was a late style. It was spectacular, certainly. But 'style' seems the wrong word for Kusama's continued obsession with covering the world with dots. What *has* changed has been people's attitudes towards and understanding of her work; among other things, they are impressed that she has not given up. Now, all round the world there are queues to enter her infinity rooms, despite the fact they are not significantly different from the one she made more than fifty years ago – although the technology she uses has improved.

Although nothing Cindy Sherman has made in the last few decades has had such an impact as her first 'Untitled Film Stills', her work has at least constantly moved

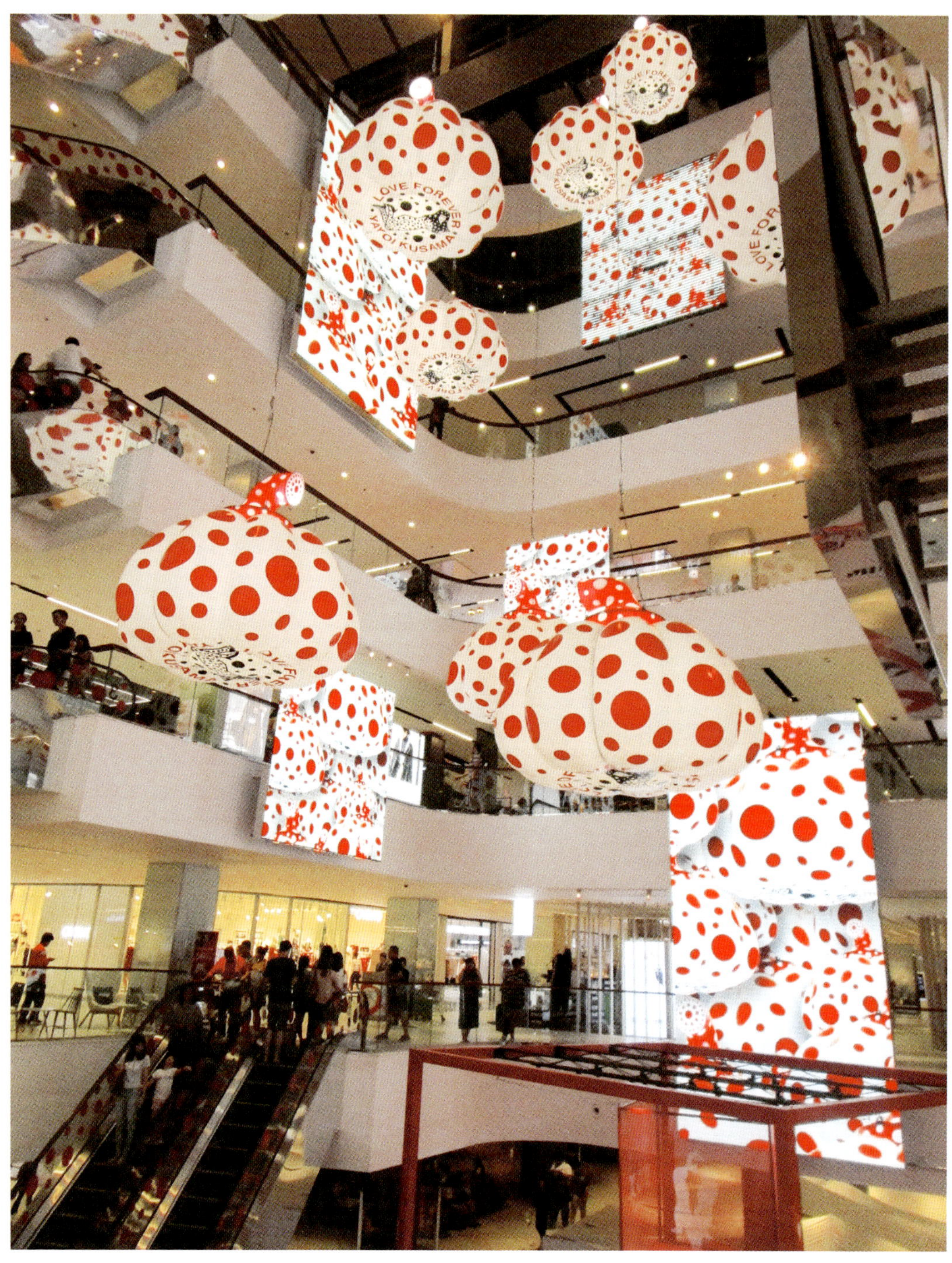

Yayoi Kusama, *Pumpkins*, 2017
Inflatable pumpkins, fabric; installation view, CentralWorld for Bangkok Biennale 2018

on, through the grotesque to the parodic (she has also used Instagram to expand her project). Recent photographs of her in outfits apparently belonging to flappers or ageing Hollywood vamps look like a child trying on its parents' or grandparents' clothes – except that *this* child is sixty-plus years old. Sherman's work, like that of Baselitz or Lassnig, is at least partly to do with ageing.

When Marina Abramović, by then aged sixty-four, staged her performance *The Artist is Present* at MoMA in 2010 – in which, dressed in a glamorous, long red dress, she sat motionless and silent at a table – 750,000 people queued to sit opposite her and stare into her eyes. For some, it was a profound and moving experience. But for others, or those who only saw photographs of the event or just read the publicity, it seemed portentous rather than profound. They started to see her as an egotist – no longer an artist, just another celebrity.

No doubt this is why Maurizio Cattelan, when asked to stage an exhibition at the Yuz Museum, Shanghai, in 2018, decided to mock Abramović and her painfully earnest authenticity. Cattelan purloined not only the title of Abramović's performance for the exhibition, but also an image of her for the exhibition poster (below). However, neither Cattelan nor the other artists he invited were present, and most of them were happy to exhibit copies of other things. The Icelandic artist Ragnar Kjartansson set up a stage with a red curtain drawn across it: every so often, the curtain would be pulled open to reveal a young Chinese woman in traditional Icelandic costume sitting in front of a large painting of mountains. She would then

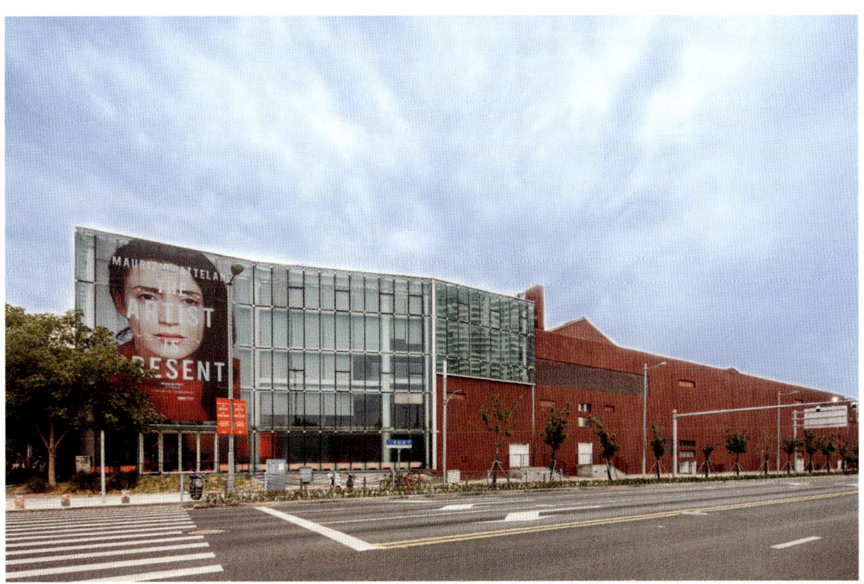

Yuz Museum, Shanghai, advertising Maurizio Cattelan's exhibition 'The Artist is Present', 2018

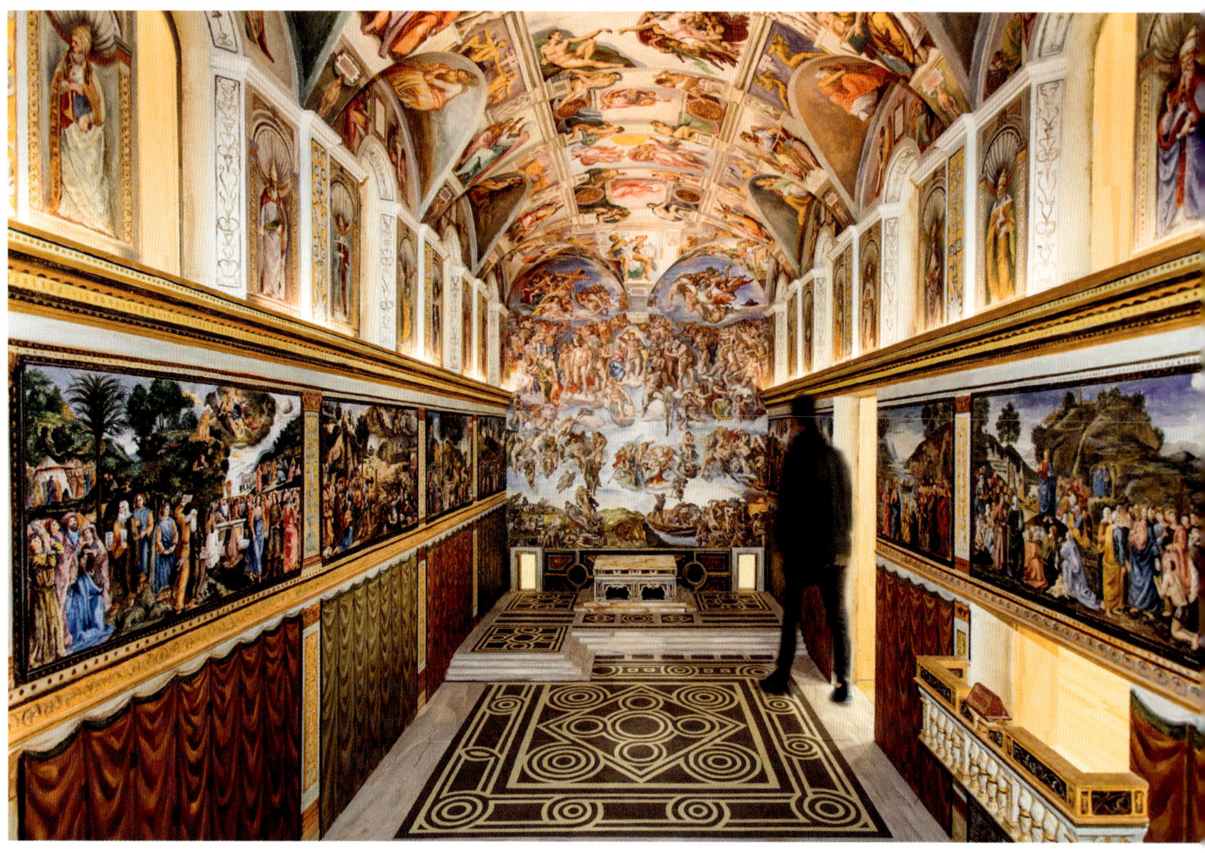

Maurizio Cattelan, *Untitled*, 2018
Fresco painting, pine wood, steel, 713.2 × 392.7 × 272.4 cm (280⅞ × 154⅝ × 107¼ in.), as installed at Yuz Museum, Shanghai

sing a melancholy song supposedly sung by Ragnar's great-great-great-grandmother. Cattelan himself employed Chinese painters to produce a miniature version of the Sistine Chapel (above). It was impeccably made, but the wonder and joy came from walking inside and being a giant in the Pope's house. Everyone who entered smiled – and had themselves photographed. The exhibition itself was sponsored by Gucci. Young women wandered around in fashionable clothes, frantically taking selfies, and didn't look out of place. Here there was certainly no dreadful sense of authenticity; and if the artist was present, he or she was laughing. The question was: is one being laughed at, or laughing with the artist?

Cattelan has been exceptional in remaining so perversely inventive. The market is happiest if an artist settles down into being reasonably predictable – if, in effect, they become a brand. Between 1989 and 1994, Damien Hirst was arguably one of the best and most inventive artists in world; but for twenty-five years now he has either repeated himself (more and still more spot paintings) or hyped himself up.

Many people would say the same of Jeff Koons or Richard Prince. With their prices so high, artists at the 'top' can also afford assistants to maximize production. It is not only the market but also the museum world that wants the same thing repeated, but, as Christian Boltanski has lamented, 'When a museum invites you to come and make an "intervention", it is no longer an intervention.'[13]

It is a challenge for an artist to develop his or her career naturally when the art market and institutions are so demanding. The pressure on an artist such as Neo Rauch to make more 'Rauchs' is enormous. His gallery has many branches and shows at many art fairs; numerous collectors want his work (as would many museums if they had not been priced out of the market). Rauch certainly produces a large number of paintings, which are always well made and often witty. Should one be asking for more variety? Or is this imaginary world he has created rich enough to sustain a career?

Ding Yi has certainly not speeded up production; in fact, by making larger paintings, he has slowed it down. No doubt for the rest of his career he will continue to paint crosses: it is the basis of what he does. Yet he succeeds in finding variety within that. Recently he has forsaken the vivid Shanghai colours for a more muted tonality, but, in the case of *Appearance of Crosses, 2018-2* (overleaf), he wanted to give the work a

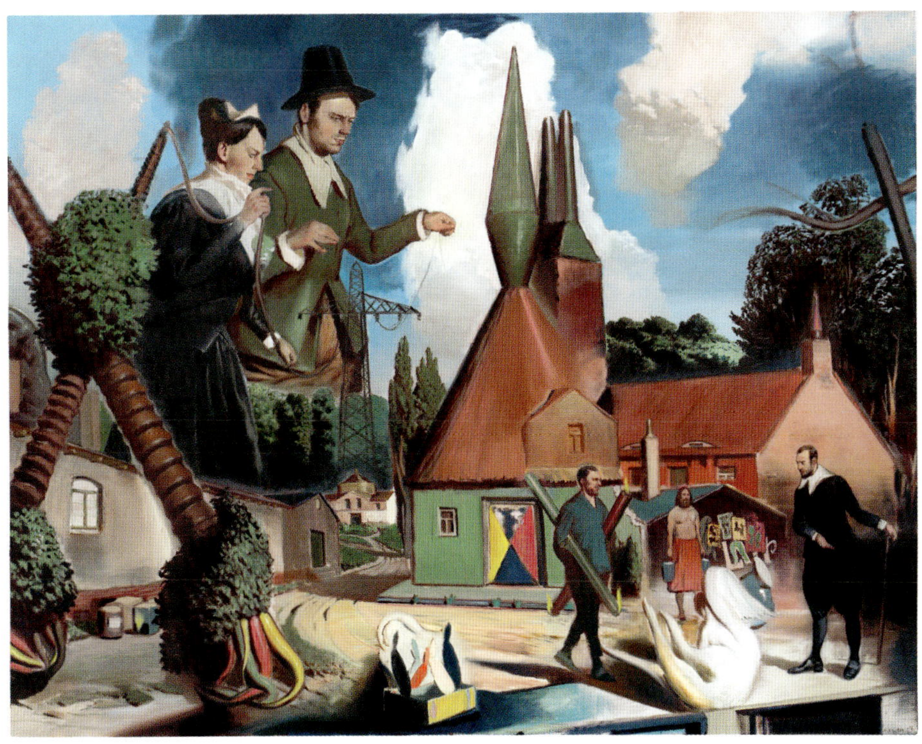

Neo Rauch, *Zustrom*, 2016
Oil on canvas, 200 × 250 cm (78¾ × 98½ in.)

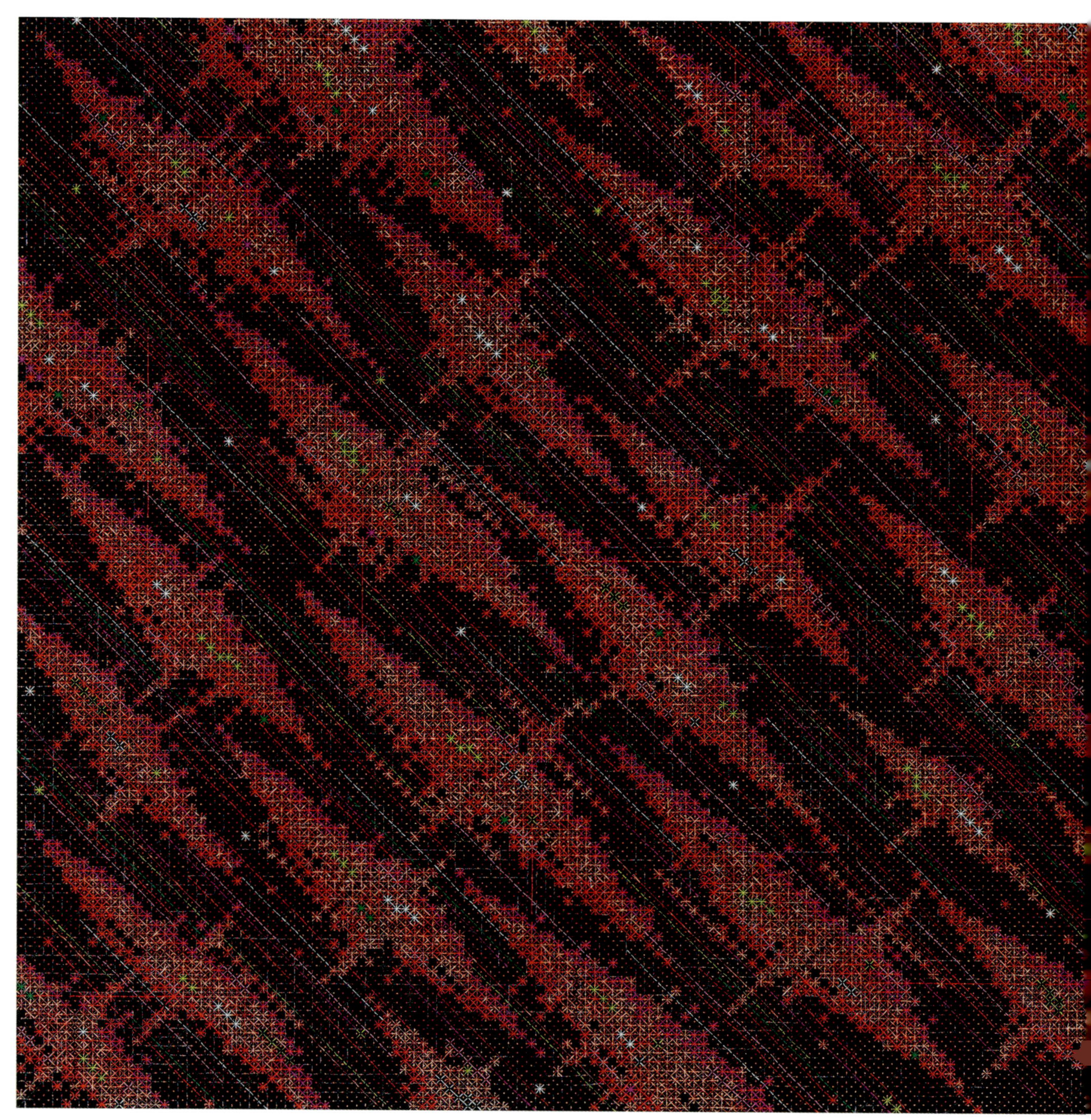

Ding Yi, *Appearance of Crosses, 2018-2*, 2018
Mixed media on basswood, 366 × 732 cm (144⅛ × 288¼ in.)

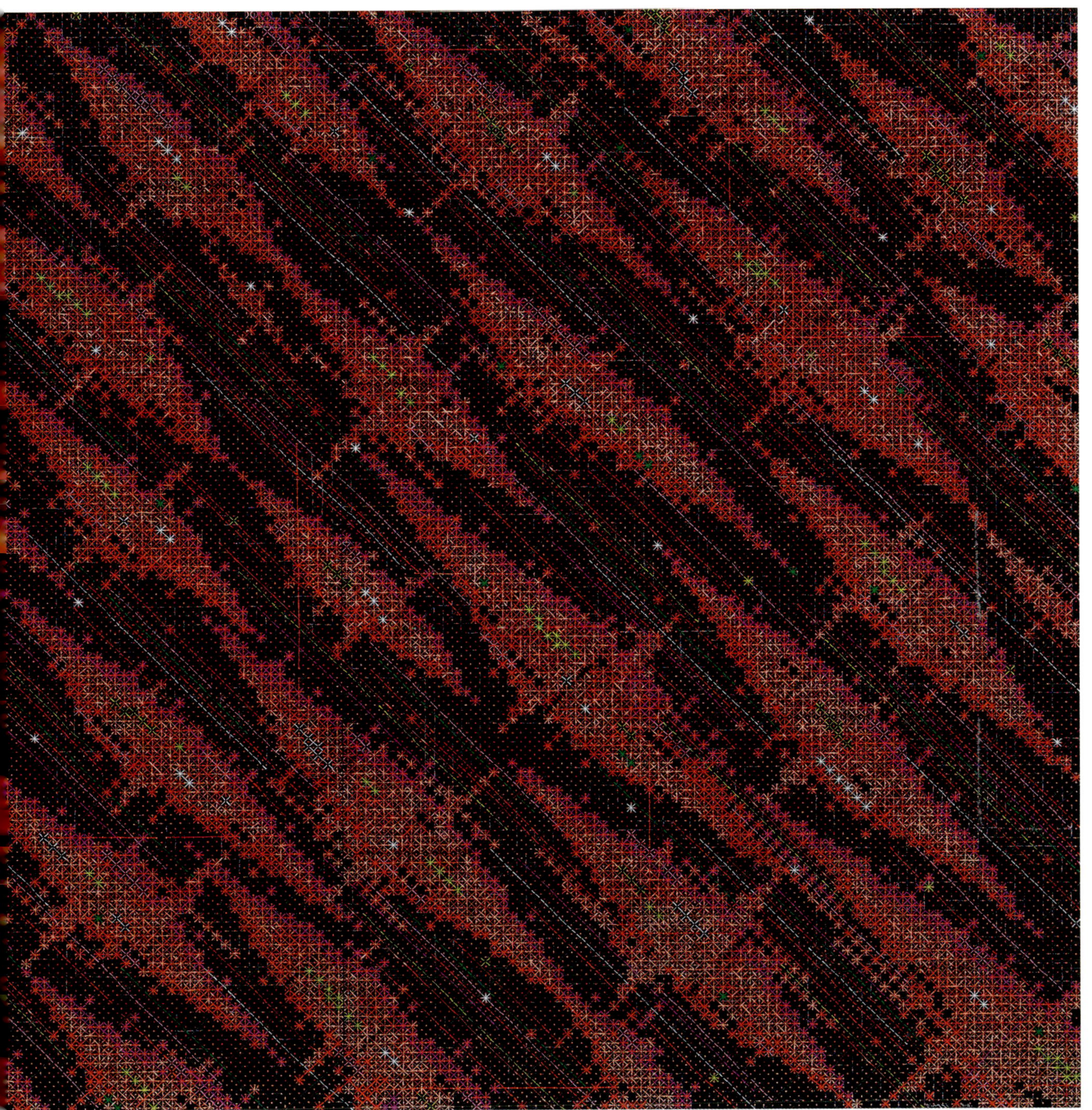

sense of power – hence the boat shapes moving together. Now he works on wood panels coated with layers of paint he can cut into and expose, as well as paint over. Ding may have assistants to produce these flat layers of paint, but it is he who makes each of the thousands of lines, crosses and dots that make up the picture, normally working long hours alone. For Ding, as for Baselitz, Rauch, etc., art is all about one individual's consciousness and creativity, about freedom and authenticity. But, nevertheless, has the age of the individual artist come to an end? Some have suggested so.

Today it has become far more common for artists to work in groups. This is not a wholly new phenomenon: several of the artists we have discussed already have worked collaboratively earlier in their careers. Teresa Margolles, for example, once worked with the artists' collective Semefo, while Marina Abramović performed with her long-time partner Ulay for more than a decade. Since the 1960s the need for artists to work alone has frequently been challenged, especially by feminist groups or those who want art to focus on social praxis; for the New York collective Guerrilla Girls, for instance, 'The concept of the individual genius artist is outdated, kept alive by an art market that needs super-expensive art objects made by "geniuses".'[14]

The Danish group Superflex admits that, like other artists' groups today, it is very much influenced by social media, where people are used to being in touch with one another to the point of blending. Perhaps working together is also a necessary reaction to the narcissistic individualism of the selfie phenomenon. The three artists that make up Superflex – Jakob Fenger, Bjørnstjerne Christiansen and Rasmus Nielsen – came together in 1993 when they were in their twenties. Their work, often with an anti-capitalist message, is normally intended for the public domain. *Flooded McDonald's* (2009), for example – a video created with the Propeller group from Vietnam, in which a mock-up of a McDonald's outlet slowly fills with water – was meant as a metaphor for the imminent ecological and economic apocalypse.

But do ordinary people always 'get' such deeper meanings?

In 2017 Superflex showed in Tate Modern's turbine hall. They provided a range of swings that people could, singly or in groups, swing on (their work often invites viewers to participate). 'The work', said a hand-out distributed at the museum, 'explores the potential of energy generated by social movements, drawing unexpected connections within, between and beyond institutions, and proposing new uses for urban public space.' Most of those who used the swings would probably have laughed at the text's portentousness: they were just having fun. It was most unlikely that many people understood that *One Two Three Swing!* (opposite) was apparently all about 'society's apathy towards the political, environmental and economic crises of our age'. Nor was it likely that many people, unless told, realized the carpet laid down nearby used the same colours as English banknotes. All too often artists and curators mistake their intentions for meanings, but the actual meaning is whatever the viewers or participants experience. We learn and experience more by reading as well, but if understanding is so dependent on reading, then it is divorced from experience.

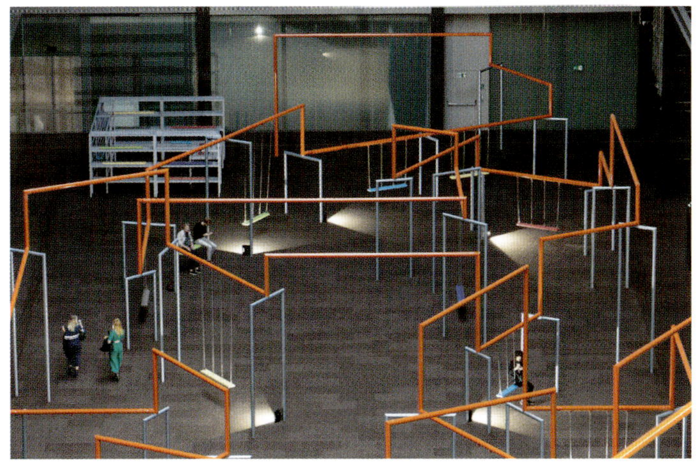

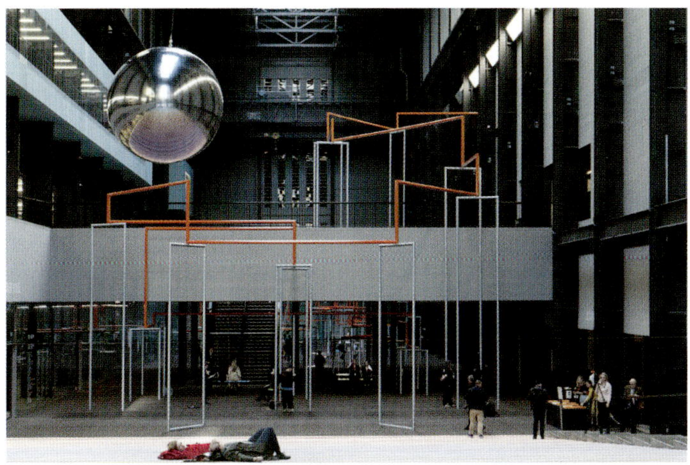

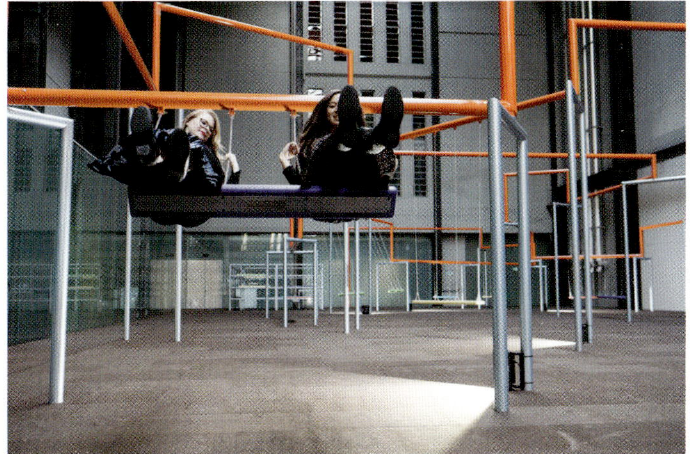

Superflex, *One Two Three Swing!*, 2017
Installation view, Turbine Hall, Tate Modern, London

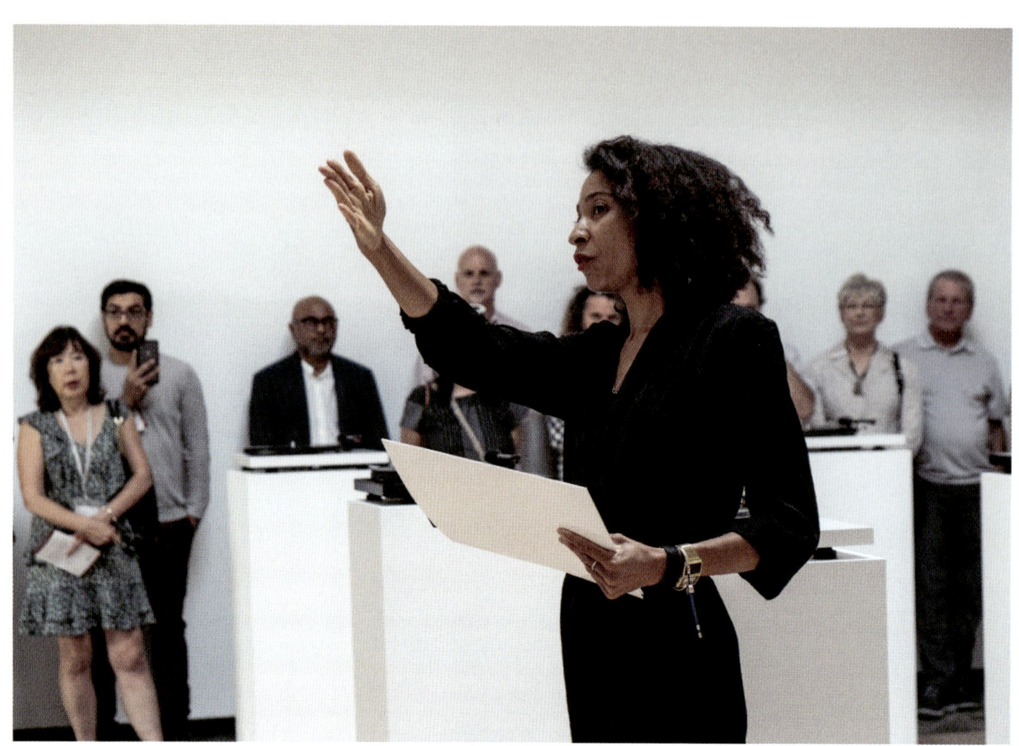

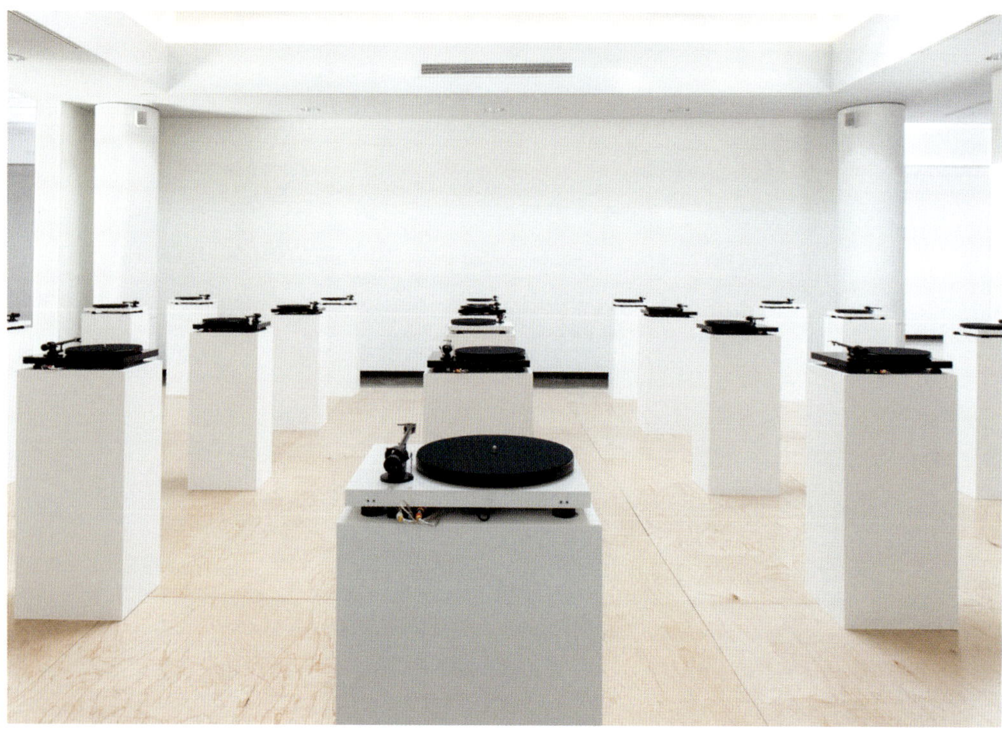

lauren woods, *American Monument, 25/2018*, 2018
25 record payers with records, 25 boxes of documents, transcripts

Much art now depends on collaboration with others, curators or institutions, to be made or staged. Have curators become more important than artists? In August 2018 the curators of the Wiesbaden Biennale placed a statue of the Turkish president, Recep Tayyip Erdoğan, in a public space, having warned no one that the work would be of such a controversial figure. The artist remained anonymous: his or her name wasn't important, we were told; the public's reaction was what mattered. The city had the sculpture removed. 'The question of authorship is not central for us,' said Martin Hammer, one of the biennale's two curators.[15] Curiously, he seemed very keen to have his own name mentioned! That may appear hypocritical to some. It is certainly indicative of how curatorial authorship has become empowered, even dominant at times. Certainly, it was Hammer and his co-curator, Maria Magdalena Ludewig, who initiated the work and staged it. For them, the actual sculpture was only one part of the work; even its removal became an aspect of it. As Ludewig said, 'Whatever your reaction is, it's already part of the artwork.'[16]

Like many other artists, lauren woods (she insists on her name being uncapitalized, by way of denying she is a 'singular, lone artist') is fascinated by history and archives, and by how they illuminate the present and show how we might change it. Her work is based on research, often into racism. woods had been invited to install her *American Monument* – a project focusing on the killing of African Americans by police officers – at the University Art Museum at California State University, Long Beach. The main element of the monument at that time (woods is adamant that it not be called an exhibition, and intends to expand it for any future manifestation) was a grid of twenty-five record players, on each of which was a 12-inch record of police reports, court transcripts and eye-witness accounts of a black man or woman being shot dead by police. Visitors were invited to play and listen to these discs.

However, six days before the official opening in 2018, the museum's curator, Kimberli Meyer, was fired. In a speech given at the opening, woods announced that the university had, by firing Meyer, 'removed my primary and most committed collaborator and institutional steward, someone integral to the existence of *American Monument*. To remove a key partner for this project from the directorship of the museum at this critical point and actually expect this project to continue indicates a profound lack of understanding about what this "work" actually is. It shows utter disregard for what the labour that manifests it actually is. There is a mythology around art production, that authorship of a work is by a singular, lone artist and that that artist is at the centre of art production. This is not an exhibition of objects. This is not a show of conceptual play. *American Monument* is a transformative process that wants to tackle the culture of police brutality through cultural production. It can only exist through collective authorship.'

The artist then read a message from Meyer: 'Racism is structural and rhizomatic ... We are called upon to disrupt the unjust system. I realize this is very hard to do, but art may help us. At its best, art has the power to redeem, to lift us out of fear and ignorance, engaging our sense of beauty and our desire to transform.' woods concluded by announcing that *American Monument* had to be paused, but not closed. She and her assistants turned off all the record players. Later, woods said, 'We can't even get to the point of discussing police brutality, if we can't consider institutional violence.'[17] One reason for the importance of art is that it offers a space where the individual, or the group, can engage with the institution.

The relationship between curator and artist has not always been such a harmonious one. Like DJs in the music world, curators have become up-front participators.[18] Arguably, this began in the 1960s with the de-skilling of artists' education, and when the presentation of art became as important as the making of it. Since the 1990s there has been an avalanche of new MAs, not only in curating but also in art business, arts management, art logistics and art theory. I am all for professionalism, but one starts to wonder if there are too many zoologists and not enough animals in the system. Are curating courses the art world's equivalent of an MBA? Or are they the more up-to-date version of a theology degree – training for people who want to make the world a better place, and who are also drawn to institutional life?

So far in this chapter, other than Steyerl and woods, we have been looking at artists whose careers were already well established. What of younger artists or those who have emerged more recently? How do they respond to today's challenges?

From the start of his career, Ragnar Kjartansson was fascinated by such artists as Marina Abramović, who made 'kinds of holy rituals. Sacred, otherworldly, *ubermensch* rituals … it was simultaneously a kind of show business. Like a Houdini stunt.'[19] Asked why so many of the artists he referred to were women, he replied: 'Because it's just a more interesting stand. It's a slightly different point of view that didn't exist in history before and it's almost like they are the first generation of it.'[20]

Kjartansson began as a musician, and still, for him, 'Music is the ultimate. I cannot breathe without music. I was in a lot of bands.'[21] But as he never felt comfortable being a musician, he moved to art: 'The ambition to do music was to be like a pop star, but the ambition to do art was just because I thought it was fun.'[22] Much of his art is to do with music and his fan-like passion for it: 'I just *really* love the National. And I *really* love the song "Sorrow". I listen to it all the time. And I just thought, Wow, wouldn't it be cool if there was just a whole day of that song played live?'[23] So he asked the band to play the song live, in public, non-stop for six hours. They obliged, and he called the piece *A Lot of Sorrow* (2013–14).

Kjartansson's *The Visitors* (opposite) is named after Abba's final album. Nine large screens are spread around the gallery, more or less in a circle; on each screen we see one of nine musicians, some from the band Sigur Rós, in an old house, each in a separate room, connected by headphones. They play a slow lament, occasionally singing words from a poem by the wife Kjartannson was in the process of being divorced from, Ásdís Sif Gunnarsdóttir: 'Once again I fall into / my feminine ways / There are stars exploding around you / And there is nothing, nothing you can do.'

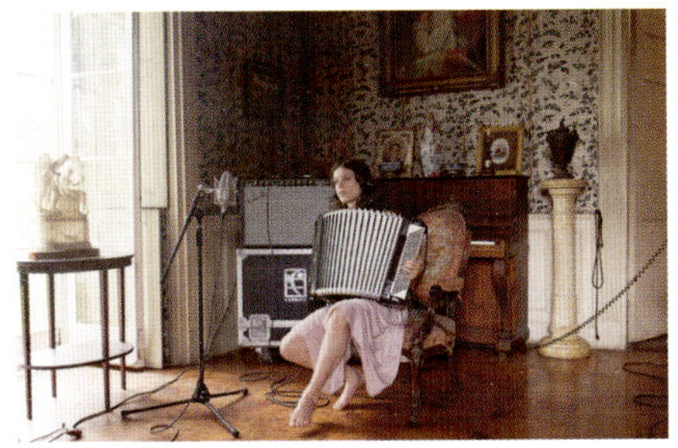
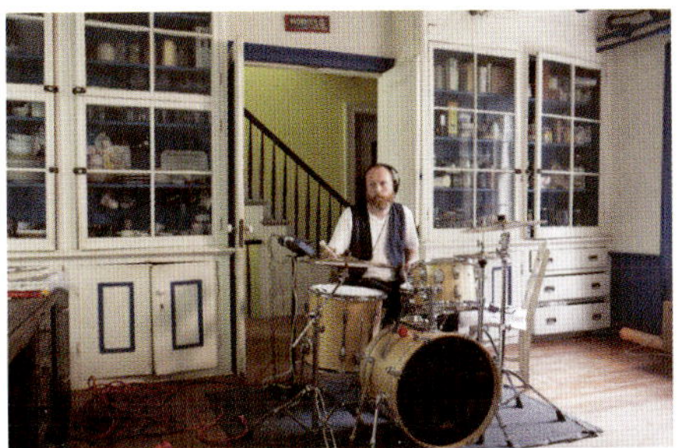
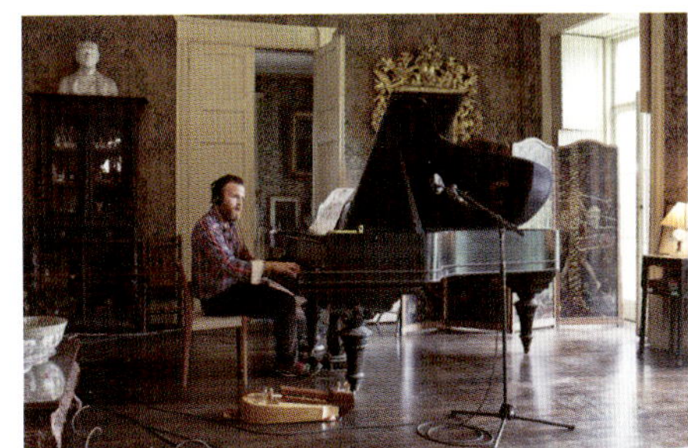
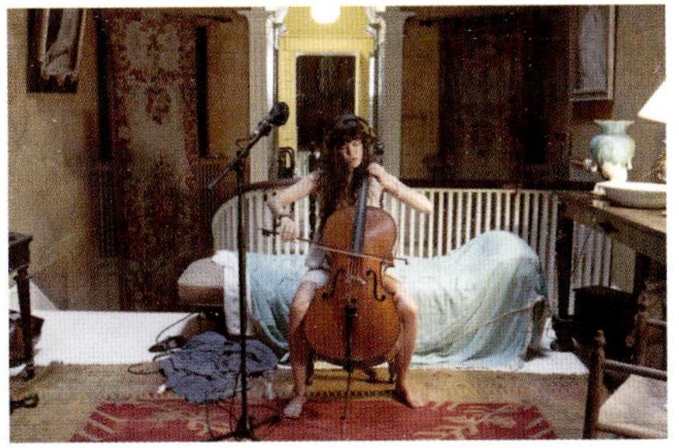
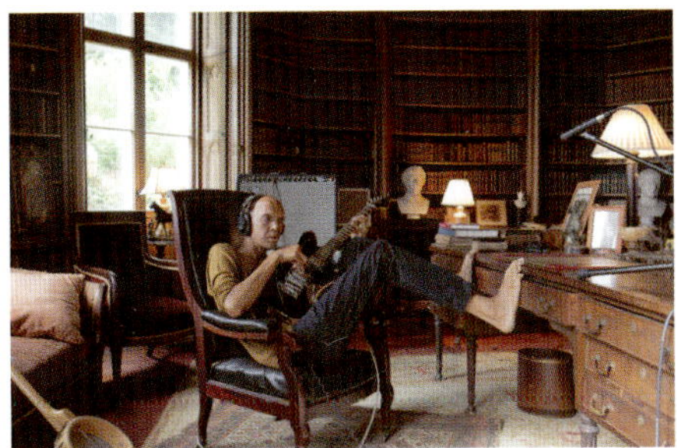
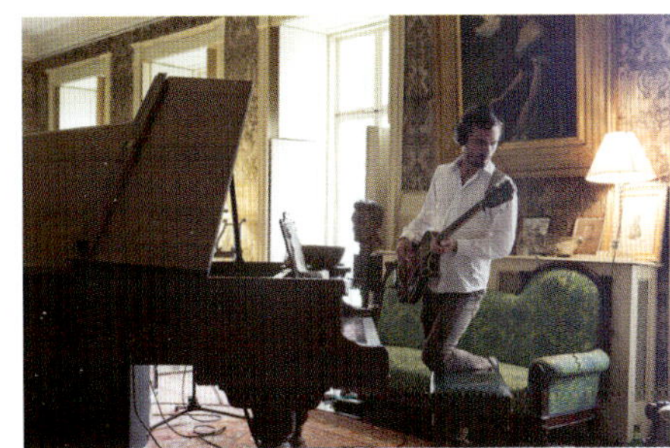
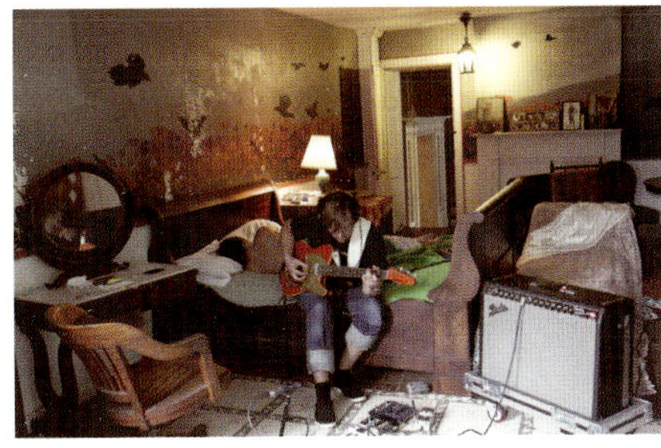
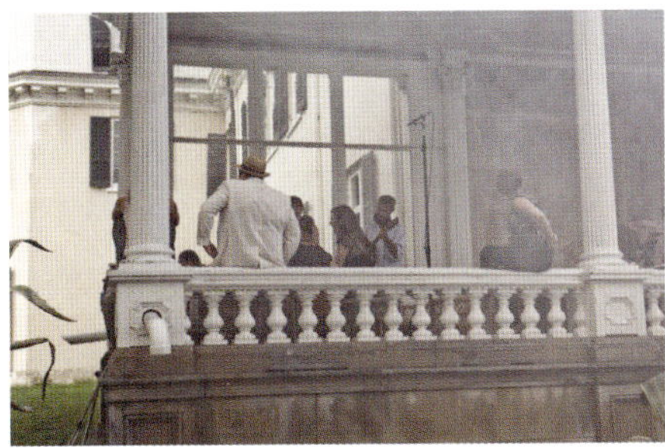
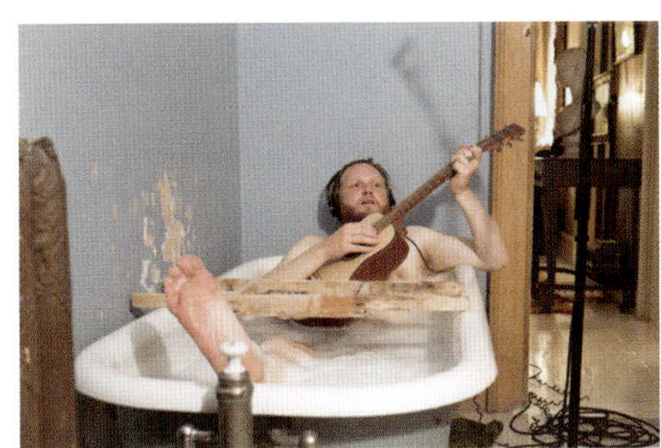

Ragnar Kjartansson, *The Visitors*, 2012
Nine-channel video, 64 minutes

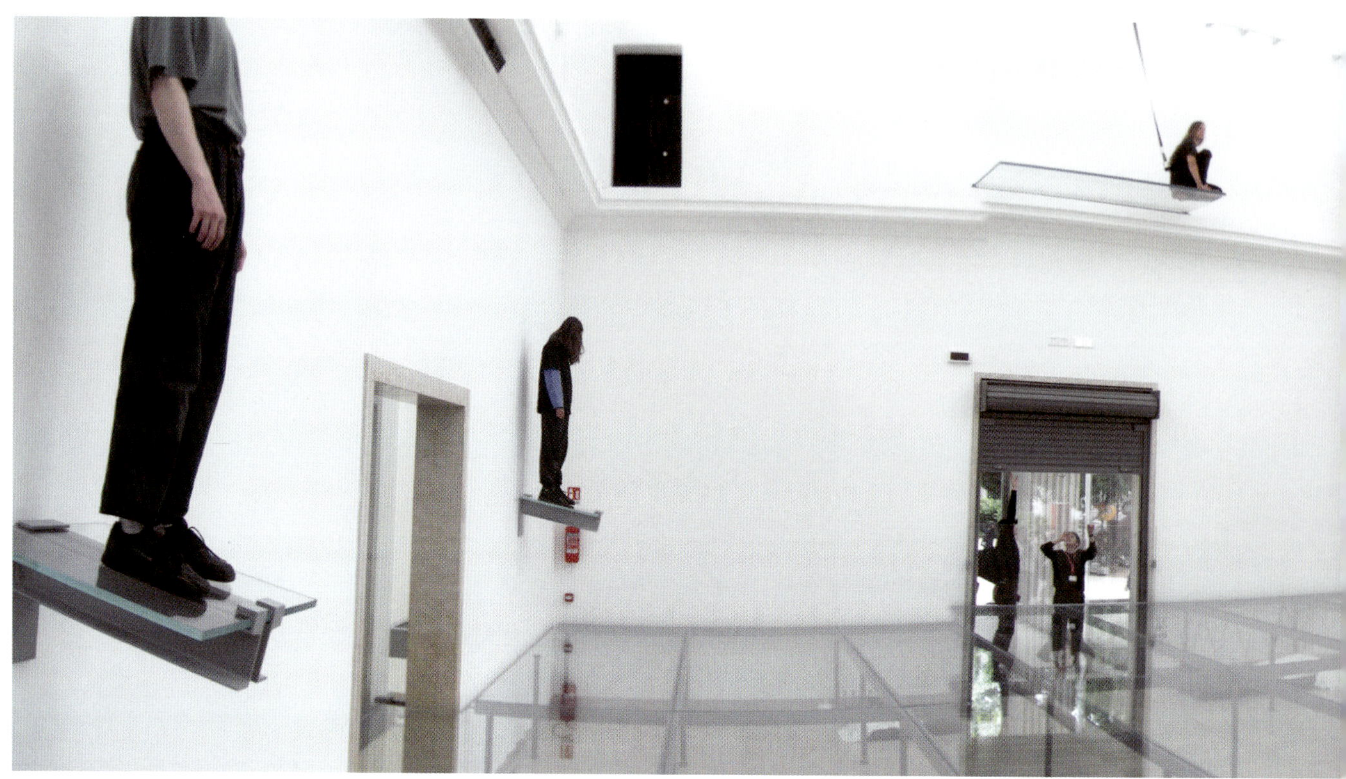

Anne Imhof, *Faust*, 2017
Performance, German Pavilion, Venice Biennale, 2017

As with Janet Cardiff's *Forty Part Motet*, you are inside the music, although you can only see a few musicians at any one time. It is melancholy, but captivating; periodically, you move to watch and hear different players. After nearly an hour you see the musicians put down their instruments, get up and congregate outside the house, then wander off into the distance as if to have a party. It is very laid back, hardly a 'holy ritual', yet it functions very well as a communal act of mourning and consolation.

Do you always know what art is supposed to mean? At the 2017 Venice Biennale, I entered the German pavilion to see Anne Imhof's work (above), but nothing seemed to be happening. About a dozen young people were standing or sitting on shelves around the central space. They did not move or smile, just stared at something beyond me – far less welcoming than the two Doberman Pinschers in cages outside. An extra floor of glass had been laid down, on which spectators walked, at first gingerly. Scattered in the space below this glass floor were water bottles, two mattresses, marker pens, catapults with metal pellets, and several mobile-phone chargers. In an adjoining room behind a glass wall were an electric guitar and a drum.

Once the pavilion was nearly full, with perhaps close on a hundred visitors inside, the young people started to get down from their shelves like animals

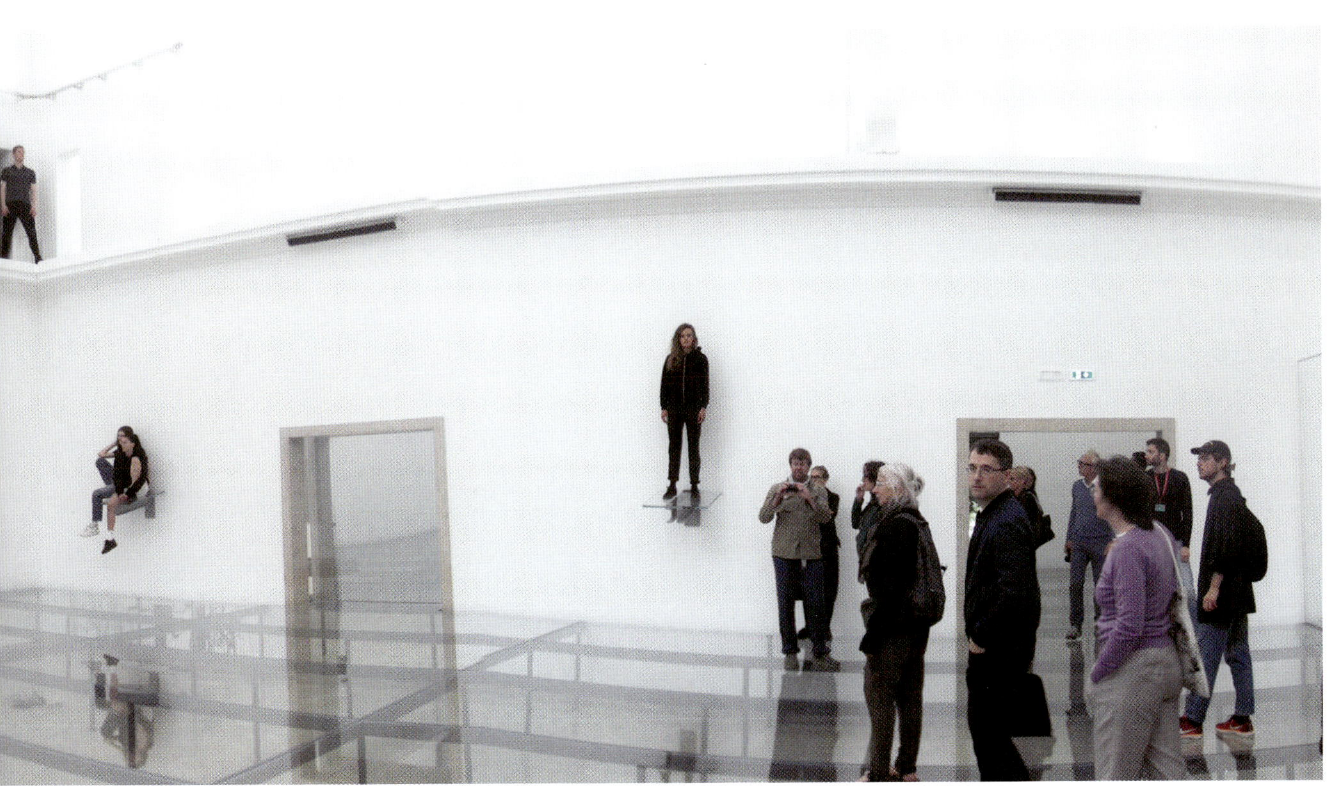

woken by the dawn. They then marched, processed, formed into lines, broke off in different directions, walked through the crowds as if they were not there, had fights or seemed to be about to have sex, sat alone or crouched alone as if thinking or sulking. Sometimes they were above, sometimes under the glass floor, crawling around beneath it. It was like being at the zoo, except we were in the cage with the animals – or maybe we were the animals and the performers the zookeepers. They, after all, were in charge. One man licked the wall obsessively; a young woman poured a line of paraffin on the floor and set it alight; another drew thick lines on the wall.

In a very abstract way, the work was about watching human activity. The performers acted like people newly born into this world and finding out what human activity is. Often, they would cling together, as if the need for company was compulsive. After an hour or so, although it was increasingly crowded, one stopped becoming annoyed at how other people kept getting in the way and started to look at them unconsciously performing too.

I was riveted, but was never really sure what it was all about. Power and abnegation? The work's title, *Faust*, didn't help much, unless your German was good enough to know it meant 'fist' as well as naming the protagonist of Goethe's drama.

‘This is a work that happens a bit like making a painting,’ said Imhof, who began as a painter and still sees painting as her core activity. ‘It’s about accidents that happen, the ability to trust. The more that is accidental, the more precise the whole thing gets. It’s happening out of impulse. Then, of course, when you work with so many good people, you can make it very elegant and repeat it.’[24] In most other contexts *Faust* would be seen as theatre or dance; certainly, it reminded me of the work of the dancer and choreographer Pina Bausch. But the art world has become so diverse, and the definition of art now so widely defined, that almost anything goes. The gallery is a spacc for many ways of thinking and experiencing.

Because Imhof uses people, mainly dancers and models, all with a strong presence, being ‘inside’ her work is an exceptionally visceral experience. But complex, puzzling and compelling experiences can also be created with such passive objects as mirrors and stones. The German artist Alicja Kwade likes puzzles: two cars, each a mirror image of the other, for example. This is her work *Nissan (Parallelwelt 1 + 2)* (2009). After buying a right-hand-drive Nissan Micra in England to match her partner’s left-hand-drive version purchased in Germany, Kwade scrupulously copied each graze and bump on her partner’s car so that hers was an exact reflection of his. Nothing unusual to note unless you look a second time ... *Unheimlich!* Uncanny!

In 2011 Kwade took 303 clock weights and hung them from a ceiling to create a room of time affected by gravity – although some of the weights seemed to sink into the floor. Titled *Durchbruch durch Schwäche* (Breakthrough through Weakness), the installation managed to seem both scientific and poetic. Kwade has also balanced porcelain models against a pile of coal, and crushed champagne bottles to make a pile of green sand, asking us to think about what connections can be made between different forms and materials. Her works are always aesthetically pleasing. ‘I’m trying to see what reality is for me, and what it is for us all,’ she says.[25]

Like many successful artists, Kwade needs assistants to make her work. However, as she and others have observed, that makes it difficult to think. ‘I have, depending on the work, two to five assistants, but during the day I always feel a little observed,’ she admitted in 2013. ‘I do my research and develop my ideas in the evening and at night [when she is alone].’[26] Creating her world is not a communal vision, but that of a single person.

What is Kwade’s work about? In 2016, she explained: ‘My interests focus on all the “paths” which lead us towards the question (or have this question as their starting point) of why the world is just the way it is. This is the oldest question in philosophy: why does the world exist, why is the Earth turning around, what are atoms ... Why do we call a table a table if it usually is a piece of wood? ... I also try to analyse more minor aspects, such as why something costs as much as it does and not more, or less. Who is creating the reality and how do we contribute to this process, namely how do we change the reality ourselves by means of our everyday activities and decisions?’[27]

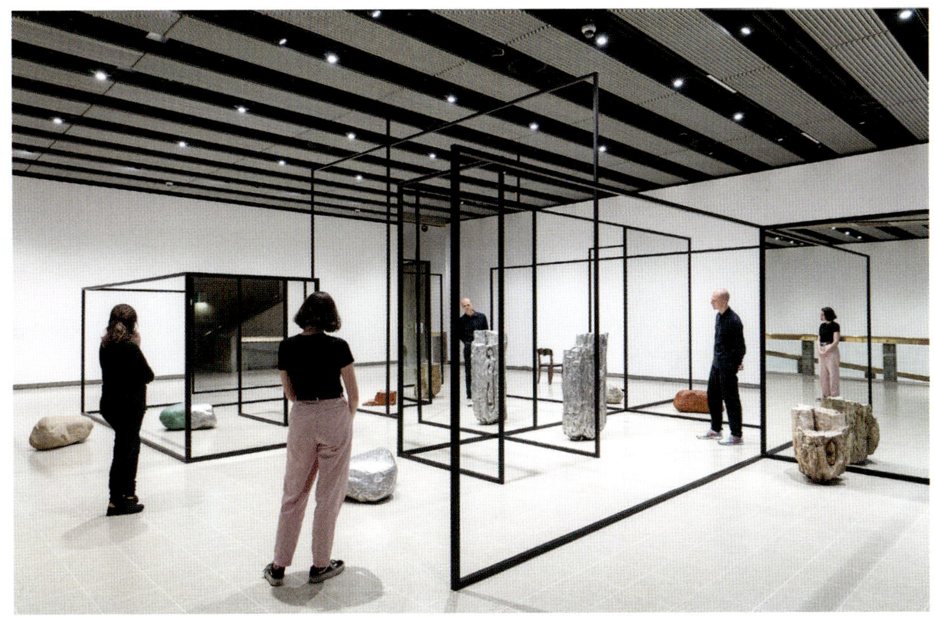

Alicja Kwade, *WeltenLinie*, 2017
Powder-coated steel, mirror, stone, bronze, aluminum, wood, petrified wood; installation view, 'Space Shifters', Hayward Gallery, London, 2018

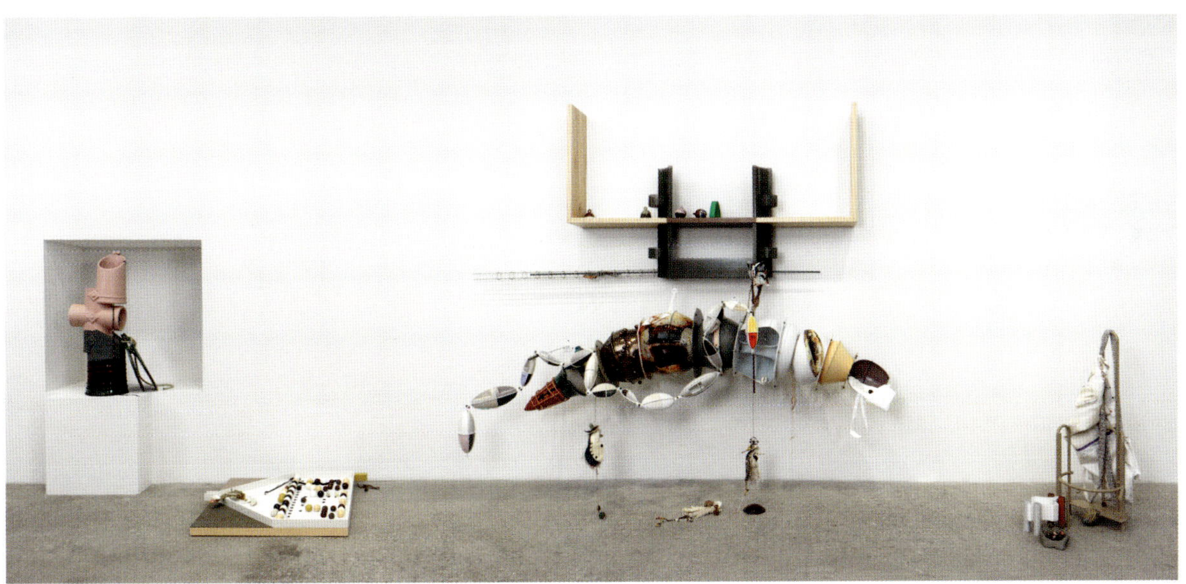

Helen Marten, *Brood and Bitter Pass*, 2015
Steel, aluminium, model board, ash, cherry, chipboard, sprayed MDF, blown glass, glazed ceramic, screen printed Latex, bucket, cast resin, cast Jesmonite, stones, cast rubber, flocked aluminium, gold leaf, cotton, nails, magnets, heating filament, lace, vinyl, twig, glass beaker, cast concrete, brass, neoprene rubber, stitched and embroidered fabric, airbrushed steel, cardboard, sand, sugar, felt, oyster shell, overall: 301 × 816.9 × 111.8 cm (118½ × 321⅝ × 44 in.)

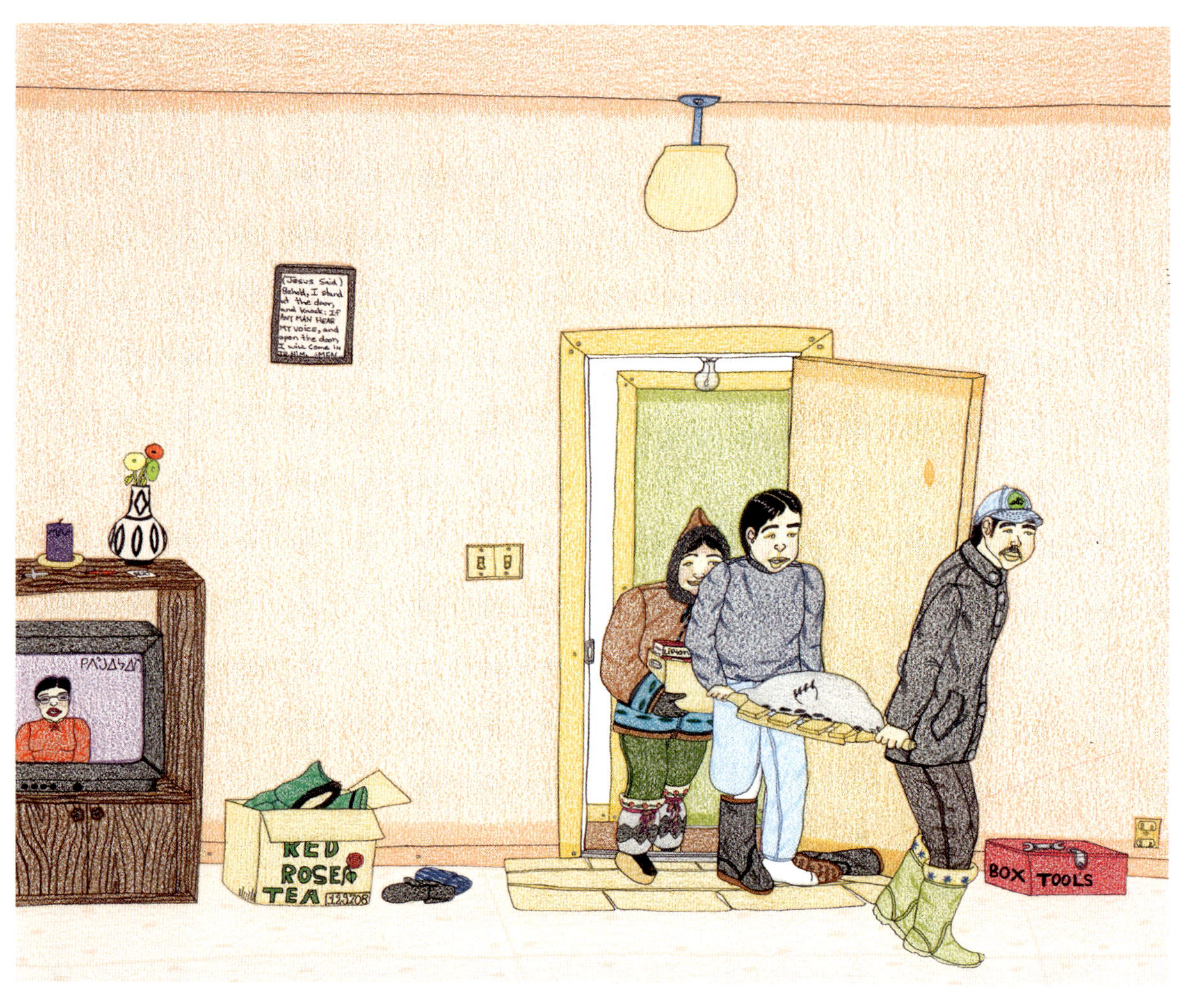

Annie Pootoogook, *Bringing Home Food*, 2003–04
Coloured pencil and felt-tip pen over graphite on paper, 50.8 × 57.8 cm (20 × 22⅞ in.)

In Kwade's 2017 large-scale installation *WeltenLinie* ('World Line'; page 249), nothing is quite what it seems. As we move around and through it, real objects and mirror images double up and un-double. We think we see in the double-sided mirrors a rock again and again, but we get muddled as the rock periodically seems to be green or silver or red when reflected. That is because they are paired objects seen for 'real', not mirrored. Speaking of *WeltenLinie,* Kwade has said: 'I hope that it is more like a feeling or an experience than a solid sculpture', more like a 'phantasm rather than an object'.[28] But aesthetically it is, as always, both pleasing and puzzling.

As with other especially inventive artists – Cy Twombly and Sarah Sze, for example – our first encounter with the art of Helen Marten can be confusing: the work looks intriguing, visually satisfying, but one hasn't the faintest idea what it's about. But, as with Twombly and Sze, we recognize a particular voice; we may not quite 'get' the world they are creating, but it feels coherent. It's a bit like hearing some new music: you don't understand it, but you know the soloist is in control.

Looking at Marten's *Brood and Bitter Pass* (page 249), it's not just that there are so many different types of object and material in the work, or that many of the objects aren't even what they appear to be (the pink drainpipe, for example, is actually a handmade ceramic). What it is about, or points to, is how we – or at least people in wealthy countries – use or own so much stuff, and where the distinctions between organic, inorganic, handmade, branded, etc., have become blurred. There is a lot to untangle in this work; indicatively, the central hanging element looks like the bride in Marcel Duchamp's *The Bride Stripped Bare by Her Bachelors, Even (The Large Glass)* (1915–23) – a work that is also like a puzzle, and of notorious complexity.

Although Marten draws on a computer, and many have written of her as exemplifying a generation for whom the virtual and the real elide continually, she prefers reading books and making. 'I'm really not into technology at all, or in media in that sense,' she explains. 'I like handling material, physically constructing, rather than working with an interface which really holds you hostage.'[29] Even if her work can sometimes look machine-made – clearly, many of the elements are bought or laser-cut and assembled by fabricators – it always looks hand-assembled, clinically clean in parts but improvised, even messy in others.

Marten writes a lot, and her writing is as teasing and slippery as her sculptures: 'Oysters. Oh ancient Jurassic barnacle! Whiffy signifier, salted pearl! You are wondrous, platitudes and all. Leather. Leather is ancient, sleazy, academic ... Skin. Skin is one surface and of one plane. It is dimensionally intelligent, wraps around us and stops blood from leaking out – like enamel of glaze on a bathtub, it is an encasement, an enclosing, a layer.'[30] She does not 'explain' her works, but gives an equivalent that is rhapsodic and witty, the words tumbling out but in well-formed sentences. She writes ecstatically about cartoons and food: 'In moving cartoons, the inorganic often becomes uncontrollably and beautifully plasmatized ... Images are made wonderfully elastic, but a complexly volumed shape can be described and solidified with a few encircling marks or flicks or a line … In all its engineered shapes, colours, flats and corrugations, pasta is one of the most fabulously playful dishes. To sit consuming a bowlful of spaghetti is to be brought face-on with material floppiness, with squiggle, softness and swelling.'[31]

One virtue of the contemporary art world is that it gives people from the margins opportunities to bear witness to their lives, and to be seen. Annie Pootoogook was born in Cape Dorset, in the far north of Canada. Her parents made the sort of traditional Inuit art that tourists like to collect, but Pootoogook started to do something very different: make pictures of the life she really lived. 'I didn't see any igloos in my life,' she once pointed out; instead, she drew her community in their actual homes doing actual, day-to-day things. Traditional life had become muddled up with all the impedimenta of Western culture: catching seals, but eating them in a neat suburban interior. She also showed the traumas of life: drawings such as *Man Abusing a Woman* and *Breaking Bottles* were of her own life.

Sadly, like many from the margins, Pootoogook found life in the footlights of artistic fame difficult. Having won a $50,000 prize, she gave the money away to her extended family. She moved to Montreal then Ottawa, slipped into alcoholism, and shacked up with men who ended up in prison or couldn't hold down a job. Eventually she was living on the street, selling drawings to passers-by for beer money. She gave birth to a child who was promptly taken into care. In 2016, at the age of forty-seven, Pootoogook was found drowned in the River Rideau. But despite all this, her drawings are memorable not only for being deceptively straightforward and formally very tight, but also for their joyfulness.

It has been argued that Pootoogook and other indigenous artists become more energized, more engaged, when they give up producing images of traditional life and begin focusing on how that tradition crashes up against the culture and economy of Western modernism. Njideka Akunyili Crosby, for example – Nigerian-born but resident in California – talks of 'contact zones': 'social spaces where cultures meet, clash and grapple with each other'.[32] Having moved to the US aged sixteen, Crosby, she says, 'felt an urgency to tell my story as a Nigerian in diaspora'.[33] Whenever she returned to Africa, she began collecting images and objects from the life she had known: 'I started collecting pictures as a way to stay connected to the Nigeria as I knew it. I became aware that people had no clue, not just about Nigeria but about Africa as a continent, or life in that part of the country, at all. I had a desire to share the Nigeria I knew with people, in a way that felt real or sincere to me … I wanted to give people a glimpse of this other space that they weren't familiar with.'[34]

The English that Crosby learnt in Nigeria is a global language, but one with many local phrases and idioms. Like those phrases and idioms, the pictures she brings from Africa are blended into her paintings, in a formally very sophisticated way. Her paintings are both Nigerian and American, but also something else: 'I'm trying to work within the tradition I inherited, but make moves that signal my difference

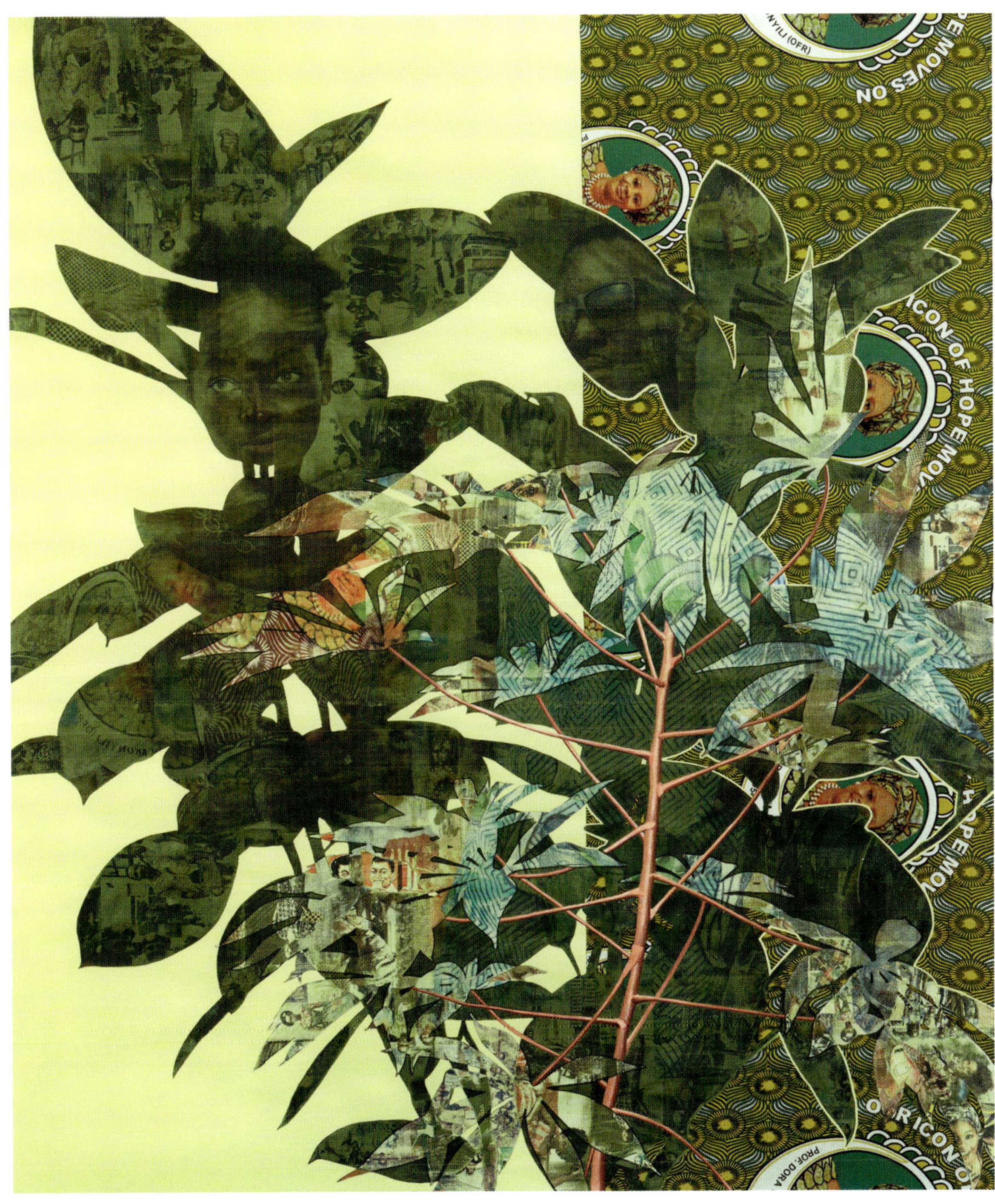

Njideka Akunyili Crosby, *Cassava Garden*, 2015
Acrylic, transfers, colour pencil, charcoal and commemorative fabric on paper, 191.5 × 160.4 cm (75⅜ × 63⅛ in.)

from it.'[35] Or, put another way, 'I wanted to root my work in a transcultural space, this weird, buzzing in-between space, a kind of no-man's land.'[36]

In Zhao Renhui's 2019 photographic project *The Pond* (opposite), we see several species of bird land on a pail of water set in a forest, drink from it, or perhaps swim or socialize with other birds. We also see a lizard climb up the pail and drink from the water. Zhao's work does not have the super-bright colours and extraordinary detail of recent BBC nature documentaries, nor does it have the hushed, reverent commentary of David Attenborough. But Zhao is fascinated by animal life. All his work is about it; however, it is also about how we think, represent and connect with wild animals. 'I think I am a "documenter" too', says Zhao, 'but a very subjective one ... We should always question everything that is given to us.'[37] The four images of the lizard shown here are as much about how we look at animals as animals themselves.

Zhao's relationship to zoology is similar to Alicja Kwade's relationship to epistemology. Tellingly, Zhao's early work was presented under the guise of the 'Institute of Critical Zoologists'.[38] His photographs of animals – dolphins swimming off Singapore, for example – were often faked. He wants to provoke: 'Let's not try to pretend that photography is still a medium we can trust ... I think that it is my job as an artist to raise questions. We have become so comfortable with lies that lies have lost their power to shock.'[39]

Zhao has also taken over houses, recreating them as the homes of fictional botanists, complete with their collections; like many artists, he is fascinated by the compulsion to collect, to surround ourselves with stuff, that many of us have. 'Most of the time, when we talk about landscapes and animals we are really talking about human concerns and human perspectives. Our interaction with nature shapes the way we approach these subjects.'[40] *The Pond* was shot with security cameras in a small pocket of wilderness close to the centre of Singapore. Although the work recorded the secretiveness and persistence of wildlife, Zhao was intrigued to find nearby an old tent in which an illegal immigrant from Myanmar had once lived. The history of animals is now always tied up with a history of people.

We began this story by travelling to Indonesia and New York to see things more globally than had other histories of art. Let's end the book on the islands of Bantayan and Cuba. Although the art market and the media that surrounds it may still be most active (and strangely self-obsessed) in New York and other Western capitals, interesting work is being made all around the world. The future can begin anywhere.

Since 2010, Martha Atienza has filmed the annual festivities on Bantayan, the small island in the Philippines where she lives. It is, she writes, 'an animistic festival Christianized and incorporated into Folk Catholicism that slowly turns into modern-day madness ... Provoked by current events and experiences – super typhoons, Manny Pacquiao's boxing match, the Papal visit, labour migration – participants take to the streets and assume another persona. Inspired by their ancestors they become powerful, god-like and mad.'[41]

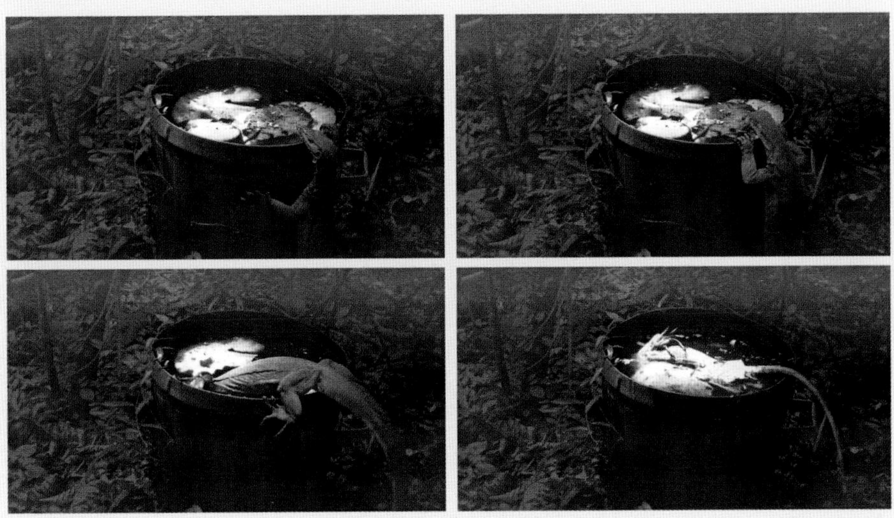

Robert Zhao Renhui, *The Pond: Malaya Monitor Lizard, Entering Pond, 1/1/2019*, 2019
Photographs taken from surveillance cameras

In her video installation *Our Islands, 11°16'58.4"N 123°45'07.0"E* (page 256), Atienza sends the festival into the sea. We see a line of strangely dressed people processing underwater: a boxer, kings and queens, men dressed as women, some carrying statues of Santa Nino (baby Jesus), doctors with survivors of typhoons, drug lords with gun-toting guards, others carrying political slogans. It's a carnival: riotous, but slowed down; amusing, but disturbing. When shown at the 2018 Taipei Biennial, which was focused on ecological issues, Atienza provided locally woven mats for people to sit on.

Atienza's work is about both Bantayan and a more universal experience of the sea: first, how it feels to be at sea, constantly moved by its waves, currents and tides; and, secondly, the life of sailors, like her father, on the ships that transport goods around the globe. Atienza also works with her brother Jake to explore, through exhibitions and a website (www.DAKO-gamay.com), not only Bantayan but also other islands in the Pacific region, the challenges to ecology, economy and local culture that Bantayan and other islands in the area face, and how their people are trying to dealing with them. In Bisayan, the language spoken on Bantayan, *dako gamay* means 'big small'.

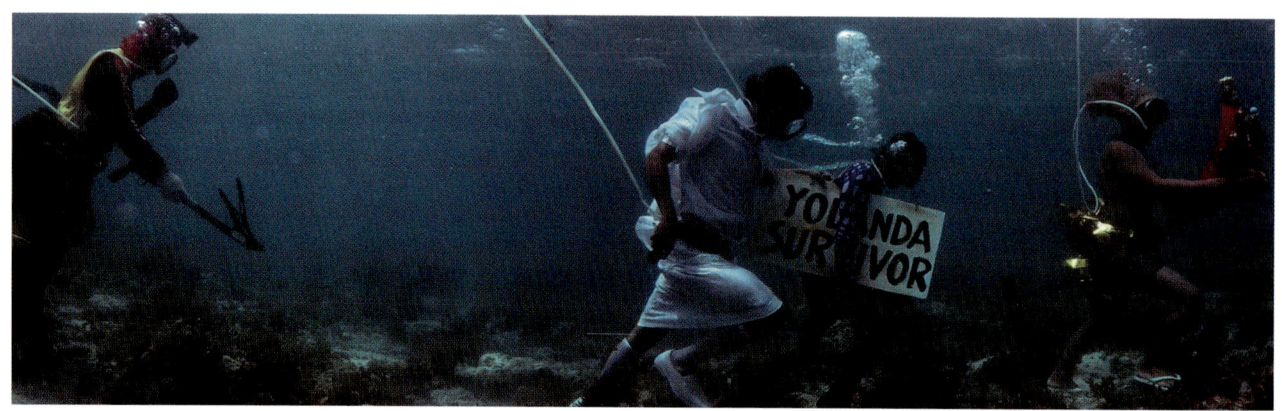

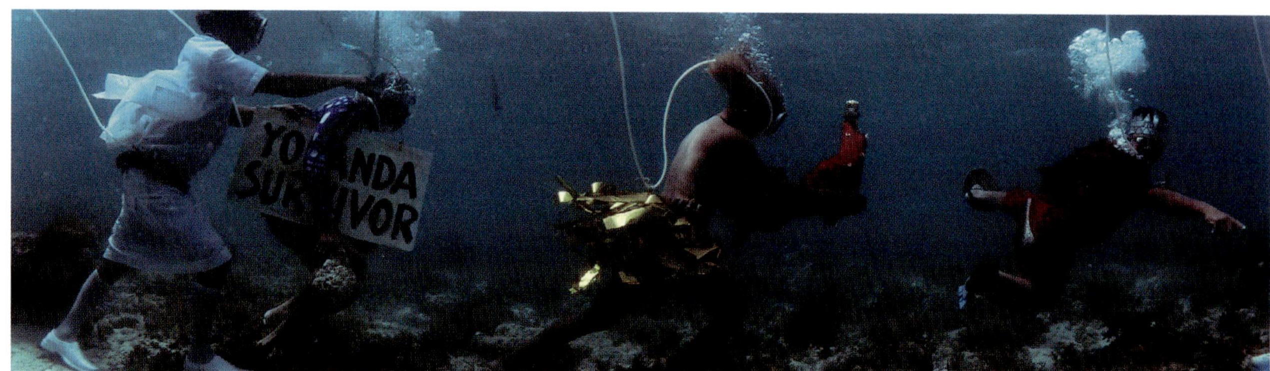

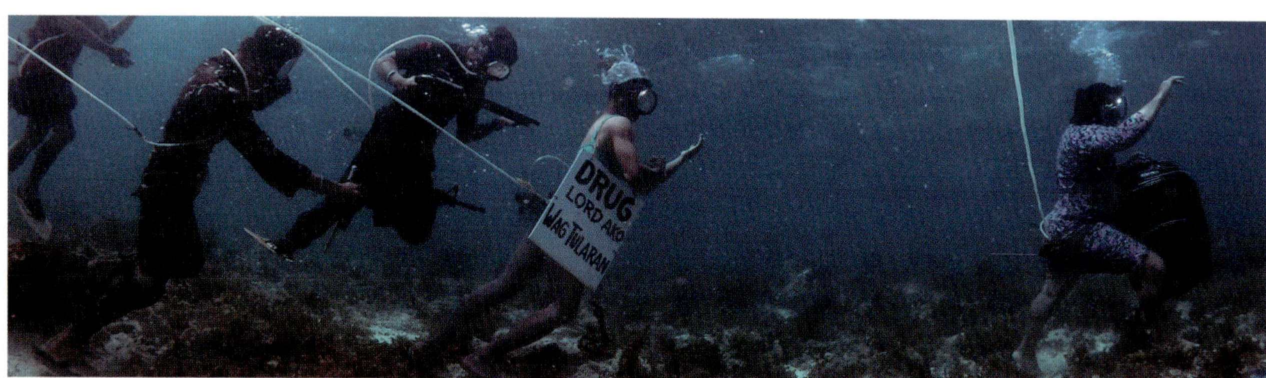

Martha Atienza, *Our Islands, 11°16'58.4"N 123°45'07.0"E*, 2018
Video intallation

It is the desire or need of many artists nowadays to be both big and small, global and local – to be rooted in a place but be part of the global conversation.

Half Filipina, half Dutch, Atienza, like a significant proportion of artists today, is mixed race or transnational. Does this give them a greater sensitivity to the state of the world? Just as Njideka Akunyili Crosby moves between North America and Africa, so Atienza moves between Europe and South East Asia. Doris Salcedo, who constantly moves between the West and Colombia, uses the word 'displaced' to refer to her own situation: 'Displaced is the most precise word to describe the contemporary artist. Displacement allows us to see the other side of the coin: indifference and war. It is obviously a position that generates tension and conflict, but I believe that from the position of displacement art derives its most powerful expression.'[42]

As it had since 1984, the Havana Biennale of 2019 sought to be a forum for artists from the Third World, inevitably with a preponderance of Latin American art. But there were artists from Asia too, including Atienza's fellow Filipina Geraldine Javier. As well as paintings, Javier has always made installations, often using textiles, crochet or embroidery. After leaving Manila to live in the countryside, she found herself impressed by the many women in her new community who worked hard to support their families, taking on numerous odd jobs to earn money. In a statement accompanying her installation *Spinning Women* (page 258) at Havana, Javier wrote: 'I live in the Philippines, a country where the majority of the population can only live on a day-to-day basis. Women especially are often faced with a difficult decision, faced with dire poverty or having to leave the family to find work abroad and provide for that family, yet knowing that the separation will damage and perhaps break the family up. Those who opt to stay but can't find permanent work have to be resourceful, finding bits of work here and there to tide them over. This work celebrates all those anonymous women who provide for and keep their families – and the country as a whole – together.'

To honour these heroines of everyday life, Javier – having made tracings of twenty-two of the women – painted the tracings, life-size, on to banners made from native pineapple fibre; then, with other women from the community, she embroidered flowers on the banners. As shown in Havana, the banners were suspended from the ceiling and the windows left open, allowing the wind to make them spin or swing about as if dancing. An accompanying wall text listed the women's names, the various jobs they undertook, their ages and the number of children they had. In any communal project, even if initiated and overseen by a solo artist, it is right and proper that all involved are named.

There were also artists from Africa at Havana, including the Mali-born Abdoulaye Konaté. At first glance, Konaté's large textile hangings looked simple, serene and decorative; but on closer inspection, you realized they were both complex and heavy with meaning. Konaté has long campaigned through his work against AIDS, pollution, war. At Havana, one hanging proclaimed: 'No to religious fanaticism!'

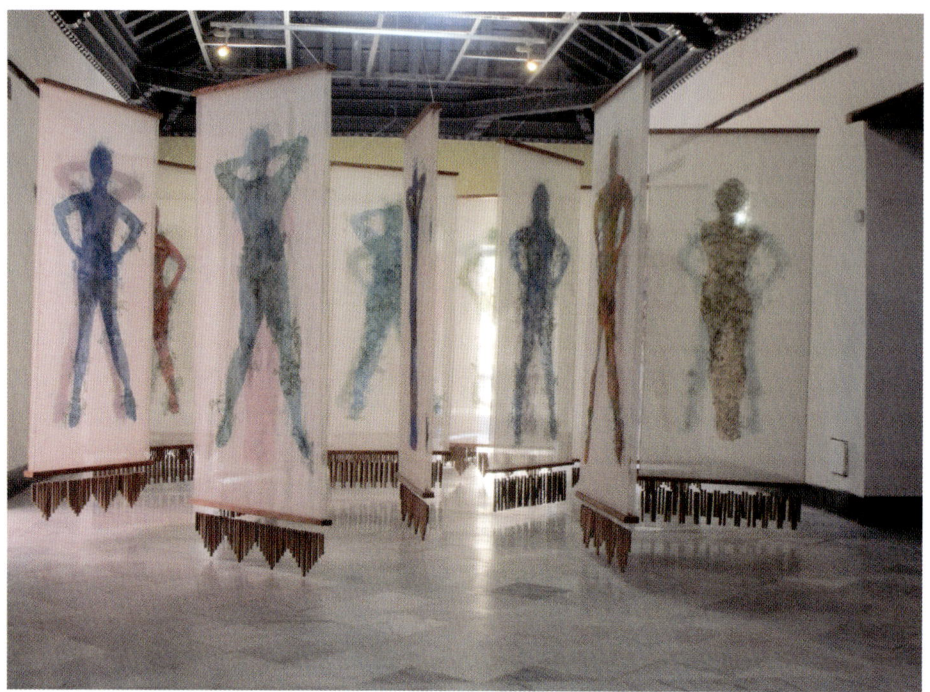

Geraldine Javier, *Spinning Women*, 2019
Installation view, Havana Biennale, 2019

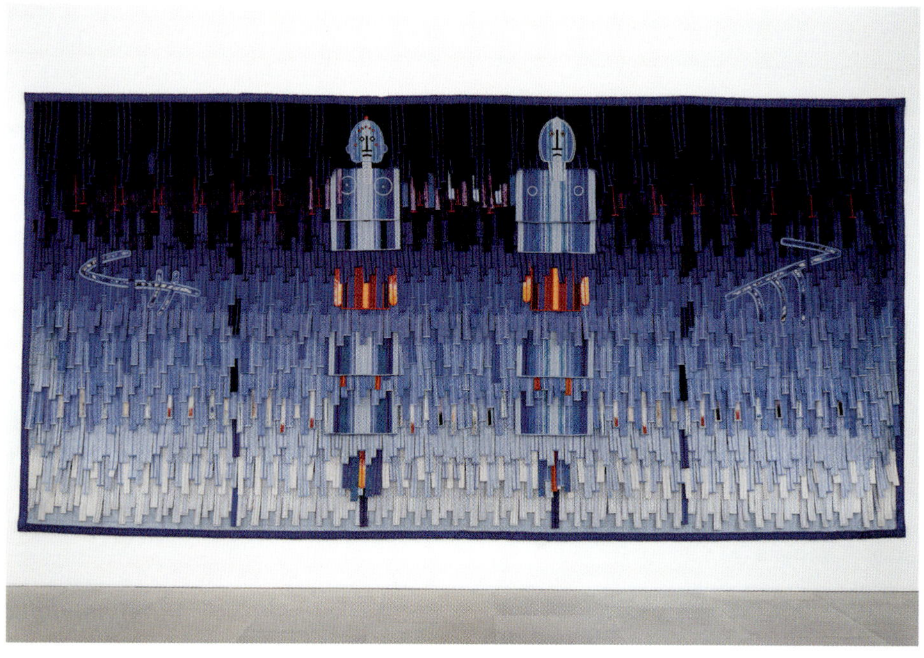

Abdoulaye Konaté, *Couple Dogon et les signes*, 2018
Textile, 291 × 595 cm (114⅝ × 234¼ in.); installation view, Havana Biennale, 2019

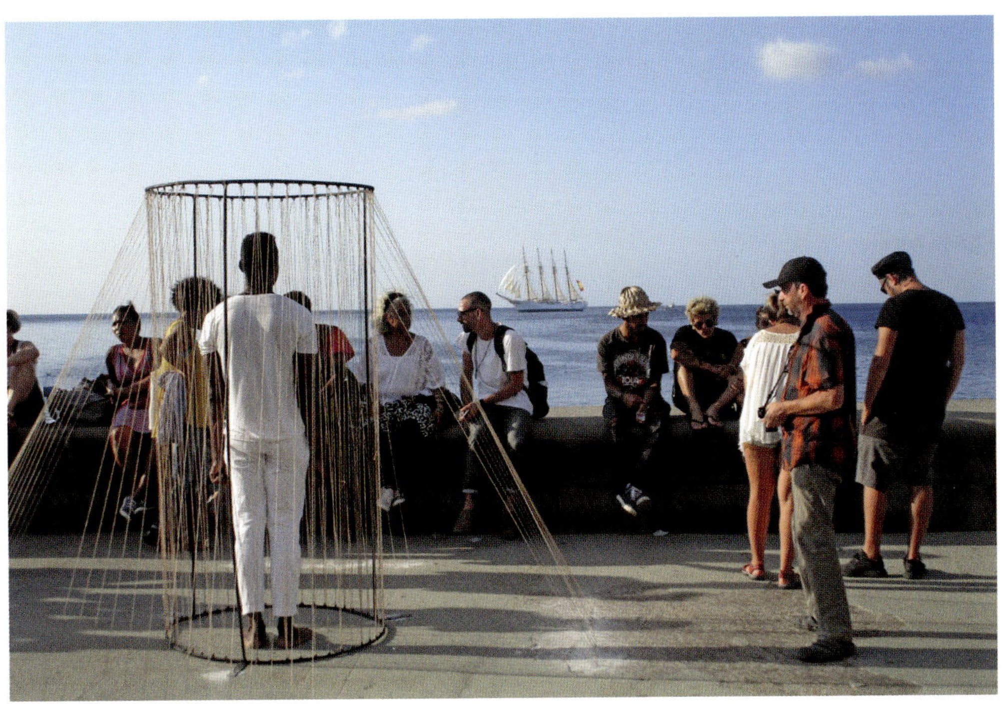

Carlos Martiel, *La sangre de Caín* (The blood of Cain)
Performance, Detrás del muro, 13th Havana Biennial, Havana, Cuba, 2019

Although shown in Western-type galleries, Konaté's work also belongs to the African tradition of commemorative textiles. He deploys signs and motifs not only from his people, the Bamana, but from all the other peoples of Mali. 'All my work is informed by my culture,' Konaté insists.[43] Although he trained as an artist in Havana, he was happy to work in the National Museum of Mali for many years. It may have limited his time in the studio, but it gave him a deep understanding of African culture.

The 2019 Havana Biennale also became a site of protest. Having been campaigning against Decree 349, a law that gives the Cuban government extraordinary powers of censorship, Tania Bruguera asked foreign artists exhibiting at the biennale to demonstrate their opposition to the law by, for example, wearing a T-shirt saying 'No to Decree 349' at the opening. It seems none did so. Not, I think, out of fear, but from a sense that it is problematic to engage in other nations' political affairs – do you really know what is going on? Would such a protest be effective or, as it would in many countries, counter-productive?

Clearly riled by this failure to elicit support, Bruguera published a letter on the website *Hyperallergic* announcing that she would not be attending the biennial and implicitly asking others to 'black' it.[44] Ironically, this was itself a form of censorship on her fellow artists, Cuban and foreign. Her defenders saw her as a model activist persecuted; others, unfairly or not, saw her as a showboating

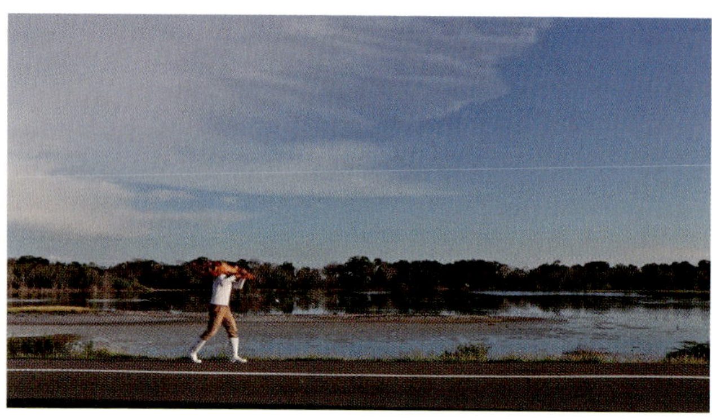

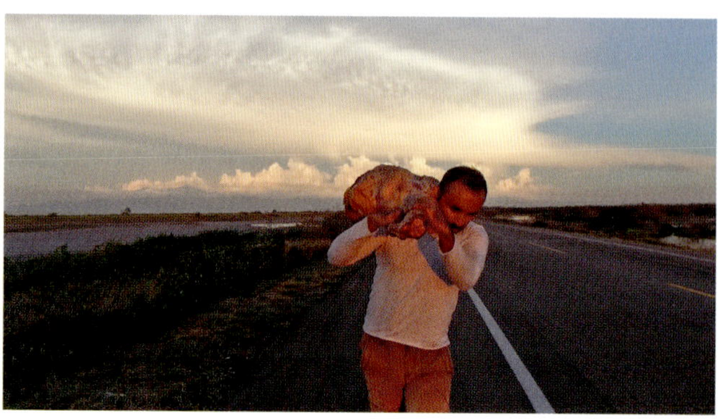

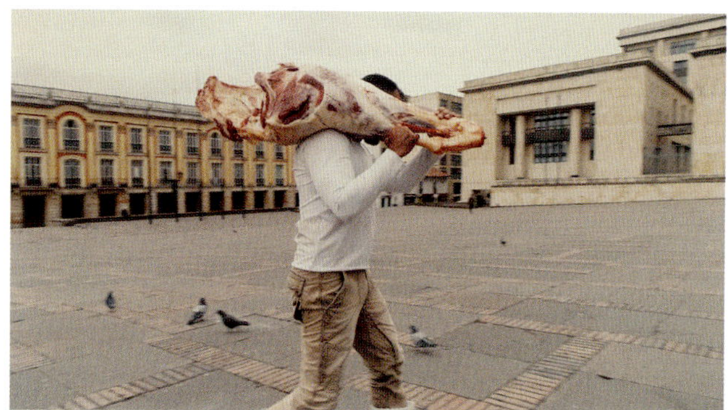

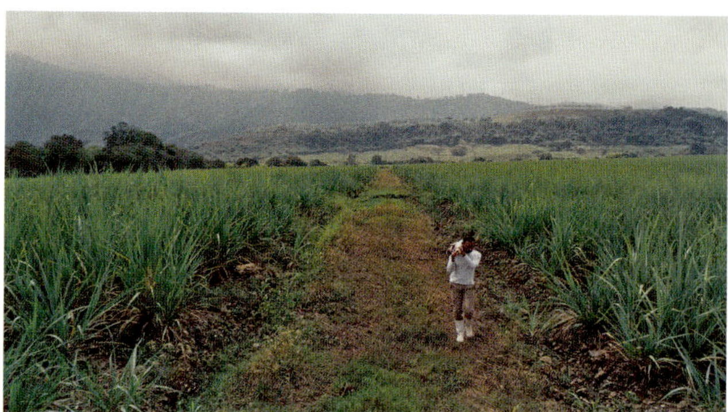

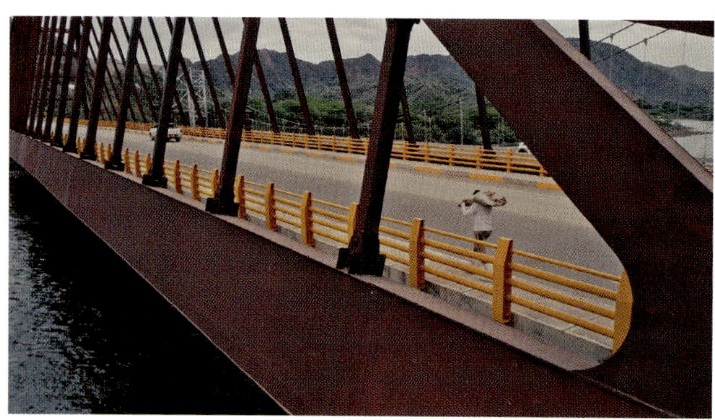

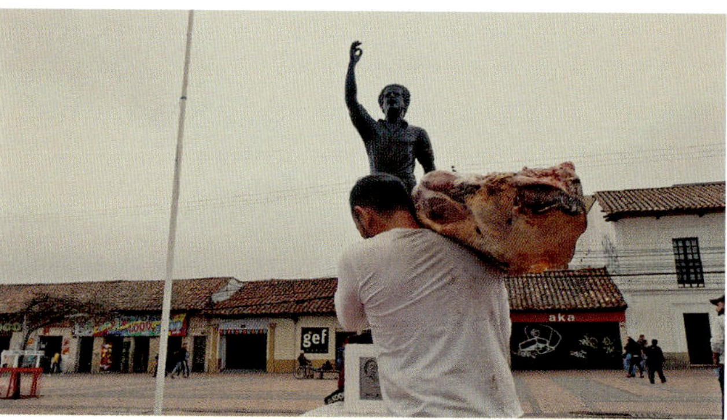

Oscar Leone, *Sequence of a Man who Walks (the Earth)*, 2018
Video performance, 1 hour 14 minutes, from the series 'Materias materiales'

egotist. Whatever the case, censorship, like restriction on press freedom, is worsening in many countries. Artists have to decide whether to protest against it or work within it, to attack the system directly or try to undermine it from within. Most, inevitably, want their work to speak for them.

One of the most striking images at Havana was that made by the Cuban performance artist Carlos Martiel. On the second day of the opening, Martiel, dressed all in white, went to the most famous street in Havana, the Malecón, entered a cage of strings anchored to the pavement, and stood absolutely still, under the sun, facing the sea (page 259). There was no information save the title, *La sangre de Caín* (The Blood of Cain). Did Martiel represent Cain, the eldest son of Adam and Eve? Or perhaps he was his brother Abel, whom he killed? Whose blood was being spilt? Clearly, the work was a protest. Only days later did one learn that the strings had been dyed with the blood of those artists protesting against Decree 349.

For *Sequence of a Man who Walks (the Earth)* (opposite), a film by Oscar Leone shown at Havana, the Colombian artist walked from his home town of Santa Marta to Bogota, a journey that took him sixteen days. Over his shoulder he carried the leg of a dead cow. In the early stages of the film, Leone looks like a worker from an abattoir, complete with white boots. But as he progresses steadfastly along the coast, through valleys, towns and over mountains, we begin to think more of Christ carrying the cross to Golgotha, or of Sisyphus endlessly rolling a stone up a mountain. We pass by ravaged and pristine landscapes, scenes of dire poverty and incredible wealth, fields of junked machinery, and properties protected by barbed-wire fences. Leone's progress is dogged; walking in silence, he looks only ahead. Periodically, a drone-mounted camera shows us what he is walking past. The film is as beautiful as any travel documentary, but with no narrator telling us what we are looking at or why.

In a statement issued at the biennale, Leone talks of 'building a relationship with the landscape', and of how the partial cadaver of the cow 'is symbolic of the tensions caused by more than fifty years of inequitable distribution of wealth in Colombia'. He hopes that viewers of the film will begin to perceive 'the religiosity, the environmental crisis, the urban and tourist developments and the latent forms of corruption that have determined the recent history of Colombia'.[45] The strength of the work is such that, while we learn a lot about Colombia, we also start to think about what else the film might mean. Leone takes on a kinship with all those whose work, like that of Sisyphus, is drudgery; but his journey to the capital is also certainly, if not a pilgrimage, a protest aimed at the centre of power. For him, it was a transformative experience – a laborious task through which he gained a sense of freedom.

In this work, as in the best of art made today, we share our experiences, thoughts and dreams; we bear witness to our times. It is through such work that we create new rituals, new metaphors, to imagine the world differently. In the age of surveillance capitalism, how best to end this book than with images of someone using their own body to inhabit and understand this world – and to make us think.

Afterword

What should you do next?

Maybe you want to read more. Maybe you want to look at some art. Or maybe you want to think about what I have written.

If you want to read more, read widely and get other opinions. There are many more books on contemporary art. The one that I have found most useful, and provocative, is Terry Smith's *Contemporary Art: World Currents*. It is genuinely global, he has a clear point of view, but it is partial: he only writes about 'biennale art'. He also tries to cover too many artists (about seven hundred), so the index looks like a telephone directory; as a result, the average reader might find the book a bit indigestible. In some respects, this book is a response to Smith's. If you want to read more about individual artists, many interviews with Western artists can be found on the Internet. Just search for the name of the artist and add the word 'interview'. Some artists, but surprisingly few, have good websites of their own.

If you want to look at art – and I hope you do! – I can't tell you where to go as I don't know where you live, but I would suggest looking at art with a friend: we learn so much by discussing our varying reactions. If you can collect, do so; you also learn much by living with art and seeing it every day. If you can't afford to buy art, collect reproductions and live with them instead. If you want to become a participant, then get involved with your local museum or gallery. Go to any lectures or discussions they hold. Go to the private views, which are less private than you might think! And if you have the chance, talk to artists themselves – not just famous artists, but younger ones, as yet unheard of, and older ones who have never had great success but have kept on working and thinking. Artists of all kinds are the most interesting people to talk to about art. If you have read Gombrich, you will know that he famously began his story by saying, 'There really is no such thing as art. There are only artists.' Artists do not exist apart from their society and culture, but they do have more freedom than most. It is they who make and ultimately define art.

This book is not a list of the hundred best artists or the hundred most valuable artists. I have tried to tell you the story of contemporary art – how it has become global and more inclusive, and how it has become perhaps the best forum for thinking about the world we live in. It is, of course, a vast, various and often contradictory story. I have tried to tell it as simply as I can, giving as examples 115 important and representative artists or artists' groups. Many of them are, I believe, the best. Some make very expensive artworks, others don't. But they are all interesting: they all represent something important in art *now*.

Perhaps you don't agree with my choices: how could I not have discussed Vija Celmins or Lucian Freud or Annette Messager or Yoshitomoto Nara or ...? Please make your own list, your own story. I want you to think for yourself: I have deliberately included differing opinions on many of the artists I've talked about so that you have to make a choice and can start to make your mind up as to who you feel is a good artist, or authentic, or even a moral one.

Today, art matters as never before. As Marcel Proust wrote in his novel *In Search of Lost Time* (1913–27), 'It is only through art that we can escape from ourselves and know how another person sees a universe which is not the same as our own and whose landscapes would otherwise have remained as unknown as any there may be on the moon.' Our world is in crisis – ecologically, politically, ideologically. Art is a place where we can share our experiences and thoughts. In fact, it might be the best place to make sense of being human in a world that seems to change so quickly and inexorably. This is the age of the Internet, but art is the place where body and mind, hand and thought are indubitably linked, not alienated. As we have seen, art can be fun, too. And enjoyable to look at, or experience. Yet art is not only about pleasure, but also the right to pleasure; not only about being thoughtful, but also the right to be thoughtful. That matters in a world where public discourse too often now becomes both angry and crass.

As Kiki Smith said, you just have to be present for life. Perhaps, above all else, this is what art today is about.

Notes

PREFACE

1 Ernst Gombrich, *The Story of Art*, 10th edn (London: Phaidon, 1960), p. 1. In writing about contemporary art, it is incredibly difficult *not* to give lists of artists. There are so many of them, and names are the currency of the art world. I once held a supper party for some art-world friends; after they had left, I asked my then partner whether she had enjoyed the conversation. 'It was like listening to people reading from the telephone directory', she replied.

INTRODUCTION

1 Agnes Martin, 'The Current of the River of Life', lecture given in 1979, quoted in Arne Glimcher, *Agnes Martin: Paintings, Writings, Remembrances* (London: Phaidon, 2012), p. 168.
2 Shahzia Sikander, interview with Ian Berry, in *Shazia Sikander, Nemesis*, exhib. cat. (Ridgefield, CT: Aldrich Contemporary Art Museum, 2004), p. 4.
3 *Ibid.*, p. 8.
4 Emily Kame Kngwarreye, interview with Rodney Gooch, 1990, quoted in Margo Neale (ed.), *Emily: The Genius of Emily Kame Kngwarreye*, exhib. cat. (Canberra: National Museum of Australia, 2008), p. 218.
5 The sculptor in question was Cathy de Monchaux.
6 Jürgen Klopp, interview with Moritz Rinke, in Rinke (ed.), *Reading the Game* (Berlin: Aufbau Digital, 2015), quoted in www.theguardian.com/football/blog/2015/nov/25/jurgen-klopp-doctor-helper-syndrome-liverpool-borussia-dortmund.
7 Mark Rothko, quoted in Jacob Baal-Teshuva, *Mark Rothko, 1903–1970: Pictures as Drama* (Cologne and London: Taschen, 2015), p. 57.
8 Donald Judd, 'On Installation', in *Documenta 7*, exhib. cat., 2 vols (Kassel: P. Dierichs, 1982), p. 164.
9 Quoted in www.kw-berlin.de/en/susan-philipsz-internationale.
10 In a subsequent chapter, I will return to this piece and how it works differently when staged in different locations.
11 See Chrystia Freeland, *The Plutocrats: The Rise of the New Global Super-Rich* (New York: Penguin Press, 2012).
12 Zeng Fanzhi, quoted in '*The Last Supper*: The Annunciation of a New Age', Sotheby's catalogue note, 5 October 2013, www.sothebys.com/en/auctions/ecatalogue/2013/40th-anniversary-evening-sale-hk0488/lot.48.html.
13 Donald Kuspit, 'Beuys or Warhol?', *C Magazine*, Autumn 1987, reprinted in Kuspit, *The New Subjectivism: Art in the 1980s* (New York: Da Capo Press, 1993), p. 403.
14 The phrase 'sophisticated entertainment' was used by the English artist Stephen Buckley. See 'Stephen Buckley interviewed by Tony Godfrey', *Artlog*, no. 2, November 1978.
15 Kuspit, 'Beuys or Warhol?', p. 403.
16 E. H. Gombrich, *The Story of Art*, 16th edn (London: Phaidon, 1995), p. 36.

CHAPTER 1

1 The country's independence was finally recognized by the Dutch on 27 December 1949. Elsewhere in the region, the Philippines had become an independent nation on 4 July 1946. More significant, perhaps, was India's declaration of independence on 15 August 1947.
2 On Kawara, quoted in Jonathan Watkins, *On Kawara* (London: Phaidon, 2002), p. 50.
3 Pere Heinrich Dumoulin, quoted in Trevor Ling, *A History of Religion East and West: An Introduction and Interpretation* (London: Macmillan, 1968), p. 413.
4 Ling, *A History of Religion East and West*, p. 413.
5 Colin McCahon, quoted in Marja Bloem and Martin Browne (eds), *Colin McCahon: A Question of Faith*, exhib. cat. (Amsterdam: Stedelijk Musuem, 2002), p. 166.
6 *Ibid.*, p. 214.
7 *Ibid.*, p. 232.
8 From my experience as a teacher, young people have difficulties relating to the 1950s, which, to them, seem very far away. By contrast, the 1960s – retro though they may seem (think Austin Powers) – seem familiar. It is in the 1960s that many of the traits of our period have their origins.
9 Donald Judd, 'Local History', *Arts Yearbook 7*, 1964, reprinted in Donald Judd, *Donald Judd: Complete Writings, 1959–1975* (Halifax: Press of the Nova Scotia College of Art and Design, 1975), pp. 148–49.
10 Was the curator of the retrospective, Pontus Hultén, playing the same game when, in 1990, three years after Warhol's death, he had carpenters in Malmö make 105 Brillo boxes (in plywood, with screen-printing) for an exhibition in Leningrad, later selling forty of them with fake certificates that claimed they were made in 1968 with Warhol's approval? Hultén later donated six of his boxes to the Moderna Museet, which accepted them as the 'real' thing. In 2006, another was sold for more than $200,000. A year later, however, Hultén's 'scam' was uncovered.
11 Christie's, New York, 10 November 2010, Lot 10. This particular box, however, was a rarer yellow, '3 cents off' version. In 2014, one of the more standard white boxes was sold for $869,000 (Christie's, New York, 13 November 2014, Lot 183), a price that may have been influenced by the box having been owned by Cy Twombly.
12 Alexandra Munroe, in Bhupendra Karia, ed., *Yayoi Kusama: A Retrospective*, exhib. cat. (New York: Center for International Contemporary Arts, 1989), p. 18.
13 Yayoi Kusama, quoted by Alexandra Munroe, in Karia, *Yayoi Kusama*, p. 18.
14 Peter Schjeldahl, *Art News*, May 1966.
15 Lee Ufan, quoted in Edan Corkill, 'Lee Ufan: Korean at the Forefront of Japan's Modern Art', *Japan*

Times, 1 August 2010, www.japantimes.co.jp/life/2010/08/01/people/lee-ufan-korean-at-the-forefront-of-japans-modern-art/#.XQJfci2ZNTY.

16 Lee Ufan, 'Stand Still a Moment', 1997, in Lee Ufan, *The Art of Encounter*, trans. Stanley N. Anderson, exhib. cat. (London: Lisson Gallery, 2004), p. 29.

17 Richard Serra, *Verb List Compilation: Actions to Relate to Oneself*, 1967–68, first published in Grégoire Müller, *The New Avant-Garde: Issues for the Art of the Seventies* (New York: Praeger, 1972).

18 By the conceptual artists' group Art & Language.

19 Gregory Battcock, quoted in Tony Godfrey, *Conceptual Art* (London: Phaidon, 1998), p. 242.

20 Richard Long, quoted in Martina Giezen, *Richard Long in Conversation: Bristol 19.11.1985* (Holland: MW Press, 1985), p. 12.

21 Richard Long, 'Words after the Fact', 1982, quoted in R. H. Fuchs, *Richard Long* (New York: Solomon R. Guggenheim Museum, 1986), p. 236.

22 Richard Long, interview with William Furlong, 1985, in William Furlong, *Speaking of Art: Four Decades of Art in Conversation* (London: Phaidon, 2010), p. 69.

23 Richard Long, quoted in Giezen, *Richard Long in Conversation*, p. 1.

24 Fuchs, *Richard Long*, p. 45.

25 Richard Long, quoted in Martina Giezen, *Richard Long in Conversation: Part Two* (Holland: MW Press, 1986), p. 16.

26 This was reputedly said by the American artist Al Held.

27 Bruce Nauman, quoted by Richard Lacayo, *Time*, 26 April 2004.

28 Art Basel was set up in competition with Kunstmarkt Köln, as Art Cologne was originally called. Art Basel Miami was initiated in 2002, Art Basel Hong Kong in 2013.

29 Robert Scull, quoted in John Tancock, 'The Robert C. Scull Auction', in *Art at Auction: The Year at Sotheby Parke Bernet, 1973–74* (New York: Sotheby's, 1974), p. 139.

30 Ana Mendieta, artist's statement, 1977, quoted in *Ana Mendieta: Earth Body – Sculpture and Performance, 1972–1985*, exhib. cat. (Washington, DC: Hirschhorn Museum and Sculpture Garden, Smithsonian Institution, 2004), p. 237.

31 Marina Abramović, interview with Hans Ulrich Obrist, 2001, in Thomas Boutoux, ed., *Hans Ulrich Obrist Interviews: Volume 1* (Milan: Charta, 2003), p. 30.

32 Marina Abramović, interview with Michael Archer, in Furlong, *Speaking of Art*, pp. 149–52.

33 *Ibid.*, p. 150.

34 *Ibid.*, p. 149.

35 Susan Hiller, interview with Rozsika Parker, *Spare Rib*, 72, 1978, reprinted in Barbara Einzig, ed., *Thinking About Art: Conversations with Susan Hiller* (Manchester: Manchester University Press, 1996), p. 28.

36 Susan Hiller, interview with Paul Buck, *Centrefold*, 1979, reprinted in Einzig, *Thinking About Art*, p. 138.

37 Susan Hiller, quoted in Einzig, *Thinking About Art*, p. 1.

38 Bill Viola, interview with Michael Nash, *Journal of Contemporary Art*, 1990.

39 Joseph Beuys, quoted in Allan Antliff, *Joseph Beuys* (London: Phaidon, 2014), p. 116.

40 Those by Donald Judd and Claes Oldenburg. A third, by Ulrich Rückriem, was re-installed and made permanent in 1986.

CHAPTER 2

1 Christos Joachimides, 'A New Spirit in Painting', in Joachimides *et al.* (eds), *A New Spirit in Painting*, exhib. cat. (London: Royal Academy of Arts, 1981), p. 14.

2 *Ibid.*, p. 16.

3 *Ibid.*

4 Georg Baselitz, interview with Peter Iden, 2003, reprinted in Detlev Gretenkort (ed.), *Georg Baselitz: Collected Writings and Interviews* (London: Riding House, 2010), p. 262.

5 In fact, by his dealer, Michael Werner, who was desperate for some press, even bad press. Sadly, the police intervention led to no sales.

6 Georg Baselitz, interview with Donald Kuspit, 1995, reprinted in Gretenkort, *Georg Baselitz*, p. 245.

7 Georg Baselitz, interview with Jean-Louis Froment and Jean-Marc Poinsot, 1983, reprinted in Gretenkort, *Georg Baselitz*, p. 66.

8 Anselm Kiefer, interview with Christian Kämmerling and Peter Pursche, 1990, reprinted in Germano Celant, *Anselm Kiefer*, exhib. cat. (Milan: Skira, 2007), p. 183.

9 Anselm Kiefer, interview with Steven Henry Madoff, *Art News*, no. 8, October 1987, p. 129, quoted in Andrea Lauterwein, *Anselm Kiefer, Paul Celan: Myth, Mourning and Memory* (London: Thames & Hudson, 2007), p. 37.

10 Anselm Kiefer, interview with Axel Echt and Alfred Nemeczek, 1990, reprinted in Celant, *Anselm Kiefer*, p. 161.

11 Julian Schnabel, interview with Donald Kuspit, 1987, reprinted in Jeanne Siegel (ed.), *Art Talk: The Early 80s* (New York: Da Capo, 1990), p. 158.

12 Philip Guston, quoted in Jerry Talmer, 'Creation Is for Beauty Parlors', *New York Post*, 9 April 1977, re-quoted in Robert Storr, *Philip Guston* (New York: Abbeville Press, 1986), pp. 52–53.

13 Manuscript note from early 1970s found in Guston's studio, quoted in Musa Mayer, *Night Studio: A Memoir of Philip Guston* (New York: Knopf, 1988), p. 170.

14 The curator was Hans Ulrich Obrist. See Tacita Dean, 'Panegyric', in Nicholas Serota (ed.), *Cy Twombly: Cycles and Seasons*, exhib. cat. (London: Tate, 2008), p. 45.

15 Cy Twombly, interview with Nicholas Serota, in Serota, *Cy Twombly*, p. 45.

16 Maria Lassnig, journal entry, 1980, quoted by Jörg Heiser, *Frieze*, November/December 2006.

17 Including myself. My 1986 book *The New Image in Painting* (London: Phaidon) mentioned no painters outside Western Europe and the US. I can only plead ignorance.

18 Nilima Sheikh, interview, 2016, www.idiva.com/news-work-life/artist-nilima-sheikh-shares-her-journey-in-art/16042733.

19 Nilima Sheikh, quoted in Hera Chan, 'Nilima Sheikh in Conversation', 28 June 2018, ocula.com/magazine/conversations/nilima-sheikh.

20 Eric Fischl, interview with Bice Curiger, *Artscribe*, no. 53, July/August 1985.

21 Eric Fischl, quoted in press release for Edward Thorp Gallery, New York, February 1982.

22 Eric Fischl, interview with Bice Curiger.

CHAPTER 3

1 See Jeff Wall, interview with Jean Wainwright, 2005, in William

Furlong, *Speaking of Art: Four Decades of Art in Conversation* (London: Phaidon, 2010), p. 257.
2 Cindy Sherman, interview with Jeanne Siegel, 1987, in Siegel (ed.), *Art Talk: The Early 80s* (New York: Da Capo, 1990), pp. 271–72. The boyfriend was Robert Longo; they were visiting David Salle.
3 Laura Mulvey, 'Visual Pleasure and Narrative Cinema', *Screen*, Autumn 1975, reprinted in Mulvey, *Visual and Other Pleasures* (Basingstoke: Macmillan, 1989), pp. 14–26.
4 Cindy Sherman, 'Artist's Statement', *Documenta 7* (Kassel: D + V Paul Dierichs, 1982), p. 411.
5 Helene Winer, quoted in Paul Taylor, 'Conversations with Art Dealers: Metro Pictures', *Flash Art*, no. 109, November 1982, p. 79.
6 Richard Prince, quoted in lot essay, lot 19, Christie's, New York, 12 May 2014, www.christies.com/lotfinder/Lot/richard-prince-b-1949-spiritual-america-5792590-details.aspx.
7 Julia Farrington, 'Case Study: Spiritual America 2014', 21 July 2015, www.indexoncensorship.org/2015/07/case-study-spiritual-america-2014/.
8 Carl Swanson, 'How Richard Prince Got Kicked Off Instagram (and then Reinstated)', 8 March 2014, www.vulture.com/2014/03/how-richard-prince-got-kicked-off-instagram.html.
9 Christie's, New York, 12 May 2014, lot 19.
10 Tehching Hsieh, quoted in Iona Whittaker, 'Doing Time: Interview with Tehching Hsieh', 19 March 2015, www.randian-online.com/np_feature/doing-time-interview-with-tehching-hsieh.
11 Tehching Hsieh, interview with Delia Bajo and Brainard Carey, 1 August 2003, *Brooklyn Rail*, https://brooklynrail.org/2003/08/art/tehching-hsieh.
12 Bernd and Hilla Becher, *Die Architektur der Forder-und Wasserturme* (Munich: Prestel, 1971).
13 Bernd Becher, quoted in Susanne Lange, *Bernd and Hilla Becher: Life and Work*, trans. Jeremy Gaines (Cambridge, MA: MIT Press, 2007), p. 219.
14 Hilla Becher, interview with Jean-François Chevrier, James Lingwood and Thomas Struth, 1989, in *Un Autre objectivité/Another Objectivity*, exhib. cat. (Paris: Centre National des Arts Plastiques, 1989), pp. 58–62.
15 Jeff Wall, interview with Mark Lewis, 1993, in *Jeff Wall: Selected Essays and Interviews* (New York: Museum of Modern Art, 2007), pp. 241–42.
16 Jeff Wall, interview with Els Barents, 1985, in *Selected Essays and Interviews*, p. 201.
17 Jeff Wall, interview with Anne-Marie Bonnet and Rainer Metzger, 1993, in *Selected Essays and Interviews*, p. 248.
18 Jeff Wall, interview with Mark Lewis, 1993, in *Selected Essays and Interviews*, p. 243.

CHAPTER 4

1 Richard Deacon, interview with Jean de Loisy, 1986, quoted in Jérôme Sans, *Richard Deacon: 10 Sculptures 1987/1989*, exhib. cat. (Paris: Musée d'Art Moderne de la Ville de Paris, 1989).
2 Richard Deacon, interview, 1997, quoted in Judith Olch Richards (ed.), *Inside the Studio: Two Decades of Talks with Artists in New York* (New York: Independent Curators International, 2004), p. 179.
3 Richard Deacon, interview with Pier Luigi Tazzi, in Jon Thompson *et al.*, *Richard Deacon*, rev. edn (London: Phaidon, 2000), p. 15.
4 Richard Deacon, interview with Ian Tromp, in Thompson *et al.*, *Richard Deacon*, p. 163.
5 Thomas Schütte, interview with Iwona Blazwick and Andrea Schlieker, 1990, in Iwona Blazwick *et al.*, *Possible Worlds: Sculpture from Europe*, exhib. cat. (London: Institute of Contemporary Arts/Serpentine Gallery, London), 1990, p. 70.
6 Thomas Schütte, quoted in Julian Heynen *et al.*, *Thomas Schütte* (London: Phaidon, 1998), p. 120.
7 Thomas Schütte, interview with Iwona Blazwick and Andrea Schlieker, in Blazwick *et al.*, *Possible Worlds*, p. 70.
8 *Ibid.*, p. 71.
9 Thomas Schütte, interview with James Lingwood, in Heynen *et al.*, *Thomas Schütte*, p. 15.
10 After a few years, Fritsch stopped selling the miniature yellow Madonnas: the point had been made.
11 The other two were Shirazeh Houshiary, born in Iran but living in the UK, and Siah Armajani, also born in Iran but based in the US.
12 Author's notes, 1987.
13 Jeff Koons, quoted in Fronia W. Simpson (ed.), *Jeff Koons*, exhib. cat. (San Francisco: Museum of Modern Art, 1992), p. 89.
14 Jeff Koons, interview with Adrian Searle, 1989, reprinted in William Furlong (ed.), *Speaking of Art: Four Decades of Art in Conversation* (London: Phaidon, 2010), p. 105.
15 *Ibid.*, p. 106.
16 See www.theguardian.com/artanddesign/2017/mar/09/jeff-koons-plagiarised-french-photographer-for-naked-sculpture.
17 Kiki Smith, quoted by Barbara Bloom, in Bloom *et al.*, *Marlene Dumas* (London: Phaidon, 1999), p. 9.
18 *Ibid.*
19 Kiki Smith, speaking in 2000, quoted in Judith Olch Richards (ed.), *Inside the Studio: Two Decades of Talks with Artists in New York* (New York: Independent Curators International, 2004), p. 236.
20 Kiki Smith, interview with Robin Winters, 1990, quoted in Petra Giloy-Hirtz (ed.), *Kiki Smith: Procession*, exhib. cat. (Munich: Haus der Kunst, 2018), p. 34.
21 Kiki Smith in discussion with Chuck Close, 1994, quoted in Giloy-Hirtz, *Kiki Smith*, p. 34.
22 Christian Boltanski, interview with Tamar Garb, in Didier Semin *et al.*, *Christian Boltanski* (London: Phaidon, 1997), p. 11.
23 Ann Hamilton, interview with Sarah Rogers-Lafferty, in John Howell (ed.), *Breakthroughs: Avant-garde Artists in Europe and America, 1950–90*, exhib. cat. (New York: Rizzoli, 1991), p. 209.
24 Ann Hamilton, 'Notes to *Indigo Blue*', in *Ann Hamilton: The Body and the Object*, exhib. cat. (Columbus: Wexner Center for the Arts, Ohio State University, 1996), p. 55.
25 Indicatively, the first book with the term 'installation art' in its title was published only in 1993.
26 See, for example, Oliver Sacks, *The Man Who Mistook His Wife for a Hat*, rev. edn (London: Picador, 2011), esp. pp. 47–58.
27 The commission formed part of 'Histoires de Musée', an exhibition marking the curator Suzanne Pagé's appointment as director of the museum. Pagé invited a number of artists, Boltanski included, to interact with the museum and its

collection. The show coincided with 'Magiciens de la Terre', the more famous exhibition of contemporary art at the Centre Pompidou (see Chapter 5).

28 Christian Boltanski, quoted in Georgia Marsh, 'The White and the Black: An Interview with Christian Boltanski', *Parkett*, no. 22, December 1989, p. 39.
29 Ilya Kabakov, press release for *The Red Pavilion*, 1993.
30 Ilya Kabakov, studio talk, 1994, in Richards (ed.), *Inside the Studio*, p. 138. The talk was given by Kabakov's wife, Emilia, as Kabakov couldn't speak English.
31 Ilya Kabakov, quoted in Boris Groys, '"With Russia on Your Back": A Conversation between Ilya Kabakov and Boris Groys', *Parkett*, no. 34, December 1992, p. 38.

CHAPTER 5

1 It was billed as the '*première exposition mondiale d'art contemperain*'. See Lucy Steeds *et al.*, *Making Art Global: Part 2 – Magiciens de la Terre*, 1989 (London: Afterall, 2013), p. 24.
2 Meschac Gaba, 2001, quoted in Hans Beltin *et al.* (eds), *Global Contemporary and the Rise of New Art Worlds* (Karlsruhe: ZKM/Centre for Art and Media, 2012), p. 214.
3 Strictly speaking, Papua New Guinea is not part of South East Asia, although Indonesia rules the western half. Culturally and racially, it belongs to Oceania. But the fact remains that no artist from the developed and sophisticated art communities of Indonesia, Philippines, Singapore, Thailand, etc. was selected for the exhibition. This book includes several from those countries.
4 Jean Fisher, 'Fictional Histories: "Magiciens de la Terre" – The Invisible Labyrinth', *Artforum*, vol. 28, no. 1, September 1989, reprinted in Steeds, *Making Art Global*, p. 255.
5 Richard Long, letter to Annie Cohen-Solal and Ella Biezunski, reprinted in *Magiciens de la terre: retour sur une exposition légendaire*, exhib. cat. (Paris: Centre Pompidou, 2014), p. 208.
6 Nicolas Bourriaud, 'Altermodern', in Bourriaud (ed.), *Altermodern: Tate Triennial*, exhib. cat. (London: Tate, 2009), p. 20.
7 The artist concerned was Xiao Lu. Both she and her then partner, Tang Song, were arrested.
8 Taiwan, Hong Kong and most overseas Chinese continue to use the traditional characters. They are the basis for Chinese calligraphy and, arguably, Chinese culture itself.
9 Cai Guo-Qiang, interview with Dana Friis-Hansen, in *Transculture*, exhib. cat. (Tokyo: Japan Foundation, 1995), p. 102.
10 Cai Guo-Qiang, interview with Octavio Zaya, in Dana Friis-Hansen *et al.*, *Cai Guo-Qiang* (London: Phaidon, 2002), p. 13.
11 Felix Gonzalez-Torres in conversation with Joseph Kosuth, in *A. Reinhardt, J. Kosuth, F. Gonzalez-Torres: Symptoms of Interference, Conditions of Possibility*, exhib. cat. (London: Camden Art Centre, 1994), p. 79.
12 Felix Gonzalez-Torres, interview with Hans Ulrich Obrist, 1994, in Thomas Boutoux (ed.), *Hans Ulrich Obrist Interviews: Volume 1* (Milan: Charta, 2003), pp. 308, 313.
13 Felix Gonzalez-Torres, interview with Tim Rollins, in *Felix Gonzalez-Torres* (New York: A.R.T. Press, 1993), p. 23.
14 Alfred Taubman, Preface, *Sotheby's: Art at Auction 1989–90* (London: Philip Wilson Publishers, 1990), p. 9.
15 Neo Rauch, interview, 2004, translated and quoted in *Neo Rauch: Para*, exhib. cat. (Cologne: Dumont, 2007), p. 65.
16 Reproduced in Mariska van den Berg (ed.), *Marlene Dumas: Sweet Nothings – Notes and Texts* (Amsterdam: Uiteverij de Balie, 1998), p. 46.
17 Marlene Dumas, 'Blind Dates and Drawn Curtains', 1993, in Van den Berg, *Marlene Dumas*, p. 78.
18 Marlene Dumas, 'Give the People What They Want', 1993, in Van den Berg, *Marlene Dumas*, p. 67.
19 Gerhard Richter, notes for a press conference, 1989, reprinted in Dietmar Elger and Hans Ulrich Obrist (eds), *Gerhard Richter Text: Writings, Interviews and Letters, 1961–2007* (London: Thames & Hudson, 2009), p. 203.
20 Gerhard Richter, interview with Jan Thorn-Prikker, 1989, reprinted in Elger and Obrist, *Gerhard Richter Text*, p. 229.
21 Gerhard Richter, conversation with Sean Rainbird, 1991, in *Gerhard Richter*, exhib. cat. (London: Tate Gallery Publications, 1991), p. 130.
22 Gerhard Richter in conversation with William Furlong *et al.*, 1988, reprinted in Elger and Obrist, *Gerhard Richter Text*, p. 212.
23 Gerhard Richter, interview with Hans Ulrich Obrist, 1993, reprinted in Elger and Obrist, *Gerhard Richter Text*, p. 300.
24 Gerhard Richter, notes, 1989, reprinted in Elger and Obrist, *Gerhard Richter Text*, p. 214.
25 Peter Doig in conversation with Kitty Scott, in Adrian Searle *et al.*, *Peter Doig* (London: Phaidon, 2007), p. 16.
26 Peter Doig, quoted in Paul Bonaventura, 'A Hunter in the Snow', *Artefactum*, no. 9, 1994, p. 12.
27 Peter Doig, quoted in Benjamin Klein and John Bentley Mays, 'The Closer You Get: An Interview with Peter Doig', 30 January 2014, https://canadianart.ca/interviews/peter-doig-interview.

CHAPTER 6

1 Hans Ulrich Obrist in discussion with Hou Hanru, *Kiasma*, vol. 5, no. 2, http://kiasma.fi/kiasma-lehti/5.php?lang=en&id=11.
2 Hou Hanru, 'Initiatives, Alternatives: Notes in a Temporary and Raw State', in Philippe Vergne *et al.*, *How Latitudes Become Forms: Art in a Global Age*, exhib. cat. (Minneapolis: Walker Art Center, 2003), p. 36.
3 *Ibid.*
4 Kimsooja, interview with Diana Augaitis, in *Kimsooja: Unfolding*, exhib. cat. (Ostfildern: Hatje Kantz, 2013), p. 88.
5 Kimsooja, interview with Gerald Matt, 2002, in *Kimsooja: To Breathe/Respirare*, exhib. cat. (Milan: Charta, 2005), pp. 99–101.
6 *Ibid.*
7 Kimsooja, interview with Diana Augaitis, p. 89.
8 T. S. Eliot, 'Burnt Norton', 1935, in *Collected Poems, 1909–1962* (London: Faber & Faber, 1963), p. 191.
9 Maurizio Cattelan, interview with Nancy Spector, in Francesco Bonami *et al.*, *Maurizio Cattelan*, 2nd edn (London: Phaidon, 2003), p. 9.
10 *Ibid.*, p. 18.
11 *Ibid.*
12 Tania Bruguera, in W. J. T. Mitchell, 'How to Make Art with

a Jackhammer: A Conversation with Tania Bruguera', *Afterall*, 42, Autumn/Winter 2016.
13 Tania Bruguera in conversation with Octavio Zaya, in *Zaya, Cuba: los mapas del deseo*, exhib. cat. (Vienna: Kunsthalle Wien, 1999), pp. 245, 253.
14 Montien Boonma, interview with Alfred Pawlin, in *Arte Amazonas: Montien Boonma*, exhib. cat. (Bangkok: Goethe-Institut, 1992), www.artdesigncafe.com/montien-boonma-interview-1992.
15 Apinan Poshyananda, 'Montien Boonma: Paths of Suffering', in Poshyananda (ed.), *Montien Boonma: Temple of the Mind*, exhib. cat. (New York: Asia Society, 2003), p. 24.
16 Montien Boonma, quoted in Poshyananda, *Montien Boonma*, p. 120
17 Job 1:22 and 38:16,17.
18 Nalini Malani, interview with Murtaza Vali, *Art Asia-Pacific*, 63, May/June 2009, http://artasia pacific.com/Magazine/63/Her CassandraComplexNaliniMalani.
19 *Ibid.*
20 Nalini Malani, interview with Anne McCoy, *Brooklyn Rail*, 5 November 2013, https://brooklynrail.org/2013/11/art/nalini-malani-with-ann-mccoy.
21 Nalini Malani, interview with Sophie Duplaix, in Duplaix (ed.), *Nalini Malani: The Rebellion of the Dead = La Rébellion des morts*, exhib. cat. (Berlin: Hatje Kantz, 2017), p. 30.
22 *Ibid.*, pp. 30–34.
23 Nalini Malani, interview with Anne McCoy.
24 *Ibid.*
25 Pipilotti Rist, quoted in Kaelen Wilson-Goldie, 'Peep Show Video', *Black Book Magazine*, Spring 2000, p. 53.
26 Pipolotti Rist, interview with Hans Ulrich Obrist, in Peggy Phelan *et al.*, *Pipilotti Rist* (London: Phaidon, 2002), p. 12.
27 *Ibid.*, pp. 18–19.
28 Sophie Calle, quoted in Angelique Chrisafis, 'He Loves Me Not', 16 June 2007, www.theguardian.com/world/2007/jun/16/artnews.art.
29 Janet Cardiff, extract from script of *Münster Walk*, 1997, reprinted in *Janet Cardiff: The Walk Book* (Vienna: Thyssen-Bornemisza Art Contemporary, 2005), p. 102
30 *Ibid.*, p. 113.
31 Tobias Meyer, 'Contemporary Art at Sotheby's', in *Sotheby's Art at Auction, 1997–98: The Year in Review* (London: Sotheby's, 1998), p. 27.

CHAPTER 7

1 Meschac Gaba, interview with Chris Dercon, 2000, www.tate.org.uk/whats-on/tate-modern/exhibition/meschac-gaba-museum-contemporary-african-art/my-museum-doesnt-exist.
2 Meschac Gaba, interview with Akiko Miki and Else Delage, 2012, http://archives.palaisdetokyo.com/fo3/low/programme/index.php?page=../editions/editions/gaba.html.
3 Olafur Eliasson, interview with Jessica Morgan, in Morgan (ed.), *Olafur Eliasson: Your Only Real Thing Is Time*, exhib. cat. (Ostfildern: Hatje Cantz, 2001), p. 17.
4 Olafur Eliasson, quoted in Markus Wailand, 'Olafur Eliasson: Neue Galerie, Graz, Austria', *Frieze*, 54, September–October 2000, p. 127, https://frieze.com/article/olafur-eliasson.
5 Olafur Eliasson, 'Dear Everybody', text accompanying *The Mediated Motion*, Kunsthaus Bregenz, 2001, reprinted in Eliasson *et al.*, *Olafur Eliasson* (London: Phaidon, 2002), p. 134.
6 Olafur Eliasson, statement accompanying *Your Rainbow Panorama*, ARoS art museum, Aarhus, 2006–11, reprinted in Studio Olafur Eliasson, *Unspoken Spaces* (London: Thames & Hudson, 2016), p. 236.
7 Norman Mailer, quoted in Calvin Tomkins, *Lives of the Artists* (New York: Henry Holt & Co., 2008), p. 133.
8 Antony Gormley, interview with Ina Cole, 2003, in Glenn Harper and Twylene Moyer (eds), *Conversations on Sculpture* (Hamilton, NJ: ISC Press, 2007), p. 134.
9 Antony Gormley, interview with Declan McGonagle, in Judith Nesbitt (ed.), *Antony Gormley*, exhib. cat. (London: Tate Gallery, 1993), p. 50.
10 Antony Gormley, interview with Ina Cole, p. 135.
11 Susan Philipsz, quoted in Lena Corner, 'The Art of Noise: "Sculptor in Sound" Susan Philipsz', 14 November 2010, www.theguardian.com/artanddesign/2010/nov/14/susan-philipsz-turner-prize-2010-sculptor-in-sound.
12 *Ibid.*
13 In 2017, when I returned to Münster, hundreds of padlocks had been fastened to the railings beneath the bridge – emblems of the love between two individuals. Whether the people who had left them there had been inspired by Philipsz's singing I do not know, but it seemed strangely appropriate.
14 Doris Salcedo, interview with Carlos Basualdo, in *Doris Salcedo* (London: Phaidon, 2000), p. 16.
15 Doris Salcedo, interview with Tim Marlow, in Honey Luard (ed.), *Doris Salcedo*, exhib. cat. (London: White Cube, 2018), p. 59.
16 Luc Tuymans, interview with Juan Vicente Aliaga, in *Luc Tuymans* (London: Phaidon, 1996), p. 8.
17 *Ibid.*
18 El Anatsui, interview with Robert Preece, 'Out of West Africa', *Sculpture*, 2006, reprinted in Harper and Moyer, *Conversations on Sculpture*, p. 314.
19 *Ibid.*, p. 317.
20 El Anatsui, quoted in Ming Lin, 'Material World: Interview with El Anatsui', 6 June 2014, http://artasiapacific.com/Blog/Material WorldInterviewWithElAnatsui.
21 El Anatsui, quoted in Brendon Bell-Roberts, 'In Conversation with El Anatsui', *Art South Africa*, vol. 13, no. 3, March 2015, http://artafricamagazine.org/the-innovation-issue-13-3-a-journey-of-materiality-and-art-practice-in-conversation-with-el-anatsui/.
22 See Peter Plagens, *Bruce Nauman: The True Artist* (London: Phaidon, 2014), p. 212.
23 Thomas Hirschhorn, interview with Alison M. Gingeras, *Thomas Hirschhorn* (London: Phaidon, 2004), p. 11.
24 Thomas Hirschhorn, interview with Hans Ulrich Obrist, in Thomas Boutoux (ed.), *Hans Ulrich Obrist Interviews: Volume 1* (Milan: Charta, 2003), pp. 396–97.
25 Do Ho Suh, quoted in Marybeth Sollins (ed.), *Art:21: Art in the Twenty-first Century – 2* (New York: Harry N. Abrams, 2003), p. 48.
26 *Ibid.*, p. 54.
27 Do Hoh Suh, interview with Christopher Turner, 2016.
28 Do Hoh Suh, interview with Art21, 2013, https://art21.org/read/do-ho-suh-seoul-home-la-home-korea-and-displacement.
29 Do Ho Suh, in *Rubbing/Loving*, video

for Art21, available online at https://art21.org/watch/extended-play/do-ho-suh-rubbing-loving-short/.

CHAPTER 8

1 William Kentridge, 1992, quoted in Lilian Tone (ed.), *William Kentridge: Fortuna* (London: Thames & Hudson, 2013), p. 15.
2 *Ibid.*
3 William Kentridge, interview with Carolyn Christov-Bakargiev, in Dan Cameron *et al.*, *William Kentridge* (London: Phaidon, 1999), p. 19.
4 *Ibid.*, p. 35.
5 Isaac Julien, quoted in Stuart Jefferies, 'Isaac Julien's Angel of Morecambe', 29 September 2010, www.theguardian.com/artanddesign/2010/sep/29/isaac-julien-ten-thousand-waves.
6 *Ibid.*
7 Keiko Okamura, 'Isaac Julien: Ten Thousand Waves', *Flash Art*, no. 274, October 2010.
8 Isaac Julien, quoted in Jefferies, 'Isaac Julien's Angel of Morecambe'.
9 Isaac Julien, quoted in Anne Dickie, 'Isaac Julien in Conversation', 11 November 2014, ocula.com/magazine/conversations/isaac-julien.
10 Shirin Neshat, interview with Arthur C. Danto, 1 October 2000, bombmagazine.org/articles/shirin-neshat.
11 Shirin Neshat, quoted in Haley Weiss, 'In Dreams', 18 August 2016, www.interviewmagazine.com/art/shirin-neshat.
12 Shirin Neshat, interview with Danto.
13 Shirin Neshat, interview with Anna McNay, 23 April 2015, www.studiointernational.com/index.php/shirin-neshat-interview-home-of-my-eyes-yarat-baku-azerbaijan-photography.
14 Shirin Neshat, interview with Danto.
15 Shahzia Sikander, quoted in Vishakha N. Desai, *Conversations with Traditions: Nilima Sheikh, Shahzia Sikander*, exhib. cat. (New York: Asia Society, 2001), p. 77.
16 Shahzia Sikander, artist's statement, in *By Day, By Night*, exhib. cat. (Shanghai: Rockbund Art Museum, 2010), p. 113.
17 See https://art21.org/watch/extended-play/shahzia-sikander-the-last-post-short.
18 Michaël Borremans, quoted in David Coggins, 'Michaël Borremans: An Interview', 25 February 2009, www.artinamericamagazine.com/news-features/magazines/michael-borremans.
19 *Ibid.*
20 Michaël Borremans, interview with Luk Lambrecht, *Flash Art*, no. 250, October 2006.
21 *Ibid.*
22 *Ibid.*
23 Michaël Borremans, quoted in Diana d'Arenberg, 'Michaël Borremans in Conversation', 17 April 2018, ocula.com/magazine/conversations/michael-borremans.
24 Neo Rauch, quoted in Elena Cué, 'Interview with Neo Rauch', 8 December 2016, www.alejandradeargos.com/index.php/en/all-articles/21-guests-with-art/41432-interview-with-neo-rauch.
25 Neo Rauch, interview with Klaus Werner, 1997, translated and quoted in *Neo Rauch: Para*, exhib. cat. (New York: Metropolitan Museum of Art, 2007), p. 55.
26 *Ibid.*, p.54.
27 Neo Rauch, interview with Holger Liebs, translated and quoted in *Neo Rauch: Para*, p. 71.
28 Translation by Richmond Lattimore, www.kenyonreview.org/programs/resources-for-teachers/konstantinos-kavaphes.
29 Christoph Tannert, in Tannert (ed.), *New German Painting* (Munich: Prestel, 2006), p. 199.
30 Stephen Ellis in conversation with the author, 2009.
31 Stephen Ellis, in David Reed interviewed by Stephen Ellis, 1996.
32 For once, I will break my rule and list some of them: Lydia Dona, Stephen Ellis, Mary Heilmann, Thomas Nozkowski, David Reed.
33 Jonathan Lasker, interview with Amy Bernstein, www.lalouver.com/html/gallery-history-images/other-resources/Lasker_Bernstein_Interview.pdf.
34 Jonathan Lasker, interview with Shirley Kaneda, in *Bomb*, Winter 1990, www.bombmagazine.org/articles/jonathan-lasker.
35 *Ibid.*
36 Jonathan Lasker, interview with David Moos, in *Jonathan Lasker: Recent Paintings*, exhib. cat. (Brussels: Maruani Mercier Gallery, 2018).
37 Beatriz Milhazes in conversation with Christian Lacroix, in *Beatriz Milhazes: Avenida Brasil*, exhib. cat. (Bignan: Domaine de Kerguéhennec, 2004), p. 71.
38 Beatriz Milhazes, quoted in Yvonne Hindle and Michael Stanley (eds), *Base & Awesome: Conversations on Contemporary Painting*, exhib. cat. (Birmingham: Article Press and Ikon Gallery, 2003), p. 32.
39 Beatriz Milhazes in conversation with Christian Lacroix, p. 64.
40 *Ibid.*, p. 83.
41 Ding Yi, interview with Tony Godfrey and Kaimei Wang, November 2018.
42 Ding Yi, interview with Tony Godfrey and Wang Kaimei, 2011, quoted in *Ding Yi*, exhib. cat. (Shanghai: Minsheng Art Museum, 2011), p. 21.
43 Grayson Perry, quoted in Marjan Boot and Grayson Perry (eds), *Grayson Perry: Guerrilla Tactics*, exhib. cat. (Rotterdam: NAi Uitgevers, 2002), p. 76.
44 Grayson Perry, quoted in R. Campbell-Johnston, 'Perry: Perturbing, Perverse or just Potty?', *The Times*, 5 April 2000, p. 18.
45 Edmund de Waal, quoted in *Edmund de Waal* (London: Phaidon, 2014), p. 175.
46 *Ibid.*, p. 170.
47 Grayson Perry, quoted by Sarah Howell in *World of Interiors*, July 1993, p. 101.
48 Grayson Perry, quoted by Louisa Buck in *Crafts*, no. 37, 1989, p. 38.

CHAPTER 9

1 Holly Peterson, quoted in Chrystia Freeland, *Plutocrats: The Rise of the New Global Super-rich and the Fall of Everyone Else* (London: Allen Lane, 2012), p. 2.
2 Freeland, *Plutocrats*, p. 5.
3 Ragnar Kjartansson, quoted in Adrian Searle, 'Death, Volcanoes and Nazis in the Family: Ragnar Kjartansson, Wild Man of Icelandic Art', 28 June 2016, www.theguardian.com/artanddesign/2016/jun/28/ragnar-kjartansson-interview-iceland-barbican-the-visitors.
4 See www.theguardian.com/business/2019/jan/21/world-26-richest-people-own-as-much-as-poorest-50-per-cent-oxfam-report.
5 Felix Gonzalez-Torres, 'Public and Private: Spheres of Influence', lecture given on 2 October 1993, reprinted in *A. Reinhardt, J. Kosuth, F. Gonzalez-Torres: Symptoms of Interference,*

Conditions of Possibility, exhib. cat. (London: Camden Arts Centre, 1994), pp. 88, 90.

6 See William N. Goetzmann *et al.*, *Art and Money* (Cambridge, MA: National Bureau of Economic Research, 2009).

7 Melanie Gerlis, 'Merry-go-round: Why So Many Art Fairs Are Planned then Shelved, *Financial Times*, 6 April 2018, www.ft.com/content/6a5a9380-3823-11e8-b161-65936015ebc3.

8 See www.biennialfoundation.org/home/biennial-map/.

9 Kimsooja in conversation with Diana Augaitis, in *Kim Sooja: Unfolding*, exhib. cat. (Vancouver and Ostfildern: Vancouver Art Gallery and Hatja Cantz, 2013), p. 97.

10 Peter Doig in conversation with Kitty Scott, in *Peter Doig* (London: Phaidon, 2007), p. 16

11 Peter Doig in conversation with Chris Ofili, *Bomb*, 101, Autumn 2007, https://bombmagazine.org/articles/peter-doig-chris-ofili/.

12 Peter Doig in conversation with Nicholas Serota, *Artlyst*, 27 May 2015, www.artlyst.com/news/in-conversation-artist-peter-doig-and-tate-director-nicholas-serota/ (acccessed June 2019).

13 Adrian Ghenie, quoted in Robin Pogrebin, 'How the Artist Adrian Ghenie Became an Auction Star', 7 November 2016, www.nytimes.com/2016/11/08/arts/design/how-the-artist-adrian-ghenie-became-an-auction-star.html.

14 Adrian Ghenie, interview with Marta Gnyp, *Zoo Magazine*, December 2017, www.martagnyp.com/interviews/adrian-ghenie.php.

15 Adrian Ghenie in conversation with Jane Neal, *Art Review*, 46, December 2010, p. 70.

16 Adrian Ghenie, interview with Stephen Riolo, 12 October 2010, www.artinamericamagazine.com/news-features/interviews/adrian-ghenie.

17 *Ibid.*

18 Peter Doig, quoted in *Cavepainting: Peter Doig, Chris Ofili & Laura Owens*, exhib. cat. (Santa Monica: Santa Monica Museum of Art, 2002), p. 14.

19 Adrian Ghenie, interview with Marta Gnyp.

20 'Zeng Fanzhi and the Rise of China's Contemporary Artists', 17 October 2016, www.abc.net.au/news/2016-10-17/zeng-fanzhi-china-art/7939656.

21 Zeng Fanzhi, quoted in 'Chinese Artist Zeng Fanzhi: "I Don't Want To Be Pigeonholed"', 4 May 2010, https://jingdaily.com/chinese-artist-zeng-fanzhi-i-dont-want-to-be-pigeonholed.

22 Sotheby's, April 2014, p. 49.

23 Liu Xiaodong, quoted in Rajesh Punj, 'The Tiger in the Forest: Liu Xiaodong Profile Piece', 2017?, www.rajeshpunj.com/the-tiger-in-the-forest-liu-xiaodong-interview/.

24 Dana Schutz, quoted in Ted Loos, 'After the Quake, Dana Schutz Gets Back to Work', 9 January 2019, www.nytimes.com/2019/01/09/arts/design/dana-schutz-painting-emmett-till-petzel-gallery.html.

25 *Ibid.*

26 Imran Qureshi, quoted in David Shariatmadari, '"Violence Is All Around Me": Imran Qureshi on His Disturbing Miniatures', 18 February 2016, www.theguardian.com/artanddesign/2016/feb/18/violence-is-all-around-me-imran-qureshi-on-his-disturbing-miniatures.

27 Imran Qureshi in conversation with Ian Alteveer and Navina Najat Haidar, in *Imran Qureshi: The Roof Garden Commission*, exhib. cat. (New York: The Metropolitan Museum of Art, 2013), p. 31.

28 Imran Qureshi, quoted in Shariatmadari, 'Imran Qureshi on His Disturbing Miniatures'.

29 Sara Sze, interview with Emma Robertson, 2018, http://the-talks.com/interview/sarah-sze.

30 Sara Sze, interview with Okwui Enwezor, in Benjamin H. D. Buchloh *et al.*, *Sara Sze* (London: Phaidon, 2016), p. 36.

31 Katy Siegel, 'Strangers on a Train', *Sara Sze: Timekeeper*, exhib. cat. (New York: Gregory R. Miller, 2018), p. 62.

32 Sara Sze, interview with Okwui Enwezor, p. 26.

33 Haegue Yang, quoted by Eungie Joo, in *Asymmetric Equality: Haegue Yang*, exhib. cat. (Los Angeles: California Institute of the Arts/REDCAT, 2008), p. 9.

34 Haegue Yang, interview with Anna Dickie, Ocula, 21 August 2014, https://ocula.com/magazine/conversations/haegue-yang.

35 *Ibid.*

36 Ayşe Erkmen, quoted in H. G. Masters, 'Ayşe Erkmen: A Reasonable Beauty', *ArtAsiaPacific*, 73, May/June 2011, p. 96.

37 Ayşe Erkmen in conversation with Danae Mossman, in *Plan B*, exhib. cat. (Istanbul: Yapı Kredi Yayınları in association with the Istanbul Foundation for Culture, 2011), interview available at www.planb-venicebiennale.com/giris_en.asp#.

38 Araya Rasdjarmrearnsook, quoted in Brian Curtin, 'Confronting Confrontation: An Interview with Araya Rasdjarmrearnsook', *Art Signal*, October 2007, www.trfineart.com/wp-content/uploads/2016/11/Art-Signal-2007-Confronting-Confrontation-An-Interview-with-Araya-Rasdjarmrearnsook-.pdf.

39 Clare Bishop, 'History Depletes Itself', *Artforum*, September 2015, p. 329.

40 Teresa Margolles, quoted in Kaelen Wilson-Goldie, 'Death in Venice', The National, 4 September 2009, www.thenational.ae/arts-culture/art/death-in-venice-1.521212.

41 Teresa Margolles, interview for the Tate, 14 September 2006, www.tate.org.uk/context-comment/video/teresa-margolles-liverpool-biennial-2006.

42 Teresa Margolles, notes for exhibition, 2009.

43 Ai Weiwei in conversation with Chin-Chin Yap, in Charles Merewether (ed.), *Ai Weiwei: Works, Beijing 1993–2003* (Hong Kong: Timezone 8, 2003), p. 51.

44 *Ibid.*, pp. 51–53.

45 Ai Weiwei, 'The Artwork that Made Me the Most Dangerous Person in China', 15 February 2018, www.theguardian.com/artanddesign/2018/feb/15/ai-weiwei-remembering-sichuan-earthquake.

46 Theaster Gates, interview, 2016, https://art21.org/read/theaster-gates-expanding-the-role-of-the-artist.

47 *Ibid.*

48 Rudolf Lorenzo, quoted in Noelle Bodick, 'A Brief History of Art Basel, the World's Premier Contemporary Fair', *Artspace*, 17 June 2014, www.artspace.com/magazine/art_101/art_market/a-brief-history-of-art-basel-52350.

49 Eric Fischl, interview with Tim Adams, 12 October 2014, www.theguardian.com/artanddesign/2014/oct/12/eric-fischl-america-art-expensive-toys.

50 Emma Crichton-Miller, in Edmund de Waal (London: Phaidon, 2014), p. 56.

CHAPTER 10

1 Eric Schmidt, quoted in Shoshana Zuboff, *The Age of Surveillance*

Capitalism: The Fight for a Human Future at the New Frontier of Power (London: Profile, 2019), p. 498.
2 Tristan Harris, quoted in Paul Lewis, '"Our Minds Can Be Hijacked": The Tech Insiders who Fear a Smartphone Dystopia', 6 October 2017, www.theguardian.com/technology/2017/oct/05/smartphone-addiction-silicon-valley-dystopia.
3 Zuboff, *The Age of Surveillance Capitalism*, p. 129.
4 'Surveillance capitalism depends upon undermining individual self-determination, autonomy and decision rights for the sake of an unobstructed flow of behavioural data to feed markets that are about us but not for us.' Zuboff, *The Age of Surveillance Capitalism*, 2019.
5 *Ibid*., p. 369.
6 *Ibid*., p. 187.
7 *Ibid*., p. 380.
8 Carl Andre, quoted in Tony Godfrey, *Conceptual Art* (London: Phaidon, 1998), p. 302.
9 Hito Steyerl, quoted in Jean Kay, 'An Interview with Hito Steyerl', AQNB, 16 April 2014, www.aqnb.com/2014/04/16/an-interview-with-hito-steyerl/.
10 *Ibid*.
11 Hettie Judah, 'Liberation Day: The Artists Fighting the Power of the Market – and the Internet', 17 October 2017, www.theguardian.com/artanddesign/2017/oct/17/artists-fighting-power-of-market-internet-hito-steyerl.
12 Kimberly Bradley, 'Hito Steyerl is an Artist with Power: She Uses It for Change', 15 December 2017, www.nytimes.com/2017/12/15/arts/design/hito-steyerl.html.
13 Christian Boltanski, talk given at Henry Moore Sculpture Studio, Halifax, 1995.
14 Guerrilla Girls, interview with Ellen Mara De Wachter, in De Wachter, *Co-Art: Artists on Creative Collaboration* (London: Phaidon, 2017), p. 25.
15 Martin Hammer, quoted at www.theartnewspaper.com/news/police-remove-giant-erdogan-statue-from-german-city-square-after-aggressive-exchanges.
16 Maria Magdalena Ludewig, quoted at www.washingtonpost.com/world/2018/08/29/artists-put-up-golden-statue-turkeys-leader-germany-spark-conversation-it-worked-too-well.
17 lauren woods, quoted in Matt Stromberg, 'After Museum Director Is Fired, Artist Shuts Down Her Exhibition on Police Brutality', *Hyperallergic*, 18 September 2018, https://hyperallergic.com/461150/american-monument-lauren-woods-kimberli-meyer-california-state-university-long-beach/?.
18 This observation is inspired by a comment made by the musician and artist Brian Eno during a lecture of his I attended in the late 1990s.
19 Ragnar Kjartansson, interview with Sabine Mirlesse, Bomb, 3 July 2013, https://bombmagazine.org/articles/ragnar-kjartansson/.
20 *Ibid*.
21 *Ibid*.
22 Ragnar Kjartansson, interview, 25 March 2015, *The Talks*, http://the-talks.com/interview/ragnar-kjartansson.
23 Ragnar Kjartansson, interview with Sabine Mirlesse.
24 Anne Imhof, quoted in Elizabeth Fullerton, 'In London, Anne Imhof Talks About Her Kicking, Screaming Venice Biennale Hit "Faust"', 30 May 2017, www.artnews.com/2017/05/30/in-london-anne-imhof-talks-about-her-kicking-screaming-venice-biennale-hit-faust.
25 Alicja Kwade, interview with Kimberly Bradley, *Art Review*, December 2013, https://artreview.com/features/december_2013_feature_alicja_kwade/.
26 *Ibid*.
27 Alicja Kwade, interview with Dobromila Blaszczyk, *Contemporary Lynx*, 15 January 2016, http://contemporarylynx.co.uk/alicja-kwade-somewhere-else-at-the-same-time.
28 Alicja Kwade, quoted in a hand-out distributed at the exhibition 'Space Shifters', Hayward Gallery, 2018.
29 Helen Marten, interview with Jan Kedves, *Travel Almanac*, no. 11, Autumn/Winter 2016, www.travel-almanac.com/blogs/travel-log/helen-marten-turner-prize-winner-2016-tta11.
30 Helen Marten, 'Lexicon', in Amira Gad with Joseph Constable (eds), *Helen Marten: Drunk Brown House*, exhib. cat. (London: Serpentine Galleries and Koenig Books, 2016), pp. 188–89.
31 Helen Marten, 'Helen Marten: My Influences', *Frieze*, no. 155, May 2013, https://frieze.com/article/helen-marten-my-influences.
32 Mary Louise Pratt, 'Arts of the Contact Zone', *Profession*, 1991, pp. 33–40, quoted by Njideka Akunyili Crosby, interview with Cassie Davies, November 2016, www.thewhitereview.org/feature/interview-njideka-akunyili-crosby/.
33 Njideka Akunyili Crosby, interview with Erica Ando, *Bomb*, 15 September 2016, https://bombmagazine.org/articles/njideka-akunyili-crosby/.
34 Njideka Akunyili Crosby, interview with Cassie Davies.
35 Njideka Akunyili Crosby, interview with Erica Ando.
36 *Ibid*.
37 Zhao Renhui, interview with Tan Boon Hau, Luxuo, 2016, http://luxuothailand.com/culture/art/interview-artist-robert-zhao-renhui.html.
38 See www.criticalzoologists.org.
39 Zhao Renhui, interview with Durriya Dohadwala, *Art Radar*, 22 February 2016, http://artradarjournal.com/2016/02/22/singapores-robert-zhao-renhui-and-the-institute-of-critical-zoologists-interview/.
40 *Ibid*.
41 Extracted from a text by Martha Atienza to accompany her video project *Anito* (2010–).
42 Doris Salcedo, interview with Carlos Basualdo, in *Doris Salcedo* (London: Phaidon, 2000), p. 35.
43 Abdoulaye Konaté, quoted in Chris Spring, Angaza Afrika: Africa Art Now (London: Laurence King, 2008), p. 164.
44 See https://hyperallergic.com/495007/why-i-will-not-go-to-this-years-havana-biennial/.
45 Oscar Leone, artist's statement, Havana Biennale, 2019.

AFTERWORD

1 Terry Smith, *Contemporary Art: World Currents* (London: Lawrence King, 2011).
2 Ernst Gombrich, *The Story of Art*, 10th edn (London: Phaidon, 1960), p. 5.
3 Marcel Proust, *In Search of Lost Time*, vol. 6, *Time Regained*, trans. Andreas Mayor and Terence Kilmartin, revised D. J. Enright (London: Chatto & Windus, 1992), p. 254.
4 Kiki Smith, interview with Robin Winters, 1990, quoted in Petra Giloy-Hirtz (ed.), *Kiki Smith: Procession*, exhib. cat. (Munich: Haus der Kunst, 2018), p. 34.

Acknowledgments

I would like to thank Roger Thorp for commissioning this book, Mark Ralph for his patient and meticulous editing, and Maria Ranauro for her determination in getting hold of the images. Without the support of my partner, Ghe, and all the people at Cuenca, this book would never have been completed. Looking at art is always more exciting when you have a companion to discuss it with. Over the years, I have learnt much from all the people with whom I have visited museums and galleries, including Gerlinde Gabriel, Mark Gisborne, Isolde Godfrey, Wang Kaimei, Anna Moszynska, Peggy Prendeville, Heloise Talbot-Godfrey, Andrea Schlieker, Annushka Shani, the students I have taught on the MA in Contemporary Art at Sotheby's Institute of Art (in London, New York and Singapore), Eugene Tan, Philip Tinari, Hermione Wiltshire and others. The first of these gallery-going companions was Jenny Godfrey, with whom I first encountered Andy Warhol in 1970. This book is dedicated to her.

Picture Credits

t = top; b = bottom; l = left; r = right; c = centre

2tl, 43: Photo Udo Dewies, courtesy Museum Abteiburg, Mönchengladbach. Joseph Beuys © DACS 2020; 2cl, 56: Courtesy Galerie Lelong & Co., New York. © Cildo Meireles; 2bl, 178: Courtesy the artist, Gladstone Gallery, New York and Brussels. © Shirin Neshat; 2tr, 165: Collection S.M.A.K. Stedelijk Museum voor Actuele Kunst, Ghent. Photo Ben Blackwell, courtesy David Zwirner, New York-London. © Luc Tuymans; 2br, 209: Courtesy the artist and Petzel, New York; 3t, 256 (all): © Martha Atienza; 3c, 260 (all): Courtesy Oscar Leone; 3bl, 231: Private collection. Courtesy Hauser & Wirth Collection Services. Photo Stefan Altenburger Photography Zuurich. © Maria Lassnig Foundation; 3br, 15: Singapore Art Museum. Photo Tony Godfrey. Courtesy the artist; 10: Solomon R. Guggenheim Museum, New York, Gift of Lenore Tawney, 1963 (63.1653). © Agnes Martin/DACS 2020; 11: Courtesy the artist and Marian Goodman Gallery. © John Baldessari; 12: Whitney Museum of American Art, New York; Purchase, with funds from the Drawing Committee (97.83.2). Courtesy the artist and Sean Kelly, New York. © Shahzia Sikander; 13: Photo courtesy Utopia Art Sydney. © Emily Kame Kngwarreye/Copyright Agency. Licensed by DACS 2020; 14: Photo Tony Godfrey. Courtesy the artist and Victoria Miro, London/Venice. © Sarah Sze; 16: Photo Roger Wooldridge. © Damien Hirst and Science Ltd. All rights reserved, DACS/ Artimage 2020; 17: Whitney Museum of American Art, New York. Purchase, with funds from the Painting and Sculpture Committee (91.13a-d). © Kiki Smith, courtesy Pace Gallery; 18: Photos Tony Godfrey. Carsten Höller © DACS 2020; 19: Photo Christie's Images Limited 2012. Courtesy Beatriz Milhazes Studio; 20–21: Permanent collection, the Chinati Foundation, Marfa, Texas. Photo Florian Holzherr, 2002. © Judd Foundation/ARS, NY and DACS, London 2020; 22: Installation view, 16th Biennale of Sydney 2008. Photo Jenni Carter. Courtesy the artist, Isabella Bortolozzi Gallery, Berlin, and Tanya Bonakdar Gallery, New York/Los Angeles; 25: © Zeng Fanzhi. Courtesy Gagosian; 26: Alexander Liberman photography archive. © The J. Paul Getty Trust. Mark Rothko © 1998 Kate Rothko Prizel & Christopher Rothko ARS, NY and DACS, London; 27: Photo Tony Godfrey. Courtesy Robert Zhao Renhui; 28: Stiftung Museum Schloss Moyland, Bedburg-Hau, Germany. Photo Ute Klophaus (JBA-F 90705)/Scala, Florence/bpk, Bildagentur für Kunst, Kultur und Geschichte, Berlin. Joseph Beuys © DACS 2020; 29: Private collection. © 2020 The Andy Warhol Foundation for the Visual Arts, Inc./Licensed by DACS, London; 32: S. Sudjojono Center Indonesia, ssudjojonocenter.com, Instagram @sscenter, Facebook S. Sudjojono; 33: Solomon R. Guggenheim Museum, New York. Gift of Elaine and Werner Dannheisser and The Dannheisser Foundation, 1978 (78.2461). © 1998 Kate Rothko Prizel & Christopher Rothko ARS, NY and DACS, London; 35: Auckland Art Gallery Toi o Tāmaki, gift of the Friends of the Auckland Art Gallery, 1960 (1960/24/2). Courtesy the Colin McCahon Research and Publication Trust; 36: © Kanayama Akira and Tanaka Atsuko Association; 38: Courtesy Srihadi Soedarsono; 39: The Estate of Pauline Boty. Image courtesy of Whitford Fine Art, London; 40: Moderna Museet, Stockholm. Photo Nils-Gören Hökby. © 2020 The Andy Warhol Foundation for the Visual Arts, Inc./Licensed by DACS, London; 42: Photo © documenta archiv/Photo Ingrid Fingerling; 44: © YAYOI KUSAMA; 46: Collection Kröller-Müller Museum, Otterlo, the Netherlands. Photo Tom Haartsen, Ouderkerk a/d Amstel; 48t, 48b: Collection Kröller-Müller Museum, Otterlo, the Netherlands. Photo Tony Godfrey; 51: © Richard Long. All Rights Reserved, DACS 2020; 52: Courtesy the artist and Marian Goodman Gallery. © John Baldessari; 54: © Bruce Nauman/Artists Rights Society (ARS), New York and DACS, London 2020; 55: Hirschhorn Museum and Sculpture Garden, Smithsonian Institution, Washington, D.C. (bought 1993). © Bruce Nauman/Artists Rights Society (ARS), New York and DACS, London 2020; 58: Courtesy Galerie Lelong & Co. © The Estate of Ana Mendieta Collection, LLC.; Licensed by Artists Rights Society (ARS), New York; 59: Photo Nebojsa Cankovic. Courtesy Marina Abramović Archives. © Marina Abramović. Courtesy Marina Abramović and Sean Kelly Gallery, New York. DACS 2020; 60: © Susan Hiller. All Rights Reserved, DACS/Artimage 2020; 61: Photo Kira Perov © Bill Viola Studio; 62: Installation view, Münster, Germany. Photo Tony Godfrey; 66: Photo © Jochen Littkemann/Courtesy Galerie Thaddaeus Ropac, London/Paris/ Salzburg. Joseph Beuys © DACS 2020; 67: Courtesy Unitel GmbH & Co.KG, Munich; 69: Sammlung Moderne Kunst in der Pinakothek der Moderne – Bayerische Staatsgemäldesammlungen, Munich (WAF PF 31). Photo Scala, Florence/bpk, Bildagentur für Kunst, Kultur und Geschichte, Berlin. Courtesy White Cube, London. © Georg Baselitz; 70: Kunsthaus Zürich (1991/0008). Courtesy White Cube, London. © Georg Baselitz; 72: Metropolitan Museum of Art, New York. Denise and Andrew Saul Fund, 1995 (1995.14.4)/Art Resource/Scala, Florence. © Anselm Kiefer; 73: Photo Atelier Anselm Kiefer. © Anselm Kiefer; 74: Speck Collection, Cologne. © The Estate of Sigmar Polke, Cologne/DACS 2020; 75: Photo Farzad Owrang, copyright Julian Schnabel Studio (P81.0010). © Julian Schnabel/ARS, New York/ DACS 2020; 76: Collection Stedelijk Museum Amsterdam. © The Estate of Philip Guston; 77: © Cy Twombly Foundation. Courtesy Archives Nicola Del Roscio; 78: © Maria Lassnig Foundation; 81: S. Sudjojono Center Indonesia, ssudjojonocenter.com, Instagram @sscenter, Facebook S. Sudjojono; 82: Private collection. Photo Roberto Ortiz. Courtesy Arte Actual Mexicano; 83 (all): Courtesy Chemould Prescott Road and the artist; 85: Photo courtesy Eric Fischl Studio. © Eric Fischl/ ARS, NY and DACS, London 2020; 88: Courtesy the artist; 90, 91: Courtesy the artist and Metro Pictures, New York; 93t: Courtesy the artist and Sean Kelly Gallery, New York. © Tehching Hsieh; 93b: Photo Michael Shen. Courtesy the artist and Sean Kelly Gallery, New York. © Tehching Hsieh; 95: Courtesy Die Photographische Sammlung/SK Stiftung Kultur - Bernd and Hilla Becher Archive, Cologne, 2019. © Estate Bernd & Hilla Becher, represented by Max Becher; 96: Courtesy the artist; 100: © Richard Deacon; courtesy Lisson Gallery. Photo Ken Adlard; 101: Harsewinkelplatz, Skulptur Projekte, Münster 1987. LWL-Museum für Kunst und Kultur, Westfälisches Landesmuseum, Münster/ Rudolf Wakonigg; 102: Salzstraße, Skulptur Projekte, Münster 1987. LWL-Museum für Kunst und Kultur, Westfälisches Landesmuseum, Münster/Rudolf Wakonigg. Katharina Fritsch © DACS 2020; 107: Photo John McWilliams. Courtesy Ann Hamilton Studio; 108: Musée d'Art Moderne, Paris. Photo Roger-Viollet/Topfoto. Christian Boltanski © ADAGP, Paris and DACS, London 2020; 109: Photo Cameraphoto Arte, Venezia. Ilya Kabakov © DACS 2020; 114: Photo Centre Pompidou, MNAM-CCI Bibliothèque Kandinsky, Dist. RMN-Grand Palais/Béatrice Hatala/Konstantinos Ignatiadis. Richard Long © Richard Long. All Rights Reserved, DACS 2020. Paddy Japaljarri Sims, Paddy Japaljarri Stewart, Neville Japangardi Poulson, Francis Jupurrurla Kelly, Paddy Jupurrurla Nelson, Franck Bronson Jakamarra Nelson, Towser Jakamarra Walker, membres de la communauté Yuendumu © Warlukurlangu Artists/Copyright Agency. Licensed by DACS 2020; 115: Courtesy Galerie

Lelong & Co., New York. © Cildo Meireles; 117: © Xu Bing Studio; 118 (all): Photo Yamamoto Tadasu, courtesy Cai Studio; 121: Gemeentemuseum, The Hague, Netherlands. Photo Peter Cox, Eindhoven, Netherlands. © Marlene Dumas; 123, 124: © Gerhard Richter 2019 (0156); 126: Private Collection. © Peter Doig. All Rights Reserved, DACS 2020; 127: Courtesy Fawbush Gallery, New York. Photo Geoffrey Clements. Whitney Museum of American Art, New York. 2019, Digital image Whitney Museum of American Art/Licensed by Scala. © Kiki Smith, courtesy Pace Gallery; 132: Collection Architekturzentrum Wien. Photo Margherita Spiluttini. Courtesy the artists and Navin Production; 134–35: Courtesy ARCO, Korea, and Kimsooja Studio; 137: Installation view, 'Italics. Arte italiana fra tradizione e rivoluzione 1968-2008', September 26, 2008 to March 22, 2009, Palazzo Grassi, Venice. Fondazione Sandretto Re Rebaudengo, Turin. Photo Zeno Zotti. Courtesy Maurizio Cattelan's Archive; 138: Courtesy Estudio Bruguera; 140: Installation at Wat Prayurawongsawas Waraviharn (Temple of the Iron Fence), Bangkok Art Biennale (BAB). Photo Konrawat/Shutterstock; 141: Performer Chad Walker. Photo Edward Woodman © Edward Woodman. All Rights Reserved, DACS 2020; 142: Art Gallery of Western Australia, Perth. Courtesy the artist; 145t: Installation view, 'Ever Is Over All', 1997, by Pipilotti Rist at Glenstone, Maryland MD, 2019. Photo Ron Amstutz. Courtesy the artist, Hauser & Wirth and Luhring Augustine. © Pipilotti Rist; 145b, 145c: Installation view, 'Ever Is Over All', 1997, by Pipilotti Rist at Kunsthalle Zürich, Zurich, Switzerland, 1999. Photo Alexander Troehler. Courtesy the artist, Hauser & Wirth and Luhring Augustine. © Pipilotti Rist; 146: Sophie Calle © ADAGP, Paris and DACS, London 2020; 147 (all): Photos Tony Godfrey; 149: A Groundwork exhibition presented by Newlyn Art Gallery & The Exchange and CAST (Cornubian Arts & Science Trust). Photo Steve Tanner; 150: Photo Tony Godfrey; 155: Photo © documenta archiv/Photo Ryszard Kasiewicz. Mechec Gaba © DACS 2019; 157: Photo Denis Jones/Associated Newspapers/Shutterstock; 158: Photo Chris Winget. Courtesy Gladstone Gallery, New York and Brussels. © 2002 Matthew Barney; 159: Photo Tony Godfrey; 161: Installation view, Torminbrücke, Münster, Germany, 2007. Courtesy the artist, Isabella Bortolozzi Gallery, Berlin; and Tanya Bonakdar Gallery, New York/Los Angeles; 162: Photo Tony Godfrey. Thomas Schütte © DACS 2020; 163: Courtesy Liverpool Biennial and White Cube. © the artist; 166: Photo Stuart Tyson. Courtesy Dia Art Foundation, New York. © Bruce Nauman/Artists Rights Society (ARS), New York and DACS, London 2020; 167: Courtesy the artist and Jack Shainman Gallery, New York. © El Anatsui; 169: Photo © documenta archiv/Photo Ryszard Kasiewicz. Thomas Hirschhorn © ADAGP, Paris and DACS, London 2020; 170: © Do Ho Suh; 175: Courtesy the artist and Marian Goodman Gallery; 176: Bayerische Staatsgemäldesammlungen, Munich. Photo Nicole Wilhelms. Courtesy the artist, Victoria Miro, London/Venice, Metro Pictures, New York and Galería Helga de Alvear, Madrid. © Isaac Julien; 179 (all): Courtesy Chemould Prescott Road and the artist; 181: Courtesy the artist and Sean Kelly, New York. © Shahzia Sikander; 182: Photo Ron Amstutz. Courtesy Zeno X Gallery, Antwerp and David Zwirner, New York/London/Hong Kong; 183: Photo Peter Cox. Courtesy Zeno X Gallery, Antwerp, David Zwirner, New York/London/Hong Kong and Gallery Koyanagi, Tokyo; 186–87: Photo Uwe Walter, Berlin. Courtesy Galerie EIGEN+ART, Leipzig/Berlin and David Zwirner, New York/London/Hong Kong. © Neo Rauch, VG Bild-Kunst, Bonn; 189: Courtesy Timothy Taylor Gallery, London/New York. © Jonathan Lasker; 190: © Ding Yi; 192–93: National Gallery of Victoria, Melbourne. Presented through The Art Foundation of Victoria by Donald and Janet Holt and family, Governors, 1995 (1995.709). © Emily Kame Kngwarreye/Copyright Agency. Licensed by DACS 2020; 196: Photo Hélène Binet. © Edmund de Waal; 197: Courtesy the artist and Victoria Miro Gallery, London/Venice; 202: The Weston Collection. © Peter Doig. All Rights Reserved, DACS 2020; 203: Photo Kerry Ryan McFate. Courtesy Pace Gallery. © Adrian Ghenie; 205: Art Jog, Yogyakarta. © Hahan (Uji Handoko, Eko Saputro); 206: © Hahan (Uji Handoko, Eko Saputro); 207: © Zeng Fanzhi. Courtesy Gagosian; 208: © Liu Xiaodong. Courtesy Lisson Gallery; 211l, 211r: Installation views, Bait al-Serkel courtyard, Sharjah Biennial, United Arab Emirates, 2011. Photo Alfredo Rubio, courtesy the Artist, Corvi-Mora, London and Galerie Thaddaeus Ropac, Salzburg; 212: Photo Angus Mill. Courtesy the artist and Victoria Miro, London/Venice. © Sarah Sze; 214: Installation view, 'The Great Acceleration', Taipei Biennial 2014, Taiwan, 2014. Photo Taipei Fine Arts Museum. Courtesy Haegue Yang; 215: Exhibition curated by Fulya Erdemci, 54th Venice Biennale, The Pavilion of Turkey, Artigliere, Arsenale, Venice, 04.06-27.11.2011. Photo Roman Mensing, artdoc.de. Courtesy the artist/Galerie Barbara Weiss, Berlin; 217: Photo Tony Godfrey. Courtesy the artist and Tyler Rollins Fine Art, New York; 218 (all): Courtesy Danh Vo; 220–21: Courtesy the artist and Lisson Gallery; 222, 223: Courtesy the artist and James Cohan, New York. © Teresa Margolles; 224: Photo © Nathaniel Willson. Courtesy Seattle Art Museum. © Theaster Gates; 228: Photo Henning Rogge. Courtesy the artist, Andrew Kreps Gallery, New York and Esther Schipper, Berlin; 230: Photo © White Cube (Ben Westoby). © Georg Baselitz; 232, 233: Courtesy Srihadi Soedarsono; 234: Photo Tony Godfrey. © YAYOI KUSAMA; 235: Courtesy Maurizio Cattelan's Archive; 236: Exhibition view, 'The artist is present', curated by Maurizio Cattelan, Yuz Museum, Shanghai, China. Courtesy Maurizio Cattelan's Archive; 237: Photo Uwe Walter, Berlin. Courtesy Galerie EIGEN+ART, Leipzig/Berlin and David Zwirner, New York/London/Hong Kong. © Neo Rauch, VG Bild-Kunst, Bonn; 238–39: © Ding Yi; 241 (all): Photo James Morris. Courtesy SUPERFLEX. *One Two Three Swing!* was commissioned by Hyundai for TATE Modern, 2017. *One Two Three Swing!* was developed in close collaboration with KWY.studio, Betar, Nupergo and Rasmus Koch studio. *One Two Three Swing!* was realized in partnership with Ege and Amorim, and support of Montana, Faurschou Foundation, New Carlsberg Foundation, Danish Arts Foundation, Beckett-Fonden, the Danish Ministry for Culture, The Embassy of Denmark in London; 242t: Photo Nicola Goode. Courtesy lauren woods and the University Art Museum, California State University, Long Beach; 242b: Photo Jason Meintjes, Courtesy lauren woods and University Art Museum, California State University, Long Beach; 245 (all): Commissioned by the Migros Museum für Gegenwartskunst, Zurich. Photos Elísabet Davids. Courtesy the artist, Luhring Augustine, New York and i8 Gallery, Reykjavik. © Ragnar Kjartansson; 246–47: Photo Tony Godfrey. Reproduced courtesy the studio of Anne Imhof; 249t: Installation view, 'Space Shifters', Hayward Gallery 2018. Photo Mark Blower. © Courtesy the artist and Fondazione Sandretto Re Rebaudengo; 249b: Courtesy the artist and Greene Naftali, New York; 250: McMichael Canadian Art Collection. Gift from the Christopher Bredt and Jamie Cameron Collection (2016.10.5). Reproduced with permission of Dorset Fine Arts; 253: Photo Robert Glowacki. © Njideka Akunyili Crosby. Courtesy the artist, Victoria Miro, and David Zwirner; 255: Courtesy Robert Zhao Renhui; 258t: Photo Tony Godfrey. Courtesy the artist; 258b: 13th Havana Biennial, exhibition 'La construcción de lo possible', April - May 2019. Courtesy the artist and Blain|Southern. Photo Peter Mallet; 259: Photo Tony Godfrey. Courtesy the artist and Steve Turner, LA.

Index

Numbers in *italic* refer to illustrations